Contents

advancing learning, changing lives

Edexcel GCE in
Applied ICT

South Sefton
6th Form College

A2 Single Award

69

Trevor Heathcote   Steve Farrell   Richard Dunn

Edexcel
190 High Holborn
London WC1V 7BH

©Edexcel 2006
Third impression 2008

ISBN-10: 1-903133-78-5
ISBN-13: 978-1-903133-78-1

Designed by HL Studios Ltd, Oxford
Index by Indexing Specialists (UK) Ltd

Printed and bound by Scotprint

The publisher's policy is to use paper manufactured from sustainable forests.

Unit 12 Customising Applications

Introduction

In the 21st century it is difficult, if not practically impossible, to avoid ICT, since almost everything we do uses it in some way or another whether we realise it or not. More and more applications of ICT are being developed, and we are now capable of harnessing its powers to an extent that was pure science fiction only a few years ago. Our increasing reliance on computer technology in all areas of our lives has made individuals with in-depth ICT knowledge an extremely valuable commodity. ICT skills are now a basic prerequisite for an increasing number of jobs and this trend will only continue.

The *Edexcel GCE in Applied ICT* AS Single Award is a means of attaining these skills in a practical manner. The qualification concentrates on empowering you to gain ICT skills and knowledge that will allow you to *do* useful things with ICT programs, rather than write such programs. The aim is to create the so-called 'power-user': an individual capable of harnessing ICT to enhance his or her effectiveness in his or her daily life.

Following on from the Single Award, this book and CD-ROM keep faith with Edexcel's aim, allowing you to gain applicable, practical knowledge in as hands-on a way as possible. The three units completed in the A2 part of this course combine with the single AS award to make one A-level qualification. Two units, Unit 7 (Using Database Software) and Unit 8 (Managing ICT Projects), are compulsory. The third unit can be chosen from Unit 10 (Using Multimedia Software), Unit 11 (Using Spreadsheet Software) or Unit 12 (Customising Applications).

Interactive CD-ROM

The CD-ROM that accompanies this book provides direct access to files for activities and assessment practice, multimedia presentations and skills demonstrations, all launched straight from the ActiveBook pages.

An icon 🖲 in the book indicates that a file is available on the CD-ROM to accompany that section. It can be accessed from the corresponding page in the ActiveBook. In many cases you will need to save the file to a folder on your PC on order to edit and use it in your work.

Security settings

You will be using the macro facility in Microsoft Excel and Access. The security settings in both these programs may prevent you from running macros as they can operate in the same way as viruses. Therefore, you may need to change the security settings in these programs. Network users may need help from a network administrator to do this. For further information see the ActiveBook help section.

Unit 7 – Using Database Software

This unit builds on the database skills you started to develop in Unit 2 (The Digital Economy). However, whereas in Unit 2 you concentrated on how to retrieve information from a database, in this unit you learn how adaptable a database can be by designing and implementing one.

You will be taken through the design of a database system from its initial inception through to its implementation in a live environment. You will learn that the effectiveness of a database system depends on its structure and that a well designed database structure will have long-term benefits both in terms of efficiency and flexibility. You will learn the principles of data modelling and design so that the databases you create are resilient and effective. You will learn to appreciate the importance of considering the user when designing a database system.

This is an externally assessed unit which means you will be given a database design/construction task to complete within a specified time (10 hours). This section of the book will prepare you for this task and provide you with the skills to complete it.

Unit 8 – Managing ICT Projects

In this unit you will learn about the ingredients which go together to make a successfully run project. You will gain the skills needed to ensure that projects achieve their goals within a set time frame and budget. You will learn about the project life cycle, and the importance of setting objectives and success criteria at the start of a project. You will also learn the importance of producing a detailed plan, and constantly reviewing this plan, to ensure that your project runs smoothly.

For the assessment of this unit you will be asked to run a small ICT project. You will be guided through the process and the evidence you need to produce at each stage. To ensure a successful project you will need to communicate regularly with everyone who has an interest in it (the stakeholders), and provide evidence of this communication. You will be shown how to handle this aspect, too.

Unit 10 – Using Multimedia Software

In this unit you will learn the skills required to produce a rich multimedia experience. You will already have gained some multimedia skills in Unit 1 (The Information Age); these will be enhanced and expanded during the course of the unit. You will learn how to use a number of key multimedia tools and techniques creatively and effectively, and will be taken through the design, development and testing of a multimedia product.

The assessment requires that you produce an interactive multimedia product for a specific audience; this section of the book will suggest the best way for you to do this.

Unit 11 – Using Spreadsheet Software

You used spreadsheets in Unit 3 (The Knowledge Worker) to model situations in order to help make informed decisions. This is just one use of what is an extremely versatile software application. This unit will show you a number of these uses and instruct you in the skills required to design user friendly spreadsheet solutions to problems.

For your assessment you are required to produce a spreadsheet solution to a problem as defined by a specific client; this unit will provide you with guidance to help you. It will take you through the development stages of providing a solution to a realistic problem.

Unit 12 – Customising Applications

In this unit you will learn to enhance the functionality of applications such as a database or a spreadsheet by creating special routines programmed by you. You will take what may well be your first tentative steps in programming, by using an event-driven programming language within an application. This will enable the application to do things that are either not possible by other means, or are not as secure or efficient by those means.

This unit will take you through the fundamentals of programming in this way. It will not only guide you through the production of a solution to a problem, but will also give you a basis of good practice should you wish to do further programming.

Assessment

Unit 7 is assessed by a 10-hour externally-marked set assignment. The number of sessions involved in completing the assignment, and the length of each session, will be decided by your school or college, but will take place over a period of three weeks. You will be given a brief for which you will need to develop a database solution; during the 10 hours you will design, build and test the solution.

Unit 8 requires you to run a small ICT project and provide evidence, in the form of an eportfolio, of its successful management. The eportfolio should include plans from different stages of the project, minutes of meetings, and the development of the actual ICT solution. It is suggested that this unit be studied in conjunction with the optional unit you choose.

Units 10, 11 and 12 require that you design, build and test a piece of software to a particular specification defined by a real or imaginary client. Each of the units requires that your evidence be submitted in the form of an eportfolio showing a prototyping approach to system development.

The *Edexcel GCE in Applied ICT* is an exciting new qualification and the authors wish you the best of luck in your studies.

Trevor Heathcote
Steve Farrell
Richard Dunn

Unit 7

Using Database Software

Databases in various forms underlie the majority of ICT applications of the Information Age. As individuals our existence is registered within a few days of our birth; from here onwards our details are stored in many databases set up for a vast array of purposes until we die, an event which is of course also captured in a database record. Even after our death the Church of Jesus Christ of Latter-Day Saints may then eventually put us into their genealogical database.

As consumers, as citizens and as employees, we interact continually with database applications. Databases and an understanding of them are therefore fundamental to modern living. Unit 7.1 will examine the many applications of databases in modern ICT and will look specifically at relational database systems, and the concepts and terminology associated with these. Finally you will build a small, but complete, database application to help you understand these concepts from a practical viewpoint.

Living with data

Figure 7.1.1 Babies' details are stored in databases from within days of their birth

The government and local authorities are among the largest users of database applications in the UK, and have been for a very long time; for example, babies are registered when born by the Registrar of Births and Deaths. These public bodies store large amounts of data about us as individuals, in databases that, although separate, could also be linked.

Your details are stored in and processed from databases at the hospital where you were born and at the doctor's surgery where you were first registered as a patient. The NHS number you are given is used to identify you on each visit to the doctor or hospital, throughout your life. Each event at NHS institutions is recorded and associated with your NHS number. Presently much of this information about you is kept in separate databases, though the government's aim is to have an electronic central national care record which would allow all clinicians access to your health history.

At school in the state sector you are given a unique pupil number (UPN); many records are attached to this, keeping together all relevant information about your school history. Your national test results, exam results, class history, reports by outside bodies and more are all potentially stored in databases that help your teachers understand your individual progress and potential. They are intended to 'facilitate the tracking of pupils' progress through the school system, yielding better information (for schools, Local Education Authorities, LEAs, and central government) on pupil performance and related factors. This information strengthens procedures for target setting and monitoring, and so contributes to raising standards'. (Source: Information on Unique Pupil Number, produced by the Department for Education and Skills.)

ACTIVITY 1 Find out your UPN ◀

If you are studying in a state school, find out and write down your UPN. Otherwise discover and write down the unique student identifer your institution uses to identify you.

If you have a UK passport your records will be stored in the Passport Office database. This allows the government to keep track of its citizens and attempt to ensure that only authorised people are allowed into the UK. When you first receive any official income you will receive a National Insurance Number and details of your income will be stored in Inland Revenue databases. If you had not earned any income prior to your 16th birthday you should have been sent your NI number anyway.

When you learn to drive your details are captured on a database at the Driver Vehicle Licensing Authority (DVLA). When you get your first car the car itself has a unique record in a database attached to a registration certificate (V5c); this in turn is linked to your driver record through your driver number, so that the DVLA can tell who is the keeper of the car (i.e. who is responsible for it). When you buy a house, the details are stored by the Land Registry. Your TV Licence details are captured in a database which can be used to check that each house has a licence.

Figure 7.1.2 Car details, driver details and insurance details are all stored on databases

DISCUSSION The DVLA database and the police ◀

How many ways can you think of that the DVLA databases may be used by the police?

How can criminals attempt to defeat database searches?

Commercial applications of databases

Virtually the whole of the high street and e-commerce retail sectors are built on database technology. Modern accounting systems, stock control systems, order processing systems and human resource systems all rely on data stored in databases.

The bar codes on most of the products we buy are keys to database records, and these are at the heart of a large database-driven application. In the high street, the bar code is scanned at an electronic point of sale (EPOS) terminal at the checkout and is then used to retrieve the price from a price look-up table. When a sale is made and the goods are paid for at the checkout, the stock record in the database is updated by deducting the item sold and the sales record is updated by adding the item sold. Some of the retailer's better-connected suppliers can then access the stock and sales records related to their products, and calculate how much to resupply, and when. A retailer's finance department can calculate sales figures per store, or even per till (EPOS terminal). A store manager can access detailed or summary statistical and financial information about staff, products and sales. The database is therefore central to how a modern store operates.

Figure 7.1.3 Scanning at the checkout is a vital part of a large database application

Databases are not simply for large public and private sector companies, however. At the other end of the spectrum, a small DVD rental store will keep records of all the DVDs in stock and of all its members in a database. It will also maintain records of all 'lending events', matching a member to a DVD. Store staff can interrogate the database, for example, for addresses so as to send out special offers to all of their customers. They can ask the database to send out overdue letters automatically to all members who have failed to return their DVDs on time. They could send out targeted special offers by finding all members who have not hired any DVDs for a year, in order to try to entice them back. Alternatively, they could search for the 10 members who have spent the most in the last year and reward them with a different form of offer.

Banks' businesses are essentially based on large financial databases. Each customer account is given a unique account number that is a key to all the records of money coming in and money going out. Interest and charges are calculated automatically by the database application. A bank statement is essentially a simple database report on the customer's account between two given dates. An automated teller machine (ATM) is a terminal that provides an interface to the database. Using an ATM it is possible to request cash, show a balance or mini-statement, even put money on a mobile phone. All these actions are linked to the core database. Online banking, similarly, is in its essence a very simple database-related process. A series of web forms are linked securely to it, allowing the customer to input their requests directly to the database application (see Fig. 7.1.4). In practice, database security – rather than functionality – is the major issue for banks worldwide.

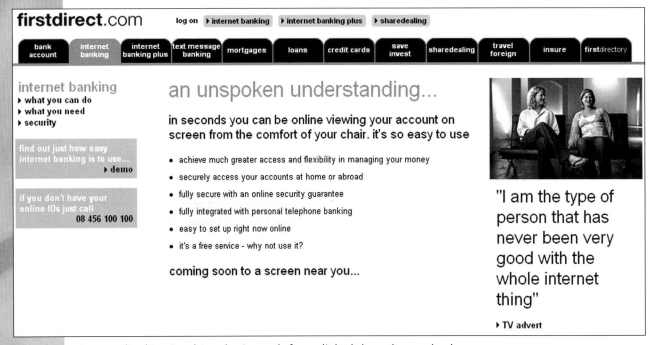

Figure 7.1.4 Internet banking is achieved using web forms linked through to a database

Each bank is allocated a sort code which identifies it as unique and distinct from any other bank in the world; the banks' database applications then cooperate via a jointly-owned 'clearing' system to ensure swift and accurate money transfers almost untouched by human intervention.

Other applications of databases

At home we can use simple database applications on our PCs such as address books, phone books and CD catalogues. Adventure games are usually based around a database containing scenes, characters, events and other features. On the internet, iTunes is a database of music; the iPod or other MP3 player with a track-searching facility are essentially databases linked to small applications that query that database, finding and playing the music we request (see Fig. 7.1.5).

Database applications are all around us, and are a fundamental part of all our lives. We are routinely entering data into databases: using manual data capture forms such as those at a Registrar of Births and Deaths; electronically via terminals such as ATMs; or selecting a track on our music player. We also query databases all the time. When we order a ticket for the latest movie, a database of available tickets is searched to find seats that are empty. When we search for a book title in a library or buy a can of beans in the local grocers, when we ask for a balance on our bank account or go online to find a cheap flight, databases are searched. When we receive a bank statement, when we get a receipt for our purchases from the supermarket, or when we play a track on iTunes we are getting a database report, of one form or another, from a database.

Figure 7.1.5 iTunes is essentially a music database application

Relational databases

There are a number of different types of database including flat-file databases, object-oriented databases and XML databases. The overwhelming majority of databases, however, are relational. You will therefore study relational databases and relational database management systems (DBMS) throughout this unit.

▶ Invention of relational databases

The concept of a relational database was revealed by an IBM researcher named Dr Codd (see Fig. 7.1.6) in 1970 in a paper called 'A Relational Model of Data for Large Shared Data Banks'. He spent 15 years refining

Key database terms

DBMS Database management system. The application that manages a database.

File How the data is physically stored, independent of the logical structure.

Database The data stored in a collection of tables.

Table A collection of records. Also known as a relation.

Record The central store of **information** – a collection of fields; a tuple or row.

Field An individual data item of a fixed type – a single piece of data – a data item or column.

Field name The unique name that is used to identify a field within a record.

Primary key A means of uniquely identifying a record (single field or composite key).

Composite key A primary key composed of more than one field.

Foreign key A data item in a second table that is used to join to a primary key in a first table.

Query An operation on a table or set of tables resulting in another table.

Logical structure The way the structure of a database appears to the user.

Physical storage The physical medium where data files are stored, e.g. the disk drive.

Presentation How the information is presented to the user (in forms and reports).

Form How data is presented to the user, primarily used for input.

Report How data is presented to the user for output.

Integrity Data is consistent and correct.

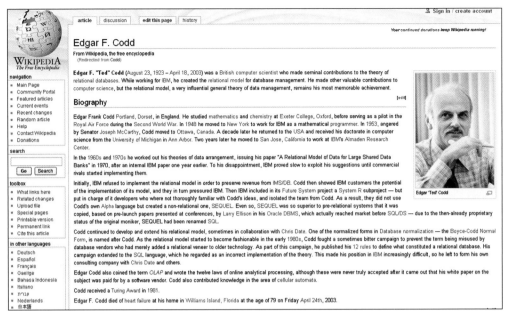

Figure 7.1.6 You can find out more about Dr Todd, inventor of relational database theory, from <u>Wikipedia</u>

the idea and in 1985 published 12 rules that a database should follow to be called relational (see <u>IT World</u> for a short explanation of each rule).

Two important principles lie behind the idea of the relational database he proposed:

- The data should be independent of any particular storage system.
- The database programs that search, sort and analyse the data should be devised automatically by the relational DBMS (RDBMS) from a simple specification given by the user.

The first principle underlies the structure of all modern databases. The second principle means that DBMSs have to be built on a solid mathematical basis and have a standard, structured language with which a user specifies the required query (now implemented as structured query language, SQL). This enables the RDBMS to work out for itself how to conduct an efficient search or mathematical operation, for example.

Structure of a relational database
Simple structure of a relational database

A relational database is at heart a very simple structure. It is made up of simple two dimensional tables, just like spreadsheet tables with headings for each column. Within the table each row has to be unique; each column must contain data of the same type; each cell must contain a single value; and each table can be related to another table only by the tables having a column containing the same information and cells containing the same value. Look at this demonstration from the ActiveBook illustrating the structure.

Microsoft Access

Throughout this unit we will use Microsoft Access for all demonstrations of relational database management systems. If you are using a different RDBMS to study this unit you must ensure that it is on the Edexcel approved list. As far as possible the text is written in a neutral manner so that the lessons learned can be applied to all RDBMSs, but inevitably specific instructions and illustrations will vary from application to application and you must use your own documentation to support these lessons.

Independence of physical files and logical data structure

RDBMSs can store their data physically in any manner they wish. They may store all tables in separate files, or have all tables and indexes in a single file. They can spread the data across physical media or have it all in one place. What matters is that to the database designer and the person querying the database, it appears as a simple set of tables. For example, it is perfectly possible to store some data in spreadsheet tables, some in database tables, and yet more in a web database, but to query the database as though all its data is in a simple set of tables. Watch this demonstration of this from the ActiveBook.

> **Number and #**
>
> # is conventionally used to represent number. So 'CustomerNumber' is sometimes written as 'Customer#'.

Tables and relations

A relational database is composed of one or more tables (called 'relations' by Dr Codd). A relation is a two-dimensional table comprising rows (records) and columns (fields). Each row is a unique record, sometimes called a 'tuple'. Each record must be capable of being identified uniquely by a field or some combination of fields within it. Each column represents a single data item or field. Each column is identified by a unique name and has a single data type (e.g. number or text).

Table 7.1.1 Customer table

Customer	First	Surname	Credit Limit
1001	John	Paul	2000
1002	Terry	Downs	1500
1003	Colm	McConway	2000
1004	Rob	Fletcher	2500
1005	Geoff	Nicholson	3000

In the customer table (see Table 7.1.1) the first row is the record for customer 1001, John Paul, who has a credit limit of £2000. Each column has a heading which is the name of the data item stored in that field. The first column is 'Customer#', which has a numeric data type. The data in this column can be used to identify a customer uniquely. 1004 therefore represents the customer Rob Fletcher, 1005 represents Geoff Nicholson, and so on.

Table 7.1.2 Order table

OrderNum	Customer#	Date
1122	1001	12/05/2005
1123	1002	12/05/2005
1124	1001	14/05/2005
1125	1005	14/05/2005

In the order table (see Table 7.1.2) the first row is the record for order 1122. The order was made by customer 1001 on 12 May 2005. This illustrates an important principle in the structure of a relational database. The two tables are related by the data in the Customer# field. We can see that customer 1001 is John Paul and so we deduce that it was John Paul who placed order 1122 on 12 May. This is the only form of relationship allowed in a relational database. There can be no physical connection between the tables, no pointer to the first record of the customer table and no hidden link between the tables. The tables are related when the value of the data (in this case 1001) in the same field (Customer#) in both tables is identical.

ACTIVITY 2 Add a new order to a database

Create a project folder and save this database into it as 'simple_order_database.mdb'. Open the file and add a new order (order number 1126) to the order table. The customer is Rob Fletcher and the date is 15/05/2005.

If you're not sure how to do this watch this demonstration from the ActiveBook.

> **Security settings**
>
> Your computer's security settings may prevent you opening this and other Microsoft Access databases and Excel spreadsheets. For information on changing these settings see the Help Section. You may need help from a network administrator.

▸ Records and keys

A record is the structure in which information about an individual or an item is stored. An employee record records details about an employee, a stock record stores details about a stock item. A customer record stores details about a customer. Each record is represented by a row in its table.

A primary key is a means of uniquely identifying a record. A single field is usually used as the primary key. In the case of the order table in Table 7.1.2 the key field is OrderNum. In the case of the customer table it is the Customer# field. Sometimes, however, a single field is insufficient to identify a record uniquely.

In the order line table (see Table 7.1.3) it can be seen that on order 1122, two of item 12 have been sold at £2.00 each and three of item 13 at £4.00 each, and again on order 1125. In this case no individual field is unique, but the combination of OrderNum and Stock# is unique when composed together. The two fields together, known as a **composite primary key**, are therefore the primary key of this table.

Table 7.1.3 Order line table

OrderNum	Stock#	QuantitySold	Price
1122	12	2	£2.00
1122	13	3	£4.00
1123	12	2	£2.00
1123	14	1	£3.00
1124	13	1	£4.00
1125	12	2	£2.00
1125	13	3	£4.00

ACTIVITY 3 Add the order lines for an order ◀

Using the simple order database from Activity 2, add the order lines for order number 1126 to the order lines table, showing that Rob Fletcher bought two of item 13 at £2.00 and four of item 14 at £3.00. If you're not sure how to do this, watch this demonstration from the ActiveBook.

A good deal of thought must be given to the construction of sensible primary keys. Where there are no obvious single fields available to act as a primary key, and a composite primary key is not desirable (see Unit 7.3 Data modelling), a unique identifier can be constructed in two ways, either of which is effective. The first is to devise a code

Figure 7.1.7 UPN Data Standard (Source: <u>Government specification of the UPN</u>)

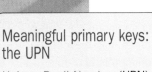

Meaningful primary keys: the UPN

<u>Unique Pupil Number</u> (UPN) (see Fig.7.1.7) is the key to student records in maintained schools from primary school onwards, and in effect is the key to the permanent record of a student.

that is composed of parts of information (e.g. a driver number which includes information about your surname, date of birth and sex; your UPN which includes your LEA, school and start year; an EAN13 barcode, such as those found on groceries and similar products which includes the country of origin, a supplier code, and a product code). The second is to invent a sequential numeric code whose only job is to be unique. OrderNum in the order and order line tables is clearly of this latter type.

The UPN is a well constructed and meaningful primary key. It consists of a 13-character code starting with a letter, followed by 12 digits. The first letter is a validation check that ensures the numbers have been entered correctly (see the section on validation and verification in Unit 7.3). The 12 digits comprise three digits for the LEA code, four digits for a school code, two digits for the academic year and three digits for the student number.

ACTIVITY 4 Match some primary keys ◀

Many databases have well known keys. Match the pairs in Figure 7.1.8.

Key	Database component
Driver number	Medical records
Registration number	Key Stage 3 results
Passport number	Price look-up in supermarket
NHS number	VAT records
UPN	Driving licence
NI number	Tax records
EAN13	Customer's bank records
ISBN	Book record in library
VAT number	Passport database
Unique Tax Reference	Bank
Account number	V5c car records
Sort code	Pay records

Figure 7.1.8 Matching pairs

Foreign keys

Table 7.1.4 Customer table

Customer#	First	Surname	CrLimit
1001	John	Paul	2000
1002	Terry	Downs	1500
1003	Colm	McConway	2000
1004	Rob	Fletcher	2500
1005	Geoff	Nicholson	3000

Avoid automated primary keys

In many instances it is useful to generate sequential numeric primary keys. For example, order numbers in an order processing system do not usually have any intrinsic meaning. They are allocated sequentially (i.e. 1122 is followed by 1123 and so on). Some RDBMSs have the functionality to generate these numbers automatically. They will ensure that no duplicate numbers are ever issued, even if a record is deleted. This can help to prevent particular types of fraud.

It is therefore tempting to use AutoNumbers for all primary keys since they guarantee uniqueness very easily – but in reality this is not good practice. Auto-generated primary keys should not normally be used for link entities (see the section on normalisation in Unit 7.3) and, indeed, should ideally only be used when the data in a manual equivalent would naturally be sequential.

Table 7.1.5 Order table

OrderNum	Customer# *	Date
1122	1001	12/05/2005
1123	1002	12/05/2005
1124	1001	14/05/2005
1125	1005	14/05/2005

In the customer table (Table 7.1.4), the primary key (which is shown underlined, as is conventional) is Customer#. This same field appears in the order table (Table 7.1.5) where it is not unique: a customer can place many orders and appear many times in the order table. We can see this with customer 1001. The Customer# in the order table can be used, as we have seen, to find information about the customer from the customer table. The customer who placed the order 1122 is John Paul. We used the key to find this information. In the primary table, where it is unique, it is called a **primary key**. In the other table, where it is not unique, but holds the same information, it is called a **foreign key**. It is a key to the information in the customer table, but it is in another (thus foreign) table.

Primary and foreign keys are fundamental to relational databases. They are used to relate tables together. A fundamental rule of relational databases is that information (excluding keys) must not be duplicated. For example, the details of the customer Rob Fletcher must only appear once in the database. Using foreign keys enables this. The details are stored once in the customer table and then the foreign key is used to relate back to this single record whenever needed.

▶ Fields and field names

Whereas records are identified uniquely by a primary key, fields are identified within a record by a field name. The order of the columns is therefore not important. The order of fields can be different in different circumstances; indeed, extra fields can be added and many fields can be taken away without affecting the integrity of the database.

All the data in a single field of a table (i.e. a column of data) must be of the same data type. You cannot store, for example, a customer number as a numeric type in the first record and as text in the second. You have to decide on the optimal data type before you start (see Unit 7.3 Data modelling), based on the range of data that will be stored in that field. If customer numbers include 1001, 1002, C101 and FX2, then the type could not be numeric; it would have to be alphanumeric text.

ACTIVITY 5 Allocate field names ◀

Decide field names for a personal address book.

Decide what data type each would be from the following list: number, text, currency, date/time.

Querying a database

Unlike custom programming solutions, when you ask an RDBMS to find information in a database you simply specify what fields you want in your answer (e.g. customer number, first name, order number, date) from what tables (e.g. order, customer) and possibly criteria you wish to apply (e.g. date >1 Jan 2005). You specify all these using either a query language that is simply a structured form of English (e.g. structured query language, SQL, pronounced 'sequel'), or by selecting the fields and tables in some form of graphical view (query by example or query by design). The database query engine will then decide how to program the query. It will devise and run the complex set of operations necessary to achieve the results – the user does not have to know any programming at all.

When you query a relational database the result, or the output of the process, is another table. This has a number of consequences. Firstly, there is a basic elegance to the whole model. Every part of the structure, including the output of operations, is simply a table. Secondly, as the output of a query is a table, this means that queries can be queried in the same way as tables. Furthermore, all the presentational techniques that can be used to format tables for input (usually using forms) and output (usually using reports) can be used on the results of queries as well.

> ## Query speed
>
> Smaller RDBMSs will program a query in a fixed way. This will usually be efficient and the result of the query will therefore usually be available very quickly. More sophisticated RDBMSs go through an extra stage, called planning. They will devise a number of alternative methods of programming the query, and will allocate a time to each operation. In doing this they will calculate which is the optimal method and run the query procedure in the most efficient manner.

ACTIVITY 6 Query a database using the Wizard ◀

Use the simple order database from Activity 3 go to Query View. Add a new query using the Wizard to show a list of customer numbers with their names. Save it as 'qryAllCustomers'. You can see a demonstration of how to do this from the ActiveBook.

Note: The result of the query is itself a table.

ACTIVITY 7 Query a database using design view ◀

Use the simple order database from Activity 6. Go to Queries, under Objects View. Create a query in Design View to show which customers have bought stock item 12 and when. Specify:

- all the tables by adding them all.
- which fields you want – stock item, first, surname, date.
- your criteria by putting 12 in the criteria row under stock item.

Save it as 'qryStockCustomers'. You can see a demonstration of how to do this from the ActiveBook.

Note: You were able to build a query by specifying what you wanted rather than by programming the database; also that the result of the query is itself a table.

Presenting the database: The user interface

The database structure and the queries are the fundamental building blocks of the database. Separate from this, and on top of this, an RDBMS will often allow the creation of very user friendly interfaces in which fields from a table or query can be effectively 'painted' onto the screen, in any position or format you choose. Virtually all RDBMSs now offer facilities to create forms (mainly to aid input) and reports (to aid output).

The simple order database has some simple user interface facilities already written into it. In this next section we will examine some of these.

Activity 8 Use a simple user interface to the database

If you are uncertain about any parts of this activity watch this demonstration from the ActiveBook.

Save and open this simple order database. Then open the main menu form (see Fig. 7.1.9).

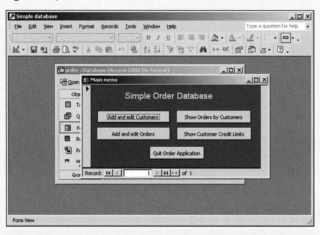

Figure 7.1.9 The main menu form

1 How does a form such as this help the user?

Increase John Paul's credit limit to £3000 and add a record for new customer John Maltby (see Fig. 7.1.10).

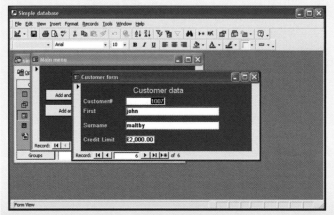

Figure 7.1.10 Adding a record for John Maltby

2 What is the difference for the user when amending data or adding a record in this way compared to entering data directly into tables?

Add an order for John Maltby (see Fig. 7.1.11).

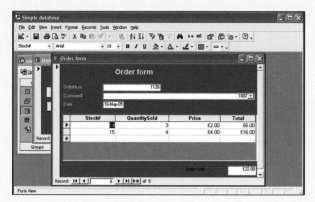

Figure 7.1.11 Adding an order for John Maltby using 'Add and Edit Orders'

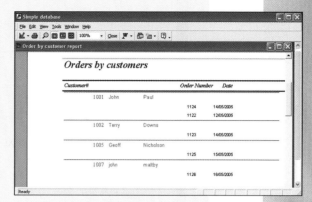

Figure 7.1.12 Orders by customer report

3 What is the difference for the user when amending data or adding a record in this way compared to entering data directly into tables? How many useful extra facilities can you identify?

Show the orders made by each customer in the form of a report (see Fig. 7.1.12).

4 What is the difference for the user when viewing data in this way compared to viewing a query? Why is this better?

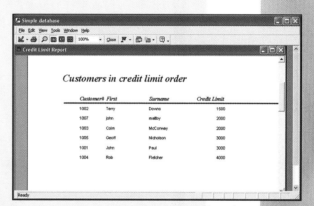

Figure 7.1.13 Customers in credit-limit order

Show the customers in order of their credit limits (see Fig. 7.1.13).

5 What is the difference for the user when viewing data in this way compared to viewing a query? Why is this better?

Conclusion ▶ ▶ ▶

In Unit 7.1 we have discovered how database applications are fundamental to the way we live today; we have examined and explained the terminology used in relational database technology and have looked at some of the practical applications of these terms in a simple database. In the following units you will reinforce this knowledge as you learn the steps of producing a database application by completing a very simple database application from start to finish, and then progress to looking at the different stages in detail.

Activity 9 Search for database terminology

Print out the wordsearch shown in Figure 7.1.14 and complete it.

M	E	N	T	I	T	Y	M	E	S	R	Y	V	Y	S
R	N	T	Q	R	F	S	T	M	G	E	T	G	R	E
U	E	A	U	I	E	I	O	W	D	F	I	R	Z	A
I	B	L	E	B	S	P	P	R	D	E	R	D	N	R
I	P	L	A	O	I	R	O	R	T	R	G	A	O	C
D	D	A	P	T	I	R	O	R	N	E	E	T	I	H
W	E	M	R	M	I	C	T	A	T	N	T	A	T	Y
E	O	P	A	A	E	O	V	T	M	T	N	B	P	R
C	L	R	U	R	M	I	N	M	A	I	I	A	A	E
N	Y	B	L	O	G	E	R	S	Y	A	K	S	C	U
S	K	D	A	A	R	O	T	Q	H	L	E	E	M	Q
S	M	B	T	T	F	G	E	E	U	I	Y	Z	P	P
N	G	I	E	R	O	F	U	M	R	Z	P	H	S	H
N	O	R	M	A	L	I	S	A	T	I	O	N	F	Y
N	D	E	T	A	L	U	C	L	A	C	F	I	L	E

ATTRIBUTE	CALCULATED	CAPTION
COMPOSITE	DATABASE	ENTITY
FIELD	FILE	FOREIGN
FORM	GROUPED	INTEGRITY
KEY	NAVIGATION	NORMALISATION
PARAMETER	PRIMARY	QUERY
RECORD	REFERENTIAL	RELATIONSHIP
REPORT	SEARCH	SORT
TABLE		

Figure 7.1.14

7.2 Database development: System and specification

Developing a database is a serious undertaking, requiring careful specification and design, implementation and testing. Careful management of a database development project leads to safer and often faster development, and most crucially ensures that the end product meets the needs of its users. Databases that are developed correctly are flexible, efficient and very fast. You saw in Unit 7.1 that databases underlie many different business processes. As an organisation or application grows, the database has to grow with it. If the database has been structured correctly this is a reasonably straightforward process. Relational databases allow the addition of fields, tables, queries, forms and reports without compromising the original integrity. However, if the original structure is not correct for the required processes, the database will be compromised. Hacks and workarounds can be employed to make the database do what it was intended to, but it will inevitably be less efficient from the start and massively harder to upgrade in the future. In Unit 7.2 we will examine the project-management life cycle for a database application and then look at the document that is the foundation of all of this: the functional specification.

Part 1: Database application development lifecycle

Any database application project will stand a greater chance of success if it is developed using sound project management techniques (see Unit 8 for a full description). We will examine a methodology that is in general use in the database development world: that of prototyping. The exact stages and sub-phases of the project may vary a little between developers, but the essence will be the same.

A property development database

Figure 7.2.1 Property site under development

A group of property managers used Microsoft Access to manage their project consultants. The structure was good but not perfect. Some programming workarounds were used to manage some of the difficulties. For a while it was used very successfully to allocate costs and expenses to different jobs. However, the number of consultants and expense categories grew eventually to a point where the workarounds failed. New database developers were brought in to deal with problem. They discovered the flaws in the original structure and suggested re-engineering the whole application. The amount of live data then in the system made this a very expensive option; however, equally, leaving it unfixed was an expensive option. If the application had been engineered correctly in the first place the upgrades would have been totally straightforward.

ACTIVITY 1 Create a list of prototypes ◀

Create a list of prototypes (see Table 7.2.1). Explain what they are used for.

Table 7.2.1

Prototype	Purpose of prototype
Clay model of car	Test look and wind resistance of shape

▶ Prototyping

The traditional approach to systems development is to have a series of sequential processes, each of which must be finished before the next starts. One such model is shown in Figure 7.2.2.

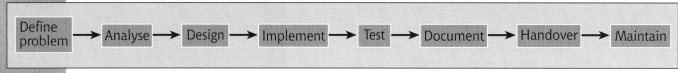

Figure 7.2.2 Traditional system development lifecycle

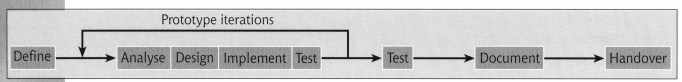

Figure 7.2.3 Design and development lifecycle

Prototyping

There are a number of variations on the prototyping approach. Traditional prototyping involves creating a model 'for show' that is subsequently thrown away when the full model is built. The approach we are using is evolutionary development in which the initial model is refined over a number of iterations rather than being discarded and rebuilt (see Fig. 7.2.3).

Using relational database design and development tools it is not essential, nor often totally desirable, to finish one stage completely before moving on to the next. One of the criticisms of large systems projects is that the users have to specify their exact requirements before they can even imagine what the final product will look like or be able to do. Using prototyping, the developer will build an early version of the product so that the users can have an initial look at it. It is then possible for the users to say what they like and dislike about it, and for it to be adjusted accordingly. They may be shown a single prototype or be given many opportunities to revise the final product until it exactly suits their needs. The developers can also test early versions of the product and be sure their ideas will work before committing their time and energy to finishing it completely.

Define

The most successful projects will start from a sound project definition. This will spell out unambiguously the problem the project intends to solve, the scope of the project (i.e. what is included and what is not), the likely costs and benefits, other resource usage, any areas of potential risk, any potential constraints, the timescale, and, most crucially, the objectives and the key success criteria the project will be judged against when it is complete.

▶ Analyse

The next stage is to analyse the users' requirements in-depth. The main aim of this is to produce a functional specification. This amplifies the initial objectives and makes them very specific. At this stage all the documentation is written in terms of the user and the tasks they will perform, rather than what the application has to do. It lists everything that is required of the application. Using prototyping it is not essential to specify absolutely every requirement in detail before development. Some of the detail – particularly the exact form of the user interface – can be negotiated at a later stage, when the user can see and understand more clearly how the database application will work. Nonetheless it is important to be as clear as possible at the outset about the data requirements and about what the application must do. It is only by having a really clear understanding that the structure and the main processes can be designed and implemented. The prototype may change the detail, but the functional specification must be clear at all times.

▶ Design

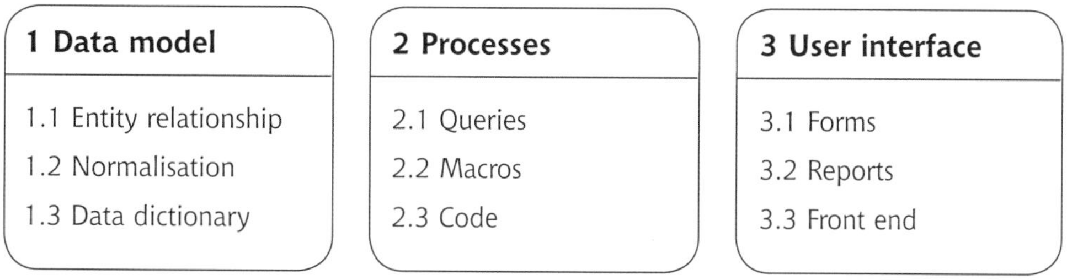

1 Data model	2 Processes	3 User interface
1.1 Entity relationship	2.1 Queries	3.1 Forms
1.2 Normalisation	2.2 Macros	3.2 Reports
1.3 Data dictionary	2.3 Code	3.3 Front end

Figure 7.2.4 Phases of design

When the requirements are understood the design can begin. This converts the users' needs into a form suitable for a database application. This can be divided into a number of sub-phases (see Fig. 7.2.4) in the database development project: the design of the data model, the design of the processes and finally the design of the user interface. It may take one or more attempts to get each of these right and complete.

In practice the data model must be completed as thoroughly and accurately as possible at the initial development stage. As with the requirements specification, the data model can be refined through successive iterations, but it is preferable to capture the most accurate model as soon as possible. The core data and relationships should be as correct as possible.

It is feasible to add extra fields, extra tables and relationships at a later stage, but it is extremely undesirable to amend existing relationships, as this will break the structure of the database. The design of processes and the user interface can, and often is, left until later iterations of the prototyping process, after the foundation structure has been built.

The first stage is to develop the data model. This involves modelling how the data will be stored in tables. There are two principal complementary techniques for doing this: **entity relationship (ER) modelling** (a top–down technique) and **normalisation** (a bottom–up technique), described in detail in Unit 7.3. The outcomes of the two techniques are an ER diagram and a set of normalised tables. These are compared to ensure they are the same. Once the results have been verified, full **data dictionaries** can then be drawn up which specify in detail the properties of each data item in each table, including the type of the data, and the validation and verification to be used (see Unit 7.3).

Aliases

Different users will see the same data in different ways. A salesman may be an employee in the database whereas a customer will see him as the salesperson who sold the goods.
The data name might be EmployeeName but it is possible to also set up an alias (or alternative name) for the customer's view so that they see it as SalesPerson.

Top–down and bottom–up techniques

Top–down techniques start with the overall picture (problem) and break it down into smaller parts (sub-problems). Bottom–up techniques start with the individual parts of a picture (problem) and join them together to form the larger picture.

Data dictionaries

Table 7.2.2

Name	Type	Length	Format	Other validation	Comments

A data dictionary (see Table 7.2.2) is a table that spells out each data item in the database. The amount of detail given varies between developers. The simplest dictionaries will merely list the data names, but commonly they will also show for each data item: the name, the type, the purpose and the different types of validation applicable to the data to ensure that the data entered is valid (see Unit 7.3). It is also common, and sometimes very desirable, to show aliases for data names, as well as examples of the data values in the dictionary, either as separate columns, or in the comments column.

The design of the database processes is usually the next phase undertaken. This involves specifying the queries, and sometimes the macros and code, that will operate on the database structure to achieve the requirements. Following this it is possible to design the user interface elements of the database project, i.e. designing the storyboards for the forms for gathering input and the reports for formatting the output. These elements, in particular, are likely to be amended as the project progresses and so will benefit most from a prototyping approach. At this time a test plan will usually be drawn up and agreed to ensure that the database fulfils all the requirements and operates correctly.

▶ Implement

1 Structure	2 Data entry and conversion	3 Processes	4 User interface	5 Security
1.1 Tables 1.2 Relationships	2.1 Initial data entry 2.2 Importing data	3.1 Queries 3.2 Macros 3.3 Code	4.1 Forms 4.2 Reports 4.3 Front end	5.1 Backing up 5.2 Archiving 5.3 User accounts

Figure 7.2.5 Phases of implementation

The next major phase of the project is to build the database from the design (see Fig. 7.2.5). The implementation clearly follows the design closely. The first and crucial phase is to implement the database structure (see Unit 7.4). This involves creating the database itself, and then building the tables from the data model; ensuring that as much of the detail of the model as possible is captured in the implementation. Once the structures have been implemented, it is common, as part of the iterative process, to test them to ensure they work as intended. Most database applications are conversions of paper systems or file-based programming applications. In the former case, this phase may involve adding new data by copying from paper sources using scanners, optical readers, or perhaps simply a keyboard and mouse. In the latter case, this sub-phase will often involve importing the data from the old system to work with the new system (see Unit 7.4).

The next sub-phase is to implement the processes (see Unit 7.5). This will involve specifying the database queries, and where necessary writing macros (sequences of pre-built common actions) and code (functions and procedures that add functionality to the database management system). Wherever possible, developers will try to avoid code-based solutions as they are inherently less flexible and more error prone than the built-in processes. However, sometimes for a fully customised solution, they are the best choice. In the case of Microsoft Access the code will be written in Visual Basic for Applications (VBA) – see Unit 12. For other RDBMS applications there will be a variety of different methods of writing code.

The next major sub-phase is to implement the user interface. This is often called the presentation layer, as it sits on top of the database functionality and structure merely adapting the way it looks, rather than the underlying way it works. It is the means by which the user will interact with the database. There are three main parts to this: forms to enter data in as usable and efficient a manner as possible; reports to view the outputs in as useful, attractive and user-friendly a manner as possible, and a front end which ties the whole application together.

The final implementation phase, often not completed until the very end of the iterative processes, is to implement the database security. This will involve implementing, and possibly automating, the back up schedule; arranging archiving of older data; and perhaps setting up individual user accounts and passwords so that different users can have different levels of access to the database.

▶ Test

The final stage of each iteration is to test the implementation to ensure it works as it should and to gather feedback from the users (see Fig. 7.2.6). If they require amendments or the tests reveal that adaptations are necessary, the whole prototyping cycle will then run again until the tests are all passed and the user has no further amendments (see Unit 7.7).

1 Iterative testing
1.1 Test structure
1.2 Test data entry
1.3 Test processes
1.4 Test output
1.5 Test to specification

Figure 7.2.6 Testing phase

▶ Finish

1 Final testing	2 Documenting	3 Handover
1.1 Meets specification?	2.1 Help	
1.2 Usable?	2.2 Technical manual	
1.3 Efficient?	2.3 User manual	

Figure 7.2.7 Finishing phase

After all the iterative processes have been completed the database application can be finished off (see Fig. 7.2.7). This will usually involve completing the sign off tests to prove that it meets the functional specification (note that the developer will be fairly sure it will at this stage, having tested it exhaustively in the iterative stages). Once this has been done the documentation can all be completed, the users can be trained and the project can be handed over to the clients.

ACTIVITY 2 List the user documentation ◀

What documentation does a user need?

List the different items of information that a user would need to accompany a database application. In what ways would this be different from the technical documentation?

Part 2: The functional specification

Having studied the overall lifecycle of a database development process it is now possible to consider the crucial document that is the foundation of the whole database design and implementation process: the **functional specification**. This states exactly what the database application is required to do. It forms the basis of the design and implementation and it is what will be used in the end as the basis of the tests that establish whether the database is successful. In the commercial world they are created from a variety of sources. The most common of these is from a brief given by a client orally or in writing. The developer will take the rather vaguer instructions from the user and draw them up into a formal document that is used as the basis of the agreement about what the developer will provide.

The functional specification will usually have at least the following five main sections:

- the tasks the database application must perform
- information the system must supply
- data to be input into the system
- processing required by the system
- required security.

The detailed lists under each of these sections will be phrased, as far as possible, in terms of the users' needs rather than in database terminology.

▶ The tasks the database application must perform

A real database application is not intended merely to store data. Its main purpose is usually to perform some specific tasks related to that data. A theatre booking system will determine availability, allocate tickets to specific areas of the theatre, and calculate the total costs of a booking. An order processing system might create order confirmations and invoices. A stock control system might reorder goods automatically when stock falls below a certain critical level. Understanding the tasks a system has to perform is crucial to understanding how the database must be structured and the processes designed into it.

ACTIVITY 3 Set up staff holiday database ◀

A company called Pure Restaurant Supplies Ltd wants a database for recording their staff holidays. Add to the following list of tasks you feel it may have to perform. The first two are done for you:
1 Store the details of staff holiday entitlement.
2 Input details of holidays taken.
3 ...

ACTIVITY 4 Set up a database for the Videobank DVD store ◀

The Videobank DVD store has decided to computerise all of its hiring and stock control functions. What tasks do you feel the database application must perform?

▶ Information the system must supply

The second major purpose of a database application is to supply information. A cinema booking database might have to supply information about what films are being shown on what dates, what seats are free and how much the seats cost. An order processing database application may supply information about

the orders to be picked and delivered to customers, the orders taken in the last month, the total value of deliveries this week, and so on.

The exact nature of the information it must supply will determine what data must be stored. If the order processing application has to supply information about the orders taken by each salesperson, then data about the salesperson must be captured. If the system is required to show the percentage of orders delivered within a promised time, then the intended and actual delivery dates must be stored in the database structure.

A full specification of this part will consider the form the information must be supplied in. It may be presented as part of a report to the management, a screen form for the customer, a letter to the customer, a print out or even as an audio or video file. In many cases the output from one database system may form the input to another system. It is essential that all this is considered in the functional specification.

Activity 5 List relevant information

1 List the information you believe the Pure Restaurant Supplies holidays' database must supply, and to whom and in what form.
2 List the information you believe the Videobank DVD store database must supply, and to whom and in what form.

▶ Data to be input into the system

The next part of the functional specification to be considered is the data that must be input to the system: the main basis for the structure and storage of the database. Again, it is important at this stage to consider it in terms of the user rather than the database. Where possible, it is also important to consider exactly what you would expect a user to input for each database operation, rather than deal in vague generalisations. For example, when a customer first joins the Videobank DVD store you would expect to collect their personal details and verify them in some way, e.g. using a source of photo ID along with a recent utility bill. When they come in to hire a DVD on future occasions you would only expect them to show a membership card to give their membership number. You should attempt to detail all of this information in this section. If possible, this section should also record the devices the user would prefer to use to capture the data, and the sources of the data. When hiring new DVDs the membership card would be the source of the membership data. Depending on the type of card used the member number could be captured by retyping on the keyboard, by scanning a barcode or by reading a smart chip on the card.

Data capture

Data capture is the means by which data is acquired into the database. It might be achieved by typing data in using a keyboard, from a data source such as a stock record card, by scanning, by optical recognition, by voice capture or by one of many other data capture methods.

Activity 6 List relevant data input

What data has to be input into the system when a member returns a number of DVDs?

What would the source of the data be? What alternate devices might be used to capture the data?

Processing required by the system

The next consideration is all of the processing that the application must perform. Any data conversion should be noted here. All other major processes should also be listed.

The major processes that can be involved are:
- converting/importing data
- searching for data
- sorting data
- grouping data
- statistical analysis of data
- calculations on data
- creation of new data (e.g. creating a new membership number)
- applying rules, such as validation rules while entering data.

> ## ACTIVITY 7 List data processes
>
> List the processes that you think will be involved in the Pure Restaurant Supplies holidays' database application and in the Videobank DVD store database.

Data conversion

When an older system is upgraded, it is necessary to convert and import existing data to work with the new system. This data may exist in many forms. It may be on paper; it may be in a spreadsheet; it may be in a text file (particularly a delimited text file). The data should be recorded as part of the data to be input; any conversion process should be noted as part of the processing requirements.

Required security

When building a database application it is very important to consider its security requirements. For a single-user database on a PC these requirements will generally be minimal, the main consideration being potential data loss. On multi-user systems not only will data loss be a larger issue, but also potential data theft and identity theft will have to be taken into account.

> ## ACTIVITY 8 Identify security issues
> ### Buncefield Oil Depot Explosion
>
> The software company, Northgate Information Solutions, was affected badly by the blast at Buncefield Oil Depot in Hemel Hempstead on 11 December 2005 (see Fig. 7.2.8). They are a leading supplier of specialist human resource (personnel) software for local authorities and industry, including payroll details for most police forces, sections of the civil service and others. The head office was seriously damaged by the fire and its back-up systems were destroyed. The company said that its ability to maintain full service for its customers had been temporarily impaired, but its data had all been backed-up off-site on the Saturday evening, and therefore could be restored from other offices around the country.
>
>
> Figure 7.2.8 Buncefield Oil Depot explosion, December 2005
>
> *Continued on the next page*

Online tax credits closed down

'The government has shut down the tax credits website after discovering it has been targeted by online fraudsters. HM Revenue & Customs (HMRC) took the decision last week to close the site, which processes tax credit claims, after discovering that civil servants' personal identities had been stolen and were being used to try to steal money from the department through false online applications.' (Source: Daniel Thomas, _Computing_, 8 December 2005)

Based on Table 7.2.3 compile a list of potential threats to a database application, along with any measures you feel could help minimise the risk.

Table 7.2.3

Threat	Measure to minimise risk

ACTIVITY 9 List security requirements

What security requirements will the holiday database require?

What security requirements will the Videobank database require?

CASE STUDY The Videobank DVD store

The Videobank DVD store hires DVDs to members. The manager wants to convert its Basic programming language based flat-file system to a database application.

He wants to store details of all members, DVDs and hires. The database will be used to log hires and returns, and for chasing overdue DVDs using standard letters. He would like the database to print out membership cards and receipts for customers when they hire a set of DVDs. The manager also wants to be able

Figure 7.2.9

to know: the number of copies of each DVD he has; the value of DVDs held; the value of DVDs not returned; the number of active members; the number of times each DVD has been borrowed. Additionally, he does not want the staff to be able to access this data. He would also like the database to update the prices of each DVD automatically when he wants to implement a general price increase.

Tasks

Create a functional specification for this case using the pro-forma provided.

CASE STUDY Pure Restaurant Supplies Ltd (PRS) ◀

PRS are a small restaurant-food wholesale suppliers business in Lemshire. They sell vegetarian and whole-food supplies to small cafes and restaurants in Lemshire. These cafes and restaurants order for their immediate needs and thus only buy from what is in stock. PRS deliver the goods, accompanied by a sales invoice (numbered the same as the order).

They have all their records stored in a spreadsheet at the moment but want to convert to a database application. They want to put their sales order processing activity onto the database. They require the following functionality from the application as a minimum:

- Create, amend and delete customer information.
- Print a list of customers.
- Create, amend and delete stock items.
- Print a stock list.
- Create and edit sales orders (from items in stock). The order should be capable of being printed if required.
- Print a list of orders between two dates.
- Archive older orders on request. Only recent orders are to be stored on the system.*
- Print a pick list for a particular order, showing the stock number, description and location for each item on the order.
- Print an invoice to accompany each customer order generated from the original order (and amended for any shortages etc.).
- Update the stock from a particular invoice automatically when the goods are delivered to a customer (goods out).
- Print a requisition for stock replenishment.**
- Print out a list of what is in stock at any time by stock location for a physical stock check; create a shortage report if appropriate and allow for the actual stock quantity to replace the recorded stock quantity.
- Report the value of the stock and the potential profit from stock.
- Report the value at cost of each item in stock, along with a running total of the value in each location.
- Print out a price list to be distributed to all customers and potential customers.
- Create an archive of dated price lists
- Increase the price of all stock items by a predetermined percentage at the push of a button, archiving the old prices at the same time.
- Create a back-up copy of the database at the push of a button.

* The system should archive orders up to a date specified by the manager.
**They buy goods from a number of large food suppliers on a regular basis. Each item is bought from a single supplier. A requisition is created for each supplier by comparing the stock level with the minimum amount that should be in stock. Where the level is too low a requisition is made for a predetermined amount called the reorder level.

Note: The old data will be converted into comma separated variable (CSV) delimited files and will have to be imported into the database.

Task

Create a functional specification for the database application using the pro-forma provided.

Conclusion ▶ ▶ ▶

In Unit 7.2 we have examined the life cycle of a database development project. We have seen how database projects are usually developed using a prototyping methodology; we have seen the impact this has on the development process, particularly in creating an end product that is as close as possible to what the user really requires. We have also examined how the user requirements themselves are listed exhaustively in the functional specification. The functional specification is the foundation of the whole database development project since it specifies in detail what the application has to do from the viewpoint of the users of the system. It enables the developer to understand in detail what is required, and thus be able to design and implement the project correctly.

We are seeing that relational database management systems (RDBMSs) are capable of being truly flexible, efficient systems with a vast variety of applications, though it is always essential that they are constructed on the basis of a correct relational structure. In order to be efficient and effective, the database itself must follow some basic rules while modelling the real-world data correctly. To achieve this database designers model the data using some well established techniques which, combined together, help ensure the integrity of the database. The main techniques used are **entity attribute relationship** (EAR) modelling (a top–down modelling approach), **normalisation** (a bottom–up modelling technique), and recording the final results in a **data dictionary** in the necessary detail. You may have to create any or all of these in your final examination for this unit, so it is important that you fully understand the processes involved. We will investigate each of these in turn in Unit 7.3.

EAR glossary

Model   A representation of a system or application in the real world; e.g. *library borrowing system*.

Entity   A real world object or concept to be modelled; e.g. *a member (or members)*.

Attribute   An individual property of an entity (*Note*: It must not be a group of data, such as a list of books borrowed). Each attribute must be for a single item of data; e.g. *a surname*.

Relationship   How one entity is related to another; e.g. *one member can borrow many books*.

Primary key   A unique identifier for an entity; e.g. *the membership number in members*.

Foreign key   The property that relates an entity to a primary key in another entity; e.g. *the membership number in a books-borrowed entity*.

The difference between ER and EAR diagrams

Entity relationship (ER) diagrams show the entities and the relationships (see Fig. 7.3.1a), but entity attribute relationship (EAR) diagrams show the attributes as well (see Fig. 7.3.1b).

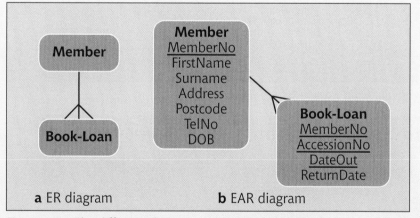

a ER diagram   **b** EAR diagram

Figure 7.3.1 The difference between ER and EAR diagrams

Chen and EAR

Peter Chen proposed EAR diagrams in 1976 in a work entitled 'The entity-relationship model: Toward a unified view of data' (published in the *ACM Transactions on Database Systems*) thereby establishing this excellent method for combining real-world meaning with relational structures.

Modelling using EAR diagrams

Entity attribute relationship diagrams are a tried and trusted technique for modelling data. They allow the designer to consider the real-world relationships while developing a pure relational data model. Each entity to be modelled is shown as a rectangle; the attributes are shown as a list inside the entity and the relationships are shown as lines with 'crow's feet'.

▶ Basic modelling tools

Figure 7.3.2 shows how to produce EAR diagrams, and Figure 7.3.3 gives an example of how this is done for a member entity in a library borrowing system.

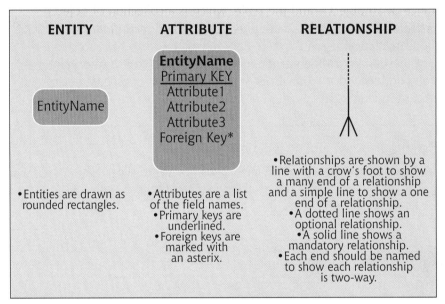

Figure 7.3.2 Style used to produce EAR diagrams

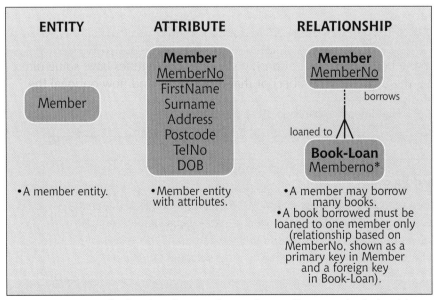

Figure 7.3.3 Example showing the member entity, attributes and relationships for a library borrowing system

A worked example: Mustoe Library

The Mustoe Library allows its members to borrow up to six books each, usually for two weeks; although some books are for overnight loan and some for four-week loans. The library stocks multiple copies of the most popular books. Each book title has a unique ID called an ISBN (e.g. the AS part of this series has the ISBN 1-903133-80-7). As there are potentially multiple copies of a book, every new book is also recorded using a unique number called an accession number.

Step 1: Identify the entities

Entities are objects or concepts from the real world that we will model as tables in the final database. In a database there is a distinction between a record – a single instance of an object – and the table, which is a collection of objects. However, entities do not need to make this rigid distinction and can stand for an individual or collection.

Two possible answers:

Possible entities, option 1	Possible entities, option 2
Member	Member
Book	Book
Title	Title
	Book-Loan

Finding entities is not an exact science. Practice and knowledge of an organisation will always help in the analysis. Option 1 shows all the obvious physical objects within the library system scenario. Option 2 shows an additional important concept that needs to be modelled, the book loan. EAR modelling is a sufficiently powerful technique to allow either as a starting point.

Step 2: Identify the relationships between entities

Each entity in the model will have some relationship with other entities. The concept of a relationship is a very simple idea. One title will relate to many copies of the book. One book will appear in many book loans. One member will take out many book loans. A relationship says that two entities have some direct connection, the degree (or number) of that connection, and how optional the relationship is.

Relationships are two-way

The other important thing to note is that all relationships are two-way. There is one relationship between a title and a copy of the book, and another between the copy of the book and the title. If you always spell out the two relationships you will not fall victim to the confusion that can arise when entities are sometimes thought of as singular and sometimes as plural.

Cardinality of relationships

There are three possibilities for the cardinality of a relationship, one-to-many (1:M), many-to-many (M:M) and one-to-one (1:1) (see Fig. 7.3.4). However, only the first of these (1:M) is usually used in data models for relational databases. M:M is not allowed, and 1:1, while allowed, is discouraged.

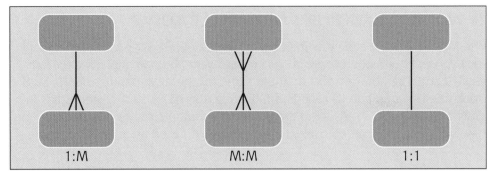

Figure 7.3.4 The three types of cardinality

One-to-many relationships

Virtually all relationships in EAR diagrams (as in relational databases) will be one to many (1:M). Figure 7.3.5a shows that one title may be stored as many copies of the same title. On the other hand one book must be stored as a copy of a single title.

Relationship names

It is good practice to name the relationships between entities, and it helps remind us that all relationships are two-way. The name does not matter too much as long as it is unique and sensible. It is useful if it conveys a sense of what is happening. 'Stored as' gives an idea that a single book title is held or stored many times as individual books. A single book is also a copy of the title.

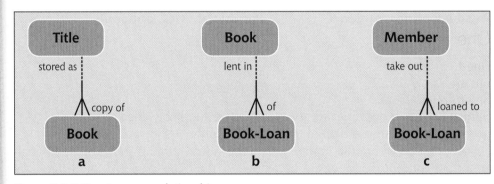

Figure 7.3.5 One-to-many relationship

The relationship between book and loans is similar (see Fig. 7.3.5b):
- One book may be lent in many loans.
- One book loan must be of one single book.

Similarly for the relationship between member and loans (see Fig. 7.3.5c):
- One member may take out many book loans.
- One book loan must be loaned to one single borrower. (*Note*: The book itself may be loaned to many borrowers, but this loan of the book is to this individual borrower.)

Many-to-many relationships

It is not possible to have many-to-many (M:M) relationships in finished ER (or EAR) diagrams as relational databases do not permit such relationships. The relationship is very common in the real world, however, as shown in Figure 7.3.6, one book may be loaned to many members and one member may borrow many books. To model this in an EAR diagram we always create a third (**intersection**) entity with two one-to-many relationships and usually give it a double barrelled name such as 'Member-Book' or 'Book-Loan' (see Fig. 7.3.7).

Naming intersection entities

It is good to give intersection entities meaningful double barrelled names such as Book-Loan, or Order-Line or Student-Enrolment, but alternatively simply use the names of the two entities they are created from.

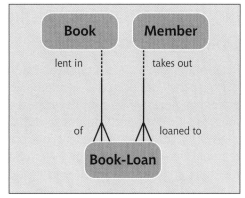

Figure 7.3.7 Example of a many-to-many relationship modelled as two one-to-many relationships

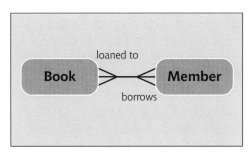

Figure 7.3.6 Example of a many-to-many relationship

So if option 1 for the found entities was chosen, the data modeller would still have arrived at a solution with a book loan included, though it might be called 'Book-Borrowed'.

One-to-one relationships

One-to-one relationships are allowed, but are rarely used. In order to be a one-to-one relationship the entities must share a primary key. This means that they are both uniquely identified by the same attribute (see Fig. 7.3.8). When this is the case, the two entities can clearly be merged. There may be reasons for not doing so, such as security, but this will be very rare. Any one-to-one relationships in an ER diagram should therefore be analysed very carefully before being allowed to remain.

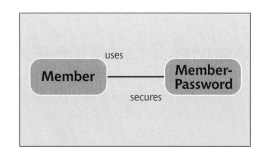

Figure 7.3.8 One-to one relationship

Relationships in relational databases

A relationship in a relational database is a very simple concept. A table may be joined to another to form a new table if they share the same value in a key field (i.e. if the foreign key of a record in one table has the same value as the primary key field in another table). The 'one' end of the EAR relationship is always the primary key and the 'many' end is always the foreign key.

ACTIVITY 1 Sketch ER diagrams ◀

Sketch the following seven ER diagrams, showing the 'one' end of the relationship at the top and the 'many' end at the bottom of each diagram.

1 A customer is allocated to an individual sales region which may contain many customers.
2 Stone College has one office for each employee.
3 ICT staff at Sir John Lawes School share one office.
4 The Principal at Bedville has two offices.
5 Customers place orders.
6 An employee may be responsible for more than one car, but each car is only managed by one employee.
7 Each car is allocated to a group of employees who can only drive that one car.

▶ How optional is a relationship?

Optional and mandatory

Relationships in a data model can be modelled in more detail by considering whether they are optional or mandatory. Many students enrol in their school or college library, but then never take a book out on loan. They still have a membership card and could take out a loan. Similarly, a book can stay on the shelves without ever being lent in a book loan; that is, without ever being in a relationship with a loan. However, a book loan must be loaned to an existing member, and must be of an existing book. The *takes out* and *lent in* relationships shown in the ER model are therefore said to be **optional**, whereas the *loaned to* and *loan of* relationships are said to be **mandatory**. Figure 7.3.9 shows how these are illustrated.

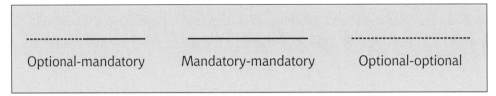

Figure 7.3.9 How to illustrate optional and mandatory relationships

Activity 2 Draw the relationship ◀

A supermarket website signs up customers who they hope will place orders in the future. Draw the relationship (including optionality) between a customer and an order and explain why it is like that.

The final ER model for Mustoe library

Figure 7.3.10 shows the final ER model for the Mustoe Library.

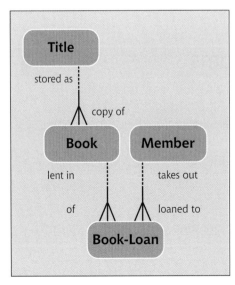

Figure 7.3.10 ER diagram for the Mustoe library

Issues with EARs

Dead crows

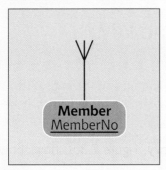

Figure 7.3.11 Example of a dead crow

Crossing lines

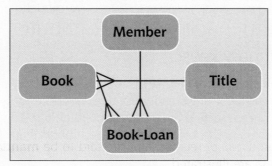

Figure 7.3.12 Crossed lines

Drawing a 1:M relationship with the 'many' end above the 'one' end (see Fig. 7.3.11) is not technically incorrect, but it is usually considered bad practice. It is called a **dead crow** after cartoon images of birds. The reason for avoiding this where possible is that it is easier to follow the logic of a drawing flowing down from the main entity to the subordinate entity, from the one to the many.

The main purpose of an EAR diagram is to untangle the data model and present its constituent parts clearly. A crossing, overlapping diagram, like the one in Figure 7.3.12, does not achieve this.

Numbering the many end

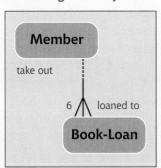

Figure 7.3.13 Incorrect numbering of the many end

Figure 7.3.13 is trying to show that one member is allowed to borrow six books at a time. This is not allowed. The crow's foot means from nought to many, and does not allow a particular number to be specified. In a relational database, the relationship is between a table that may be empty or have a large, but undefined, number of records. This is the structure allowed; if you wish then to impose a limit to the records this must be done programmatically, rather than through the structure.

ACTIVITY 3 Sketch more ER diagrams ◀

Sketch the following five ER diagrams resolving M:M relationships where necessary:

1. Students are taught Unit 7 by Liz, Unit 8 by Steve and Unit 10 by Kate. (Show lecturers and students.)
2. Consultants have many projects to work on and projects can have more than one consultant.
3. Customers place sales orders against stock. Orders may contain many lines of stock.

4 Employees are managed by a single manager who can manage at most eight staff.

5 A DVD hire shop allows customers to borrow four DVDs at a time.

▶ Step 3: Identify the attributes and keys
Primary keys

The job of a primary key is to identify uniquely one instance of the entity. This will usually be a single entity but does not necessarily have to be so; indeed, whenever a concept such as an intersection entity (e.g. Book-Loan) is used, then a composite primary key (a key made up of a number of attributes) should be used.

In this case we have four entities, and thus need four primary keys, as shown in Table 7.3.1. The ISBN, AccessionNumber and MemberNo are all obvious candidates for being primary keys. An ISBN uniquely identifies a book title, an accession number uniquely identifies a copy of the book, and a member number uniquely identifies a member.

Table 7.3.1 Entities and their primary keys for Mustoe Library

Entity	Primary key
Title	ISBN
Book	AccessionNumber
Book-Loan	AccessionNumber, MemberNo, DateOut
Member	MemberNo

The Book-Loan, however, is dealing with an underlying M:M relationship between a member and a book, and thus ought to have both keys in it. Yet the two attributes together would still not uniquely identify the loan. If you borrowed the book today and then borrowed it again next year, the loan would have the same MemberNo and AccessionNumber. But if we add the date the problem can be solved. Thus the primary key for the Book-Loan entity is a composite key made up of MemberNo, BookNo and DateOut. The primary keys are shown in Figure 7.3.14.

Foreign keys

A foreign key is the attribute used to relate one entity physically to another. The foreign key is at the many end of a relationship with the associated primary key at the other. This makes them very easy to identify and write into our EAR diagrams. You simply go to the one end of a relationship, find the primary key and add it to the many end as a foreign key. The ISBN is added to the Book entity; AccessionNumber becomes a foreign key in Book-Loan as does MemberNo. Title and member are not at the many end of a relationship and therefore they cannot have foreign keys. The primary and secondary keys are shown in Figure 7.3.15.

At this stage we have the basic structure of the data model. If the entities, primary keys and foreign keys (and thus the relationships) are correct, the structure of the data model will be correct and the database built on this foundation will be correct.

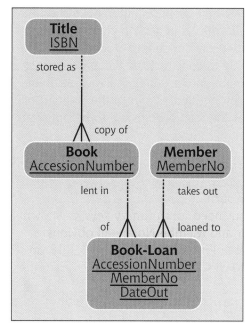

Figure 7.3.14 Mustoe Library System and its primary keys

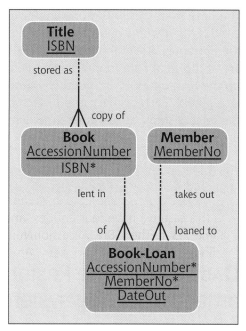

Figure 7.3.15 Mustoe Library System and its primary and foreign keys

Other attributes

The other attributes can now be added to make a complete EAR diagram (see Fig. 7.3.16). This process may take the longest, but can be done in stages. It can be refined and reviewed as the work progresses and prototypes are implemented, provided that the basic structure is correct. You do not want to capture incorrect attributes, but it is not essential to capture every single one at this stage.

▶ The final EAR diagram

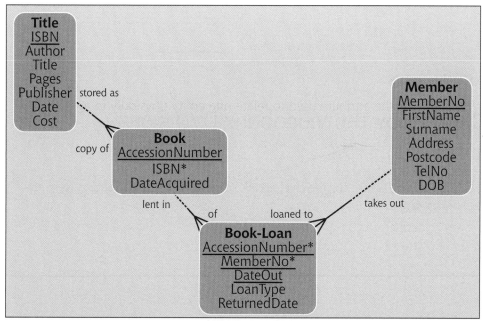

Figure 7.3.16 Mustoe Library EAR model

You have seen that EAR modelling takes the whole scenario, attempts to find the entities, then works out the relationships, allocates keys and finally identifies all the attributes. It is therefore known as a top–down modelling process. Once you are at this final data model stage it is possible to construct the database and set up the relationships. Each entity is simply made into a table, and each attribute into a field. Each primary and foreign key is identified as part of the creation of the relationships; at the same time, whether the relationships are to be optional or mandatory is implemented.

For this Applied GCE course a CASE tool (see panel) is not actually necessary. The authors' preferred solution is a 'smart drawing tool', which will allow smart linking of text and arrows to chart symbols. It is, however, quite possible to create them with any drawing package, including with simple drawing tools in your word-processing or spreadsheet applications.

Drawing the data model

The professional way of creating EAR diagrams is to use a computer-aided software engineering (CASE) tool. This will allow you to create the diagrams, check their logic and help you build a data dictionary automatically for the database. The diagrams in this book are based on the SSADM methodology, which is probably the most popular systems analysis and design methodology in the UK. An SSADM case tool such as Select SSADM could be used.

SSADM

Structured systems analysis and design methodology is a complete set of tools and techniques designed by representatives from UK industry, education and government for use in major system projects in the UK.

CASE STUDY Pure Restaurant Supplies order processing system

Task

Pure Restaurant Supplies are a wholesaler to the vegetarian and whole-food restaurant trade in Lemshire. Work out and draw the EAR diagrams for an order processing system derived from the order shown in Figure 7.3.17 and the case study notes in Unit 7.2. Ensure you include all main attributes. Mark the primary key by underlining, and any foreign keys by suffixing an *. All relationships should be named both ways.

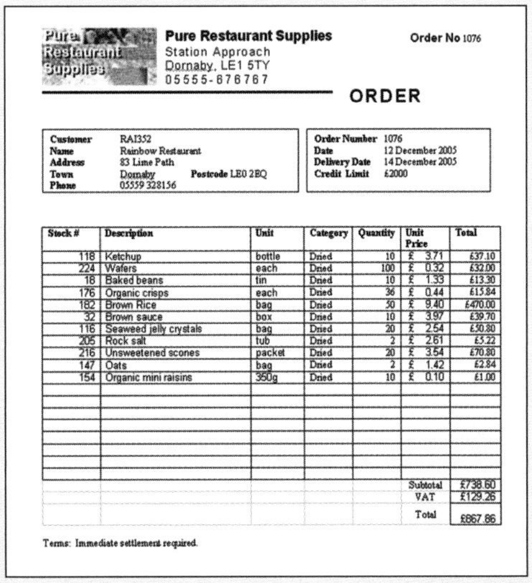

Pure Restaurant Supplies
Station Approach
Dornaby, LE1 5TY
05555-676767

Order No 1076

ORDER

Customer RAI352
Name Rainbow Restaurant
Address 83 Lime Path
Town Dornaby Postcode LE0 2BQ
Phone 05559 328156

Order Number 1076
Date 12 December 2005
Delivery Date 14 December 2005
Credit Limit £2000

Stock #	Description	Unit	Category	Quantity	Unit Price	Total
118	Ketchup	bottle	Dried	10	£ 3.71	£37.10
224	Wafers	each	Dried	100	£ 0.32	£32.00
18	Baked beans	tin	Dried	10	£ 1.33	£13.30
176	Organic crisps	each	Dried	36	£ 0.44	£15.84
182	Brown Rice	bag	Dried	50	£ 9.40	£470.00
32	Brown sauce	box	Dried	10	£ 3.97	£39.70
116	Seaweed jelly crystals	bag	Dried	20	£ 2.54	£50.80
205	Rock salt	tub	Dried	2	£ 2.61	£5.22
216	Unsweetened scones	packet	Dried	20	£ 3.54	£70.80
147	Oats	bag	Dried	2	£ 1.42	£2.84
154	Organic mini raisins	350g	Dried	10	£ 0.10	£1.00
					Subtotal	£738.60
					VAT	£129.26
					Total	£867.86

Terms: Immediate settlement required.

Figure 7.3.17 Pure Restaurant Supplies Ltd order

CASE STUDY The Videobank DVD store

Task

Create an EAR diagram for the Videobank store using the information from the case study in Unit 7.2.

Normalisation

▶ Atomic data

Data in each field of a relational database must be **atomic data**. That is, it must be a single value and not be a group of data such as an array, a list or indeed another set of records.

For example, if a customer has three phone numbers then it is *not correct* to store a list of them as a single field. To even attempt this it would be necessary to store them as a textual list rather than as phone numbers proper. Doing this would prevent the database engine from searching efficiently for a phone number or sorting them properly. You might have to write your own code to search for a telephone number or indeed to display a number (which would be less efficient and more error prone than using the DBMS). Having two identical records with different phone numbers is also not allowed as the key would not then uniquely identify a single record (see Table 7.3.2).

Table 7.3.2 Two identical records recording different phone numbers aren't allowed

Custno	Name	Phone
sf@sjl.co.uk	S. Farrell	07986 765 431
sf@sjl.co.uk	S. Farrell	01582 122 123

If a contact in your address book has two email addresses (see Table 7.3.3) they *should not* be stored in a single field for very similar reasons to the phone numbers. Furthermore, if any of the email addresses were later to be used in relationships the structure of the database would fail.

Table 7.3.3 Two identical records recording different email addresses isn't allowed

First name	Surname	Email
Fred	Forsell	ff105@gymail.com fredforsell25@yahoo.comn

If a customer places a single order for three different stock items these *cannot* be stored as arrays of data in the order record (see Table 7.3.4) without wrecking the functionality of the database altogether.

Table 7.3.4 A record cannot include an array of data

OrderNo	CustNo*	DateOfOrder	StockNo	QuantitySold	Price
1205	sf@sjl.co.uk	1/5/2006	9875 4865 2514	12 1 5	£1.20 £1.40 £9.70

In each of these cases a new table should be created for the lists of repeated data rather than storing the data in the original table. Normalisation attempts to identify and deal with this situation.

▶ Integrity, duplication and redundancy

Good databases are said to have integrity and poor databases are said to lack it. A poor student-information management system may store a student's address in an enrolment record, a timetable record, a course record and an examinations record. If the student changes address part way through a course, the database clerks would have to update all the records containing the student's address. In practice this often means that the student ends up with one address stored in one record and another in other records. Clearly the same could happen to customers in an order-processing database and in countless other scenarios. If customers of a mail-order business can have multiple entries it will be quite simple to have a 'Mr S. Farrel'l, a 'MrS Farrell', a 'Mr S Farell', a 'Mr S Farel' etc. all in the same database, all referring to the same person. The unfortunate Mr Farrell would, and does, then receive countless identical email offers to his various unintended pseudonyms.

The essence of a good relational database is that data is never duplicated in this way. Keys can be, and indeed must be, duplicated in order to join together related tables, but other attributes must never be.

If data is stored more than once in the database, the database is said to have **redundant data**. Redundant data lacks integrity. For a database to have integrity the data must be stored once, in one table. When the data is updated, it is updated in that table alone. Thus a customer's address will be stored once in the customer table, perhaps using the email address as the key (see Unit 2). If an order is placed by that customer, the email address is stored in the order table and whenever the customer's full name and address are needed that email address is used to reference the customer record which is the only place the full name and address are stored. If the customer's address changes it will therefore be changed for all orders, for all invoices, for all deliveries, and for all mail shots, as they will all refer back to the one customer record.

The normalisation process

Normalisation starts with the data and attempts – through a rigorous, systematic process – to build up to the final tables required in the database. If this and the EAR modelling are performed correctly then the results of the two models will be identical. Unlike EAR modelling, however, this process starts with the data and works bottom upwards to the tables. The overall process is straightforward but strict. The unnormalised data is first processed into what is known as **first normal form**. Data in first normal form (1NF) is then processed into **second normal form** (2NF). Data in second normal form is then processed into **third normal form** (3NF). This is data that is suitable for a relational database, with the vast majority of the redundancy removed. It is not possible to complete the process in any other order. It must follow all the steps in this one order. This is summarised in Figure 7.3.18.

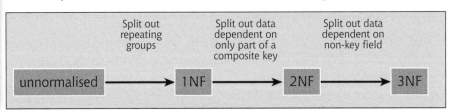

Figure 7.3.18 The normalisation process

Worked example: training course database

The staff in a large organisation attend a number of training courses each year as part of their continuing professional development. The details of these courses are recorded in a spreadsheet at the moment; an extract of which is shown in Table 7.3.5. (*Note*: No employee is allowed to go on the same course twice.)

Table 7.3.5 Training course records

E#	Name	Address	Dept#	Deptname	Loc	Salary	C#	Desc	Date	Cost	Prov#	Name	Address
1	Steve	The Hovel	1	ICT	Mi5	£9000	121	Internet	12/5/05	1200	1200	LTea	Euston
							155	Teaching	14/5/05	900	1001	WDC	Markyate
2	Andy	2 Wheel St	1	ICT	Mi5	£8999	155	Teaching	14/8/05	945	1001	WDC	Markyate
3	Sue	5 The Place	2	Finance	SOPs	£29000	122	Bus.Net	13/5/05	1200	1200	L.Tea	Euston
							123	Adv Bus	14/10/05	1250	1200	L.Tea	Euston
							121	Internet	12/5/05	1200	1200	LTea	Euston

Activity 4 Achieve data integrity ◀

1 Identify the repeating groups of data in Table 7.3.5 that must be eliminated.
2 Identify the redundant information in this table.

Step 1: Identify the unnormalised data

This step simply involves identifying every single atomic piece of data and giving each a sensible data name. Repeating groups of data should ideally be marked (overlining is the conventional way of doing this).

Employee {EmployeeNum, Name, Address, Salary, DeptNo, DeptName, DeptLocation, CourseNum, Description, Date, Cost, ProviderNum, ProviderName, ProviderAddress}

At each step from now on there are two sub-processes. Firstly, there is a rule as to how to split the tables into two in order to eliminate the redundancy. Secondly, there is a rule as to what the foreign key will be to enable the new table to join back to the original table when required.

Step 2: Convert to 1NF

- Split any repeating group of data into a separate table.
- Add the key of the original table to act as a foreign key.

Employee {EmployeeNum, Name, Address, Salary, DeptNo, DeptName, DeptLocation}
Employee-course {EmployeeNum*, CourseNum, Description, Date, Cost, ProviderNum, ProviderName, ProviderAddress}

The primary key for the table made from the repeating group will have a composite key made up from the original primary key along with the main identifier for the repeating group, in this case EmployeeNum and CourseNum.

Note that in this case these two fields will uniquely identify each record. If the employees could take the same course twice then it would be necessary to add the date fields as well.

Step 3: Convert to 2NF

Once the data is in first normal form it is possible to convert it to second normal form:
- Split out data dependent on only part of a composite key field.
- The foreign key will be the part of the composite key that is being processed.

Employee {EmployeeNum, Name, Address, Salary, DeptNo, DeptName, DeptLocation}

In this first table there isn't a composite key, so as the table is already in 1NF it must also be in 2NF.

Employee-Course {EmployeeNum, CourseNum, Description, Date, Cost, ProviderNum, ProviderName, ProviderAddress}

In this second table there is a composite key: EmployeeNum was part of the original entity so we need not process this. We therefore concentrate on CourseNum. Some of the data changes in the same way every time the CourseNum changes. For example, CourseNum 121 is an internet course provided by Ltea; '155' is a teaching course provided by WDC etc. This is the case whatever the EmployeeNum, therefore we can say that the Description, ProviderNum, ProviderName, ProviderAddress are all more dependent on CourseNum than on the composite key EmployeeNum, CourseNum. In practice this means simply that this is course data rather than attendance data.

The process in detail:
- Create a new entity based on part of the composite key called 'Course'. Look at each attribute in turn and see if it belongs to attendance (Employee-Course) or course alone.
- We end up with the following tables at 2NF:

Employee {EmployeeNum, Name, Address, Salary, DeptNo, DeptName, DeptLocation}
Employee-Course {EmployeeNum*, CourseNum*, Date, Cost}
Course {CourseNum, Description, ProviderNum, ProviderName, ProviderAddress}

Step 4: Convert to 3NF

Once the data is in second normal form it is possible to convert it to third normal form:
- Split out data dependent on a non-key field.
- The foreign key will be the non-key field left behind.

This sounds difficult, but is actually relatively simple in practice. We are essentially looking for an entity within another entity. Within Employee we can see there is a department. Within Course there is a provider. Identify the field that could be used as a key field for these entities. This will be used as a primary key in the new table and a foreign key in the original table. The other fields, which are more dependent on this than the containing entity, are removed to the new entity.

For example:

Employee {<u>EmployeeNum</u>, Name, Address, Salary, DeptNo, DeptName, DeptLocation}

This clearly contains a department entity. The candidate primary key for a new department entity is DeptNo.

A new entity is created called 'Dept' with the key DeptNo, and fields DeptName and DeptLocation, which change with DeptNo more directly than EmployeeNum. DeptNo is also left behind as a foreign key.

Employee {<u>EmployeeNum</u>, Name, Address, Salary, DeptNo*}

Dept {<u>DeptNo</u>, DeptName, DeptLocation}

The final 3NF data model

Employee {<u>EmployeeNum</u>, Name, Address, Salary, DeptNo*}

Dept {<u>DeptNo</u>, DeptName, DeptLocation}

Employee-Course {<u>EmployeeNum</u>*, <u>CourseNum</u>*, Date, Cost}

Course {<u>CourseNum</u>, Description, ProviderNum*}

Provider {<u>ProviderNum</u>, ProviderName, ProviderAddress}

ACTIVITY 5 Draw the EAR diagram ◀

Draw the EAR diagram for the training course data model.

ACTIVITY 6 Normalise data ◀

Given the data in the data model for the Mustoe Library system normalise to 1NF, 2NF and 3NF showing each stage and the final data model. Ensure the final data model matches the final EAR data model.

Unnormalised data:

Member {<u>MemberNo</u>, FirstName, Surname, Address, Postcode, TelNo, DOB, AccessionNumber, DateOut, LoanType, ReturnedDate, DateAcquired, ISBN, Author, Title, Pages, Publisher, Date, Cost}

ACTIVITY 7 Normalise athletes in races ◀

One athlete can take part in many races.

Unnormalised data:

Competitor {Comp#, Name, Address, Club#, ClubName, Race#, Description, RaceRecord, StartTime}

Some sample data is shown in Table 7.3.6.

Table 7.3.6 Sample data for an athelete

Comp#	Name	Addr	Club#	ClubName	Race#	Desc	Race Record	Start Time
1	Steve	The Hovel	100	SJL raiders	1	Egg and spoon	1:21	13:00
					2	Sack	1:45	13:30

Normalise to 1NF, 2NF and 3NF, and create an EAR diagram from the final data model.

ACTIVITY 8 Normalise MP3-player playlist ◀

Note: The playlist has many tracks, each played by one artist.
Unnormalised data:

Playlist {List#, Name, DateCreated, Author, TrackNo, TrackName, ArtistNo, ArtistName, Size, Genre}

Some sample data is given in Table 7.3.7.

Table 7.3.7 Sample data from an MP3 playlist

List#	Name	Date Created	Author	TrackNo	TrackName	ArtistNo	Artist Name	Size	Genre
1	OMIGOD	12/12/05	Steve	1	Hallelujah	1	J.Buckley	4:55	alternative
				2	Into My Arms	2	N.Cave	3:02	alternative
				3	Wild Roses	2	N.Cave	3.05	alternative

Normalise to 1NF, 2NF, 3NF and create an EAR diagram from the final data model.

ACTIVITY 9 Normalise magazine articles ◀

One magazine has many articles; each is written by one author. (*Note*: The article may be used more than once in different magazines.)
Unnormalised data:

Magazine {Magazine#, Title, Issue, NumPages, Article#, Title, Topic, WordCount, AuthorID, AuthorName, BankAccountNum, BankNum, VatRegNo}

Normalise to 1NF, 2NF, 3NF and create an EAR diagram from the final data model.

CASE STUDY Pure Restaurant Supplies ◀

Given the following data derived from the information in the previous case studies, normalise the data for PRS and verify the solution against your EAR diagram.

ONo, Date, DeliveryDate, DeliveredDate, CustomerID, Name, Number, FirstLine, Town, County, Postcode, Phone, CreditLimit, Stockno, Quantity, Description, Unit, Location, Category, Quantity, Cost, Price, Min, Reorder, SupplierNum, SupplierName, SupplierHouseNumber, SupplierFirstLine, SupplierTown, SupplierCounty, SupplierPostcode, SupplierPhone

CASE STUDY Videobank ◀

Derive the fields using information from the previous Videobank DVD store case studies, normalise the data and verify the solution against your EAR diagram.

Nailing down the data

Once the EAR diagram and the normalisation have been completed and verified by checking against each other, the database designer can really begin to nail down the data: specifying the data in as much detail as possible in order to make the database as robust as possible. The main tools for doing this are by data naming, data typing and validation. The results of this are all contained in a data dictionary (see Table 7.2.2), which is a repository for all the decisions about the data in the database.

▶ Data names

Naming the data appropriately is often seen as somewhat tedious, but it is an important task. The data should be given meaningful names rather than shorthand symbols; equally the name should not be overlong or cumbersome. It is possible to have data names that are very long and descriptive such as 'the quantity in stock' but such names are hard to use, and so it is best to use short descriptive names with no spaces.

Ideally designers will use a naming convention for all names. Spaces are not good practice and should be avoided by, for example, capitalising each successive word: (e.g. StockLevel) or using an underscore in each gap (e.g. stock_level). Some designers incorporate the data type in the name (e.g. intStockLevel), but this may be unnecessary and indeed may even give undue prominence to the physical database at the expense of the data model. The exact naming convention does not matter so much as consistency. If you are consistent with your names, eventually you will use these naturally and be able to refer to them fluently throughout the development process.

▶ Data types

Data typing is the most effective and widely used method for ensuring the accuracy and correctness of the data in the database. If the correct data type is chosen the database can automatically ensure that a great deal of poor data is automatically excluded from the database. For example, if a date data type is chosen for a DateOfBirth field the database will exclude any entry of purely textual or numeric data. It cannot prevent all errors, such as entering a date that is too young or too old, but it does avoid many errors caused by mistyping or misunderstanding. Similarly, setting a Wage field to currency will ensure that only currency data is entered and not date/time data, for example.

Different relational database management systems will allow different data types. It is important therefore that you learn the data types your system will use. The basic types are **character** (char or text), **Boolean** (yes or no) and **numeric**. Microsoft Access allows a very wide range of data types including many different numeric types. Table 7.3.8 summarises these.

Table 7.3.8 Summary of the main data types allowed in Access

Type	Range	Examples	Comments
Text	0 to 255 chars	152 The Parade	
Number: integer	-32 768 to +32 767	10 000	2 bytes
Number: byte	0 to 255	100	1 byte
Number: long integer	-2 147 483 648 to 2 147 483 647	125 000	4 bytes
Number: decimal	$-(10^{28}-1)$ to $10^{28}-1$	12.56	
Number: single	7 decimal places or large numbers	1.765472	

Continued on the next page

Type	Range	Examples	Comments
Number: double	15 decimal places or very large numbers	3.333 333 333 333	
Currency		£152 758.20	Accurate to 15.4 digits (15 digits before the decimal point and 4 after)
AutoNumber	As for long integer	1230	Automatically created long integer (sequential or random)
Date/time		12 May 2000	Stored numerically; displayed as a date
Boolean	Yes or no	Yes	Boolean, true/false 1 bit field
Hyperlink		http://www.msn.com	[text], address, [screentip] up to 64k characters
Object		An image	Linked or embedded object
Memo	Up to 65 536 characters	An essay on the ...	Non-searchable notes field

Once data is properly typed it is also possible to validate it further in order to ensure that the data entered is as accurate and correct as possible. Text fields can be validated using length, existence, list and picture checks as you learnt in Unit 2. Numeric fields can be validated further using existence checks, range checks and so on.

ACTIVITY 10 Match data and data type ◀

Match the data in the list with its data type.

Data	Data type
765 789	Text
Paul Allen	Long integer or AutoNumber
£100 000.00	Date/time
25	Number: single
Yes	Currency
Robin Hood	Text
17/05/1987	Boolean
12.7	Number: byte
1005	Long integer
70 000	Integer

▶ Verification and validation

Verification and validation are both means of helping to ensure that the data entered into the database is accurate and correct. Verification usually involves some sort of double check to ensure that the data entered is correct, whereas validation will involve a check to ensure that the data entered is valid data (though the data may still be incorrect).

Verification

Verification attempts to check the accuracy of the data entry. In data entry this usually involves utilising some form of double check. When you change your password you are usually asked to verify it by entering it twice. A meter reader will often put two readings onto a card, or straight onto a PDA. The first will be a mark on a dial, which will be read by an optical mark reader. The second will be a copy of the actual digits written into a set of boxes that will be read by an optical character reader. The processor will compare the two inputs: if they are the same, this is unlikely to have occurred by chance; if they are different they are rejected and checked by a person to see if it is possible to decide which is correct.

Figure 7.3.19 A meter reading

Validation

Validation also attempts to ensure good data entry but it works in a different way to verification. Validation will apply a set of rules to the individual item of data entered to ensure that it is of the right form or type. This idea essentially extends the concept of data typing. A quantity in stock field will probably be numeric. It will most probably be an integer data type. This restricts it to being a whole number between -32768 and +32767. A quantity in stock cannot ever be negative; also, it may be that the company never holds more than 1000 of any stock item. So it is possible to extend the idea of the data type to say it is an integer between 0 and 1000 inclusive. If a data entry clerk enters data such as -9 or 1100 as the quantity in stock, whether deliberately or accidentally, the DBMS will know this is invalid data. If the clerk enters data between 0 and 1000 there will be no way of knowing merely by validation that this individual piece of data is actually correct; that it represents the real stock situation. However, the RDBMS can at least reject other incorrect data out of hand. In Unit 2 you learnt about the five commonly defined forms of validation; these are summarised in Table 7.3.9. These all have different parts to play in ensuring the integrity of the database.

> **File-look up check validation**
>
> Another form of validation that is sometimes employed is file look-up check validation. This is a variation on list validation in which the list to be checked is held in another file or table. Valid entries can only be those that match an entry in the specified table or file.

Table 7.3.9 Validation checks

Type	Checking	Typical field	Example
Length	Maximum length of a text field	Surname	20
Presence	Whether a value has been entered into a field	Email	Required
Range	Whether the value entered is in the acceptable range for the field	StockQuantity	>0 and <1000
List	Whether the value entered is one of a list of acceptable values	Title	Mr, Mrs, Miss or Ms
Picture (input mask)	Whether the entered value is in the right format	SupplierNum	S099

ACTIVITY 11 Validate length for Videobank database

For each of the textual items of data in Table 7.3.10, determine their actual character length. Remember to count the spaces as characters.

Table 7.3.10

Field	Example data	Length
Postcode	HP22 5XY	8
Surname	Smith	
Telephone number	01442 225525	
DVD title	The Perfect Storm	
Rating	12A	

ACTIVITY 12 Identify potential problems validating data for Videobank database

Find the potential problems with the data in Table 7.3.11.

Table 7.3.11

Field	Data	Problem
Postcode	AL5 4QPRS3	
Date of birth	12/12/2020	
Date due back	12 May	
Cost	£15.375	
DVD returned?	<no data>	

ACTIVITY 13 Write validation rules for Videobank database

Write, in words or symbols, a validation rule for the fields in Table 7.3.12.

Table 7.3.12

Field	Validation Rule
Date of birth	Members must be older than 18 years
Title (Mr/Mrs etc.)	
DVD length (in minutes)	
Gender	
DVD returned?	

ACTIVITY **14** Create data dictionary entries ◄

What name, data type and validation should be applied to the fields in Table 7.3.13?

Table 7.3.13

Field	Name	Type	Validation
Age on a driving licence form			
Date of birth for an employee of a large organisation on joining			
Annual salary for a clerk in the civil service			
Quantity in stock for a small shopkeeper			
Cost of an item of stock			
Price of an item in stock			
Gender field in a personnel table			
Credit limit on an order			
Order date			
Delivery date			
Delivered date			
ID field for a book			
Person's weight			
Person's eye colour			
Number of items bought of one barcode at an EPOS			
Number of stars seen by a telescope in a night			

CASE STUDY PRS data dictionary ◄

Using this table, create a data dictionary for each of the tables in the Pure Restaurant Supplies case study.

CASE STUDY Videobank data dictionary ◄

Using this table, create a data dictionary for each of the tables in the Videobank database.

ACTIVITY 15 Complete the database crossword ◀

Print out and complete the crossword in Figure 7.3.20.

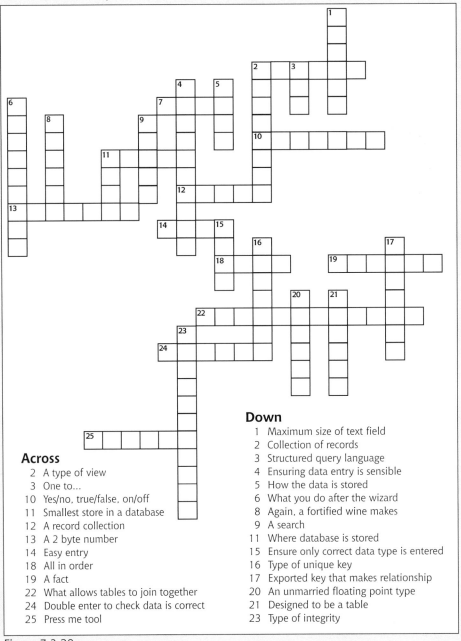

Across
2 A type of view
3 One to...
10 Yes/no, true/false, on/off
11 Smallest store in a database
12 A record collection
13 A 2 byte number
14 Easy entry
18 All in order
19 A fact
22 What allows tables to join together
24 Double enter to check data is correct
25 Press me tool

Down
1 Maximum size of text field
2 Collection of records
3 Structured query language
4 Ensuring data entry is sensible
5 How the data is stored
6 What you do after the wizard
8 Again, a fortified wine makes
9 A search
11 Where database is stored
15 Ensure only correct data type is entered
16 Type of unique key
17 Exported key that makes relationship
20 An unmarried floating point type
21 Designed to be a table
23 Type of integrity

Figure 7.3.20

Conclusion ▶ ▶ ▶

In Unit 7.3 we have examined in some depth how to create a data model with integrity to underlie a database. We have looked at how to create an EAR diagram. We have seen why we normalise and how to normalise to third normal form. We have discovered that these two processes reach the same point via different routes and thus they can be used to verify each other. Finally, we have looked at how to construct a solid set of data dictionaries to firm up the data model ready for the next stage.

Having written the functional specification and created a correct data model, it is possible to build, populate and test the relational structure for the database. In Unit 7.4 we will investigate how to do this using the Pure Restaurant Supplies case study that we have used earlier. Creating the structure is essentially a simple process of inputting the data model in the manner required by the RDBMS. In the first part we will examine how to create the tables, how to add the fields and apply all the different validation rules. In the second part we will look at how to define the relationships between tables correctly, in order that the RDBMS can use these rules to maintain the integrity of the database.

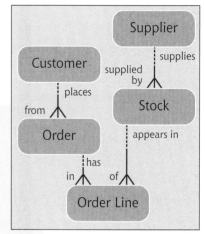

Figure 7.4.1 An ER diagram for PRS

CASE STUDY Pure Restaurant Supplies

Look at the full data model. The ER diagram is also shown in Figure 7.4.1.
1 What tables are required?
2 Name the primary key of each table.
3 Name the foreign keys required for each table.
4 Look at Table 7.4.1. Briefly identify what validation is to be applied to each field.

Table 7.4.1 Data dictionary the PRS stock table

Stock					
Name	**Type**	**Length**	**Format**	**Other Validation**	**Comments**
StockNo	Number		Long		PK
Description	Text	30			
Unit	Text	20			
Location	Text	2	L0		
Category	Text	10		Dried or fresh or frozen	Combo box
Quantity	Number		Integer	>=0	*Default=0
Cost	Currency		2dp	>=0	
Price	Currency		2dp	>=0	
Min	Number			>=0	
Reorder	Number			>0	
SupplierNum	Text	4	LL00		FK

Key PK: primary key; FK: foreign key; *: required

The first stage in any process of creating a new database application is to create the database itself.

ACTIVITY 1 Create a new PRS database

Open Access and create a new blank database. Any sensible name can be given to the database file. In this case, call it 'PRS.mdb'.

Figure 7.4.2 The new database

Part 1: Create the tables and fields to match the data dictionary

▶ Creating the tables

The first task having created the database is to add each table as defined in its data dictionary. There are five tables defined in the data model for Pure Restaurant Supplies (see Fig. 7.4.1).

Table 7.4.2 Object naming conventions

Object	Prefix	Example
Table	tbl	tblCustomer
Query	qry	qryAllCustomers
Macro	mcr	mcrShowInvoice
Form	frm	frmNewCustomer
Report	rpt	rptInvoice

ACTIVITY 2 Name the tables ◀

Write down the names of the five tables required by the data model, using the naming conventions described.

Virtually all modern RDBMSs have a user-friendly facility for entering the details of field names, types and validations from the data dictionary. (The alternative is to create the whole structure using SQL which, while more cumbersome, is still relatively straightforward once the data model is fully defined. SQL is often used for web databases.) To create the tables you will use the Design View, which will allow you to define all the fields in exactly the manner you need, and will allow you to implement virtually all facets of the data dictionary in a user-friendly manner. The first table you will implement is the stock table (see Table 7.4.1). The important thing to note is that you will simply be translating the various parts of the data dictionary into a form suitable for Access. All the inventive work should have been completed while designing the data model.

ACTIVITY 3 Enter field names for the stock table ◀

Look at this demonstration from the ActiveBook showing how to create a new table.

Now create a new table in Design View. Enter all the data names from the data dictionary into the field name column of the Table Design View (see Fig. 7.4.3).

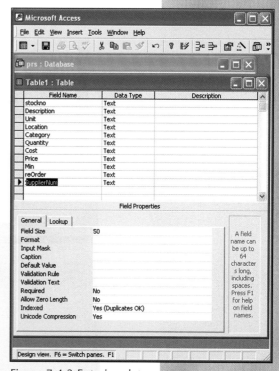

Figure 7.4.3 Entering data names

At this stage each field has the data type set as text, at the default length for a text field (usually 50 characters in Access). Clearly this is not how they will end up. It is quite possible to define each field fully, changing the type and the validation before moving on to the next field. However, when the data model has been fully defined, this is not necessary and is less efficient. We will concentrate on explaining how to implement a single element of the data dictionary at a time. This also has the advantage that the developer can concentrate on a single task at a time, and so, potentially, be more efficient. When developing databases for yourself, it is a matter of taste whether you take this approach or the alternative of fully defining a single field at a time.

▶ Defining the primary key

Once the field names have been entered, the next task is to define the primary key and save the table definition. The primary key is the field, or fields, that define uniquely each record. It is central to a relational database structure that each record is unique and that it is identified by a key, and thus it is an extremely important step in

Naming fields

Access is very flexible as to how fields are named. It permits almost any combination of letters, spaces, digits and even some punctuation. However, this is by no means universal in RDBMSs and is not always sensible in Access. We advise that names should be restricted to letters and numbers, starting with a letter, and that spaces should not be used. Multi-word identifiers should use the normal convention of capitalising the first letter of second and subsequent words. This will prevent many common problems at later stages of database development. The Caption field property can be used to display the field using spaces if desired.

the process. If no key has been identified when you save the table definition, the RDBMS will even ask if you want to create one. If you accept this, it will add an extra ID field of an AutoNumber type. This is fine if you are developing a quick temporary application on the fly, but totally unacceptable for a properly managed project. The primary key should already be defined in the data model as keys are the basis of the relationships in the model. In the case of the stock table the key field is the StockNo. Each StockNo is unique and identifies one product in the table.

ACTIVITY 4 Define the Primary Key and save the table

Figure 7.4.4 shows how to set the primary keys and save a table. You can also see a demonstration from the ActiveBook.

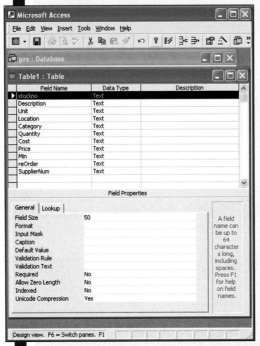

1 Highlight the required field and press the key tool icon on the toolbar

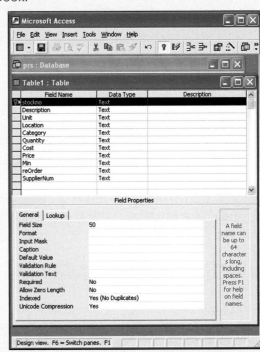

2 A key appears in the left cell showing that the StockNo field is the primary key

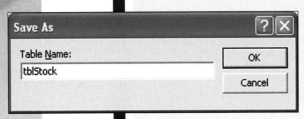

3 Now save the table using the proper naming convention as 'tblStock'

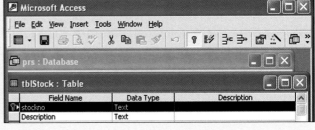

4 The name will now appear at the top of the image

Figure 7.4.4 Setting primary key and saving the table structure

Composite primary keys

To define a composite primary key, the process is exactly the same as for defining a single field primary key. Simply drag the mouse (or use 'Shift-click' or 'Ctrl-click' as appropriate) over each field in the composite key before setting the key with the tool icon (see Fig. 7.4.5).

Saving the structure

It is preferable to save the structure as early as possible in case of problems at any stage. It is not possible to save the table definition without any fields defined and it is not desirable without the primary key defined, so it is suggested that the first save is immediately after the data names have been entered and the primary key defined. The structure should then be saved as regularly as possible as part of your standard working practice.

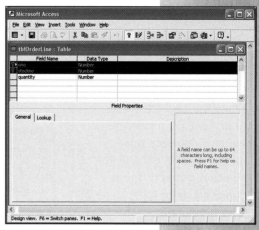

Figure 7.4.5 Setting composite primary keys

AutoNumbers

An AutoNumber is a special data type. It is essentially a numeric field whose value is determined (generated) automatically by the RDBMS. In its default mode an AutoNumber field in each new record entered into a database will have its value incremented by one. The first record will have a field value 1, the second 2, the third 3 etc. Furthermore, and crucially, if a record is deleted the AutoNumber value will not be reused. This is intended to automate similar processes in manual sequential numbering systems.

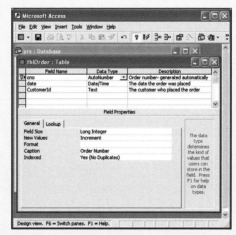

Figure 7.4.6 AutoNumber data types

Access allows some customisation of the auto-numbering process. It is possible to assign random values rather than sequential numbers (using the NewValues property that can be seen in Figure 7.4.6). By careful use of Append Queries (see Unit 7.5) it is also possible to start the sequential auto-numbering process at numbers other than one.

Manual sequential numbering systems

A very simple form of manual numbering system is the duplicate pad such as those used by small traders for receipts. These have a number on the top right of each page that increments by one for each page. No two receipts, therefore, will ever have the same number.

At a more sophisticated level, manual sales, purchase order, invoicing, accounting systems etc. often use a similar numbering system. The sets of paperwork are pre-printed with incrementing numbers that are never duplicated. These are invaluable in ensuring that all goods sent out are invoiced, and that all documents are accounted for. They also help to prevent a wide range of frauds as each number can only be used once and its use can be verified.

Defining types

The next stage in creating the structure from the data model is to enter the data types for each field. Again, with a well defined data dictionary this is a very straightforward process. The data type for each field is simply selected using the combo box in the 'Data Type' column.

ACTIVITY 5 Select the data types

1 Select the appropriate data types for each field in the stock table using the data dictionary. If the field is numeric set the appropriate Field Size property as well.
2 Save the table structure.

This process is shown in Figure 7.4.7. You can also watch this demonstration from the ActiveBook.

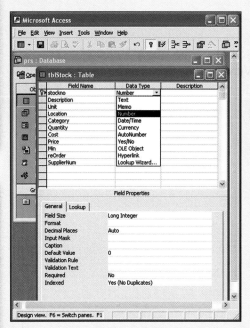
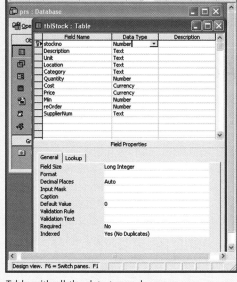

Select the data type for each field in turn   Table with all the data types chosen

Figure 7.4.7 Selecting data types

Defining the validation

You saw in Unit 7.3 that there are five main types of validation you normally need to enforce.

ACTIVITY 6 Identify data validation types

What are the five main types of validation? As a reminder, a word describing each of the images in Figure 7.4.8 sounds like one of the types of validation.

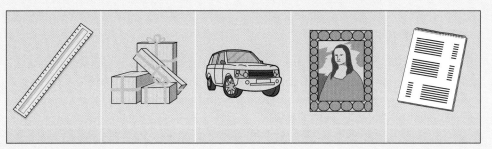

Figure 7.4.8 Sounds like ...

Presence validation

For some fields in the database it is essential that data is entered, whereas other fields can sensibly be left empty. A customer record without the name of the customer is quite useless, whereas it would be quite reasonable not to know the telephone number of a customer whom you dealt with entirely by mail. Presence validation states whether or not the value is required or must be present in the record. If it is required, it will enforce this by not allowing the user to add or amend a record if the data is not there. Primary key fields clearly have to be present, but these are enforced automatically. In the stock table, the data model states that the Quantity field is required. To enforce this, all that is necessary is to set the field properties at the foot of the Design View so that Required is 'Yes'.

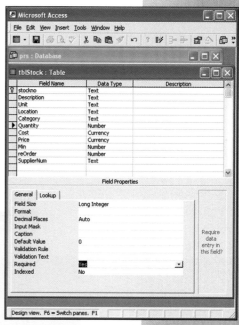

Figure 7.4.9 Presence validation

ACTIVITY 7 Set presence validation ◀

Set Quantity so that Required is 'Yes' (see Fig. 7.4.9). Then save the table structure.

Test the validation by trying to save a record with the field empty and with data in.

You can also see a demonstration of this from the ActiveBook.

Setting the maximum length of the text fields

The critical factor here is what is required by the data model. The usual method when creating the data model is to allocate the amount of space required by the single largest data value in the domain of possible values. Clearly then, any data entry longer than this will be invalid. This is a simple but extremely effective means of validating input of text fields.

ACTIVITY 8 Set the length of text fields ◀

Set the Field Size (length) of each of the text fields in the stock table (see Fig. 7.4.10). Then save the table structure.

Test the validation by attempting to add values with lengths less than, equal to and more than the maximum length set.

You can also see a demonstration of this from the ActiveBook.

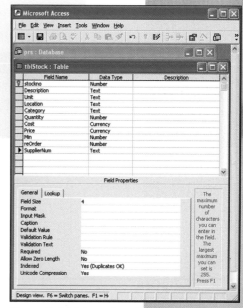

Setting the format (picture) validation

The Format column of the data dictionary defines the formats for the data input. This may be of two distinct types:

1 For text fields it is possible to define an input mask that will only allow specific characters, or types of characters, to be entered in particular positions in the field. This is **picture validation**.
2 For fields with other data types it may be used to specify the format the input data is displayed in. For example, a currency data type may be specified to have two decimal places; a date may be

Figure 7.4.10 Length validation

formatted to be displayed as a medium format date (e.g. 24 Mar 2006). This does not actually validate the input, although it may make data entry simpler and so more accurate, and so is included in the data dictionary.

▶ Input masks

Input masks are a well established means of controlling data input very precisely. In Access they have two main parts. There are masking characters (see Table 7.4.3) that are used to control what data may be input at each position in the text string, and there are action characters that transform the input data in some way (see Table 7.4.4). These are used in combination to create a powerful method of controlling textual data entry (see Table 7.4.5).

Table 7.4.3 Masking characters for input masks

Description	Required	Optional
Digit (0 to 9) only	0	9
Digit, space, + or -	n/a	#
Letter (A to Z)	L	?
Letter or digit	A	a
Any character or a space	&	C

Table 7.4.4 Action characters for input masks

Character	Description
<	All succeeding characters are converted to lower case
>	All succeeding characters are converted to upper case
\	The succeeding character is displayed as itself (For example, \L is displayed as L)
Password	Setting the **Input Mask** property to the word **Password** creates a password box (all characters are displayed as *)

Table 7.4.5 Examples of input masks

Field	Example	Mask
A customer number made up from 3 letters followed by 3 digits	MAR123	LLL000
A customer number made up from 3 letters followed by a number between 1 and 999	MAR12	LLL099
A customer number made up from between 1 and 6 digits	123456	099999
An EAN13 product number made up from 13 digits	3273498365204	0000000000000
'Male' or 'Female'	Male	>L<LLL??
A password of between 6 and 10 characters containing letters and numbers	Ch1efta1n	AAAAAAaaaa

ACTIVITY 9 Work out some input masks ◀

Work out the mask for the fields in Table 7.4.6.

Table 7.4.6

Field	Example	Mask
A national insurance number comprising 2 letters, 6 digits, 1 letter	YE234555C	
A name that could be between 2 and 10 letters; first character upper case and rest lower case	Heathcote	
An employee number that is the first letters of the surname, then 4 digits (the year of hiring) then a unique letter; all letters must be in upper case	FAR2003A	
A mask that allows Mr, Mrs, Miss, Ms or Dr; first character uppercase and rest lower	Mrs	
A mask that allows numbers between 1 and 999	23	
An ISBN	1-55555-555-1	

ACTIVITY 10 Create some input masks ◀

Create the input masks for the Location and SupplierNum fields of the stock table (see Fig. 7.4.11). Then save the table structure.

Test the validation of the fields by entering valid and invalid characters and seeing what happens.

You can view a demonstration of how to do this from the ActiveBook.

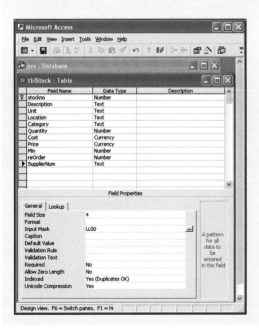

Figure 7.4.11 Picture validation

Input Mask Wizard

Access provides a Wizard to help with the creation of the input mask. It allows you to change the placeholder character and test the mask prior to deploying it. It also allows you to name the mask as an object in the database and thus reuse it as necessary. However, it does not help you to select the characters to be used, which is really the essential part of the task. In practice, therefore, it is rarely necessary to use the Wizard.

▶ Setting the range validation

Range validation checks that the data entered is within a range specified in the data model. A quantity in stock, for example, cannot actually be negative. Allowing a user to enter a negative number will allow nonsense data (or garbage) into the database. A numeric data type will normally allow positive and negative (signed) numbers. Unless your DBMS allows you to specify unsigned numbers as a data type, then it will be possible for the user to enter nonsense data. Range validation prevents this.

To set the range validation it is a simple case of putting the validation rule in the Validation Rule field property (see Table 7.4.7), then putting the text you want to appear when the rule is violated in the validation text property. This field should not be left blank as the RDBMS will then supply a default message which will be a somewhat technical error message that your users will probably not understand.

Table 7.4.7 Operators used with range validation

Operator*	Meaning	Example
<	Less than	< £10
<=	Less than or equal to	<= 100
=	Is equal to/forces the value	= 0
>=	Greater than or equal to	>= 0
>	Greater than	> 0
Between	Between two numbers	Between 1 and 10
And	Both conditions must be true	>= 0 and <= 100
Or	One condition must be true	> 10 or < -10
Not	Condition must be false	Not(<10)

*Note: These operators may also be used with text fields, where the field is compared alphabetically, but this is less useful.

ACTIVITY 11 Write validation statements ◀

The following are examples of validation rules that might appear in a data dictionary; write the equivalent validation statement for Access:

1 between £10 and £20 inclusive
2 less than 50
3 less than or equal to 0.333 333 333 333 3
4 over 1000
5 over zero up to £100 000.00
6 at least 18 years old
7 between 2 weeks and 3 weeks from now
8 between 16 years old and 65 years old.

▶ Range validation on dates

Dates are treated as special cases by most RDBMSs. They are extremely commonly used, but are formatted as though they are structured data types (i.e. that they are made up from three or more fields, e.g. 28/05/2005). In practice, as was seen in Unit 2, a date value is stored in Access as a decimal number with the whole number part representing the days since the end of December 1899 and the decimal part the seconds since midnight. The result of this is that extra care must be taken when validating dates.

For example, a delivery date might have to be between 1 and 14 days from today. The simplest idea is to let the data entry clerk enter the two dates directly: '> #2 May 2005#' and '< #16 May 2005#'. (*Notes*: The # symbol signifies the start and end of a literal date. Also it is best to enter the dates in this medium date format to avoid confusion between American and English dates – remember that Americans read 6/8 as 8 June). Of course, this leaves the data entry clerk with a lot of responsibility for calculating the dates correctly. If you know today's date you can ease the data entry process and create a better structure. This is given by a function commonly used in Microsoft packages called now(). The validation rule will then be '>= now() + 1 and <= now() + 14' as each number represents a whole day more since 31 December 1899.

Another special problem with dates is that it is conventional and sensible to store dates of birth rather than ages, since the latter are subject to annual change. If a club member must be over 16 years old, then the validation has to take into account a number of factors: the member's date of birth, the date today, and the number of days in 16 years. 16 years converted into days is 16×365 days plus an extra 4 days to allow for leap years. Thus a method of validating a date of birth field to ensure a member is over 16 years old would be '<=now()-(365*16+4)' (see Fig. 7.4.12). This is fine for most purposes but is not foolproof. A more flexible solution will use the DateDiff() function in combination with the Format() function: DateDiff("yyyy",[dob],Date())+Int (Format(Date(),"ddmm")<Format([dob],"ddmm"))>=16).

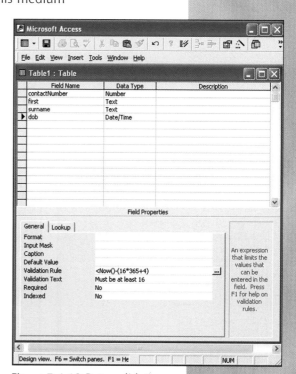

Figure 7.4.12 Date validation

ACTIVITY 12 Validate dates ◀

Write down the Access validation rule for the date ranges in Table 7.4.8.

Table 7.4.8

Range	Rule
Over 18 years old	
Between 18 and 65 years old	
Greater than 10 days from now	
Less than 14 days from now	
Within 12 hours	
Before 1 Jan 2000	

Activity 13 Set range validation

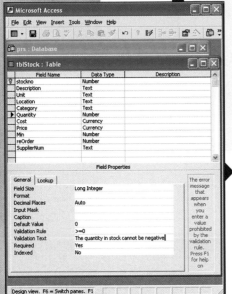

Set the range validation for the stock table from the data dictionary. Add an appropriate error message for each validated field (see Fig. 7.4.13). Then save the table structure.

Test the validation for each of the validated fields by adding valid values, invalid values and values right on the boundary between valid and invalid.

You can view a demonstration of this from the ActiveBook.

Figure 7.4.13 Range validation

List validation

List validation is a more specific variation on range validation. It forces the user to enter data belonging to a specific list of values, for instance only PS2, PSP, XBOX or PC. It is implemented in the same manner as range validation in that the list of values is entered into the validation rule field property. There are two main ways of doing this:

1 as a list of values separated by OR (e.g. PS2 OR PSP OR XBOX OR PC)
2 using the operator IN with a list of values in brackets (e.g. IN(PS2, PSP, XBOX, PC).

An alternative method of list validation in Access

Another method of list validation is shown in Figure 7.4.14.

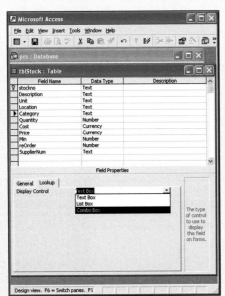

1 Select the 'Lookup' tab and then choose 'Combo Box' as the display control

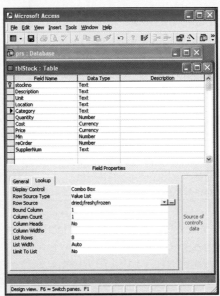

2 Set the Row Source Type to 'Value List' and then put the list of values separated by semicolons in the Row Source property

3 Set the Limit To List property to 'Yes'. *Note*: Doing this means that only values from the list can be entered. It is this that makes this validation; else it is simply an aid to input.

Figure 7.4.14 Alternative method of list validation

ACTIVITY **14** Validate lists ◀

Write the validation for the lists in Table 7.4.9.

Table 7.4.9

List	Validation
Gender	
Title	
3 primary colours: red, green or blue	
The following types of car: saloon, estate, coupe, cabriolet, hatchback	

ACTIVITY **15** Set the list validation for the stock table ◀

Set the list validation for the stock table from the data dictionary (see Figure 7.4.15). Add an appropriate error message. Then save the table structure.

Test the validation by entering values from the list and values not on the list.

▶ ## Finishing off the table structure

To complete the table structure from the data dictionary it is only necessary to add any default values that may be useful and write descriptive comments in the description field of the table definition. Strictly speaking, neither of these is necessary to the structure, but they do help in the construction and maintenance of the database and so should be completed whenever possible.

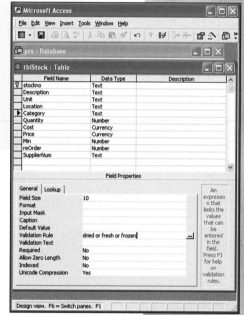

Figure 7.4.15 Setting the list validation for the stock table

Indexing fields

The RDBMS can be forced to create an index for any field by selecting 'yes' for the Indexed property to speed up searches and sorts that involve the field. This can be very useful for a database administrator when looking after a database with very large numbers of records. The index can be set to allow no duplicates (the same as a primary key) or to allow duplicates, which is the default state.

Setting default values

It is useful to give a field a default value if possible as this will simplify data entry and make errors a little less likely. In the case of our stock table we will set the default quantity to '0' as it is the likely value when a new item is first entered, before it has been delivered. In the customer table the default county can be set to 'Lemshire' as virtually all the customers are located there. It is a default value, not a mandatory one, and thus the user can change the value if required.

Activity 16 Set a default value for the quantity field

Set the default value for quantity in the stock table to zero (see Fig. 7.4.16). Then save the table structure.

Adding comments

The final task is to add descriptive comments for each field to aid in the future maintenance of the database. These will be derived directly from the final column of the data dictionary, although they may be embellished with any further points that have arisen during the development process. Adding full comments is good practice, as they make everything that much easier to understand when a developer looks at the work at a later date.

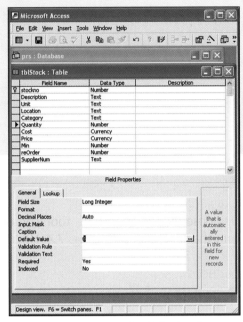

Figure 7.4.16 Setting the default value to zero

> **Description column**
>
> Access uses the description column to provide the status bar text that appears at the foot of the window when the user enters data.

Figure 7.4.17 A completed table with comments

Activity 17 Add descriptive comments to the stock table

Add comments as in Figure 7.4.17 to the stock table. Then save the table structure.

Activity 18 Define the other tables

Repeat these stages for the other four tables in the PRS database.

Part 2: Create the relationships from the ER diagram

A database structure comprises two main parts:
1 The first is the set of tables themselves.
2 The second is the relationships between them, as shown most clearly on the data model by the ER diagram. (The normalised tables and the data dictionaries also show the relationships through matching primary keys with foreign keys.)

In the second part of Unit 7.4 we will examine how to define the relationships in the RDBMS and how to set up referential integrity between tables to achieve a mandatory relationship. Access has a particularly user-friendly graphical interface for defining relationships that makes the process very straightforward.

ACTIVITY **19** Select the tables to define the relationships ◄

You can view demonstration of Activities 19 to 22 from the ActiveBook.

Choose the 'Relationships' tool icon or choose 'Relationships' from the Tools menu (see Fig. 7.4.18).

In the Show Table dialogue box that appears, select all the tables that need to be related. Choose 'Add' to add them to the view.

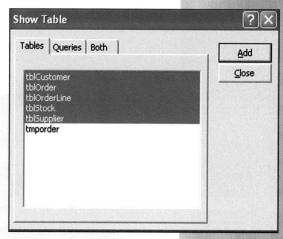

Figure 7.4.18 Choosing the tables before defining their relationships

ACTIVITY **20** Rearrange the tables to match the EAR diagram ◄

Drag the tables into the same positions as the ER diagram (see Fig. 7.4.19). Resize the table rectangles so that it is possible to see all the field names.

Referential integrity

Setting referential integrity forces the RDBMS to check entry of records at the 'many' end of the relationship. If the foreign key field entered does not have a corresponding primary key in the table at the 'one' end of the relationship, the RDBMS will not allow the creation of the record. For example, it would mean that an order could not be made for a customer who has not been entered into the database (a mandatory relationship). Note that a customer can be entered without an order (optional). Unless there is a very good reason to the contrary from the data model, referential integrity should always be set.

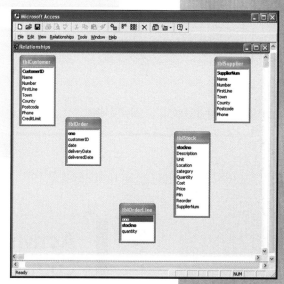

Figure 7.4.19 Rearranging the tables to match the ER diagram

► Cascaded updates and deletes

If a record in a table with the primary key in a relationship is deleted, there could be many records at the other end of the relationship related to this one record. One customer could have placed many orders. In turn these orders could each have many lines. With referential integrity set, it is not possible to delete the one record without first deleting the many records. Setting cascaded deletes allows the RDBMS to delete all of these many records automatically when the one is deleted, cascading down through as many relationships as necessary. Similarly with a key change, all the 'many' records' foreign keys can be updated automatically.

> ### Synonyms and homonyms
>
> When a primary key from one table is used as a foreign key in another table it does not have to have the same name (**homonym**). The field names can be different provided they are referring to the same values (**synonyms**). The customer table can be given a primary key of ID, which is called CustNo in the order table. These are valid synonyms and are thus quite acceptable.

This is a very useful facility, but it is also a very powerful and potentially destructive facility that should be used with care. For example, if cascade delete is set to on, when a salesperson leaves the company the DBMS might delete all his customers and then all their orders from the database.

ACTIVITY 21 Add the relationships

Select the primary key of the customer table and drag it onto the same field in the order table (see Fig. 7.4.20).

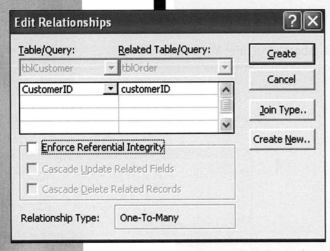

When the Edit Relationships dialogue box appears check that it relates to the correct fields

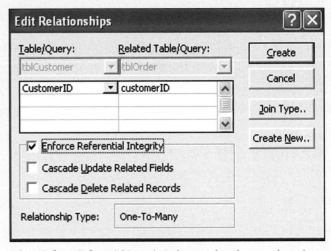

Select 'Enforce Referential Integrity'; do not select the cascade options

Figure 7.4.20 Adding the relationships

ACTIVITY 22 Complete the relationships

Complete all the relationships from the data model. Your completed relationships diagram should look like Figure 7.4.21.

Notes:
- Always drag from the primary key to the same foreign key and check that the correct fields have been selected.
- A 1:M relationship is shown by an infinity symbol (∞) at the 'many' end to signify infinite number of records there could be at this end of the relationship.

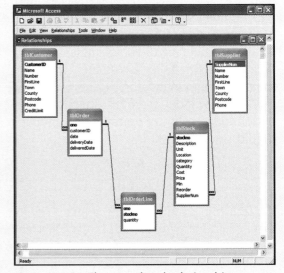

Figure 7.4.21 The completed relationships diagram

The relationships are now all set up and can be used by the RDBMS to check the data in the database and help with processing and the user interface.

Extension activity Toddling Tots Toy Library ◀

Look at the data model for Toddling Tots Toy Library. Implement this as a relational database structure.

Conclusion ▶ ▶ ▶

In Unit 7.4 you have seen how to construct a relational database structure. You have examined how to translate the data dictionary into a solid table structure. You have then seen how to translate the relationships from an ER diagram into the database itself. The end result is a relational database structure that will form the foundation of a flexible and efficient database. If this stage is done correctly, the database can be extended easily without compromising the structure. Extra processing and user interface facilities can be added on a systematic or even an ad hoc basis, and the database application will work without problems. If the database structure is incorrect, however, it is akin to building on sand. There will be a lot of shoring up to do and it may fail at any moment. Therefore it is very much worthwhile spending the time necessary to ensure this stage is done as well as possible.

Once the relational database structure has been established, the next stage of the development process is to build the queries that will implement most of the processing for the database. One of the principles of an RDBMS is that the user should simply specify what they want the query to do, and the RDBMS should then write the program. The user can specify the query using a simple English-like language called structured query language (SQL, pronounced 'sequel') or using a graphical interface.

CASE STUDY Pure Restaurant Supplies

Normalised tables for PRS in 3NF:

Customer {CustomerID, Name, Number, FirstLine, Town, County, Postcode, Phone, CreditLimit}
Order {ONo, Date, DeliveryDate, DeliveredDate, CustomerID*}
OrderLine {ONo*, Stockno*, quantity}
Stock {Stockno, Quantity, Description, Unit, Location, Category, Quantity, Cost, Price, Min, Reorder, SupplierNum*}
Supplier {SupplierNum, Name, Number, FirstLine, Town, County, Postcode, Phone}

Task

Ensure that your relational data model matches the data model presented in Unit 7.4. Save these test data CSV files from the ActiveBook into the tables that you created in Unit 7.4:

- the customer table
- the supplier table
- the stock table
- the order table.

(*Remember*: You imported data in this manner in Unit 2.)
Make sure you save all the files you create in Unit 7.5 systematically as you'll be returning to them.

Naming of queries

In order to work through all of the exercises in Units 7.5 and 7.6, it is simplest if the names used when saving queries and macros are exactly the same as those used by the authors. Later exercises build on exercises already completed and any changes in names of objects would have to be carried through to these exercises.

Basic queries

For any basic query all you have to specify are:
- the tables to be used
- the fields to be used (in the order you want to display them)
- any criteria you want matched
- any order you want values to be displayed in.

The RDBMS will then do the rest. It will work out the order in which to process the fields and tables and apply the criteria, and as you saw in Unit 7.1, it will attempt to do this in the optimal manner. For example, Pure Restaurant Supplies completes a regular physical stock check by comparing the actual stock against the quantity in stock in the database. To do this, they do not want to have all the detail of the whole stock table, so they write a query that only displays the fields they actually need.

To specify this query you simply write:

Tables to be used: tblStock

Fields to be used: <u>Stockno</u>, Description, Unit, Location, Quantity

Criteria:

Sort order:

There are two ways of implementing this design specification in most RDBMSs:

- SQL
- using a graphical editor (Query By Example, Design View etc.).

In SQL this is simply:

SELECT   <u>Stockno</u>, Description, Unit, Location, Quantity

FROM   tblStock;

In the Design View in Access the same result is achieved graphically. You can see a demonstration of this from the ActiveBook (see Fig. 7.5.1).

Views

As was seen in Unit 7.1, the result of all queries is another table. This is a virtual table, often called a 'view' as they are an alternative view of the same information. In almost every way, views act like a normal physical table and may be used in the same manner as normal tables. They can usually be edited, and act as the basis for further queries, and for reports and forms. As will be seen in Unit 7.6, 'qryStockCheck' will act as the basis for an efficient and useful stock check form.

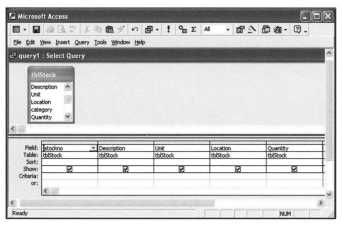

Figure 7.5.1 Setting up 'qryStockCheck' from Design View

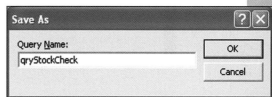

Figure 7.5.2 Naming and storing a query for reuse

The query can be saved for reuse. It should be named using standard naming conventions (see Fig. 7.5.2).

Running the query yields the results shown in Figure 7.5.3.

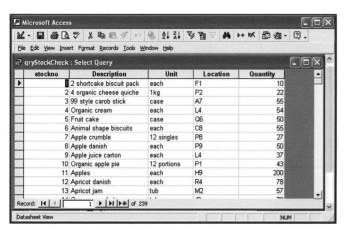

Figure 7.5.3 Results of running 'qryStockCheck'

SQL and the examination

SQL is not a required skill for the examination. It is, however, a very useful and portable tool that is easier to use than many people realise. In some cases it is easier to use than the Design View to achieve the same results; and can always act as a double-check on the output of the Design View. It is therefore worth a little extra effort to learn.

ACTIVITY 1 Create 'qryStockCheck'

Create the stock check query using the Design View. Save it as 'qryStockCheck'. Use the Datasheet View to run the query and view the output.

From the Design View, you can select 'SQL View' from the tool icon on the top left (see Fig. 7.5.4); you can then simply type the SQL directly into the window.

Use the SQL View to view the SQL that Access automatically generates from the Design View. (*Note*: Access gives full table.field names to each field.)

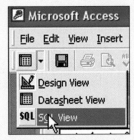

Figure 7.5.4 SQL View

ACTIVITY 2 Create basic lists for reports

1 Create a query 'qryCustomerList' that lists all customer details.
2 Create a query 'qryStockList' that lists all stock details.
3 Create a query 'qrySupplierList' that lists all supplier details.

ACTIVITY 3 Create 'qryPriceList'

We will create a price list showing the stock number, the description, unit and price for all the stock items. Save it as 'qryPriceList'.

1 Fill in the specification:

The tables to be used: tblStock
The fields to be used: Stockno, Description, Unit, Price
Criteria:
Sort order:

2 Create the query in SQL View or in the Design View.
3 Save it, then run it.

Shortcut to showing all fields

If you want to show all fields of a table in the output you can, for speed and convenience, select the * symbol in place of the field names (see Fig. 7.5.5).

Sorting in a query

To sort the output in a query is simply a matter of specifying which field or fields you want to sort on and whether you want to view the output in ascending or descending order. *Note*: When sorting on multiple fields, fields to the left are sorted prior to those to the right.

You may want to view the price list sorted into price order, with the lowest price first. To do this you would take the following steps:

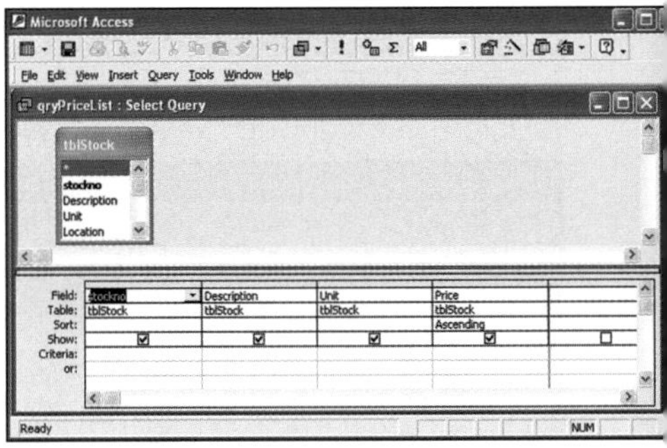

Figure 7.5.5 Query Design View

1 Specify:

Tables to be used: tblStock
Fields to be used: Stockno, Description, Unit, Price
Criteria:
Sort order: Price ASC;

2 Either enter the SQL directly into the SQL View:

SELECT <u>Stockno</u>, Description,
Unit, Price
FROM tblStock
ORDER BY price ASC;

or enter the information into the Design View as in Figure 7.5.5.

ACTIVITY 4 Create a sorted price list ◀

1 Create a price list showing it in price order with the lowest price first.
2 Create a price list showing it price order with the highest price first.
3 Create a price list by category, then description. Show all the dried goods, then the fresh ones and then the frozen ones, each in alphabetical order.

ACTIVITY 5 Enter SQL into Access ◀

Create a new query, without choosing any tables. Select 'SQL View' as described in Activity 1. Type the following SQL into this window:

SELECT TOP 5 tblCustomer.Name, tblCustomer.Number, tblCustomer.CreditLimit
FROM tblCustomer ORDER BY tblCustomer.CreditLimit DESC;

Test it.

The top and bottom of a sorted list

It is possible to select the topmost records from a sorted list using the expression 'Top x'. For example, to choose the two most expensive products in stock use the following statement:

SELECT TOP 2 description, price FROM tblStock ORDER BY price DESC;

To choose the five customers with the highest credit limits use the following:

SELECT TOP 5 tblCustomer. Name, tblCustomer.Number, tblCustomer.CreditLimit FROM tblCustomer ORDER BY tblCustomer.CreditLimit DESC;

Searching (restriction or filter queries)

One of the most useful facilities of database queries is the ability to search for data by specific criteria. It is very straightforward to ask the RDBMS to look, for instance, for all the products where there are less than 10 in stock, all the items supplied by Cheerful Food Ltd, all the customers from Dornaby, all the dried goods in stock or all the orders not yet delivered. For example, to find all the frozen goods in stock you set Criteria for Category as 'frozen' (see Fig. 7.5.6). You specify the query in the same way as always (see Table 7.5.1).

Wildcards

The wildcard character * can be used to replace sets of characters in queries using the LIKE operator. To find all customers whose name starts with 'a' use the criteria 'LIKE "a" & "*"'.

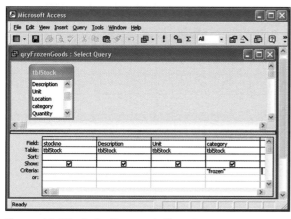

Query with Criteria for Category is 'frozen'

Figure 7.5.6 Using criteria

Results of the query

Table 7.5.1 Operators that can be used in the WHERE clause of queries

Operator	Meaning	Examples
>=	Is greater than or equal to	Wage >= 120 000
>	Is greater than	Wage > 120 000
=	Is equal to	Name = 'Roberts' County = [which county?]
<	Is less than	Quantity < minimum
<=	Is less than or equal to	Price <= cost
<>	Is not equal to	Quantity <> 10
LIKE *	Contains	Description LIKE 'chocolate*' Description LIKE * [product?] & '*'
IN	Is in the set	Title IN (Mrs, Ms, Miss)
BETWEEN	Is between	Wage BETWEEN 1 and 10
IS (NOT) NULL	Is (not) empty	Name IS NOT NULL DeliveredDate IS NULL

The tables to be used: tblStock
The fields to be used: <u>Stockno</u>, Description, Unit, Category
Criteria: Where Category is 'frozen'
Sort order:

ACTIVITY 6 Create WHERE queries

Using the table of operators that can be used with Criteria:
1   Decide on the Criteria for each item in Table 7.5.2.
2   Create queries for each using these Criteria.

Table 7.5.2

Question	Criteria
List all the stock items with no stock	
Find the products that have a price greater than £5	
Find the products that have less stock than the minimum they should have	
Find the stock items with a price between £1 and £2	
Find all the things stocked that include carrot	
Find all the fresh and dried goods	
List all the goods in locations starting with A	
List all the suppliers starting with A to K	
List everything not sold in a bottle or jar	
What is the most expensive product?	
List all the customers from Bisham, Boxbridge and Dornaby	

Activity 7 Create goods not yet delivered query ◀

List all order numbers that have not been delivered yet. Save this as 'qryGoodsNotDelivered'.

Parameters

A query can ask for information from a user to form part of the query. The sales office may ask for the quantity of stock of a particular item. The particular item obtained from a user is called a parameter. Writing this in the query is as simple as writing in a new field name in the Criteria row (see Fig. 7.5.7). It is usually phrased as a question.

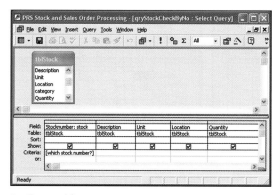

1 Query with parameter

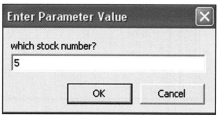

2 Enter parameter value '5'

Stocknumber	Description	Unit	Location	Quantity
5	Fruit cake	case	Q6	50

3 Result where stock number is 5

Figure 7.5.7 Using parameters

Activity 8 Find orders between any two dates ◀

List the orders between two dates given by the user. Save this query as 'qryOrdersBetweenDates'.

Find the stock number, description, unit, location and quantity for a stock item specified by the user. Save it as 'qryStockCheckByNo'.

Multiple conditions

You can query a database using multiple criteria, combined together in different ways using AND, OR and NOT operators:

- Combining with AND will mean that all the conditions must be TRUE (see Fig. 7.5.8).

- Combining with OR means that only one of the conditions needs to be true (see Fig. 7.5.9).
- Using NOT means that the condition must be false (see Fig. 7.5.10).

Note: For relational queries on the same field you can write the operator as part of the criteria: e.g. 'Bisham' OR 'Dornaby'.

You can see a demonstration of this from the ActiveBook.

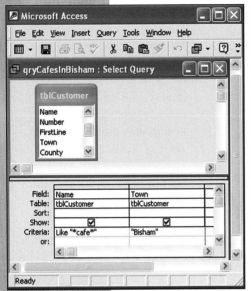

Figure 7.5.8 Query to find all the cafes in Bisham (*Note:* The criteria are written on the same row for an AND query)

```
SELECT Name, Town
FROM tblCustomer
WHERE Name like "*cafe*"
AND Town = "Bisham";
```

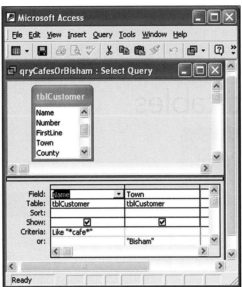

Figure 7.5.9 Query to show all cafes or customers from Bisham (*Note:* OR criteria are written on different rows)

```
SELECT Name, Town
FROM tblCustomer
WHERE Name Like "*cafe*"
OR Town="Bisham";
```

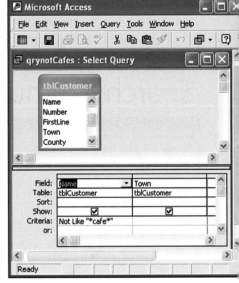

Figure 7.5.10 Query to show everything but cafes (*Note*: NOT criteria simply invert the existing condition)

```
SELECT Name, Town
FROM tblCustomer
WHERE NOT name like "*cafe*"
```

AND and OR

The meaning of AND and OR in relational queries is very precise, whereas the way we use it in everyday conversation is not.

'Show all the dried and frozen products' should be expressed as:

SELECT Name FROM tblStock WHERE category = 'dried' OR category = 'frozen';

It should not be expressed as:

SELECT Name FROM tblStock WHERE category = 'dried' AND category = 'frozen';

To use AND *all* conditions must be true; whereas to use an OR *only one* must be true. When we speak, we use AND to mean either of these.

▶ Relational queries

Table 7.5.3 lists the relational operators that can be used in queries.

Table 7.5.3 Relational operators used in queries

Operator	Meaning	Example
AND	All conditions must be true	Wage > 12 000 AND holidays > 21
OR	One condition must be true	Wage > 15 000 OR holidays > 42
NOT	Condition must be false	NOT (wage < 12 000)

ACTIVITY 9 Create queries with multiple conditions ◀

1 Show all the frozen products where there are less than 10 in stock.
2 Find all the dried foods that contain chocolate.
3 List all the dried and frozen foods that contain chocolate.
4 Show all the goods where there are less than 10 in stock and those with more than 90 in stock.
5 Show the suppliers from Kirkham or Boxbridge.
6 Show the customers from Boxbridge with a credit limit of greater than £4000.

Search on multi-tables (JOIN queries)

Another feature of relational database queries is how easy it is to search on multiple tables. When the data model is first constructed, the tables are designed in such a way that data is never duplicated, and so that it is easy to join tables back together again by matching the foreign key from the 'many' end of a relationship with the primary key of the 'one' end of a relationship.

Our order table may show that order 1013 was placed by KIR749 on 4 October. To find who customer KIR749 is, you simply look for the primary key KIR749 in the customer table, where it is a unique record: that of Kirkham Cafe. Effectively, you join the two tables by showing the customer name where the primary key=foreign key and the foreign key='KIR749'. In the Design View, simply selecting the two tables is sufficient as the RDBMS automatically joins the tables in this way. This means that to construct a query from multiple tables, you specify it in exactly the same way as before: you say which tables you want to use, which fields you want to use and what criteria you want to apply (see Fig. 7.5.11).

To select all the orders made by Kirkham Cafe:

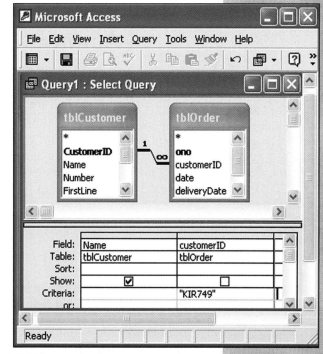

Figure 7.5.11 Multi-table searches

The tables to be used: tblCustomer, tblOrder, tblOrderLine, tblStock
The fields to be used: Name, ONo, Date, StockNo, Description
Criteria: Where Name is 'Kirkham Cafe'
Sort order:

Figure 7.5.12 shows how this query is implemented. You can see a demonstration of this from the ActiveBook.

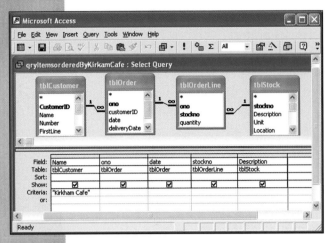

Creating the query

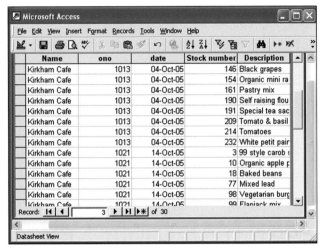

The results

Figure 7.5.12 Multi-table queries

SQL basic joins

Using SQL a basic join can be written in two ways:

SELECT Name FROM tblCustomer, tblOrder WHERE tblOrder.CustomerID = 'KIR749' AND tblOrder.CustomerID = tblCustomer.CustomerID;

or

SELECT tblCustomer.Name FROM tblCustomer INNER JOIN tblOrder ON tblCustomer.CustomerID = tblOrder.CustomerID WHERE tblOrder.CustomerID = 'KIR749';

ACTIVITY 10 Create JOIN queries ◀

1 Show all the items ordered in October.
2 Show all the items supplied by the company whose name begins with Bio.
3 List all the orders for customers in Dornaby.
4 Show the order number, date, stock number, description, quantity sold and price for all orders by Kirkham Cafe.
5 Show the suppliers' names and addresses where the stock level is less than the minimum.
6 Show all the customers who have ordered Bakewell Tart, which has the stock number of 19.

Join types

So far we have just looked at the basic join, which also called an INNER JOIN. Table 7.5.4 lists the other types.

Table 7.5.4 Different types of JOIN

Operator	Meaning
INNER JOIN	The basic join that returns all rows from multiple tables where the join condition is met
OUTER JOIN	Returns all the rows from the first table and those rows from the second table where the join condition is met (e.g. to show all customers and their orders whether they had placed an order or not – see Figure 7.5.13)
LEFT [outer] JOIN	All rows from the left table with joined rows from the right
RIGHT [outer] JOIN	All rows from the right table with joined rows from the left

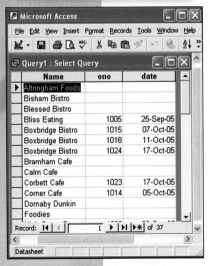

Figure 7.5.13 Typical outer join

Using Database Software

Calculated fields

When processing a database one of the most useful facilities is to be able to calculate information from existing information. If you want to know the total cost value of each item of stock, you do not store this information in your database structure, but calculate it.

The tables to be used: tblStock

The fields to be used: StockNo, Description, Unit, Quantity, Cost, Quantity*Cost AS CostValue

Criteria:

Sort order:

ACTIVITY 11 Explain why you calculate fields ◀

Why do we usually not store information in our basic relational structure that we can calculate from existing fields? Use the words 'integrity' and 'redundancy' in your answer.

Figure 7.5.14 shows how you can calculate the value of stock from existing fields. You can see a demonstration of this from the ActiveBook.

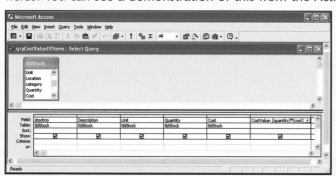

Query using a calculated field

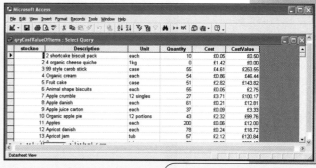

The results of the query

Figure 7.5.14 Calculated fields

ACTIVITY 12 Create queries using calculated fields and aliases ◀

1 Show the value, if sold, of each item in stock.
2 Calculate the total cost of each line of order 1010 showing the total cost, VAT at 20%, and the grand total for each line of the order.
3 Calculate the number of items in stock over the reorder quantity.
4 Show all the orders that were delivered later than promised.

ACTIVITY 13 Create a query to calculate the cost value of items ◀

Create a query called 'qryCostValueOfItems' that shows the stock number, description, unit, quantity, cost and [Quantity]*[Cost] AS CostValue.

Using an alias

When using calculated fields it is necessary to create a name for the field so that the results table is meaningful. In SQL you simply name the field by adding the phrase 'AS *name*' to the field:

> SELECT StockNo, Description, Unit, Quantity, Cost, [quantity]*[cost] AS CostValue
> FROM tblStock;

In the Query Design View write NAME: before the name of the field, as in:

> CostValue: [Quantity]*[Cost]

The same techniques may be used to rename any field in a query.

ACTIVITY 14 Create a requisition query ◀

Create a query that will act as requisition for new stock when the amount of stock falls below the minimum. It should show all the supplier details, the stock number, description, unit, the amount to reorder as quantity, the cost and the total cost (quantity × price). Save it as 'qryAutoOrder'.

ACTIVITY 15 Show the potential profit of each item ◀

Show the total potential profit of each item as the sale value-cost value. Save it as 'qryProfitPerItem'.

Hint: Cost value is cost × quantity in stock; sale value is price × quantity in stock.

ACTIVITY 16 Make a query that will create an invoice ◀

Create a query that will form the basis of an invoice report. It should contain the following fields:

tblCustomer.CustomerID	tblOrder.DeliveredDate AS [Invoice Date]
tblCustomer.Name	
tblCustomer.Number	tblOrderLine.StockNo
tblCustomer.FirstLine	tblStock.Description
tblCustomer.Town	tblOrderLine.Quantity
tblCustomer.County	tblStock.Price
tblCustomer.Postcode	[tblOrderline.Quantity]*[Price] AS Total
tblOrder.ONo	tblOrder.DeliveryDate
tblOrder.Date AS [Order Date]	

It should show the invoice for an order number specified by the user. Call it 'qryInvoice'. As always, add the tables required, add the fields required and add the parameter criteria. Do not worry about how it will be formated at this stage.

It is also possible to use built-in functions in calculations. For example, when calculating the number of items in stock over the reorder quantity, you get minus figures for those that should be reordered. To set these to zero, you can use the IIF() function as follows:

Number until reorder: IIF([Quantity] - [Min] > 0, [Quantity] - [Min], 0)

This works in the same way as the IF() function in a spreadsheet. There are three terms in the brackets. Term 1 is the condition which can be *true* or *false*. If the result is *true* the second term is evaluated and shown, and if *false* the third term is evaluated and shown. *Note*: If you do not want to display items when they are zero or below, you would use a criteria for the calculated field of >0 rather than an IIF() function.

Aggregating (totals)

There are a number of common aggregation (total) functions including Sum, Count, Average, Maximum and Minimum. These can be used with a whole table, or on groups of data within a table. To find out how many customers there are, use:

    SELECT count(CustomerId) FROM tblCustomer

To work out the number of individual items in stock use:

    SELECT Sum(Quantity) FROM tblStock

The same technique works with calculated fields as well. So to work out the total value of the stock at cost use:

    SELECT Sum(Quantity * Cost) FROM tblStock

Figure 7.5.15 shows how to calculate the potential profit from the stockholding.

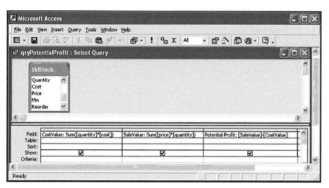

Aggregate functions and calculated fields

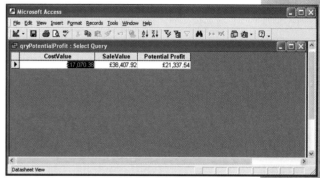

The potential profit from the stockholding

Figure 7.5.15 Aggregate functions

ACTIVITY 17 Create queries using aggregate functions

Part 1

Calculate the potential profit from the stock holding as in the example above and save it as 'qryPotentialProfit'.

Part 2

1   How many orders have been placed?
2   What is the total value of orders in October?
3   What is the cheapest item sold?
4   What is the most expensive item sold?
5   What is the first order number?
6   What is the average quantity held in stock of each item?

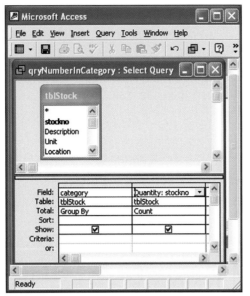
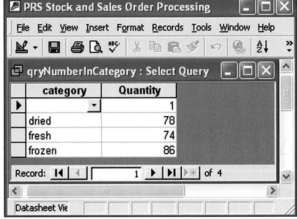

Query showing how the category is grouped and how the StockNo field is totalled using count

Results of running the query

Figure 7.5.16 Grouping in queries

Grouping

Aggregation (total) functions are very powerful when used in combination with grouping. This allows a database designer to group the data in any way desired and then use the function on the group. You can see how many different dried goods you have by grouping the data by Category and then counting the number of records in each Category by, for example, counting the primary keys (see Fig. 7.5.16). As always creating a grouped query is simply a matter of specifying the query.

All fields but the field to be aggregated have to appear in the group by statement. In Design View, selecting 'Totals' from the View menu will achieve this and put an extra row into the design grid in which the aggregation function can be chosen. The order is important when there are many fields involved in the query, since the field in the leftmost column will be the major item grouped. In Figure 7.5.16, Category is on the left so the query will group by Category. With grouped queries always consider first what the grouped field(s) should be, and then decide what field has to be aggregated to achieve the desired result. When counting it will most often be the primary key. Sums, averages, minima and maxima can be of any numeric or indeed calculated field. *Note*: When criteria are used with groups the SQL keyword is HAVING rather than WHERE.

You can see a demonstration of this from the ActiveBook.

ACTIVITY 18 Use grouping in queries

1 What is the average number of goods supplied by one supplier?
2 What is the total value of goods in each location?
3 What is the total value of each order?
4 How many lines are there on each order?
5 What is the least expensive line on each order?
6 What is the value of orders that are sent to Dornaby?

ACTIVITY 19 Create a query using grouping

Create a query that shows the tblStock.Location, tblOrder.ONo, tblOrder.CustomerID, tblOrder.Date, tblOrderLine.StockNo, tblOrderLine.Quantity, tblStock.Description, tblStock.Unit HAVING the order number specified by the user. Save it as 'qryPickByOrderNo'. This works in precisely the same manner as when using WHERE criteria, with the one additional step of selecting 'Totals' from the View menu to establish the groupings. Add the fields in the order stated, choose 'View Totals' to set up the groupings, and finally add the parameter criteria [ONo?].

Action queries

Although the most common processes on the database will be the searches, sorts and groupings already described, there is another very important set of processes that you must learn. These are called action queries because they perform an action such as making new tables, appending new records to the database, updating existing records in the database and deleting records in the database. These queries should always be developed on a back-up copy of a database and only migrated to the actual database when complete and fully tested as they are usually destructive and the previous status irretrievable!

> ## Make Table queries

You will quite often want to create a new table from an existing table. For instance, you may not want to keep all order records forever in the main working database as it can slow processes after a while. You may want to archive parts of the database that change, but want to keep a record of those parts before the change. You may want to have temporary tables storing information for as long as it is necessary before deleting them. Make Table queries are ideal in these circumstances.

For example, you may want to have an archive of all of your price lists. To archive the current prices you need to create a query that lists the prices and then stores the list in a new table (see Fig. 7.5.17). You can see a demonstration of this from the ActiveBook.

Check the SQL

When constructing action queries it is fine to create them in Design View but it is always worthwhile checking the SQL to ensure that it has interpreted the design grid correctly. Even if you could not have created the SQL you should be able to understand it sufficiently to see if it is updating, inserting into or deleting the right fields from the correct tables. The query editor in Microsoft Access does sometimes misunderstand your intentions. If you want to be really careful always use SQL.

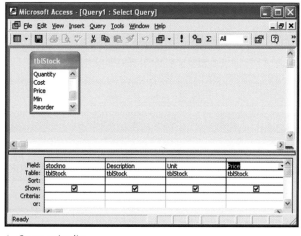

1 Create price list

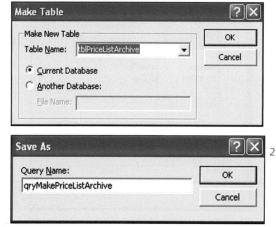

2 Select 'Make Table Query ...' from the Query menu. Name the table 'tblPriceListArchive' and save the query as 'qryMakePriceListArchive'

Fig. 7.5.17 continued on the next page

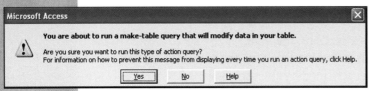

3   Run the stored query; you will now have a new table

Figure 7.5.17 Make Table queries

ACTIVITY 20 Create a price list archive ◀

Create the query 'qryMakePriceListArchive'.

ACTIVITY 21 Create actual stock table ◀

Create a Make Table query to make a table, called tblStockCheck, that can be used for recording the physical stock quantity after a stock check. It should initially contain the stock number, location and the stock amount counted as actually being in stock. Call it 'qryCreateStockCheckTable'.

▶ Update queries

Update queries do exactly as they say. They update the contents of the database. If there is a price increase - for example 10 per cent on all frozen goods in stock – this can be added very simply and quickly using an Update query (see Fig. 7.5.18). Choose the stock table and the Price and Category fields. Select 'Update Query' from the Query menu. This adds an extra row to the design grid. Put '[price]*1.1' into the update row of the Price field. Put 'frozen' into the criteria row of the category field. Save the query, qryUpdateFrozenPrices, and test it by looking at the Datasheet View. You can see a demonstration of this from the ActiveBook.

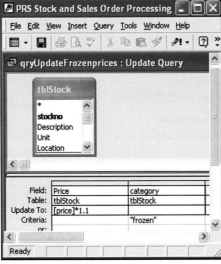

Specifying the update query

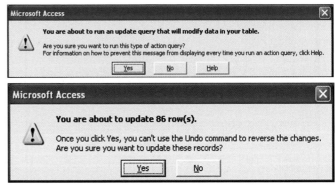

Updating the records using the query

Figure 7.5.18 Update queries

Action queries do not work unless they are run from stored queries, so when you are satisfied it will work correctly, run the query from the stored query. Make sure you have a list of the prices before and after the update and compare them, ideally by archiving using the method described earlier.

ACTIVITY 22 Update prices ◀

1 Update the price of dried goods by 5 per cent.
2 Update the price of fresh goods by 10p each.

ACTIVITY 23 Update prices using SQL ◀

Create a query called 'qryUpdatePrices' that updates all prices by an amount specified by the user using the following SQL:

UPDATE tblStock SET tblStock.Price = [Price] * (1 + [Amount to update by?]);

(or you can enter the same update query using the Design View). Test it to ensure it works.

▶ Using queries as views to update another table

It is possible to create an update query to update the goods in stock from an invoice generated in the query 'qryInvoice' for an order specified by a user. This should reduce the amount in stock by the amount of each stock item on the invoice. The SQL for this simply updates the stock table Quantity field to the invoice quantity, where the invoice number is the order number given by the user:

UPDATE tblStock INNER JOIN qryInvoice ON tblStock.StockNo = qryInvoice.StockNo
SET tblStock.Quantity = [tblStock].[Quantity] - [qryInvoice].[Quantity]
WHERE (((qryInvoice.ONo) = [order no?]));

ACTIVITY 24 Update another table ◀

Create the update query described and save it as 'qryGoodsOut'.

▶ Delete Queries

Occasionally you will want to delete rows from tables according to some criteria. In this case you can use a Delete query (see Fig. 7.5.19). For example, you may want to archive old orders and delete them from the current database. To achieve this you would write an Append query to copy the records up to a certain date into an archive table from the order table and the order line table. You can then delete the records in the order line table and then the records in the order table.

You can see a demonstration of this from the ActiveBook.

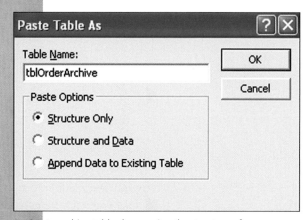

1 Create archive tables by copying the structure of the order and order line tables

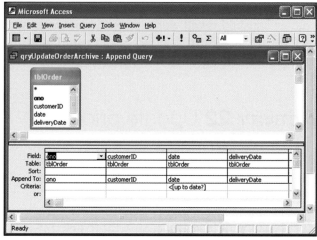

2 Create an Append query for the order table using a parameter [up to date?] to set the limits for the date

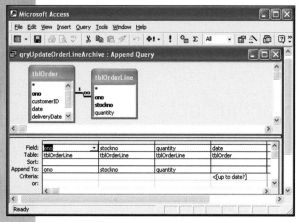

3 Create an Append query for the order line table using a parameter [up to date?] to set the limits for the date

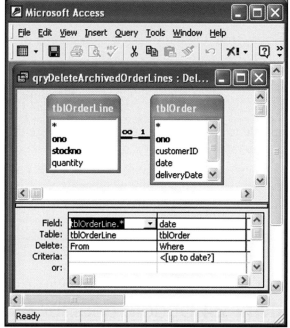

4 Create a Delete query for the order line table using a parameter [up to date?] to set the limits for the date

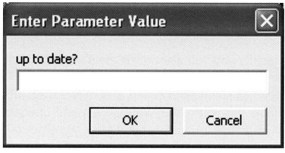

5 Create a Delete query for the order table using a parameter [up to date?] to set the limits for the date

6 Run them in sequence. Ideally write a macro that runs the queries one after the other (see later). Ensure you enter the same date each time!

Figure 7.5.19 Delete queries

DISCUSSION

Why do you have to delete the records in the order line table before the records in the order table?

ACTIVITY 25 Archive old orders

Create empty archive tables by copying the structure without the data. Then create the queries:

   qryUpdateOrderArchive
   qryUpdateOrderLineArchive
   qryDeleteArchivedOrderLines
   qryDeleteArchivedOrders.

Run them in the correct order. Test them.

Macros

A macro (mcr or mac prefix) is a short sequence of commands that can be executed by the RDMBS to perform a set of operations. They are commonly used to automate tasks that would otherwise require the user to perform a number of operations in a particular sequence. Macros both speed up the processing and make it more reliable. For example, to create an archive of old price lists, it is quite possible for the user to run the Make Table query that creates the archive table 'tblPricelistArchive'(see Activity 20), and then to rename it manually. However, it is preferable to combine these two actions into a sequence that can be replayed upon request; this saves the user the effort and ensures that the archive is maintained correctly with the correct date. (see Fig. 7.5.20).

Date functions in Access

The now() function returns the current date and time in Microsoft Office products. Remember that this is a decimal number with the integer part representing the date and the fractional part representing the time. Int(Now()) will return the integer part of the date only, i.e. the date itself. This can be added to a string such as a table name by using the concatenation (string add) operator '&'. Thus '= "tblStock" & Int(Now())' will yield a result such as 'tblStock12/12/2005'. *Note*: You may also use the function '=date()' to achieve the same effect.

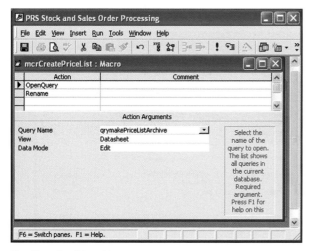

Run the price list archive query

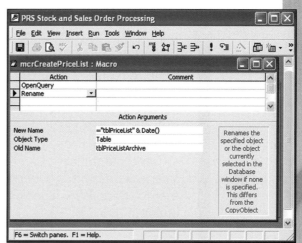

Rename it to the latest date so that there is a continuous archive of price lists at different dates

Figure 7.5.20 Price list macro

ACTIVITY 26 Create a macro to archive price lists

Create a macro called 'mcrMakePriceListQuery' that creates a dated archive of price lists. The New Name property should be set to '="tblPriceListArchive" & Int(Now())' (see Fig. 7.5.20)

ACTIVITY 27 Create a macro to update prices safely

Open 'mcrMakePriceListQuery' and append another action which runs the update price query ('qryUpdatePrices'). Call it 'mcrUpdatePrices'. This can now be used when updating prices to ensure that an archive copy of the old prices is maintained first.

▶ Combining actions

Macros are extremely useful for running a set of operations that should be combined together. Often in a database, a group of operations will together form a single transaction. If the system crashes between one operation and another, that is within a transaction, it can be in an unstable state. The archiving and updating of orders queries clearly should be done together to minimise problems. Putting the operations together in a macro means that they will be run immediately one after another and thus the risk of part the transaction being left undone will be reduced enormously.

Transactions

A transaction is a sequence of SQL (action) queries that must be run together or not run at all. If the system fails in the middle of a transaction, the database will lose integrity. It is possible to set macros to run SQL statements in transactions to ensure full database integrity.

ACTIVITY 28 Create a macro to archive old orders

Look at this demonstration from the ActiveBook and at Figure 7.5.21.

Create a macro 'mcrArchiveOldOrders' using the queries created for archiving and deleting.

This could still be smartened up with a better user interface. We will look at this in Unit 7.6.

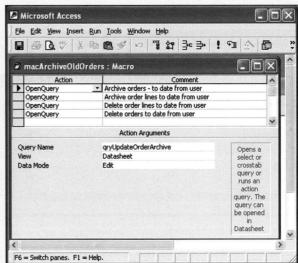

Figure 7.5.21 Archive old orders macro

Every month PRS check the products physically in stock against the stock records. There are occasional differences because of mistakes, breakages and possibly pilfering. They keep an archive copy of the stock table at the date when it was checked. They do not directly change the stock table in case the computer fails halfway through the operation; thus they create a new list of stock which they update from the stock check report. They then update the whole stock table in one go from the stock check table. The temporary stock check list is then deleted. Tables 7.5.5 and 7.5.6 show the steps in this process.

Table 7.5.5 Phase 1: Manual stock check

Step	Process
Create a stock check report and do a physical stock check	Print report based on 'qryStockCheck' and do manual stock check
Create a new stock list (table) called 'tblStockCheck' with just the stock number, location and quantity	Run Make Table query 'qryCreateStock CheckTable' to create the temporary table 'tblStockCheck': SELECT tblStock.stockno, tblStock.Location, tblStock.Quantity INTO tblStockCheck FROM tblStock;
Update 'tblStockCheck' record by record from the stock check report sheet	Use 'frmStockCheck' based on 'tblStockCheck' to update all the records one by one

Table 7.5.6 Phase 2: Automated update

Step	Process
Create a dated archive copy of the stock table (tblStock)	Use macro action to copy 'tblStock' and rename it 'tblStock & int(now())' – see margin box 'Date functions in Access'
Update 'tblStock' using an update query from 'tblStockCheck'	Run update query 'qryUpdateStock': UPDATE tblStock INNER JOIN tblStockCheck ON tblStock.stockno = tblStockCheck.stockno SET tblStock.Quantity = tblStockCheck.Quantity;
Delete 'tblStockCheck'	Use macro action to delete the temporary table named 'tblStockCheck'

The steps in the second part of the process can all be automated using a macro as no human intervention is required at any stage of this process (see Fig. 7.5.22).

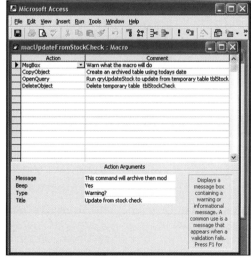

1 Write the Message

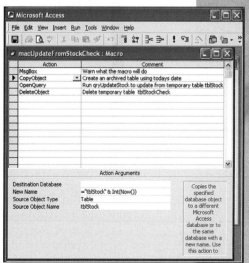

2 Copy the object using the date appended to the original name

Fig. 7.5.22 continued on the next page

 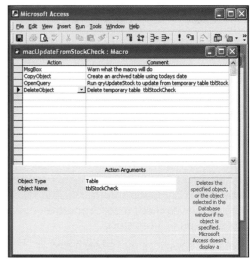

3 Run the update query to update the original stock query

4 Delete the temporary table.

Figure 7.5.22 Update from stock check macro

ACTIVITY 29 Automate the backing up of the database ◀

PRS want to keep dated archives of their main tables. It is usually possible to back up all the data and the database objects (queries, reports, macros etc.) by using the built in facilities of the RDBMS. To archive only the data it is also possible to use a macro (e.g. mcrBackUp) that backs up the data required.

1 Create a blank database called 'PRSBackUp.mdb' and close it.
2 Create a macro in the PRS database, 'mcrBackUp', that backs up all the tables of the database into 'PRSBackUp.mdb'. Append the date to the names of the tables in the back-up database.

ACTIVITY 30 Review the implementation of the database ◀

Consider the case study for PRS on page 25. Ensure you have created the queries and macros for the main processes involved, and named them as in Table 7.5.7. These queries and processes will form the basis of the user interface created in Unit 7.6.

Table 7.5.7 Queries and macros for the PRS database

Required process	Query and/or macro
Print a list of customers	qryCustomerList (Activity 2)
Print a stock list	qryStockList (Activity 2)
Print a list of orders between two dates	qryOrdersBetweenDates (Activity 8)
Archive older orders on request. Only recent orders are to be stored on the system	mcrArchiveOldOrders (Activity 28) qryUpdateOrderArchive (Activity 25) qryUpdateOrderLineArchive (Activity 25) qryDeleteArchivedOrderLines (Activity 25) qryDeleteArchivedOrders(Activity 25)

Continued on the next page

Required process	Query and/or macro
Print a pick list for each order	qryPickByOrderNo (Activity 19)
Print an invoice to accompany each customer order	qryInvoice (Activity 16)
Update the stock from the invoice automatically when the goods are delivered (goods out)	qryGoodsOut (Activity 24)
Print a requisition for stock replenishment	qryAutoOrder (Activity 14)
Print out a list of what is in stock at any time by stock location for a physical stock check	qryStockCheck (Activity 1) qryCreateStockCheckTable (Activity 21)
Report the value of the stock and the potential profit from stock	qryPotentialProfit (Activity 17)
Report the value at cost of each item in stock, along with a running total of the value in each location	qryCostValueOfItems (Activity 13)
Print out a price list to be distributed to all customers and potential customers	qryPriceList (Activity 3)
Create an archive of dated price lists	qryMakePriceListArchive (Activity20)
Increase the price of all stock items by a predetermined percentage at the push of a button, archiving the old prices at the same time	mcrUpdatePrices (Activity 27) qryUpdatePrices (Activity 27)
Create a back up copy of the database at the push of a button.	mcrBackUp (Activity 29)

Conclusion ▶ ▶ ▶

In Unit 7.5 we have examined a wide variety of processes that can be created for a database application. The most important aspect of executing them correctly is to be really clear about what you are trying to do. For an ordinary query, this simply involves specifying what tables, fields and criteria are to be used, and what order to display the results in. We have examined and applied a wide range of these criteria and seen that they are relatively easy to use – provided you are clear what you are trying to achieve. We have seen that it is also possible to perform calculations on rows of data, tables of data and groups of data within a table. Finally, we have looked at action queries and macros, which when used together are a very powerful tool for designing and implementing database processing such as creating new tables, updating existing tables and deleting whole tables or records within them.

By now you have created a functioning database application, but it is still quite basic. In Unit 7.6 we will examine the techniques that can be used to add a user-friendly interface to this basic application.

7.6　The user interface

Wizards

Database Wizards are different, but no less powerful, than traditional wizards

Wizards are small programs that guide the developer through a task in as user-friendly a manner as possible. They should be used where possible to create the basic user-interface elements, such as forms and reports. The output of the Wizard should then be customised to meet the exact requirements of the application. Note that Wizards often require a little care, especially when used with joins.

At this stage the project has been specified, the data model defined, the relational structure implemented and the basic processes all designed. There is, in effect, a working database application. The next phase is to add a layer to the database which will make it easier to use. This is the presentation layer, or the human–computer interface. The aim is to make it as user-friendly and automated as possible. This has the dual effect of reducing the number of errors the user will make, and making the database easier and more efficient to use.

There are three main aspects to master in a user interface: forms, reports and menus. In Unit 7.6 we will build further on the Pure Restaurant Supplies database to see how these three elements are implemented. Firstly, we will investigate how making data input into a user-friendly process is achieved through forms. Secondly, we will examine how output is formatted and presented using reports. Finally, the front end of the database – the menus and controls that help the user navigate and manage it – will be explored.

Creating user-friendly data input forms

Using the Form Wizard

Wherever possible, you should use the Form Wizard to construct a form for inputting data into a table. The Wizard will link the form to the table, it will create labels automatically from the field or caption names specified in the Table Design View, it will order the fields on the form as you specify, and will give you some default controls such as a navigation bar at the foot of the form. In practice the end result is not usually a perfect interface, but it is a very solid and usable basis from which to customise, as in Figure 7.6.1. You can also see a demonstration of this from the ActiveBook. The Wizard starts you off on the right track; tweaking can be done later.

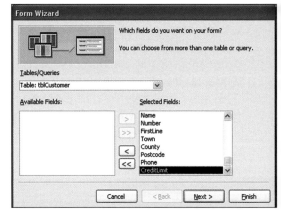

Fig 7.6.1 continued on the next page

1　Select the customer table to base the form on

2　Choose the fields that will be added to the form in the order you want them to appear on the form

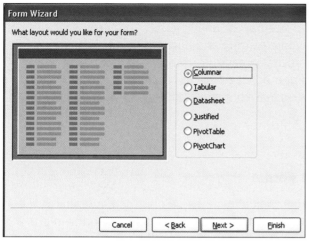

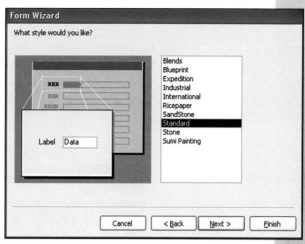

3 Choose the format the records will be displayed in – columnar usually

4 Select a style; keep it simple as you will modify it yourself

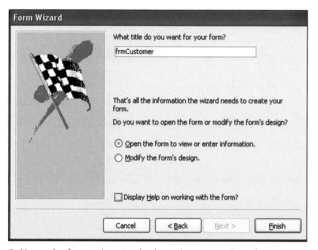

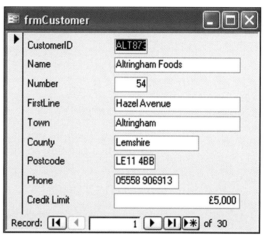

5 Name the form using standard naming conventions (e.g. frmName)

6 Output of the Form Wizard – a good starting point

Figure 7.6.1 Using the Form Wizard to create the customer form

Activity 1 Create the basic customer form ◀

Create 'frmCustomer' using the Wizard.

▶ Customising the form

The rest of the work is in customising the form to your exact needs. As always, the clearer you are about what is required the simpler this process will be. If there is a form design to copy, or a storyboard already drawn at an earlier design stage, use this; otherwise it is best to sketch a storyboard to show the design. This can be drawn by hand or in a computer package, as shown in Figure 7.6.2. It can be very quick, and it will save you time when you come to implement the form. Customisation is completed in Design View (selected by clicking the 'Design View' tool icon (see Fig. 7.6.3). In most cases the steps required to customise comprise:

- setting form properties such as caption
- altering the form itself: the size, layout and colours
- altering the fields: rearranging, resizing and aligning fields
- adding the static controls such as images, rectangles and lines and labels
- changing text boxes to combo boxes where appropriate
- adding advanced controls such as command buttons and option groups.

The following section will examine these processes.

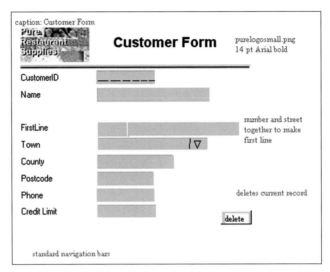

Figure 7.6.2 Simple storyboard of the customer form created in a painting application

Figure 7.6.3 Design View tool icon

Set form properties

The name that appears in the blue title bar of the form window will be the name of the form by default, which is useful for the developer, but unfriendly for the user. Changing this involves changing the Caption property of the form. To access the form properties window, the simplest method is to right click on the square on the top left of the form design window to access the menu, and then select 'Properties'; find the property for the Caption and amend it as required (see Fig. 7.6.4).

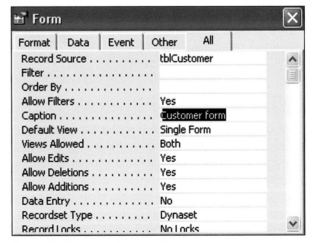

Select 'Properties' Change the Caption to 'Customer form'

Figure 7.6.4 Setting the form caption

There is quite an extensive range of properties to set. In general the defaults work well, but properties can be set to remove or add the navigation buttons, scroll bars, various standard buttons on a form and to change the behaviour of the form. We will examine some of these in context later, but as you become more familiar with your RDBMS you should experiment with the various properties in order to gain total mastery over the user interface.

Customise the form itself

The form will usually have to be made taller and or wider and the colours adapted to the standard colours of an organisation, or simply to match the storyboard. Use the resize cursor shown in Figure 7.6.5 to make the form larger or wider. Then right click in the background to access the formatting menu for the form. Select 'Fill/ Back Color' to change the background colour. Select the colour itself from the colour palette.

Customising the fields

It is nearly always necessary to customise the fields created by the Form Wizard. The most crucial aspect of this is to resize the fields; firstly so that they give a visual cue to the input length and secondly to make the whole form look balanced and attractive. This second aim is achieved by using the format menu to align the fields and make them the same size and equally spaced (see Fig. 7.6.6). The combination of tools provided means that it is very straightforward to create neat and well laid out forms to meet the user's requirements.

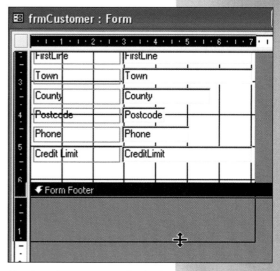

Use the resize cursor to make the form larger, move footer down, or to select all fields and move them

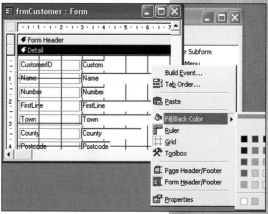

Select 'Fill/Back Color' to change the background colour

Figure 7.6.5 Customising the form size and colours

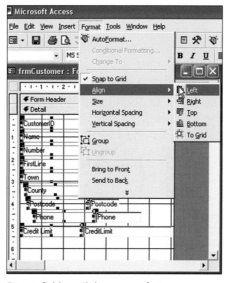

Resizing a field

Format fields until they are perfect

Figure 7.6.6 Resizing, arranging and aligning the fields

Adding static controls

The styling of the form can be improved dramatically by adding static design elements such as a logo, lines or shapes, and styled text. This can be achieved by using the toolbox controls on images, lines, rectangles and labels (see Fig. 7.6.7). Images can also be inserted by selecting 'Picture...' from the Insert menu, or pasted in directly from the clipboard.

Paste in 'purelogosmall.png'

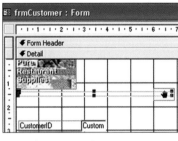
Add a filled rectangle to act as the line

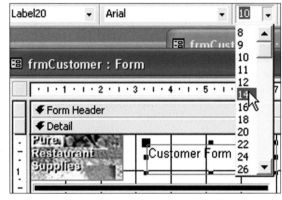
Add a label and use the font controls to customise it

Figure 7.6.7 Adding a logo, a rectangular line and label

ACTIVITY 2 Customise the customer form ◀

Customise the customer form using the stages described (see Figs 7.6.4–7).

Creating combo boxes

In the storyboard we specified a requirement for a combo box (a combination of a text box and a pull-down list). These are extremely useful devices for data entry as they allow the user to select from a list rather than entering in free text. This restricts the scope for error in the input. They are also extremely useful to users in circumstances such as choosing a number like a stock number on an order form as the numbers may not mean a great deal to them on their own and so it would be very difficult to enter the appropriate value in the field. Using a combo box it is possible to display more than one field in the drop-down list, and yet the selected value will be bound to a single field in the table (usually a key field). In addition, it is possible, but not necessary, to limit the data entry to the list, which is useful if the combo box is to be used for list validation. In the customer form we require a drop down list of towns as shown in Figure 7.6.8.

Using the Combo Box Wizard

The Combo Box Wizard can be used to add a pull-down list that enables the user to find and display it on a form. It is a very useful facility for allowing the user to edit forms. Activity 19 uses the Combo Box Wizard.

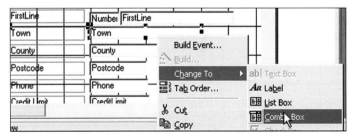

1 Select the Town field; right click and change to a combo box

Fig 7.6.8 continued on the next page

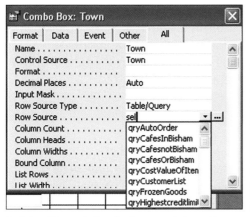

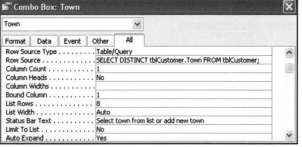

2 Select 'Properties' and select an existing table or query, or write a new query using the Design View or by writing SQL directly

3 In this case, write a new SQL query to show the towns

4 The working combo box

Figure 7.6.8 Changing the Town field to a combo box

ACTIVITY 3 Add a combo box ◀

Add a combo box for the Town field.

Add advanced toolbox controls

In addition to the static controls, the Toolbox (see Fig. 7.6.9) provides a number of other controls that work with the data in the database or enable more advanced operations in the database. It is possible to add groups of option buttons, check boxes, and toggle buttons, and indeed more advanced controls. The most common of these by far is the command button. The Command Button Wizard will connect a button to the most common operations, including record navigation, form printing, deleting, showing a report, or calling a custom macro or even application. If this is not enough then it is possible to customise a button control further by cancelling the Wizard and writing any code required in VBA.

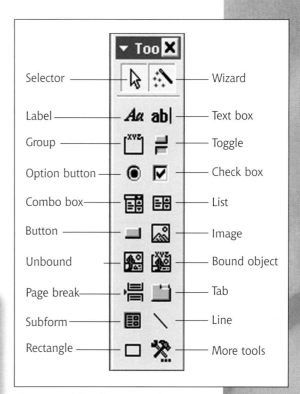

Figure 7.6.9 Toolbox controls

Bound and unbound controls

A bound control is a control that is linked to a field in the database. When the data in the control is updated the data in the database will be updated. Similarly when the data in an underlying table or query is updated the data in the control will be updated. Unbound controls can be used for calculated fields, for holding data temporarily before it is used to update a bound control and for capturing user preferences in dialogues.

Choose the operation

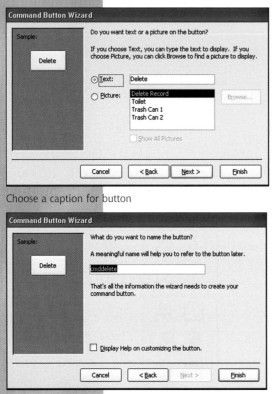

Choose a caption for button

Give the button a name using standard naming conventions

Figure 7.6.10 Command Button Wizard

To use the Command Button Wizard to place a button on the form which will delete the current record is a simple matter of drawing the button in the required position, choosing the appropriate operation in the Wizard, deciding on a caption for the button and finally giving the button a name as in Figure 7.6.10.

Meeting the requirements

The result of all this is a form (see Fig. 7.6.11)) that matches the storyboard we started out with. Now all that is required is to test it to ensure it fully meets the requirements and that all the validation, defaults and expected behaviours are functioning correctly. If they are not then the form will simply be adjusted in Design View until it is correct.

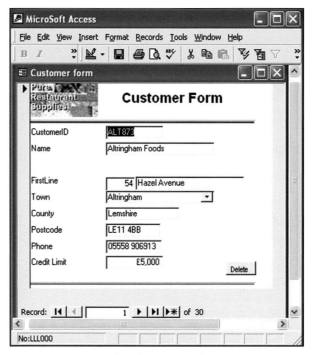

Figure 7.6.11 Completed customer form

ACTIVITY 4 Create supplier and stock forms ◀

Create a supplier and a stock form using the same techniques.

▶ Further techniques

In the following section we will examine further useful techniques for customising forms, including conditional formatting, using the tabular rather than columnar view, using subforms to show data in a related table, and using calculated fields. In practice the vast majority of these simply build on the techniques just described. These fundamental tools will be useful in creating forms, form-based menus and indeed reports. The basic principles are the same in every case with only minor variations to achieve a great variety of results.

Conditional formatting

Conditional formatting is used to format a control differently, depending on the contents of the control. The concept is also used in spreadsheet design. It is very useful to highlight fields when they contain exceptional or odd data. In the stock form the quantity field is to be highlighted when the stock item falls below the minimum stock level and it is therefore ready to be reordered. To set conditional formatting on a field, highlight the cell and select 'Conditional Formatting ...' from the Format menu. Then simply change the conditions and the formats using the dialogue box provided (see Fig. 7.6.12).

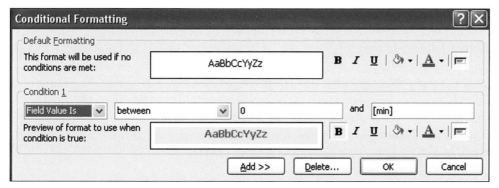

Set conditional format to red on a yellow field if the quantity field is less than minimum

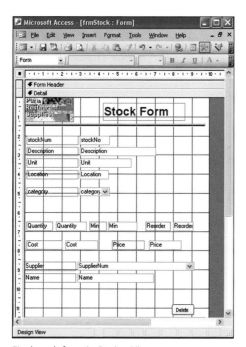

Final stock form in Design View

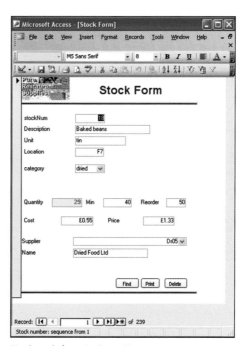

Final stock form in Form View

Figure 7.6.12 Using conditional formatting

ACTIVITY 5 Add conditional formatting to the stock form

Add conditional formatting as described in Figure 7.6.12 to the stock form.

Tabular view

Most users will be used to seeing forms in the columnar view used for the customer and stock forms already discussed. Sometimes this view is less useful than a list-type view, as shown in Figure 7.6.13. The stock check form has been created to allow the results of the physical stock check to be transferred from a paper report to the file as quickly as possible. The only field that is to be updated at all is the quantity field and thus the other two are locked and not enabled (from form properties). A tabular view allows the user to enter the new quantity and/or press return to move on very quickly to the next cell. It has the further advantage that it is very similar in layout to the stock check report and thus once again there is less likelihood of making data-entry errors. The tabular view is simply selected using the Form Wizard (see Fig. 7.6.1, step 3). Similar adaptations can be made to the tabular view as the columnar view. Any data that should be shown just once for all the records, such as the logo and user instructions, will be placed in the form header rather than in the body of the form, as the body is essentially now a table (see Fig. 7.6.13).

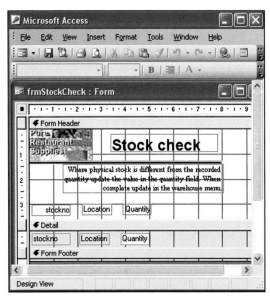

Set StockNo and Location to locked and not enabled   The result

Figure 7.6.13 The tabular view

ACTIVITY 6 Create a tabular stock check form

Using the table created when running the query 'qryCreateStockCheckTable' (Activity 21, Unit 7.5) as the basis of the form, create the stock check form as described in Figure 7.6.13.

Forms with subforms

The order form, as was seen when initially constructing the data model for PRS (see Unit 7.3), is a complex entity comprised of data from many tables. In this situation we need one form for the order – which includes the main order details with the related customer details (there is one customer to one order) – and another as a form within a form (a subform) for the order lines, which includes the order-line information and any necessary stock information such as description, unit and price (there are many order lines for a single order).

The Form Wizard allows you to choose from any number of tables and/or queries, and it then uses the relationships defined while creating the relational database structure to decide how different elements of the form are to be related. There are a number of different views it is possible to take on the same set of tables. For example, it is possible to view the customer and order for a particular order line; or it is possible to view the order with all of its order lines.

There is one more important consideration when using the Form Wizard with this complex type of form. The order in which you select fields can have an impact on the way the Wizard interprets the data. It is best to start with the data that is pivotal to the main form and then add the data from the 'many' relationship later. In the case of the order form, add the fields from the order table, then the customer table, then the order lines and finally the stock, as shown in Figure 7.6.14. This ordering gives the Wizard the best chance of establishing the correct relationship between the subform and the main form. Finally the naming convention we suggest for subforms is to use the form name, e.g. 'frmOrder' with Subform as a postfix, i.e. 'frmOrder Subform'.

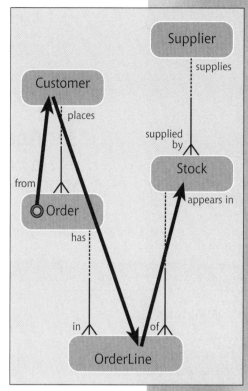

Figure 7.6.14 Selection path through EAR diagram

Choosing the table order for form–subform relationships

Use the ER diagram to guide you. Start with the table that represents what the form is about (see Fig. 7.6.15). Then go up to capture any M:1 relationships, then follow the diagram down to capture any 1:M relationships and on from there as necessary.

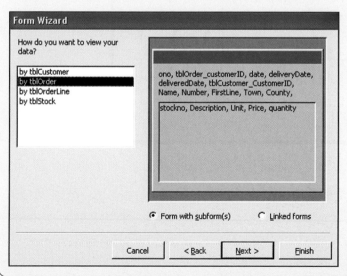

Figure 7.6.15 Selecting subform while using the Wizard

Customising the form and subform is essentially the same process as for a single form. It is only important to remember that the subform is potentially showing many records to the one record for the master form. When designing the subform, it is preferable to open the subform itself in Design View rather than adapt it inside the main-form design. As with any form it is possible to set the subform up as a columnar form using the form properties, but the default behaviour is as a datasheet, as this is by far the most commonly required layout.

ACTIVITY 7 Create an order form with a subform

Look at these demonstrations from the ActiveBook. Now create the order form and customise it in the same manner as the other forms.

▶ Calculated fields

> ### Control sources
>
> A control source is a property of a control, stating where the value in the control is being derived from. For bound controls it will be from the table. For calculated controls it will be a formula, usually comprising one or more field names, functions, operators or values. The field need not be on the current object (form, report etc.), but if it is not then it is preferable to use the Expression Builder (see later) to specify the name of the field, as it can be quite complex. The control source is displayed in the field itself in Design View and can thus be easily edited.

An essential item of most database applications is the use of calculated fields. These are fields that are calculated from the values in other controls rather than bound to data in a table. The calculations can take the form of almost any that we have seen so far in examining queries, and more. In the order form an extra field is required to display the total for each row in order line, which is calculated as the price × quantity. To add this field it is only necessary to add a text box using the toolbox, name it using the properties window and then add '= price * quantity' as the control source for the field, as shown in Figure 7.6.16.

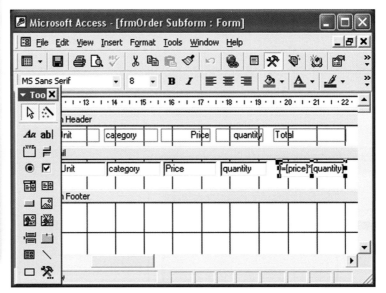

Add a new text field on the subform. Enter the formula '= price * quantity' to act as the control source

Figure 7.6.16 Adding a simple calculated field

ACTIVITY 8 Add a calculated field ◀

Look at this demonstration from the ActiveBook. Now add a calculated field for a total on the subform.

▶ Values from subforms

One of the more difficult commonly needed operations when implementing a form is calculating a total (or average or any other function) from the rows of a subform, to be displayed on the main form. This is essentially a three-step process, as shown in Figure 7.6.17.

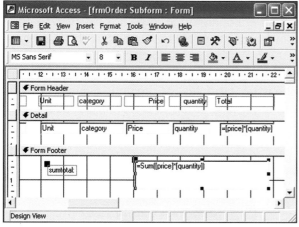

1 Add a new field in the footer of the subform called 'SumTotal'

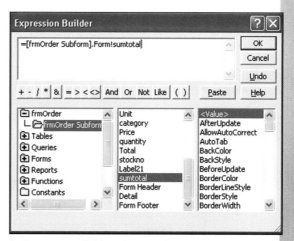

2 Create a new field on the main form, use Expression Builder to select the correct field, then copy the result into the field to act as the control source

First, the total of the required rows is computed in a new calculated field in the footer of the subform itself (where it will not be displayed but will be available for further calculation). Note that you cannot use functions, such as Sum(), on the values in calculated controls; thus on the order form it is essential to calculate the sum of the quantity × price rather than the sum of the total field, i.e. '=Sum(quantity * price)'. Step 2 is to close the subform and add a new text field to the main form which will be used to pick up the value from the field in the footer of the subform. Step 3 is to right click on the field, select 'Build Event', and then select 'Expression Builder'. The Expression Builder can then be used to find the field in the footer of the subform. It will write the correct syntax for the field which can then be copied into the control source of the field in the main form. This is a complex expression and developers have to gain a good deal of experience before they can write the correct syntax by hand, and thus Expression Builder should be used for all such operations.

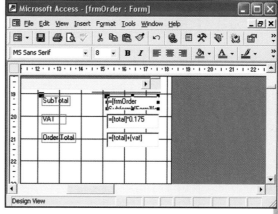

3 Copy the result into the field to act as the control source, then add extra fields calculated on this field

Figure 7.6.17 Calculating a total from rows on a subform

ACTIVITY 9 Create a calculated field dependent on a subform

Look at this demonstration from the ActiveBook. Now add the total, VAT and grand total fields.

▶ Completing the form and its subform

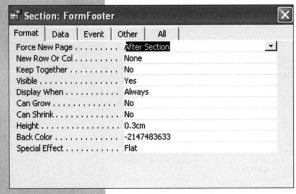

Figure 7.6.18 Customising for print – force a new page after the footer

Customising the order form into a finished state can be a time-consuming business. The final two calculated fields are simple to add, but the exact layout can sometimes be a little awkward. If the form is to be printed, which it is in the case of the PRS Order to act as an order confirmation, then it is essential that each order form takes exactly one page. To ensure this, simply change the Force New Page property for the form footer so that it forces a page break after the section (see Fig. 7.6.18). The final results can be really satisfying, as shown in Figure 7.6.19 where the finished order form matches the printed order form nearly exactly.

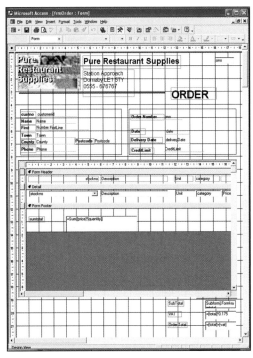

In Design View

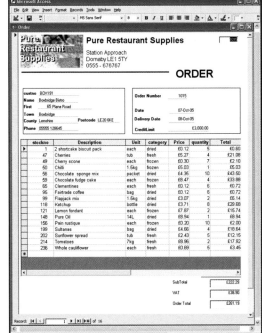

In Form View

Figure 7.6.19 Completed order form

Complete the order form and test it.
  Print it out and adjust margins and field widths as necessary.

Creating attractive and useful reports

Reports are the main media for outputting information in an attractive and user-friendly manner in a database application. They work in almost exactly the same manner as forms, with the exception that the bound data is not meant for editing. As they are built for outputting to screen and paper, there is a little more control over the layout using a series of different headers and footers, including, most crucially, headers and footers for groups of data, which can all be used for different purposes within the overall report. This gives a really flexible means of producing output.

  Reports are usually built with a Report Wizard (see Fig. 7.6.20). This binds the report to the queries and/or tables chosen. It aids in grouping the data. If there are any numerical fields it allows aggregation of these fields automatically. It helps define the sort order of the data. It helps in establishing a basic layout and style to customise from and allows a name to be chosen for the report.

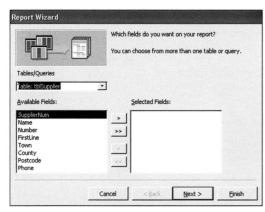

1 Choose the tables, queries and fields

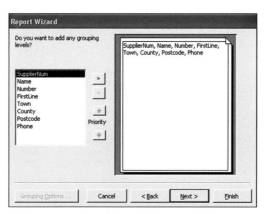

2 Set any grouping of data; this is essential for reports displaying one to many relationships

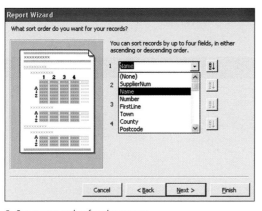

3 Set a sort order for the report

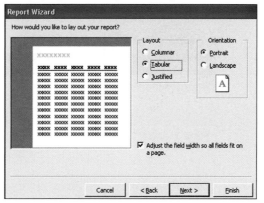

4 Set a layout for the report

Fig 7.6.20 continued on the next page

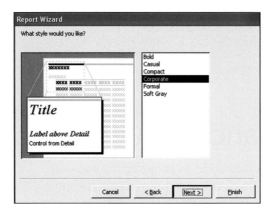

5 Set a style for the report

6 Name the report using standard naming conventions

Figure 7.6.20 Using the Report Wizard to create the supplier list

As with forms, Wizards should be used wherever possible, but the same caveats apply to the order in which tables and fields are chosen. Customising a basic report uses all the same techniques as customising a form, including changing captions, backgrounds, field widths, and adding controls and calculated fields. This is shown in the demonstration you can view from ActiveBook. It leads to the finished report shown in Figure 7.6.21.

Figure 7.6.21 Tabular view of completed supplier list

▶ Report sections

Table 7.6.1 shows the different components of a report.

Table 7.6.1 Parts of a report

Section	Position	Content
Report Header	At the top of the report Prints before page header	Cover page type information – logo, title, date, overall aggregate info
Page Header	Prints at the top of every page	Page title Aggregate functions do not work
Group Header	Prints at the start of each new group of records	Group information, e.g. customer and order name Aggregates over current group
Detail	The main body of the report Prints once for each row	

Continued on the next page

Section	Position	Content
Group Footer	Prints at the end of each group of records	Summary information for a group Aggregates over current group
Page Footer	Prints at the foot of the page	Footer info – date, page number etc. Aggregate functions do not work
Report Footer	Prints at the end of the report	Summary information for the entire report

Note: You have to select a group to have a Group Header; you have to select Group Footer in the Groups dialogue box to have a Group Footer.

Activity 11 Use columnar view ◀

Use the Report Wizard to select the potential profit query (qryPotentialProfit); select columnar view; customise the report to match Figure 7.6.22.

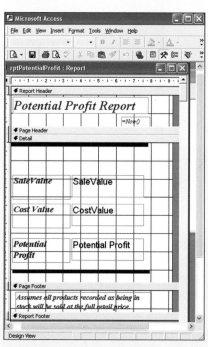

The final design   The result

Figure 7.6.22 Potential profit report

ACTIVITY 12 Add a blank textbox to control to a report

1 Use the Report Wizard with 'qryStockCheck' to create a basic report.
2 Group the records by location.
3 Customise it as required to match the output in Figure 7.6.23.
4 Add a blank text box in the final column to act as a space for the warehouse staff to write down the actual level of stock against the recorded level.

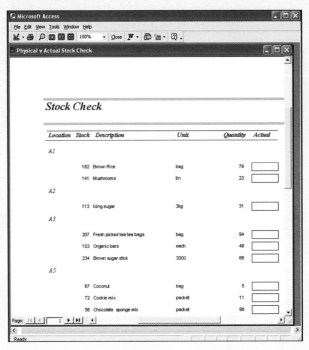

Figure 7.6.23
Stock check report

Multi-table reports

The most challenging reports are those that are required to display a one-to-many relationship within the report, as in the order requisition that is created automatically by PRS. The first important difference from the single table/query reports is that the Wizard will try to use the relationships created from the EAR diagram to help layout the data in groups.

In Figure 7.6.24, the Report Wizard has deduced the relationship in 'qryAutoOrder', laid out the supplier information in a group header and the stock information in the detail. It is possible to do this manually using groups – you can see some demonstrations from the ActiveBook showing how 'rptInvoice' is built from 'qryInvoice', which has a much more complex structure and is built with stock as the first field. It is, of course, much simpler when the RDBMS can deduce the groupings itself as could be seen from the demonstration.

Having established the correct groups, customising the report itself is very similar to customising a form. To add the total field of the report to the correct position at the foot of the Total column (which is a value that was originally created in the underlying query) it is necessary to create a Group Footer to match the header using the sorting and grouping dialogue that is accessed by right clicking in the top left of the Group (name) Header.

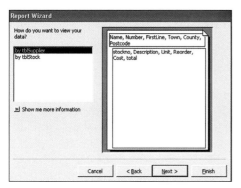

1 Ensure the correct grouping is selected

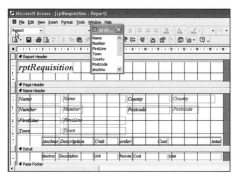

2 Layout as created by the Wizard

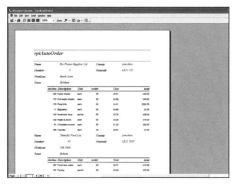

3 Layout with a Group Header (name)

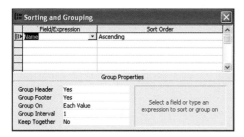

4 Sort Order can be set in the report's sorting and grouping view

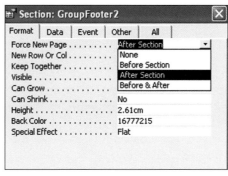

5 To add the calculations for the total requisition value, add a Group Footer for the Name group

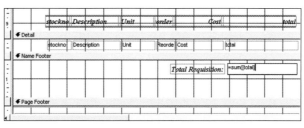

6 Add the calculated field and write in the function '= Sum(total)' to add up the total column

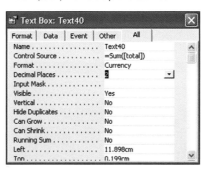

7 Change the field properties to 'Currency' with two decimal places

Figure 7.6.24 Key stages in creating and customising multi-table reports

8 Final requisition design

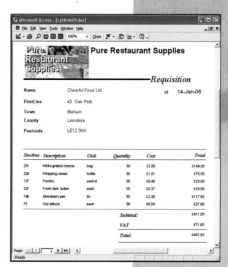

9 Final requisition

ACTIVITY 13 Create multi-table reports

1 Create the requisition report to match the report shown in Figure 7.6.24.
2 Create an invoice report from 'qryInvoice'.

Note: The use of so many sections in a report means that it does become a little more complex to decide where to force the use of a new page. Good design, or trial and error (iterative testing), will ensure the correct position is chosen

▶ Aggregate calculations

Access reports permit a multitude of methods for calculating values on reports. The one that should be used first is to perform the calculations in the underlying query. This is the most portable and efficient method, and means that the calculations are reusable across different reports. Secondly, formulas can be written directly into a Text Box control as the control source, as shown in the first part of Figure 7.6.25. In this case a formula is concatenating (adding) today's date to the string 'Value of stock at cost at'. Aggregate functions such as Sum(), Count(), Min(), Max() and Average() can be written in headers and footers (with the exception of page headers and footers). The Report Wizard also has a facility for summarising numerical data, when it finds data that can be summarised. Another interesting and important facility is that of calculating a running or a cumulative total as demonstrated in Figure 7.6.25.

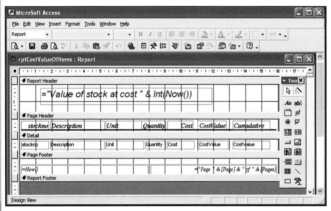

1 Draw in the extra text boxes 1 and 2 with the correct control source

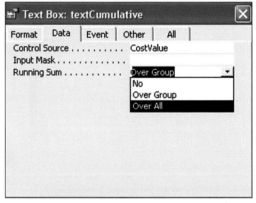

2 Select properties for the cumulative total

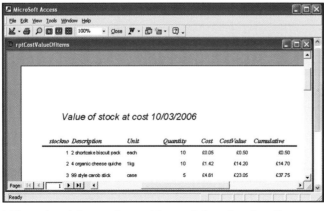

3 The end result is a running total (a cumulative value of stock)

Figure 7.6.25 Running totals

Using Database Software

Creating a user-friendly front end using menus

The final part of creating a user interface is to connect all the forms and reports together using a front end built around menus. It is possible to create this semi-automatically using the 'Switchboard Manager' from 'Database Utilities' on the Tools menu. However, although this is a clever and very useful tool it does not have the flexibility to achieve everything a client may require from a front end, and so it is essential to learn how to build menus on forms from scratch.

▶ Storyboards

As always, a little time spent designing saves a great deal of time later. Designing using storyboards allows the developer to ensure that all the required functionality is implemented through the menu system, and makes it really clear how this is to be done. Another advantage is that it allows a standard look and feel to be developed, which helps the user by introducing some consistency and helps the developer because a fair amount can be achieved by copying and pasting.

A quick look at the functional specification for PRS from the ActiveBook shows that there are too many functions for a single form. A rough guide is that 10 controls are about as many as you should have on one menu. Having established that submenus are necessary there are a number of choices as to how they might be implemented. The most important principle is that they should be grouped in a manner that is right for the user, not the developer. For PRS we specified a menu for the sales staff, one for the warehouse staff, and one for the managers and administrative staff. There is also a main form which pushes control to one of the other menus and allows the user to exit. Having established the look and feel of the menu system (see Fig. 7.6.26), the actual implementation work is relatively straightforward.

- The first step is to create a form that can be used as the basis of all four forms in the menu system. This will then be copied to create the other forms. Menu forms do not usually contain bound data and thus they can be created in Form Design View without using the Form Wizard.
- The second step is to add the basic controls that do not require further macros, such as the combo boxes, and the buttons that can use the Command Wizard.
- Finally, simple macros must be developed for all instances where the built-in behaviours are not sufficient; then the controls must be added to the forms in Design View in the manner described for data input forms.

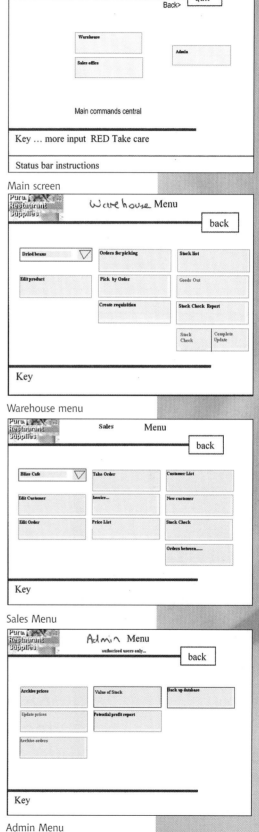

Figure 7.6.26 Storyboards for the menus

▶ Creating the basic form

The steps in creating the basic form vary depending on how complex the storyboards are. In this case they have been designed to be simple.

ACTIVITY 14 Create the basic form ◀

Create the basic form. The main stages of this process are shown in Figure 7.6.27.

1 Create the main form

Figure 7.6.27 Creating the main menus from the storyboards

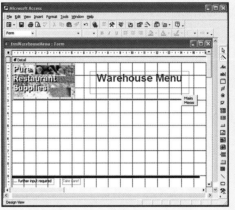

2 Copy it and add main menu button linked to the main form

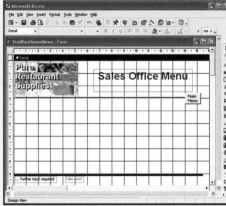

3 Duplicate this twice to create the other two menus

1 Create a form about 17 cm × 10 cm in Design View.
2 Change the background to match the storyboard.
3 Save and insert the logo.
4 Insert a rectangle to act as a line (or insert a line).
5 Add a label and format it for the title.
6 Add labels for the key at the bottom.
7 Add a command button using the Wizard and choose 'Quit Application' from the Application category and type the Caption 'Exit'.
8 Change the properties of the form to those you wish to have for all the forms (e.g. remove navigation buttons etc.).
9 Save this is as 'frmMainMenu'.
10 Now copy this form and save it as 'frmWarehouseMenu'.
11 Delete the 'Exit' button and replace it with a 'Main Menu' button that opens the 'frmMainMenu' form.
12 Save this and copy it 'frmSalesMenu' and 'frmAdminMenu'.

ACTIVITY 15 Add the basic controls to the main menu ◀

Open 'frmMainMenu'. Add three buttons to match the storyboard (see Fig. 7.6.27). Use the Command Button Wizard in each case to open the appropriate form by selecting 'Form Operations' from the Categories list.

Test that the menu system works by navigating between them and quitting the application.

◄

DISCUSSION Alternative menu systems

What other menu system could there be?

Propose your favourite and explain the advantages and disadvantages of this method.

ACTIVITY 16 Implement the warehouse form ◄

Open 'frmWarehouseMenu' in Design View. List which buttons can be implemented from existing reports and macros. Implement these using the Command Button Wizard.

▶ Building actions with macros

The Command Button Wizard will automate a good deal of the functionality required for the linking buttons to forms, reports and the macros that were written as part of developing processes (see Unit 7.5). Where it does not, it is necessary to design and implement custom macros to achieve the desired functionality.

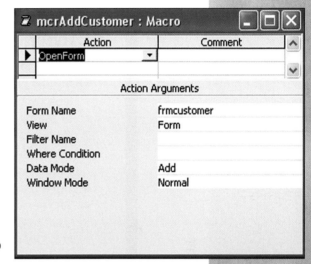

Figure 7.6.28 Add customer macro

Link to a form to add a new record

When the sales staff want to add a new customer they could simply open the customer form and select the '>*' control on the navigation bar to show the blank form for a new customer. It is simpler for the customer, however, if the form automatically opens in Add mode. To achieve this with a macro is simple (see Figure 7.6.28).

ACTIVITY 17 Create the required macros ◄

1 Create the macro shown in Figure 7.6.28.
2 Create a similar macro for orders called 'mcrOrder'.
3 Create a similar macro for suppliers called 'mcrSupplier'.

Link a form to a value in a combo box

The sales menu has a combo box which allows the user to pull down the customer name. This is then used by the 'Edit' buttons in Activity 18 to find the appropriate record and display it for editing, as in Figure 7.6.29.

1 Add the combo box to the form

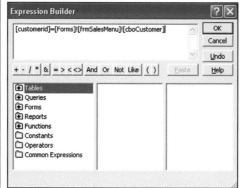

2 Use the expression builder to get the full syntax for the Where condition

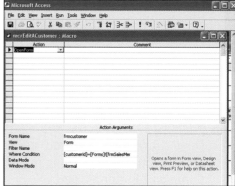

3 Set the OpenForm properties

Figure 7.6.29 Using a combo box in a dialogue box to open a form for editing

ACTIVITY 18 Implement the sales form

Refer back to Figure 7.6.29 as you do this activity.

1 Add a combo box. Either create it directly and add an SQL expression to look up the names from the customer table, or use the Combo Box Wizard to display the name in the customer table.
2 Name the combo box 'cboCustomer'. No caption is required. Note that it is wise to set the AutoCorrect property of the combo box to 'No' so that the RDBMS does not add an accent to 'cafe', which will cause problems.
3 Open a macro and call it 'mcrEditACustomer'.
4 Set the action to 'OpenForm'.
5 Use the Expression Builder to find the full syntax for the name of combo box and use it in the where condition property:
([customerid] = [Forms]![frmSalesMenu]![cboCustomer])
6 Set the data mode to edit and save it.
7 Create the button and connect it to the 'mcrEditACustomer' macro.
8 Create a similar button below for editing an order form based on the customer name called 'mcrEditOrder'.
9 Create a similar facility on the Warehouse menu to look up a stock record based on the description called 'mcrEditStock'.

ACTIVITY 19 Create combo box on a form

1 Look at this demonstration from the ActiveBook of the Combo Box Wizard.
2 Copy the supplier form and paste it as 'frmEditSupplier'.
3 Cut the name 'textbox' and replace it with a combo box.
4 Use the Wizard to enable the combo box to find a record based on the supplier name.
5 Add the button on the Warehouse menu to allow editing of Suppliers by opening this form.

ACTIVITY **20** Assessment task: Automate the goods out process ◀

Create 'frmGoodsOut' and the necessary macro.

ACTIVITY **21** Extension exercises: Finalise and test the menus ◀

Complete all the menus and test that they work correctly.

Startup procedures

Once every part of the application is working and the navigation using the menus is functioning as required, the Startup properties of the application can be set. Once again, Access provides an easy way of managing this. Select 'Startup ...' from the Tools menu and set the title of the application and the form that will be displayed when the application starts up (see Fig. 7.6.30). As can be seen by examining the dialogue box, it is possible to customise the application a great deal, including removing all the built-in menus and dialogues so that the users' experience is very tightly controlled. It will not be necessary for you to do any more than set the Startup form unless specifically instructed to in the examination.

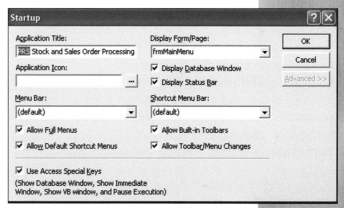

Figure 7.6.30 Start up procedures

Conclusion ▶ ▶ ▶

In Unit 7.6 we have examined how to add a user-friendly interface to the database application. The three main steps are to add forms for user-friendly input, add reports for highly tailored and attractive output, and finally to add menus as a front end to these elements. We have demonstrated how the same techniques can be used at every stage of this process, and thus techniques learnt for forms can be applied to reports and menus. At this stage a user-friendly database has been developed. The next stage is to ensure that it does do everything that it was required to do at the initial stage of the project.

Testing glossary

Test plan Table specifying the tests that will be performed.

Test log Table recording the results of applying the tests in the test plan.

Debugging Checking for errors while creating a program.

Test data Data that fully tests the item under consideration. It will include a test for valid data that should not give an error and invalid data that should give an error. It will also test the boundary between these.

Functional or black-box testing A system or module is tested from outside by feeding it inputs and checking the output. No consideration is given to how it works inside (it is black so you cannot see inside). The purpose is to check the application meets the specification.

Logical or white-box testing A system or module is tested by considering paths through it to ensure all possibilities are considered. The purpose is to ensure that the logic of the application is correct.

Performance testing Testing the application performs adequately in terms of speed with the required volume of data or with the specified number of users.

Requirements testing Testing that the application does what it is required.

Top–down testing Testing that the whole system works. If it does not then check each module. If one of these does not then check each part of the module.

Bottom–up testing Testing that each part of a module works; then when it does combine them and check the whole module works; then when it does this check the whole system works.

Recovery testing Testing to check that the data still has integrity after a crash.

Normal data Data within the expected valid range.

Boundary/extreme data Data at the boundary between normal and abnormal – the place where most problems occur.

Abnormal data Data outside the expected valid range – erroneous data

Testing is normal and essential when building a database. After each object is developed you will almost certainly test it. If you create a table you will put some data in to see if it works; if you create a form you will see if it looks like it should and enter some data and press some buttons to see if it works as it should. When you write a query or run a report, you will test it to see if it displays the output you were expecting. Any developer, even the least experienced, will do all of this without being instructed to.

The difference between an experienced and skilful developer and a novice is in the quality and coverage of the tests designed. In Unit 7.7 we will examine the testing techniques used by developers to ensure a quality project. Quality tests are designed to ensure that the database works properly when normal, extreme and abnormal data are input; that the output from the database is complete, accurate and in the required format; that the front end and the rest of the user interface is both user-friendly and works properly; and perhaps most critically, that the solution meets all the requirements of the functional specification. In Unit 7.7 we will examine each of these areas and examine how to document these tests effectively.

Testing data input

Usually the first tests that will be performed in any project will be data input tests. When a table is first created it is important to test that it works properly. The way to do this is simply to enter data into each field and check that it works. It is tempting simply to enter random data of the correct type into each field and, if it all works, assume that the table is correct, leaving proper testing until later. However, a little planning and good technique can ensure that the table is tested properly right from the start, without a great deal of extra effort in the short run and saving an enormous amount of time in the long run.

An experienced developer will test each field by using carefully chosen sample data rather than random data. For example, if a wage can be within the range £4.50 to £25.00 per hour inclusive, then the following test data will form the basis of a really rigorous plan:

£4.49	£12.00	£25.01
£4.50	£25.00	£100.00

Good test data provides evidence both that the database accepts data that is valid, and that it rejects data that is invalid. A common mistake is to test many numbers in the range of £4.50 to £25.00, but this only proves that the database accepts valid data. By testing once for normal data, once for abnormal data and testing at the boundary between the two, it is possible in most cases to see the entire range of behaviour of the field.

ACTIVITY 1 Test quantity in the stock table ◀

In the stock table for PRS, the integer numeric field quantity cannot be less than zero. What test data would you use to be sure that your field is behaving correctly? Copy and complete Table 7.7.1.

Table 7.7.1

Test class	Test data
Normal	
On boundary	
Just outside boundary	
Abnormal data	

What would happen if you entered 32 800, and why? (If you cannot work it out, do the test!)

Would a user ever enter 32 800? What implication does this have for our tests?

ACTIVITY 2 Write down why we test ◀

Write down all the different reasons we test products.

ACTIVITY 3 Test the location field ◀

The location field of the stock table must be one letter followed by one number. Although there is no obvious boundary in this case it is worth considering what might be considered the extreme 'acceptable' and 'just beyond acceptable' in this case. The lowest letter in a computer's character set is 'A' and the highest is 'z'. The lowest digit is '0' and the highest is '9'. 'A0' and 'z9' are therefore at the extreme ends of the valid range. A plus symbol is often used with numbers so it is worth testing in the numeric position. For example you may test for C+, which it should, but might not, reject.

Continued on the next page

Boundary testing

A heuristic (rule of thumb) for locating possible errors in data input, particularly of a numeric type, is to look for data which is at the extremes of acceptability. If a person has to be at least 18 years old to join a club then the most likely place to find an error in the rules for the database is by testing for a person exactly 18 years old, and one of 18 years and 1 day old (and possibly one day less). If the test passes at the boundaries it is likely that it will be correct for normal and abnormal data.

Feedback

You must get the end users to test your work and give you feedback even if you think your application may be perfect. Developers knows what data should be input and what should happen. Their tests will unconsciously take this into account and may neglect how a real user will use the application, missing really glaring problems.

Copy and complete Table 7.7.2.

Table 7.7.2

Test class	Test data
Normal	
Low boundary	
High boundary	
Beyond boundary (number)	
Abnormal data	

ACTIVITY 4 Test the reorder level

The reorder field of the stock table is an integer field that should have a value greater than zero. Write the test data to test it thoroughly by copying and completing Table 7.7.3.

Table 7.7.3

Test class	Test data
Normal	
Low boundary	
High Boundary	
Below low boundary	
Beyond high boundary	
Abnormal data	

Documenting the test plan

Documenting the tests to be undertaken is an essential part of sound project development. If the tests are all documented thoroughly it is both easy to repeat them if necessary and possible to spot if there were any flaws or omissions in the test procedures. In testing the reorder field it is essential that zero is entered as the low boundary, as this is where most errors will occur. If a bug is reported in the requisition report where zero is ordered on more than one occasion, then the test plan and log can be examined to be sure this boundary was tested. If not, then it will be an easy job to correct. If it was tested then the error may be more deep seated. The presence of good documentation may therefore save a lot of time.

There are many methods for documenting test plans but the most common are tables that spell out the test class (i.e. the purpose of the test), the actual input that will be used in the test and the expected output of that test, as shown in the test plan table in Figure 7.7.1.

Test plan glossary

Object Database object, such as a table, form, query, report.

Control Input/output object such as a textbox, combo box, check box, button.

Test number A number for the test to be used for referencing to the test log when the tester performs the tests.

Test class Purpose of the test; the range that is being sampled.

Actual input Actual data, event or file that is to be input to represent the test class.

Expected outcome If the data is accepted then the input is the outcome. If it is not accepted then what error or error message is expected. Creating a table of possible errors is a very useful tool.

Database name: PRS Object type: Table Name: tblStock		Tester name: S. Friedel Date: 12/5/2005		
Test number	Control	Purpose/test class	Actual input data/file/event	Expected output/file
1	Reorder	Normal	50	50
2	Reorder	Boundary	0	0
3	Reorder	Beyond boundary	-1	Err#1
4	Reorder	Abnormal	99999	Err#33

Err#1: It is not possible to order a negative amount
Err#33: The value you entered is not valid for this field.

Figure 7.7.1 Typical test plan table

Testing using the plan

The most obvious means of testing to the plan is for a tester to simply work through the test plan one test at a time, and enter the results of the tests into a log to show what actually happened. Assuming that the test plan was designed correctly and the actual outcome matches the expected outcome in each case, then the product passes the tests. If there is any variation, as in Test 2 of the test log shown in Figure 7.7.2, the product is passed back to the developer for investigation. Either the test design could be wrong or the product will need to be corrected. If it is the latter then the product will be re-engineered and a new set of tests designed and implemented to ensure that it does meet the criteria.

Database name: PRS Object type: Table Name: tblStock	Tester name: J. Jones Date: 12/6/2005	
Test number	Actual onput/data/event/file	Comments
1	50	☐
2	Err#1	Failed at boundary.
3	Err#1	☐
4	Err#33	☐

Figure 7.7.2 Typical test log

Automating testing with a test file

In database applications, it is easy to use a file to test your input. You can design a test plan, put all of the test into a file, run them all in one batch and note the results. The test data is put into a single file which will test what the developer wishes to look at. The file will then be imported into the database. The database may reject some of the records. These rejected records will be compared to the records that the developer expected to be rejected. If they are the same the product passes the test; otherwise the developer will investigate further and possibly retest.

Test log glossary

Test number A number for the test to be used for referencing to the test plan when the tester performs the tests.

Test class Purpose of the test; the range that is being sampled.

Actual output Actual data, event or file that is output (exactly as is).

Comments If the expected outcome does not match the actual outcome then comments should be written to explain what is to be done.

Plans and logs

The test plan and test log shown are variations on very common documents used in testing databases in industry. It is equally acceptable to create the test log by adding two extra columns to the test plan (actual output and comments).

ACTIVITY 5 Test using a test file ◀

Save and import this text file of test data, shown in Figure 7.7.3, into this test database and attempt to append it to 'tblStockTest'.

Take a screenshot of 'tblStocktest' and 'tblStock_ImportErrors'.

Security settings

Your computer's security settings may prevent you opening this and other Access databases. For information on changing these see the Help Section. You may also need help from a network administrator.

stockno	Description	Unit	Location	category	Quantity	Cost	Price	Min	Reorder	SupplierNum
1001	a	each	Z1	dried	10	£0.10	£0.10	40	50	Wh09
1002	b	each	Z2	frozen	6	£1.42	£4.31	40	50	Th72
1003	c	each	Z3	dried	55	£4.61	£14.36	40	50	Ve33
1004	d	each	Z4	fresh	0	£0.86	£3.01	40	50	Ve33
1005	e	each	Z5	frozen	-1	£2.82	£9.25	40	50	Bi95
1006	f	each	Z6	dried	999999	£0.05	£0.41	40	50	Ve33
1007	g	each	Z7	frozen	27	£0.00	£11.45	40	50	Co04
1008	h	each	Z8	frozen	50	-£1.00	£0.87	40	50	Bi95
1009	I	each	Z9	fresh	37	£20.00	£0.52	40	50	Re20
1010	j	each	Z1	other	43	£2.32	£7.76	40	50	Th72
1011	k	each	Z2		200	£0.06	£0.44	40	50	Re20
1012	l	each	Z3	frozen	78	£0.24	£0.00	40	50	Co04
1013	m	each	Z4	fresh	57	£2.12	-£1.00	40	50	Re20
1014	n	each	Z5	fresh	70	£3.83	£999	40	50	fa14
1015	o	each	Z6	dried	66	£0.19	£0.91	0	50	Wh09
1016	p	each	Z7	fresh	71	£3.00	£9.96	-1	50	Fa14
1017	q	each	Z8	frozen	50	£0.06	£0.47	999999	50	Bi95
1018	r	each	Z9	dried	29	£0.55	£2.04	40	0	Dr05
1019	s	each	Z1	frozen	50	£1.70	£5.22	40	-1	Bi95
1020	t	each	Z2	fresh	43	£0.47	£1.82	40	999999	Wh09
1021	u	each	Z3	frozen	4	£2.39	£7.71	40	50	Th72
1022	v	each	Z4	fresh	57	£2.63	£8.49	40	50	Ve33
1023	w	each	Z5	fresh	12	£1.16	£4.05	40	50	Ve33
1024	x	each	Z6	dried	6	£0.28	£1.20	40	50	11
1025	y	each	Z7	frozen	50	£3.15	£9.60	40	50	aa

Light blue: validation errors; yellow: type or format errors

Figure 7.7.3 Stock-test text file annotated to show planned errors

Look at this demonstration from the ActiveBook if you are unsure about how to import from a CSV file.

stockno	Description	Unit	Location	category	Quantity	Cost	Price	Min	Reorder	SupplierNum
1001	a	each	Z1	dried	10	£0.10	£0.10	40	50	Wh09
1002	b	each	Z2	frozen	6	£1.42	£4.31	40	50	Th72
1003	c	each	Z3	dried	55	£4.61	£14.36	40	50	Ve33
1004	d	each	Z4	fresh	0	£0.86	£3.01	40	50	Ve33
1006	f	each	Z6	dried		£0.05	£0.41	40	50	Ve33
1007	g	each	Z7	frozen	27	£0.00	£11.45	40	50	Co04
1009	I	each	Z9	fresh	37	£20.00	£0.52	40	50	Re20
1011	k	each	Z2		200	£0.06	£0.44	40	50	Re20
1012	l	each	Z3	frozen	78	£0.24	£0.00	40	50	Co04
1014	n	each	Z5	fresh	70	£3.83	£999.00	40	50	fa14
1015	o	each	Z6	dried	66	£0.19	£0.91	0	50	Wh09
1017	q	each	Z8	frozen	50	£0.06	£0.47		50	Bi95
1020	t	each	Z2	fresh	43	£0.47	£1.82	40		Wh09
1021	u	each	Z3	frozen	4	£2.39	£7.71	40	50	Th72
1022	v	each	Z4	fresh	57	£2.63	£8.49	40	50	Ve33
1023	w	each	Z5	fresh	12	£1.16	£4.05	40	50	Ve33
1024	x	each	Z6	dried	6	£0.28	£1.20	40	50	11
1025	y	each	Z7	frozen	50	£3.15	£9.60	40	50	aa
					0					

Figure 7.7.4 Screenshot of imported table

Error	Field	Row
Type Conversion Failure	Quantity	6
Type Conversion Failure	Min	17
Type Conversion Failure	Reorder	20

Figure 7.7.5 Screenshot of 'tblStockTest_ImportErrors'

In this case, comparing the screenshots in Figures 7.7.4 and 7.7.5 with Figure 7.7.3, it is clear that the database correctly rejected all seven records with validation errors. It rejected three fields with type errors and noted these in the import errors table. It did not reject the final two records as expected.

ACTIVITY 6 Analyse the results

Examine the records and the table structure and decide why errors were not picked up. Decide whether it is an error or a misunderstanding. If the former, then correct and retest.

Testing with a file in the examination

There is a high probability that you will be asked to test your table structure in the examination by importing a pre-written file. You may then be asked to provide evidence of the records imported by including a screenshot of your imported records and evidence of the rejected records. It is important that you are familiar and comfortable with this method of testing.

Testing output

There are two aspects of an application's output that must be tested. The first is that the correct data is output; the second is that it is output in the correct format. The first of these is very similar to the tests for input and will be tested and evidenced in exactly the same manner. The second will be tested by comparing the actual output with the required format from the output specification and design; it is normally evidenced using screenshots and witness statements signing that the output matches the specification.

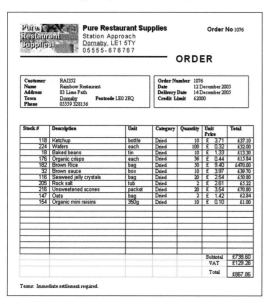
Original order

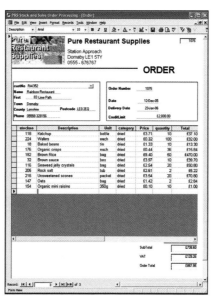
Order as rendered in the database

Figure 7.7.6 Testing the PRS order form

Figure 7.7.6 shows the order form that was used to derive the original data model for PRS. This should be compared with a printout of the order form from the database application and checked for correct output, and that the format is correct. By replicating the order in the test database it is possible to see that the correct items are chosen, that the calculations are correct, and how closely the final output matches the required format as shown in the original form.

Planning for tests

It is sensible to plan your tests so that the expected value is simple to see. This might mean using a spreadsheet to create tables, calculate totals etc., in advance of entering your data into the database. A simpler method that can be employed is to use very simple test data to make it obvious what the answer should be, and so that deviations from it can easily be seen, as is shown in the test on the potential profit report in Activity 8. Beware, however, that this heuristic should not be used for testing input, and that a really careful tester will still test the boundaries of the output.

ACTIVITY 7 Test the goods out process

1 Replicate this order in the test database and perform the test shown in Figure 7.7.6.
2 Open the form 'frmMainMenu'. Go to the 'Warehouse Menu' and run the 'Goods Out' process, choosing 'Order 1076' on the drop-down menu.
3 Test that the invoice is printed correctly, with the correct calculations and today's date.
4 The initial stock of each item in 'tblStock' on the invoice is 100; test what it is after the process.
5 Copy and complete the expected value in the first column of Table 7.7.4. Compare it with the actual quantity in stock after the process.

Table 7.7.4

Stock number	Expected value	Actual value

ACTIVITY 8 Test a query

Task 1

Test whether 'qryPotentialProfit' works correctly. Create a CSV file with a known amount of sale value (£200) and a known cost value (£150), and thus a profit of £50. Check that when run, this is the output.

stockno	Description	Unit	category	Cost	Price	quantity	supplierNum
1	a	each	dried	£1.00	£2.00	10	Bi95
2	b	each	dried	£1.00	£2.00	10	Bi95
3	c	each	dried	£1.00	£2.00	10	Bi95
4	d	each	dried	£1.00	£2.00	10	Bi95
5	e	each	dried	£1.00	£2.00	10	Bi95
6	f	each	dried	£1.00	£2.00	10	Bi95
7	g	each	dried	£1.00	£2.00	10	Bi95
8	h	each	dried	£1.00	£2.00	10	Bi95
9	I	each	dried	£1.00	£2.00	10	Bi95
10	j	each	dried	£1.00	£2.00	10	Bi95

Original table

Potential Profit Report

21 January

SaleValue	£200.00
Cost Value	£100.00
Potential Profit	£100.00

Report output

Figure 7.7.7 Profit-test text file and its output

Delete all the records from 'tblStock' in the test database. Save, then import this text file of test data shown in Figure 7.7.7.

Note: Deleting the records from 'tblStock' will also require that you delete the records from 'tblOrderLine' (consider why this is so). You may wish to do these quite radical actions on a copy of the database to preserve the original for further testing. The following two tests can be performed on the new 'tblStock' or the original one, but will probably be easier to perform on a smaller set of data.

Run the report 'rptPotentialProfit' (see Fig. 7.7.7). Check the results.

Task 2

What happens when you make the potential profit very low (e.g. less than £0) or very high (e.g. more than £10 million)?

ACTIVITY 9 Test price updating ◀

Test to see if the update price facility works correctly by adding 10% to the price of all stock using the query 'qryUpdatePrices'. Provide evidence of this test.

ACTIVITY 10 Test the order requistion ◀

Plan some simple tests for an order requisition by adjusting the minimum quantity, actual quantity, the reorder quantity and the cost fields for a number of stock items. Check the expected output against the actual output from running the report 'rptRequisition'.

Testing the user interface

The final aspect of the application to be tested is the human–computer interface (HCI) of the database. This involves testing whether the buttons do what they are expected to, such as navigate to the expected sub menu, or delete the record chosen, or perhaps print the requested invoice, or indeed exit the application. It involves checking whether the application starts up in the specified state (e.g. with the main menu onscreen, maximised etc.). Using the same pattern as for checking input, it is essential that it is tested to see if it does what it is expected to do, and that it does not do anything that it is not expected to do. For example, does pressing the 'Esc' key make it quit unexpectedly? The techniques learned so far can all be applied to this phase of testing.

Comparing actual against expected using manual or automated tests is a fundamental technique of testing, and should be used extensively during development to ensure the work is progressing correctly, and at the final stages of the project when it is used to ensure that the work has been completed correctly and meets the functional specification. The other major technique to confirm that the application works correctly is to have a third-party witness the operations. This is particularly useful to back-up screenshots and actual printouts to confirm that the output is genuine and from the input stated. A witness statement or signed checklist can be used on its own to confirm different aspects of the operations of the database, such as how the application starts up, the operation of controls such as buttons, and the speed and user-friendliness of the application.

ACTIVITY 11 Test the main form ◀

Create a test plan and test log for the buttons on the main form.

Compare the specification and design (storyboard) for the main form against a screenshot you take of 'frmMainMenu'.

ACTIVITY 12 Test the application meets the requirements ◀

Run the test application and sign off against the extract of the requirements shown by completing a copy of Table 7.7.5, which you can print out from the ActiveBook.

Table 7.7.5 HCI start up (and 'frmMainMenu') requirements checklist

No	Requirement	Y/N	Signed	Date	Comments
1	Starts with 'frmMainMenu' maximised	Y	Sf	1/1/06	
2	'frmMainMenu' matches specification				
3	Button to 'frmWarehouseMenu' works				
4	Button to 'frmSalesMenu' works				
5	Button to 'frmAdminMenu' works				
6	Exit button on 'frmMainMenu' quits application				
7	The application has sufficient user instructions to make it easy to follow				
8	No unexpected behaviour from pressing keys or mouse buttons				

Conclusion ▶ ▶ ▶

Before any data is imported into the application it is essential that the objects have all been tested thoroughly; this is part of the iterative prototyping process. Choosing good test data is vital here; indeed you may be expected to provide evidence of the test data you use. It is not the quantity of the test data that is important but its quality. It is important to test that the database will accept valid data and will reject invalid data.

Imported data will usually contain errors and it is vital these are detected. In the examination this will be a major method used to demonstrate the quality of your testing; you must therefore be comfortable with the process and be sure that your validation is spot on.

After this, the tests will to a large extent be comparing the specification or requirements against the actual processes and output. Good planning is also vital here so that wherever possible simple data with clear results are used to make the comparison straightforward, whether the evidence is from screenshots, test logs or witness statements. The final tests in a project should only be undertaken when the developer is certain that they will all be passed. At this stage a final checklist can be prepared and the results witnessed by the client or by a third party (or an invigilator in an examination situation).

The examination

Unit 7 is an examined unit. However, the format of the examination will be different from most you will take: it is a practical examination that will be taken over a lengthy period – 10 hours. You will be tested on your ability to work under the examination constraints of time and pressure, creating solutions totally independently. You will, however, have the chance to prepare as you will probably be able to see the scenario in advance of the examination itself. Furthermore, you will have a number of sessions in the computer room to complete the examination.

In Unit 7.8 we will give some advice about preparing for and tackling the examination, about the evidence you will be asked to provide for the examiners, and about the type of answers they will be looking for. There is also a full mock examination you can view from the ActiveBook, along with some help on the answers.

Part 1: Preparing for the examination

It is probable that you will receive a scenario in advance of the examination giving you details of the problem that must be solved, without specifying the tasks that you will have to perform during the examination itself. It will usually be a case study or extended briefing detailing the current situation of an organisation and giving some idea of the input, processing and output requirements, without necessarily giving all the information. It should nevertheless be possible from this to give some thought to the data model and how you might go about fulfilling the requirements you are likely to be asked to meet. In addition, you may be given some of the data files, in which case there will be ample opportunity to consider the actual data model you might use in the examination.

▶ Examination tasks

In the examination itself you will be given a set of tasks to perform. These will vary from examination to examination, but a typical breakdown of the type of tasks you will be asked to do is shown in Table 7.8.1.

Table 7.8.1 A typical examination structure by task area

Area	Possible percentage
Functional specification	10%
Database model and structure, including importing data from CSV files	25%
Input, including processing queries, macros and forms	25%
Output, including processing queries, macros and reports	30%
Front end and macros	10%

The tasks quite clearly follow the project lifecycle identified in Unit 7. You will first be given all the information for a functional specification. You may be asked to rewrite this into a pro-forma (a form designed to present the functional specification in a standard manner). This will mainly involve identifying clearly what are the tasks, inputs, processes and outputs for the system.

In the data modelling and structure phase, to achieve top marks you will have to normalise correctly to third normal form, apply appropriate validation and import data from a given set of CSV files. The final phase of this stage will be to import data from the files. This may involve using action queries to place the data in the appropriate tables in your database structure. (*Hint*: This will usually involve the repeating group of data that was identified during normalising to first normal form.) The CSV files, at least some of which you are likely to be given at the start of the examination, will provide the final information required to construct the data model and specify the data dictionary in full.

Even if you are only asked to provide evidence in the form of screenshots of the tables, relationships and validation in operation, it is essential for you to have designed the data model well and tested it thoroughly. You need to show that the import can be carried out correctly, and that you can provide evidence of which records have been accepted and which have been rejected. Furthermore, as the build progresses, the output of the database will then be predictable and the examiners will easily be able to compare the output of your application with what it should be given the data in the tables.

In the input phase you will create input forms, and possibly action queries and/or macros, to implement the input functionality required by the specification. It is important that you consider carefully the different parts of the input specification. You should take into account which data is specifically to be input, and what device is to be used to achieve the input. You will be expected to use a Wizard as the basis of your forms and then to customise the results to match your input specification and design closely.

You will usually be given fairly specific requirements. These might include placing a logo on the top left, the organisation's name and address centrally at the top, and the customer's name and address below. Marks will be gained for each correct placement of such elements, and generally for good use of formatting techniques such as alignment, same size fields, and for not truncating captions or the values of input fields. In addition, marks will be gained for following the specification closely with regard to devices and controls. If the specification calls for a combo box then it must be used; if it calls for a check box this must be used.

The scenario may not, however, spell out all of the requirements so clearly. The following two examples are from the PRS case study. Firstly, a requirement could be to offer a user-friendly method of selecting the category field when entering stock. The device might be a mouse, but the form could contain a drop-down list, check boxes or radio buttons. Note that the latter two cases would require modelling a little differently to the method used in the text. Secondly, the requirements might state that the sales office needs to be able to edit the orders for a particular customer. In this case there would be an implicit requirement that the edit facility only allows editing of orders by a selected customer, not all customers.

In the output phase you will create one or more queries and one or more reports based on these. This is also the part of the examination most likely to include calculations. In most respects this will follow the same pattern as the previous phase. You will design queries and then use the Wizard to create reports. The queries will be assessed on the tables and fields chosen, and the criteria, sorting and grouping employed. You will be awarded marks for accurately following the specification and using sound formatting techniques including layout, sizing, alignment, field widths and labelling, and appropriate use of report, page and group headers and footers. You will also gain marks for accuracy in your calculations.

The final phase will usually be to design and implement a menu system, possibly including controlling how the application starts up. You will be awarded marks for design and functionality, including marks for appropriate use of macros to open forms and/or reports in the manner required.

During any of these stages you could be asked to provide test data, or evidence of actual testing, in the form of screenshots and/or witness statements. You will, unless otherwise stated, be encouraged to gather feedback from others during the development as part of this testing. It is, of course, essential that these comments are restricted to testing and evaluative feedback as the development work must be entirely your own.

▶ Evidence

Database files are not, at the time of writing, on the list of permitted evidence formats and this position is unlikely to change. The evidence that is submitted will therefore be document based. It will comprise screen prints of designs, database tables, relationships, queries, forms, reports, macros and menus, along with annotations and/or commentary about what has been done and witness statements evidencing particular functionality in the application.

It is also possible that you may be asked to provide evidence of your sound working practices. This is a consistent theme throughout the qualification and should not be ignored simply because this is an examined unit. Indeed, the fact that there are constraints of time, system specification and also the pressure of the exam itself means that following quality standard working practices are even more important than usual. The full list of the expected practices is available on page 128 of the Edexcel specification, but perhaps the most crucial aspects you should keep reminding yourself of include:

- saving work regularly
- using naming conventions
- using sensible folder structures
- making regular backups
- using readme files and available sources of help where permitted
- creating and using a plan of your time
- checking and proofreading work carefully
- seeking and using feedback
- keeping within legal and moral frameworks
- working safely, including taking regular breaks, sitting correctly etc.

Scope of the examination

The PRS case study used in Unit 7 encompasses a great deal of functionality in order to allow you to learn about the variety of techniques and tools that may be necessary in the different examinations throughout the lifetime of the qualification. The whole PRS study would clearly take more than 10 hours to complete. In any one examination, therefore, candidates will be asked to demonstrate their ability to create forms a limited number of times. The same applies to macros and menu forms. Although the overall scenario could be very similar to this, the tasks to be performed are more likely to concentrate on particular aspects of the scenario such as ordering, goods out and invoicing, or alternatively, on stock control and requisitions. The overall menu system is in most cases likely to fit comfortably on a single form.

Part 2: A mock examination

Activity 1 Create a data model and functional specification

Open the Toddling Tots Toy Library scenario.
   Make notes on it and make an initial attempt at a data model. Make an informed attempt at the functional specification using the pro-forma provided as part of the preparation.

Activity 2 Create a final data model

Copy the following CSV files to your disc:

- toys
- members
- hires.

Analyse these files and create a final data model for Toddling Tots Toy Library.
   Make a plan as to how the data will be imported into the actual tables at a later stage.

Activity 3 Complete the exam tasks

Open the zipfile containing the Toddling Tots Toy Library exam tasks file from the ActiveBook. Read the tasks carefully. Complete the examination tasks under examination conditions.

ACTIVITY 4 Review your results

Compare what you did with the suggestion in the Toddling Tots Toy Library review file you can view from the ActiveBook.

Conclusion ▶ ▶ ▶

In Unit 7.8 we have examined how to prepare for and tackle the exam. We have looked at how the examination may be structured, what the examiners will look for and what evidence you will be asked to provide. If you have worked conscientiously through the exercises and activities in Unit 7 and attempted the mock examination, you should now be in a very strong position and totally ready for the examination, as well as being well prepared to be a proficient database user.

Unit 8

Managing ICT Projects

Success in project management

Introduction

The purpose of Unit 8 is to teach you how to manage projects. In one way or another you have been managing projects since year 10 at school (and possibly before), so actually you already have some experience of this. However, you may not have put much thought into the management of the projects, you simply got on with them in the time you had available. Your projects may or may not have been wholly successful but the fact that you are here studying for this higher-level qualification means that some of them were at least partially so.

What, therefore, is a project?

A project is simply a task or a series of tasks which combine together to form some kind of outcome; as such almost any particularly complex task could be called 'a project'.

In Unit 8.1, you are going to study several projects from the real world, some of which you will know about already. While you do so you should keep in mind the key questions about projects that are set out in the unit specification.

1 What characteristics do projects have in common?
2 What are the critical factors that make a project a success?
3 What are the reasons why some projects fail?

Let's start by looking close to home.

We've all done it ...

All of the authors will admit to having burnt the midnight oil having misjudged an assignment deadline at some point in their lives. It is quite easy to do if you are not careful. Your assignments may be substantial pieces of work, especially at A-level; because of this your teacher is likely to give them to you some weeks in advance of the deadline. At this point it is very easy to say to yourself, 'I have plenty of time'. The problem is that time has a nasty habit of passing; life also tends to throw up many interesting alternatives to doing coursework. ICT is probably not the only subject you study and examination boards tend to want the marks for all your assignments at about the same time. If you manage your assignments properly this should not be a problem, but if you leave everything to the last minute you may find you have to do three 30-hour assignments in less than a week (see Figs 8.1.1 and 8.1.2).

If things go wrong it may be tempting to blame your teacher for not reminding you of delivery dates, but essentially it is your responsibility to manage your time.

Mark bands

For each portfolio unit in this qualification the marks allocated are split into five or six strands covering different aspects of the syllabus. In each of these strands the student's work is judged to be in one of three mark bands, and marks are allocated within the range of a mark band. The qualification is awarded, which effectively means that the grades are assigned each year, so it is difficult to say what the banding will do to your grade. However, as a rule of thumb you could reckon that mark band 1 will get you a 'U' or an 'E', mark band 2 a 'D' or a 'C' and mark band 3 a 'B' or an 'A'.

Each strand in a unit is marked independently and there is nothing to stop you getting mark band 1 marks in one strand and mark band 3 marks in the rest.

One of the strands in each unit of this qualification will contain something about 'independent working' and if your teacher has to keep reminding you this can be seen as 'frequent prompting' which will restrict you to mark band 1.

Managing a project, even one as simple as getting your assignments in on time, is not an easy business and the effects of getting it wrong can be disastrous. Bad management of your assignments could cost you your qualification; in the world of work, bad management of a project can cost millions of pounds. It is no wonder that good project managers are often said to be worth their weight in gold.

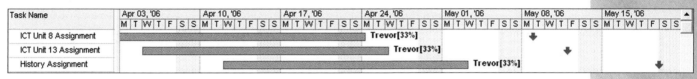

Figure 8.1.1 Gantt chart at the start of the projects

Figure 8.1.2 Gantt chart at the end of the projects

CASE STUDY 1 The 2012 Olympic Games

The initial euphoria shown when the 2012 Olympics were awarded to London masked the fact that the country was taking on a huge project. Behind the smiles, Sebastian Coe and the rest of his team were fully aware that they had taken on a massive task. Anyone who knows London will have some idea of the challenge involved in hosting the Olympics. In excess of seven million people live in the British capital; nearly three million of those live in Inner London. Add to that the hundreds of thousands more who commute into work every day from places as far away as Leeds, not to mention thousands of tourists, and our biggest city becomes a pretty crowded place. A seat on a tube train or bus is a rarity, the average speed of traffic is less than 30 miles an hour and the pavements are always crowded. How will London's infrastructure cope with hosting the Olympics? This is not to mention finding venues for 30 sports, and accommodation for all the athletes.

The benefits to London will be huge: not only will the Games attract even more tourists than usual, they will also help revive poor areas of the city and should also leave London with a transport infrastructure that is second to none. To make the London Olympics successful, however, there is a lot of work to do and only a few short years in which to do it. The London 2012 team cannot ask the International Olympic Committee for an extension: failure is not an option.

Using the internet, research the London Games:

- Make a list of as many things as you can that will need to be done prior to the opening ceremony.
- Include changes that will need to be made to London's infrastructure, buildings that will have to be constructed, and existing venues that might have to be refurbished.

Figure 8.1.3 Athlete Kelly Holmes celebrates London winning the 2012 Olympic Games

Continued on the next page

- Don't forget the organisation of the Games themselves – planning the order of events, recruitment – and accommodation for all the participants.
- As you do this activity try to categorise the tasks. There may be other tasks you can think of that are not mentioned above.
- Spend no more than 45 minutes in total on this activity.
- Suggested websites:
  BBC website, London 2012 website, London website

After 45 minutes you probably have quite a substantial list. If the truth be told, however, you have probably only scratched the surface. Ensuring all these tasks are completed before the opening ceremony takes place requires a tremendous amount of organisation. At the time of writing (late 2005) the London Olympic Team were in the process of recruiting senior management positions. Effectively, these individuals will be project managers; the success of the 2012 Games will depend on their ability to manage their areas of influence. By the time you are reading this book we may have an initial idea of how successful these appointments have been.

To err is human ..but to really louse things up you need a computer

What makes a successful project?

The 2012 Olympics project will have to be successful. What then makes a successful project? Let us look at a few projects and see if we can decide. We will look at a number of IT projects which were perceived as failures and see if we can learn from their mistakes.

CASE STUDY 2 The London Stock Exchange Taurus Project

Figure 8.1.4 The London Stock Exchange

The picture many of us have of the London Stock Exchange (see Fig. 8.1.4) – young men shouting at the top of their voices and swapping scrappy bits of paper – is not totally accurate but does demonstrate the somewhat old-fashioned view we still have of how stocks are bought and sold. In the late 1980s the Exchange attempted to use technology to bring this chaotic trading into the modern age. The Taurus project (Transfer and Automated Registration of Uncertificated Stock) was to be the computerised system that would put an end to a centuries old tradition.

However, it is probably no exaggeration to say that the Taurus project was an almost complete disaster. Missed deadlines and spiralling costs were reported almost from the start, and the whole project was finally shelved in early 1993 at an estimated cost of £400 million.

There are lessons to be learnt from a failure such as this. Research the Taurus project and see if you can come up with reasons for its failure.

Suggested websites:

Practical Law Company

School of Computing & IT, University of Wolverhampton

The Taurus project managers committed the basic sins of missing deadlines and overspending. The concept, however, was sound and should have been possible to implement. Perhaps the biggest problem was trying to please all the parties involved. There were a lot of stakeholders in the Taurus project, including some extremely powerful financial organisations. Each of these stakeholders seemed to have a slightly different view of what they wanted from the system. The expression 'you cannot please all of the people all of the time' was especially apt in this case. In an attempt to please everyone the project became so complex as to be beyond the technical limitations of the time. As Taurus could not fulfil the needs of all its clients it was probably doomed to failure from the start.

A successful project must, therefore, fulfil the needs of its customers or clients. If it does not do what they want it to do, it cannot be regarded as successful. *It must conform to requirements*. If it does more than the client wants, you will have wasted time and effort and therefore your own company's money; if it does less, you may even not get paid.

CASE STUDY 3 The London Ambulance Service Computer Aided Dispatch System

The London Ambulance Service is one of the largest ambulance services in the world. The service needs to cover around 600 square miles and has some 400 ambulances with which to do this. The well-being of over seven million people is in its hands: it receives between 2000 and 2500 calls per day, of which 1500 are emergencies.

Anyone who has driven anywhere in London will be fully aware of what this entails. Even with a siren going full blast, passage through the crowded London streets can often be slow (see Fig. 8.1.5). Although vehicles may want to get out of the way of an ambulance, there is often nowhere for them to go. London does have an air ambulance service, but to have 400 such machines would be inordinately expensive, not to mention the considerable piloting skills it would take to land in Oxford Street during the rush hour.

In a medical emergency speed of response is often critical and if little can be done about the amount of traffic on the road, it stands to reason that the shorter the distance an ambulance has to travel the quicker it will arrive. In the early 1990s the London Ambulance Service decided to invest in a Computer Aided Dispatch System. Put simply, the idea was that ambulances would be kept track of using automatic radio messages every 13 seconds. When a call came in the ambulance dispatchers would be 'offered' a choice of the three nearest ambulances to dispatch to the destination of the call.

The new system went live, on schedule, in October 1992, but far from improving the situation it seemed to make things worse: response times actually seemed to go up. There were even claims in the media that the system had costs lives. If this was the case then the project clearly was not a success.

So how was it that a system designed to cut response times ended up increasing them? More importantly, what mistakes were made in the management of the project which led to such disastrous results? Use the internet to research the London Ambulance Service Computer Aided Dispatch system and see if you can ascertain what went wrong.

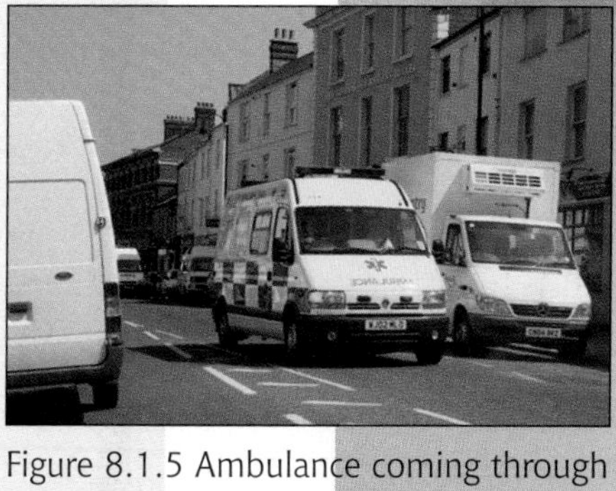

Figure 8.1.5 Ambulance coming through

Continued on the next page

Suggested websites:
Unofficial London Ambulance Service website
Report of the Inquiry into the London Ambulance Service (Feb. 1993)
Case study from the University of Iceland
Case study from the Department of Electronic, Electrical and Computer
Engineering, University of Birmingham.

So what went wrong? The developers were all working to extremely tight deadlines and were under the impression that these were non-negotiable. In an effort to meet the deadlines the system went live without adequate testing being done. In this situation the system could not cope with the load and problems occured. When these problems arose there was no time to fix them. If the problems of this system can be traced to one mistake it was agreeing to the deadlines in the first place. Hindsight is a wonderful thing: in this case, it tells us that a system of this complexity needed more development time. Fundamentally it would appear that no one actually realised the complexity of the system required to cope with the demand of so many emergency calls each day.

The lesson in these situations is 'Don't make promises you cannot keep'. One thing you can almost guarantee about any project is that somewhere, somehow, something will go wrong and extra time ought to be scheduled in any plan to cope with this. When you tender for a project it is tempting to underestimate both cost and time in order to win the contract. This is not good practice, as most contracts these days come with 'penalty clauses' which involve hefty fines if deadlines or targets are missed. Even if there are no penalty clauses a disaster doesn't do your reputation as a project manager any good, and will have a knock-on effect of making future project tenders difficult to win. It is better to lose a contract than take on one with impossible deadlines.

CASE STUDY 4 Swanwick Air Traffic Control Centre ◀

Anyone who has travelled on Britain's roads will know that the traffic jams and road accidents are, unfortunately, all too frequent these days, and that the traffic bulletins broadcast by our national and local radio stations are almost required listening for drivers. What is not so obvious, yet is equally true, is that in comparative terms our skies are just as crowded. At peak periods Heathrow alone is coping with over 80 take-offs and landings per hour. Throw into the mix Gatwick, Stansted and Luton, and there is an awful lot of metal suspended over the south of England. Of course, the sky is three-dimensional so there is a lot more space available up there than on the roads. On the other hand, whereas a 'near miss' on a road would be a metre or so, in the air it is a few hundred metres because of the speeds involved.

In the early 1990s the air authorities realised that if traffic continued to increase at its then-present rate, air traffic control facilities would not be able to guarantee public safety. A plan was developed to build a highly-computerised facility (at Swanwick in Hampshire), which would incorporate the latest technology and would be designed to cope with a 30% increase in air traffic in the south of England.

Continued on the next page

The project was expected to cost around £340 million, of which £163 million would be spent on the computer systems alone. The facility was opened in early 2002 but has not been universally regarded as a success.

How much did the system finally cost? Why was there so much bad press? If this was not a successful project what went wrong? Research the Swanwick Air Traffic Control system and see if you can discover reasons for its perceived failure.

Suggested websites:

BBC website

VNU Network

Department for Transport

At Swanwick, the actual cost of the system far exceeded the initial estimates. Again, there is probably a case for saying that the original estimates were too low. There were also problems with missed deadlines. By far the biggest cause of the bad press, however, was that the system just did not seem to work properly. The software had a huge number of bugs and in the early days of the centre there were many reports of the system crashing. The significance of this was increased, of course, by the perceived consequences of such a failure: that air traffic in the UK was not safe.

Part of this problem may have been caused by the NATS (National Air Traffic Services) changing its mind about what it wanted, a phenomenon known in project management circles as 'moving the goal posts'. For a project to be regarded as successful, the product has to work to the customer's satisfaction. This is such an important concept that it is always essential to agree with your customer right from the outset by what criteria the project will be regarded as a success. Technology is not perfect and it sometimes does less than we might demand of it. This is inevitable and everybody accepts that there may be glitches and imperfections.

The question is, how many glitches and imperfections are acceptable and how many are not? The answer to this question is simple: whatever the product of your project is, it must work to your customer's satisfaction. Testing is therefore an important task that will need to be scheduled into your project development time; it is a good idea here to involve your customer in this process.

All of our examples have one thing in common, apart that is from being perceived to have failed in some way. In each case someone, usually in a government department, has looked back on the project in an attempt to discover what actually went wrong. There are valuable lessons to be learned from evaluating projects after the event. If the reasons why a project went wrong are known they can be avoided next time. However it is often difficult when a project fails to get to the root of its failure. This is largely because an evaluation of this kind is often perceived to be an attempt to find someone to blame, and those involved tend to try to hide their mistakes. Learning from one's mistakes is difficult if one is unable or unwilling to be self-critical.

We have looked at a number of projects and have seen a number of reasons why a project can be deemed a failure. Are we any nearer to being able to answer our three key questions?

What characteristics do all projects have in common?

- **All projects produce a product of some kind** A project must achieve something that has a function. There will be one or more objectives of that function, all of which need to be met.
- **All projects have a customer** You will always be trying to achieve something on behalf of someone, even if that someone is yourself. Often you have many customers, not all with the same objectives. Pleasing them all is not easy.
- **All projects are constrained in some way by time** There will be a target date by which the project must be complete, because that is when the customer needs the product. By definition, therefore, all projects have an end time.
- **All projects will have a budget** If costs are allowed to spiral there will eventually come a point when the costs are perceived to outweigh the potential benefits of the project.

What are the critical factors which make a project a success?

Whether something is a success or failure is often a subjective decision. For example, Swanwick is now a fully-functional Air Traffic Control Centre ensuring the safety of millions of people as they head off on or return from holidays or business. Essentially though, if a project delivers a high-quality product within the time frame and budget allowed for its development, then it is undoubtedly a success.

Why do some projects fail?

On the face of it, this question is a little easier to answer. Projects are total failures or partial failures when they do not deliver a quality product, or do not do so on time, or do not do so within budget. Before we settle on this definition, however, take a look at one more project: this one a little closer to home.

CASE STUDY 5 The new network project ◀

The demands of new ICT qualifications (such as this one) have caused a few problems for schools in that they need more equipment to run new applications. A school in Berkshire recently found that its plan to run some new courses were thwarted because its present network was unable to run the applications required. The head of the ICT department, the network manager, the head teacher and the chair of governors met to discuss the situation. Funds were made available to provide a new server, fully re-equip four computer rooms with brand new machines, and provide the infrastructure to enable the machine to work.

The network manager was given the job of managing the project. He and the head of ICT decided what equipment to buy and duly ordered it. One of the main issues the network manager faced was that the rooms designated for this facelift were already equipped with machines which were currently being used to

Continued on the next page

teach. He planned that the rooms would be fitted out during the Easter holidays when there would be two weeks in which no lessons took place.

All the equipment currently in the room would be removed and stored under the stage, ready for distribution to other departments. The old cabling, both power and networking would be removed. The new server would be installed and the new upgraded cabling laid. A firm of electricians would install power points; another company which supplied networking equipment would make the rooms ready for the new equipment.

All of the above would happen in the first week. The new computers would be delivered for the second week and the network manager and his three staff would spend the second week putting them together and connecting them to the network.

The project started well and in the first of his nightly conference calls to the head teacher and the head of ICT the network manager was able to report that all the old equipment had been removed and the electricians and networkers had started work. However, the first problem occurred midway through the first week. The networking firm reported a faulty switch and had to order another one, which was not expected to be delivered until the middle of the second week. Nevertheless, the network manager informed his colleagues that his staff could build the machines first and connect them to the network and load the software later on, once the new switch had been installed.

Then came the real bombshell. The supplier of the new machines would be unable to deliver the new machines until the first day of term. Lessons had to take place and currently there were no computers for the ICT lessons. The network manager realised that the only possible way forward was to reinstall the old machines on the new network and start the term that way. The new machines could then be installed a room at a time once the term was underway. He informed the head teacher and met with the head of ICT to organise a timetable so that teaching could take place while one room was out of action.

But in the second week a further problem occurred. The old machines appeared incapable of talking to the new network. Long discussions with the network firm and the supplier of the switch ascertained that this was actually the wrong switch for the job; a much more powerful (and more expensive) piece of equipment was required. Curiously, however, this new piece of equipment could be delivered the next day. The network manager and the head of ICT got the go-ahead for this purchase from the head teacher and the chair of governors and the new equipment was installed.

At the start of term three of the rooms were functioning with old machines, and the school stage, much to the annoyance of the drama department, was full of boxes.

Over the next two weeks the new machines were installed to the schedule worked out by the network manager and the head of ICT. One of the old machines was given to the drama department; some software was bought so that they could use the machine to program the lighting for drama productions.

Overall the project 'came in' two weeks behind schedule and about £1000 over budget, yet everyone involved, even the head of drama, considered the project a success.

What do you think were the critical factors which made this project a success?

Conclusion ▶ ▶ ▶

To round off Unit 8.1, we can conclude that a successful project is a project *that has been managed well*. Such a project will demonstrate the following characteristics:

- the tasks have been undertaken in as efficient a manner as possible
- the resources required to undertake the various tasks have been made available when needed
- the product has been produced to a standard acceptable to the customer, within the required time frame, and within the required budget
- the customer has been involved every step of the way and has been kept informed at all times about the project's progress.

'11 million chimneys at .0032 seconds per chimney that's ...'

Introduction

In Unit 8.1 you looked at a number of projects of varying success. A well-run project is a little like a referee in a football match: if he is doing a good job you don't notice him. If a project is successful you will probably never hear about it. All the projects we looked at involved a number of people and involved a number of areas of development. This qualification, however, requires you to undertake a small ICT project. In most cases the only human resource you will have will be yourself.

Choosing your project

For your assessment you will be expected to manage an ICT project and provide evidence, in the shape of an eportfolio, that you have done so. Unit 8, like all the other units in the qualification, is designed to be delivered in 60 guided learning hours. In other words you should have round about 60 hours of lessons on Unit 8. Your teacher will need about half of that to take you through the various aspects of project management which will leave you 30 hours to implement and write up your project (see Fig. 8.2.1).

Figure 8.2.1 Project title page

The project you have to choose is an ICT project and this offers you a chance to kill two birds with one stone. The A2 qualification requires you to undertake Unit 7 (Using Database Software) and Unit 8 (Managing ICT Projects) plus one other taken from:
- Unit 10 (Using Multimedia Software)
- Unit 11 (Using Spreadsheet Software)
- Unit 12 (Customising Applications).

Unit 7 is assessed by examination but the optional units are assessed by eportfolio. Each of the optional units requires you to design and implement a solution to a problem. This solution will have to be project managed and could therefore be the project you choose to manage for Unit 8.

A similar structure with regards to guided learning hours applies to the optional unit: of the 60 guided learning hours about half will be needed for teaching. If, however, you decide to combine the two units it will give you 60 hours to complete and produce evidence for both assessments. However, you must also bear in mind that the examination board is looking for different things from the two units. For Unit 8 they will be looking at your ability to manage a successful project, whereas for the optional unit they will be looking at your ability to design and build a solution to a problem.

ACTIVITY 1 Choose your project

Most of the activities for the rest of Unit 8 will require you to undertake some aspects of project management. You will be given examples based on our project (Atha's Ice Cream), but you will be asked to repeat this based on whatever you choose as a project. At this point, therefore, you need to put some thought into choosing what you are going to do. You don't need a lot of detail, just note down a few descriptive comments about what you intend to do, and file them away.

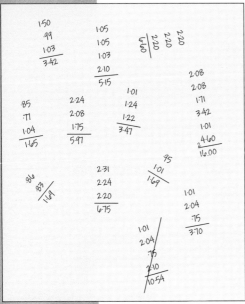

Figure 8.2.2 '1 + 1 = ...'

Atha's Ice Cream – background

To give you an idea of the sort of project to tackle we will give a brief description of the project we are going to use throughout the book. Our protagonist is Adrian Kennett, a second year Applied GCE student, whose project will be based on a problem experienced by his neighbour, Paul Atha.

For many years Paul has run a couple of ice cream vans at the local county cricket ground and other venues when needed. Paul has looked after one of the vans while his wife Shelagh has looked after the other. Looking forward to an early retirement, Shelagh and Paul have started to take their two 19-year-old sons (Paul Jr and Lee) along with them in the hope that in the not too distant future the sons may take over the vans.

After only two days of this Paul realised that he had a problem. Neither of his sons is particularly good at mental arithmetic. At the height of summer when long queues develop, speed is of the essence and customers will not wait while sums are done on little scraps of paper. The paper method isn't infallible either: the boys keep making mistakes (see Fig. 8.2.2). Paul realises that his business will not last long if he hands it over to his sons in the present state.

When Paul heard that Adrian was looking for a project for his Applied GCE he suggested that Adrian might be able to help him. Adrian felt that he could use Excel to develop a till system which would calculate the cost of each transaction and even work out the change due. He decided to present a proposal to his teacher.

Stakeholders

During the course of any project the project manager will have to liaise with a number of interested parties so that the project runs smoothly. Anyone associated with a project, no matter how small a part they play, is called a stakeholder. There are many different types of stakeholder but it is important that the project manager knows who they are and can deal with them. One of the most important attributes for a good project manager is that they are able to communicate. Stakeholders come in many shapes and forms and each have different roles in the project. Here are a few of them.

Project manager

For the purposes of the assessment exercise, you are the project manager. As the name suggests the project manager's job is to manage the project, and this may include:

- planning at the outset how the project will be brought to fruition
- assigning and managing tasks and resources (human and material)
- tracking and managing budgets
- ensuring that deadlines are met
- planning for contingencies
- liaising with all the stakeholders.

The project manager may not be involved directly with the nitty-gritty production of the product; he or she may assign tasks to other members of the team. In your particular case you do not have this luxury as essentially *you* are your own project team.

You must be able to communicate effectively with other stakeholders in the project!

Customer/client

Normally this will be the person or people for whom you are doing the job. The customer may or may not be the person who will use your product directly, often the job will be commissioned by management for use by someone else. It is important that the views of the client are taken into account, as in the end it is they who are going to pay you.

Senior management

There are two forms of senior management. Firstly, if you work for a consultancy firm your senior management will have to approve your plans as they are committing resources to the project. It is also possible that your client may have senior management; they too will also have to approve your plans.

▶ User

The user or users are the people who will actually use the product on a daily basis. Their requirements will therefore concern the nitty-gritty of the product. They should therefore be consulted very closely about what they need it to do for them.

▶ Supplier

Throughout a project various equipment and supplies will be needed. Obviously you will need the physical equipment on which your product will be run, but also you will need supplies of consumables such as paper and CDs. The project manager has to ensure these supplies are available when needed and will have to negotiate with the suppliers to make this happen. The late delivery of supplies can cause projects to miss deadlines, so good project management skills are needed to deal with suppliers.

▶ Team member

If you are lucky you will have team members to undertake project tasks for you. The project manager will assign tasks to them. Each team member will have specialist skills, so you need to know their abilities before you assign the tasks. In every project there are some tasks that no one will want to do. Someone has to do them, however, so you will need considerable diplomacy. For this project, note that you will most likely be your sole team member.

▶ Peer reviewer

Whenever you are undertaking a task professionally, it is always helpful to have someone to go to who will give you their opinion on what you are doing and tell you how they think it can be improved. The examination board calls such a person a 'peer reviewer'. Giving constructive criticism is actually a very difficult skill. You need to find someone whose opinions you trust and who will provide you with the feedback you require.

ACTIVITY 2 List the stakeholders ◀

Make a list of all the stakeholders in your project and describe what their roles will be. Your teacher will have to approve your project to ensure that it is suitable. This is a similar situation to getting approval from your senior management: you can think of your teacher as your senior manager.

Atha's Ice Cream – stakeholders

▶ Adrian Kennett – project manager

Adrian is a second year Applied GCE ICT student at Faraday College who has been asked to undertake a project on behalf of Atha's Ice Cream. Adrian has a number of relevant skills including project management, database, spreadsheet, multimedia and a little programming.

▶ Mr F Phelps – senior management (teacher)

Mr Phelps is a teacher with 15 years' experience and is currently head of ICT at Faraday College; he has the responsibility of ensuring that the project chosen is suitable for Applied GCE.

▶ Paul Atha (Snr) – client/senior management (of the client)

Mr Atha has commissioned the project. He is the owner and manager of two ice cream vans. Currently, he is also the operator of one of them but hopes to hand over the operation of the vans to his sons.

▶ Paul Atha (Jnr) and Lee Atha – users

Paul and Lee are Mr Atha's sons and will be the users of the system. Paul and Lee will be operating the vans when Mr Atha retires.

▶ Shelagh Atha (Snr) – management

Shelagh Atha is Paul's wife and also currently operates an ice cream van. She, too, intends to retire when the sons take over. Her role in the project will be to back up Paul (Snr) in the decision-making activities of the client.

▶ Sophie Bendix – peer reviewer

Sophie is also a second year Applied GCE ICT student at Faraday College. She has agreed to act as a sounding board and supply constructive criticism at each stage of the development. In a reciprocal arrangement Adrian has agreed to perform a similar role for Sophie's project.

▶ Mrs Rose – team member

Mrs Rose is one of the administrators at Faraday College and will undertake data entry tasks for the students. Mrs Rose is very busy and has to be booked well in advance.

The project proposal

The next stage in our process is the project proposal. So far we have identified a problem or situation and many of the people who would be involved. Getting together a project proposal involves some further research to get an overall view of the project and how it will be organised.

The purpose of the project proposal is to give the decision-makers enough information about the project so that they can make an informed decision about whether to go ahead.

Decisions, decisions!

What you need to bear in mind at this point is that not everyone you will be presenting this proposal to will be as expert with computers as you. You therefore have to pitch your proposal at a level that the layperson will be able to understand it; on the other hand you mustn't appear arrogant or patronising. Communicating at this level is a difficult skill and one that has to be practised.

The project proposal is doubly important for you as it is the first part of the project which will be assessed. Strand (a) of the marking grid allocates 6 marks out of 90 to the proposal.

If you look back at the examples in Unit 8.1 there were a couple of occasions when we thought that perhaps if the costs were known beforehand, the project may not have gone ahead. It is always tempting to maximise the positives and skip over the negatives. In the long term, this can have a disastrous effect on your reputation, so it is always as well to give the full picture as honestly as you can.

The specification for the qualification states: 'A project proposal can be presented on paper, electronically or verbally' (Edexcel Applied GCE in ICT, p. 125). This infers that a project proposal isn't necessarily a document, and in the outside world, this is often the case. But here are two reasons we would suggest that for your coursework, you create a document.

Firstly, the purpose of a project proposal is to elicit, from the people in charge, (your client and your management), permission to proceed with the project. As you will see later you are also describing in the project proposal, in general terms, what your project will achieve and how it will be accomplished. By giving you the go ahead your management are agreeing that that is what they want the project to achieve. A document can therefore be very useful if there are arguments later about what was agreed, i.e. you would be able to produce the document in your support.

Secondly, you will need to provide evidence for your eportfolio and a document is quite simply the easiest method of doing this. You can also include space in your document both for your teacher and client to sign and make comments when giving you the go ahead.

Having said that you need a document, it is always nice to meet your clients face to face at this point. You will have to present your project proposal to them, so why not do this as a presentation? You will need to communicate with your client throughout the project so this will be the first of a number of meetings.

Writing a project proposal

Before you write the project proposal you will need to meet with your client to find out, in general terms, what he or she wants. This initial fact-finding meeting is the first of many meetings you will attend.

The examination board states in the specification that the following should be included in your project proposal:

- What the project is about
- What it will deliver
- What the benefits and potential risks are
- What the impact will be on personnel and practices
- What the functional requirements are
- Who will use the product/services that are produced
- How long it will take
- When the deadline for completion is
- What resources will be needed
- Who else will be involved
- What ways there are of tackling the project including recommendations.

 Open this project proposal template which gives a structure to the proposal. Notice that there are spaces for your senior management (your teacher) to sign and make comments; similarly, the same for your client. Otherwise it is largely split into five sections:

1. Introduction (Terms of Reference)
2. Problem
3. Summary
4. Details
5. Conclusion.

▶ Introduction (terms of reference)

The introduction should always start off with a sentence explaining why, and to a lesser extent how, you became involved with the project. For instance "I was approached by Mr Paul Atha of Atha's Ice Cream to see if I could supply a solution to a problem he was experiencing with his ice cream vans".

The introduction should then in a couple of sentences summarise what both the problem and your proposed solution are. These will be expanded later in the 'Problem' and the 'Details' sections, so a couple of sentences for each are at this stage sufficient. You should also clearly state in this section the date the project was initiated and the final deadline date. It is worth noting, at this stage, that the final deadline date for your portfolio project is the deadline your teacher sets you. This date, in this case, is non-negotiable as your teacher will set it based on when he has to get the portfolios to the examination board for moderation.

ACTIVITY 3 Fill in the project proposal template ◀

 Open the project proposal template and fill in the banner cells (Name, etc.). In the section below the 'Introduction Header' type your introduction. Remember to save your work in a suitable place and give it a suitable title.

▶ Problem

In the problem section you will need to write in more detail about what the problem is. Describe how your client became aware of the problem and when and why the problem occurs. How do things work at the moment and what things have been done to try to solve the problem?

ACTIVITY 4 Describe the problem ◀

Open your project proposal document and in the section under the heading 'Problem' describe the problem and how it occurs.

Summary

This section is as much a statement of intent as anything else. It is really a short description of how you intend to solve the problem. What is it that your project is going to achieve and how are you going to approach the solution?

Describe all the functions your product will have to perform, who will perform them and any connections between these functions. A diagram showing the chronological order of these functions would be helpful.

ACTIVITY 5 Summarise your solution ◀

Open your project proposal document and in the section under the heading 'Summary', summarise your solution.

▶ Details

This section is the longest and should naturally be the most detailed. At this stage we are not expecting a complete design specification, just enough detail so that your management and your client can make an informed decision on whether to go ahead with the project. The following sub-headings are a guide only; depending on your project some may not be relevant.

Hardware and software

State what application software or combinations of software you are going to create your solution in. You may like to detail some alternatives but make a recommendation of your final choice and the reasons for it. Also state any hardware you may need. Be aware of the environment the hardware must work in and suggest products based on that. If the product will run on hardware and software the client already has, state this.

Use of the product

Describe the different users of the product and what they will have to do to make it work. How will the system appear to them and what actions will they take? How will they use it in the environments within which they work? What benefits will it bring to the users and are there any potential problems? What constraints would using the product place on the users and what changes to working practices will this require? Remember you will have different types of user so you will have to supply this detail for both.

Resources

In this section you need to describe the resources you need to undertake the project. These can be human resources as well as physical resources. Remember this is the project proposal and we are only really looking at rough estimates at the present time.

Costs

If your project is going to incur some costs you must give your client an idea of what these will be. At this stage you may not know them all, but a reasonably well thought out estimate is essential if you want your client to make a decision about whether to go ahead.

Implementation

It is unwise suddenly to change over from one system to another overnight. Generally, implementation is a gradual process which is done over a period of time. There are a number of reasons for this. No matter how good your testing, and for your optional project it will have to be very good, you never really know how effective a product is until you try to use it live. You therefore need a fall-back position in case anything goes wrong. The users will also have to get used to the system and may need training. You need to think about all these things when you describe how you are going to implement your system.

Deliverables

What is the project going to deliver exactly? Firstly, you are going to produce some software, so an installation disk must be supplied. A user guide must also be written so that the customer will be able to use the system; this could be online. Maybe you should supply some training. You need to detail what you expect to deliver in this section. A clear idea of the quality to be delivered should be included. This section is probably open to negotiation depending on what your client wants.

Timeline

Later on in Unit 8 we are going to be setting deadlines but for the moment we are looking at rough estimates. Firstly, you must say how long the project will take and when it must be completed. Try to be realistic. If you can split your project into stages and give an estimated completion date for each stage, so much the better. Unit 8.4 will talk about the stages of a project and you may wish to use that as an initial breakdown.

The details section is the most complex section of the proposal and can easily descend into technical gobbledegook. You must be careful that you do not do

'You want it back WHEN!'

this as your audience may not be technical. Use diagrams wherever you can as these are easier to understand than reams of text.

▶ Conclusion

In this section you wrap up by describing the main details of your project again. This gives you another opportunity to sell your project.

ACTIVITY 6 Describe your solution ◀

Open your project proposal document and in the section under the heading 'Details' describe the detail of your solution and in the section headed 'Conclusion' write your conclusion.

 Look at Adrian Kennett's proposal.

Presenting your proposal

You have to present your project proposal both to your teacher to get his or her approval and to the client to get the go ahead. You will have to arrange meetings to get this done. It would be effective if you could create a presentation to present your project at these meetings, as it will look more professional.

Both your teacher and your client may have contributions to make and you will have to make a note of these at the meetings and incorporate them into your plan.

ACTIVITY 7 Create a presentation ◀

Create a presentation and arrange meetings both with your client and your teacher. In these meetings make notes of any suggestions they make. At the end ask them to make comments and sign the approval part of the form. When you return from these meetings write up these comments and send copies to all interested parties.

Conclusion ▶ ▶ ▶

The project plan is an important phase of a project as it can be the defining moment of how the project will develop over the coming weeks or months. If in presenting your proposal you can get everyone behind you in the most convincing way possible, you will not only get the go ahead but will also ensure that management buys into the project psychologically. This can be vital during the development process, since one thing you can be sure about is that there will be glitches of one kind or another along the way. If your client and management believe in the project and are enthusiastic about it, negotiations to resolve these problems will be much easier. However, if they are not fully behind the project it will be very easy for them to take an 'I told you so' attitude. Your proposal needs to be detailed enough so that all parties can see that its targets are reasonable and that it has many benefits.

Introduction

You have presented your project proposal and you have the go-ahead to undertake the project. Before you start, however, you need to make sure that everyone is 'singing from the same Hymn Book'. It would only take one of your stakeholders to have a slightly different idea of what the project should achieve, and you could have serious problems on your hands. You need everyone's agreement about exactly what the aims of the project are and, more importantly, how the success of the project will be measured. This can all be done in a document called a 'definition of scope'. The document itself is signed by all the interested parties and becomes the basis upon which future arguments are resolved. In real life this will extend itself into a binding contract. Before we start producing our definition of scope, however, we are going to look closely at the project life cycle.

Singing from the same Hymn Book

The project life cycle

If you have studied ICT at GCSE level you will probably have come across the idea of the 'system life cycle'. The 'project life cycle' is very similar, in that it allows us to form a view of the stages a project needs to go through for successful completion. In Unit 8 our aim is to manage an ICT-related project, so probably the best way we can think about the cycle for our project is to use a combination of the two cycles. The stages they are broken down into will vary slightly depending on which book you read, though all of them go through similar phases.

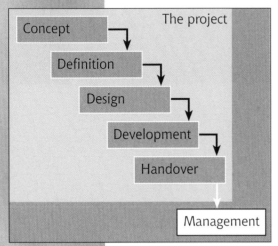

Figure 8.3.1 Phases of the project life cycle

Project life cycle phases

Fundamentally, the project life cycle is a series of activities sorted into five or six chronological phases. The six phases can be labelled 'concept', 'definition', 'design', 'development', 'handover' and 'management' (see Fig. 8.3.1). The project is usually considered complete once the product has been handed over. At this stage, the project manager's job is over and he or she has little to do with the management phase, except that many of the management procedures agreed for the running of the completed project will have been written during the design phase.

Concept

The concept phase of the cycle is essentially thinking about what the overall aim of the project is. An idea is conceived and investigated until such time as the project takes shape. The concept phase largely concerns what we did in Unit 8.2. We have identified a situation where a project could be of benefit to someone. We have identified who is involved, and have put forward a few ideas on how to proceed.

▶ Definition

This phase is what we are about to do. We are going to find out exactly what our project should achieve. We are also going to decide what our success criteria are: What would constitute a successful project?

▶ Design

It is tempting to think of the design phase of the project life cycle as being the actual designing of whatever product our project is going to produce, e.g. sitting in front of a computer screen designing software. Although this is part of what we will have to do, we have to actually design the project itself, first. This is what we mean by 'design' in the project life cycle: planning the project at the theoretical level (What will our product do, and how?), deciding on review points, deciding when and how things will be done, deciding what resources we need and how long we need them for, deciding who will do what within the project, and when.

▶ Development

As part of your project you will be creating something to do with ICT, e.g. a spreadsheet or database system, or maybe a multi-media experience. The key element of the development section of the project life cycle is to build this system or experience; in the real world, this will mainly be done by members of your team. As project manager, your job now will involve you for example in reviewing your plan at regular intervals and adjusting it to take into account unforeseen circumstances.

▶ Handover

This is an often-forgotten phase in a project and involves much more than simply saying to your customer, 'here you are, the finished product'. Your customer will need to be confident that your system, whatever it is, will not let him or her down. They will need to be involved in procedures that test the system. The term 'confidence testing' is a good one for this situation. Your customer will also need to implement your solution in a way that will protect them from disasters. A phased introduction of your product may therefore be advisable. You can use 'parallel running' – the old system and new system running together – until confidence in the new system is raised. You could have a phased introduction – moving one department onto the system to start with, and adding others as confidence in the product grows. Whatever method you choose it will have to be planned, and is an important part of the handover process.

▶ Management

As already stated, the project should be over at the handover point, though some of the deliverables at handover could be documents related to this stage, the management phase, e.g. documents concerning the running of the system such as user guides. Your hope is that this management part of the cycle is so successful for your client that your name is at the top of the list when it comes to them thinking about commissioning the next project.

System life cycle phases

The system life cycle follows much the same sequence, though once again the titles of the phases and even the number can vary depending on who you listen to. The phases we will show here will be called 'identification', 'feasibility study', 'analysis', 'design', 'implementation' and 'maintenance'. The traditional systems life cycle is shown as being cyclical (see Fig. 8.3.2). The idea behind this is that, if and when a problem occurs once the system is live or the business has moved on and the system no longer conforms to the requirements of the company, the whole process starts again.

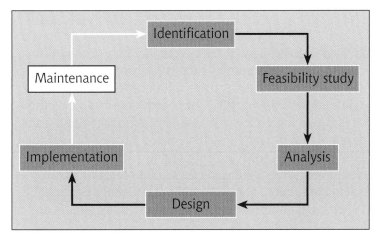

Figure 8.3.2 The system life cycle: a cyclical view

▶ Identification

This phase is based on the fact that the writing of a piece of software is often a response to an identified business problem, hence the name identification. This is very much in keeping with the concept phase in the project life cycle. The concept phase is more about seeking a better solution whereas the Identification phase says that if you want to provide a solution, you must first identify a problem. To quote Charlie Drake, 'If you want your boomerang to come back, then first you've gotta throw it!'.

▶ Feasibility study

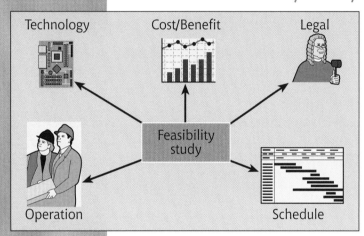

Figure 8.3.3 Elements of the feasibility study

This section is about whether an ICT solution is possible. There are a number of questions to ask here (see Fig. 8.3.3). Firstly, does the technology exist to solve your problem? These days it would be unlikely if it did not.

Technology, however, especially new technology, tends to be expensive. So, secondly, is the system we build going to involve set-up and even running costs? Do the benefits we gain outweigh these costs?

We have to look at legal aspects too. Is what we propose going to break any laws? Do we need to make special arrangements to comply with laws such as the Data Protection Act?

The system is not going to run itself. Do we have the people to enable it to run? If not, can we retrain our current staff? If we need specialists, where do we get them from?

Finally, we have to decide whether we have the resources to get the project finished on time. The term 'on time' is obviously negotiable but as we saw in Unit 8.1, time and costs are pretty directly related. In statistical parlance, they have a 'strong positive correlation'.

System life cycle – the waterfall view

The traditional cyclical diagramatical view of the system life cycle does not fit easily with the concept of a project. Because it is shown as being a circle there is no obvious end; yet if a project never ends there will never be a point when you can evaluate it and decide whether or not it has been successful. The other issue with the traditional system life cycle is that it is also difficult to apply to the method of software development promoted by the Edexcel Applied ICT syllabus.

The syllabus promotes a method known as 'prototyping', whereby you create a bit of your system, test it, get some feedback, create a bit more and so on, until you have a fully working system. If we follow the traditional diagram it appears to suggest that we would have to create a feasibility study after every bit of feedback.

A new view of the system life cycle has therefore been developed which is much more useful for our approach, called the 'waterfall view'. The phases are much the same, but they are aligned linearly and the model shows backward steps as well as forward ones (see Fig. 8.3.4). This means that we can effectively go back to wherever we want from whichever phase we are in. Although the traditional view allows for this the diagram does not show it.

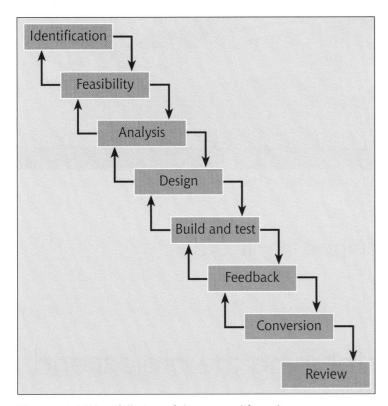

Figure 8.3.4 Waterfall view of the system life cycle

Not only does the waterfall view fit the prototyping approach better, it also has an end point as there is no connection back to the start. The final phase, 'review', also fits in well with our project life cycle as it would form part of our end of project review, which will be part of our handover phase.

The waterfall view, in fact, looks so like our project life cycle that it is easy to think they are essentially two ways of describing the same thing. This is not the case: they are two different cycles, and you will be using both of them when you do the project, so the distinction is important.

The easiest way to differentiate these is by looking at the two roles you will be undertaking in your portfolio work. We have already recommended that you use whatever you have planned for your optional unit as a basis for your project. You therefore are not only the project manager but also the developer, and probably the data entry clerk, technical writer and general dogsbody as well. With your project manager's hat on it is your job to run the project and make sure it finishes on time. In this role you will adhere to the project life cycle. With your developer's hat on, it is your job to design and build the system. In this role you must adhere to the system life cycle.

'It's an example of cross-curricular cooperation – Chloe is combining her ICT portfolio creation with her performing arts coursework'

ACTIVITY 1 Combine the life cycles ◀

Create a list showing which phases of the system life cycle would occur in which sections of the project life cycle.

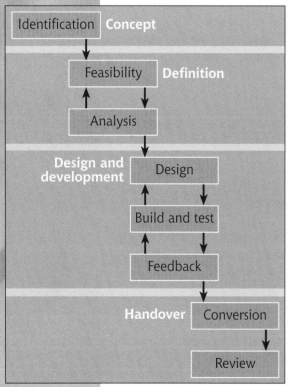

Figure 8.3.5 Combining life cycles

Combining the project and system life cycles

Although they may look the same, the system and the project life cycles do not actually fit together well, even with the waterfall view. The problem is that the waterfall view has arrows going back to the previous section in all its phases, whereas the project life cycle does not. We therefore have to create a few rules so that they can work in harmony. Let us start by trying to see which phases go with which.

We can only combine the two life cycles by using a compromise. Firstly, in the project life cycle we have to combine the design and development phases to take into account our prototyping approach (see Fig. 8.3.5). This isn't a huge problem except that the planning and timing of the project is a design function. However, if we get some feedback and have to change things this is probably going to change our plans too. Other than that, we have had to remove arrows pointing backwards between the project phases. We can explain this by saying that any changes requiring us to go back a phase in the project life cycle are likely to mean that the goalposts have been shifted so far that the project actually needs re-starting.

How far have we got?

In Unit 8.2 we produced a document which we called the project proposal. This didn't necessarily have to be a document, but it did elicit the go-ahead from the senior management and the client. The approval of this document signalled the end of the concept phase. In system terms, the document identifies the problem we are trying to fix and roughly outlines a solution method. It would be nice if we had another document, the approval of which signals the end of the definition phase. In fact, we do – this is known as the 'definition of scope'; usefully, a lot of the information in the statement of scope could form the 'project specification' required for your Optional Unit Assessment.

Producing the definition of scope
▶ Why produce this?

An important concept when drawing up a definition of scope is that of 'conformance to requirement'. What this means is that the project will deliver **exactly** what the customer wants, no more, and definitely no less. If the project does not deliver this, the customer will be rightly difficult about paying up. Often overlooked is the opposite point. You may feel that the product would be enhanced by an extra little function; however, if your customer does not want that function, then you will have wasted time, resources and effort in creating it. A definition of scope will also protect you if the customer moves the goalposts. If at the end of the project they decide that your product did not fulfil a particular requirement, they cannot insist that you implement the requirement unless it was part of the scope at the outset. In this situation you would start to negotiate an amendment to the project to upgrade what the original project produced. Situations like this may cause bad feeling so it is best to try as hard as possible to find out exactly what the customer wants at the outset.

▶ What could a definition of scope contain?

Definitions of scope vary but all should contain the objectives of the system and the criteria by which success should be measured. To make it a coherent document, however, we suggest you use the following headings as a template.

Purpose of the project

In a section headed 'Purpose of the project' you should give a brief introduction to what the project is going to achieve, why you are doing it and who you are doing it for. You will be repeating a lot of the information from the project proposal but this should be considered 'scene-setting' for the rest of the document.

Benefits to the organisation

Obviously there must be some benefits to the organisation you are undertaking the project for. Let us start by looking at straightforward financial savings. It is possible that the system will mean that the organisation can employ fewer people. The new system may save power or do something in-house instead of requiring that an external company do it. All of these situations will be of direct financial benefit to the organisation.

Many benefits, however, are not directly financial. The image a company wishes to project may be to suggest that they are at the forefront of technology, in which case a new ICT system (e.g. e-commerce website) may enhance this image. There would be an implied financial benefit as the company's improved image brings in new customers. The reverse of this argument is also true. A company may feel it is necessary to bring in a new system if its main competitor already has something similar, and the company is in danger of losing customers because its image is less up to the minute.

The project may deliver a more efficient way of undertaking a current process. This will save the company time which in itself will save money by enabling staff to do other things; it may even allow a company to reduce its workforce. It may also enable the company to deliver in a more timely fashion, which may increase sales. Or the project may deliver a system that is less prone to errors, meaning that less time is spent dealing with complaints.

Part of the feasibility study was a cost/benefit analysis and this section is half of that. We will look at costs more closely a little later.

Objectives of the project

Along with the next section, this is probably the most important part of the definition of scope, since it sets out what the project has to achieve in the form of objectives. A good objective must be quantifiable and objectively measurable. It should also be defined in conjunction with your customer because you are attempting to describe exactly what your customer wants.

Objectives depend to a large extent on the type of project being undertaken, though the aim when you set them is that there is no room for doubt whether the objective has been achieved or not. Let us look at one example connected with our Atha's Ice Cream project.

'The system will provide a method of storing, adding, editing and deleting all the different products sold in the van.'

Initially, this looks quite a reasonable objective but think about what may happen.

ACTIVITY 2 Correct an objective ◀

Can you see anything wrong with this objective? What is a possible problem?

Imagine that currently our ice cream van sells 140 products. During our investigations we find this. As you will see later, our testing will require us to test extreme data. So we will test that the system can hold 140 different products. If during the course of the project the ice cream supplier brings out a new product which Mr Atha wants to sell, our system is not tested for 141 products and may well fail. If it does we have failed to meet the objective because the system does not hold all the products. Our objective wasn't specific enough and consequently left us open to argument. A better objective would have been:

'The system will provide a method of storing, adding, editing and deleting 140 different products.'

Unfortunately not all objectives can be as black and white as this one. There must be some objectives that attempt to provide targets for ease of use and fitness for purpose. The problem with these is that they involve subjective judgement; consequently, a part of the system that one person thinks is easy to use will seem difficult to another. If you can define these objectives with targets, so much the better. Perhaps you could relate ease of use to the number of transactions a user can complete within a certain time. Unfortunately, this is not always possible. If it is not and it is a matter of opinion, then make sure it is the opinion of your client that is used as the measuring stick.

Key success criteria

This section defines under what circumstances the project could be considered successful. The first of these must always be that the system achieves all the objectives.

Other things that may be listed as success criteria are:
- A date by which the project should be completed
- A maximum cost
- Performance targets, such as how many transactions could be completed in an hour.

At the end of the project review these will be looked at again; your project will be judged a success depending on whether or not these criteria were met.

Deliverables

This section defines what you are going to deliver and how you are going to deliver it. Obviously the first deliverable is the system itself. Will you supply it on a disk with an installation program, or will the customer be able to download it from your website? Alternatively, will you install it for them?

Similarly, what documentation are you going to supply? Will it be hard copy or electronic? A user guide is a must, but you will also have to think about a system manual and an installation guide. Are you supplying the customer with the source code of your programs? Will you be committing to any training or maintenance?

Constraints

This section defines the parameters under which you will be working. There will probably be a maximum cost. There may be the constraint that any externally purchased software should already be available currently. The users may have special needs, which preclude the use of certain devices. (In the case of the ice cream van the hardware must fit in a small area and will probably have to have back-up batteries in case the power source is not available.)

Areas of risk

How is your product most likely to go wrong, and in what circumstances? This section is asking you to be a prophet of doom and say where your schedule is weak. What sort of effect would the late delivery of supplies have? What if it rains? What if you have underestimated the time it takes to do things? Is there any leeway in your project for things to go wrong?

Where exactly is your project heading?

Project roadmap

In this section you break the project down into activities and assign time and resources to them. You look at which activities require the completion of other activities before they themselves can begin, and which activities can be run in parallel. We will look in more detail at how we do this in Unit 8.4; it is by comparing progress with this roadmap that you can gauge how well a project is going.

Project resources

A definition of a manager's job is to achieve the tasks he or she is set using the resources available. Again, we will look at resources in more detail in Unit 8.4, but here is where we list what we have available to us. This may be people, space, equipment and raw materials.

Target completion date

This is the date that your system will be handed over. It should be a bland statement saying that the system will be available for live use on the specific date.

ACTIVITY 3 Write a definition of scope ◀

Write a definition of scope for your project based on the template shown above. For the moment leave out the project roadmap.
  Look at this definition of scope for the Atha's Ice Cream project.

Conclusion ▶ ▶ ▶

During your project you will be adhering to two 'life cycles'. One will define the management of the project and the other will define the management of the product the project is to supply. The project life cycle normally has five phases – concept, definition, design, development and handover. In order to incorporate the prototyping approach used by the examination board, we have merged the design and development phases. The concept phase is concluded by the production of the 'project proposal'. Similarly, the definition phase is concluded by the production of the definition of scope.

The definition of scope document defines **exactly** what the project is to achieve and what the project has to do to be considered a success.

'... now let's see Joe, your definition of scope defined this as a computer-contolled mousetrap'

Introduction

Thinking back to our project life cycle, we have finished the concept phase with the production of our project proposal. We have produced a definition of scope which should signal the end of the definition phase. 'Great!' you may be thinking, 'the next phase is design and development, at last we are going to do something!'. Sadly this is not the case just yet – we somewhat skimmed over the surface of the 'project roadmap', which is so important to our project that we need to look at it in a lot more detail.

The project roadmap is the plan of the project; it is against this that the project is measured. As such, it is probably the most important document you will produce in Unit 8. It is not a static document and will change during the course of the project as you hit unforeseen difficulties, or even because sometimes things go better than you thought they would.

The project roadmap

▶ What are we mapping?

The project roadmap maps the activities which combine to make up your project. It assumes that each activity will take a set amount of time, require a finite amount of resources, and may be dependent on the completion of other activities. The examination board requires you to supply your project roadmap in graphical form which leaves you with two choices: the Gantt chart or the PERT chart. There may be others but these are the most common.

▶ Gantt charts

Item 1

A Gantt chart represents, using a bar on a calendar, the length of time an activity will take (see Fig. 8.4.1). The longer the bar the longer the activity will take. The activity in Figure 8.4.1 will take four days and will start on 23 January. Each activity in a project is represented by a separate bar (see Fig. 8.4.2).

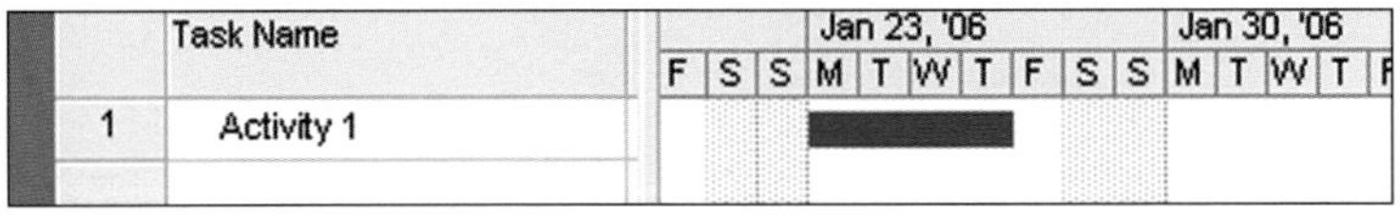

Figure 8.4.1 Length of time of an activity

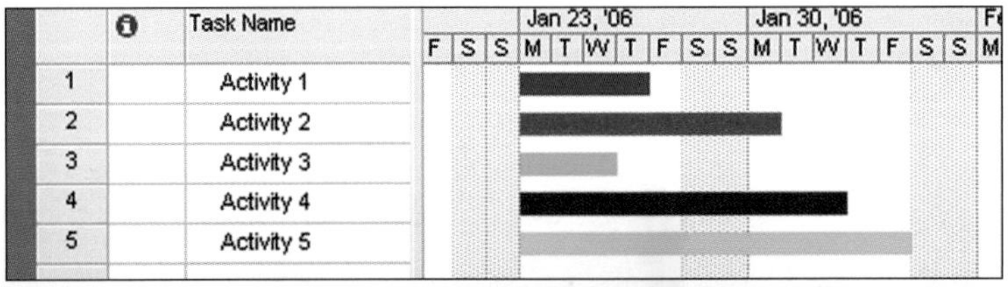

Figure 8.4.2 Multiple activities

The example in Figure 8.4.2 shows a project with five activities. Each of these five activities can be done independently of the others and we have enough resources to do them. This means that the entire project will take the length of the longest activity, in this case activity 5, which requires 10 days. The whole project will therefore finish on 3 February.

Most projects are usually more complicated than this, however. Imagine that to complete activity 4 we require the hire of a JCB vehicle, which is not available until 30 January. Also imagine we cannot do activity 5 until activity 2 is finished, nor activity 3 until activity 1 is finished. As you can see in Figure 8.4.3, the project now doesn't finish until 13 February.

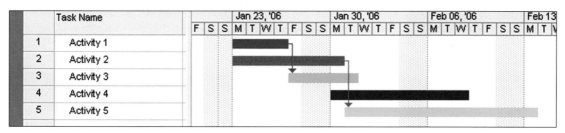

Figure 8.4.3 Project end date

The examination board's requirements for your portfolio mean that you will have to find a way of showing, at any particular time, how well you are doing with each activity. There are a number of ways you can do this. The simplest is usually to draw a black line along the bars to represent the proportion of that activity that has been completed (see Fig. 8.4.4).

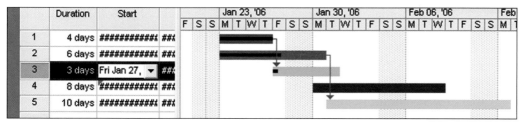

Figure 8.4.4 Completed activities

▶ Pert charts

Item 2

An alternative to the Gantt chart is the PERT chart. PERT stands for Program Evaluation and Review Technique. There are similarities with the Gantt chart in that the information it supplies you with is more or less the same. The PERT chart takes the form of a network chart where activities are represented by lines and milestones by circles, known as nodes. Note, however, that the length of the line does not reflect the length of time the activity will take. Producing a PERT chart requires a number of steps, as follows.

Step 1 – Identify your activities

Firstly, like Gantt charts, a number of activities need to be identified, but because there is less space for labels than there is in a Gantt chart, we assign each activity a letter. We also need to make estimates of how long each of these activities will take. Using the example we used for the Gantt chart, these are as follows:

A	Activity 1	4 days
B	Activity 2	6 days
C	Activity 3	3 days
D	Activity 4	8 days
E	Activity 5	10 days

Our activities are measured in days but larger projects may be measured in terms of weeks, months or even years. One of the advantages of a PERT chart is that it can use different time measurements in the same chart, because the line length between nodes does not correlate with time.

Step 2 – Identify your milestones

A milestone is a significant point in the project. Obvious ones are the project start and the project finish. Other milestones are things that have to happen before an activity can start, such as the end of a related activity or the delivery of a piece of equipment. Milestones in the network diagram are represented by nodes. These nodes have numbers in them so that we assign numbers to our milestones. Convention says that our network diagram should be drawn from left to right with the earliest node (the start of the project) being to the far left, and all others arranged to the right of this, depending roughly on how far through the project they occur. The 'end of project' node will be the furthest to the right.

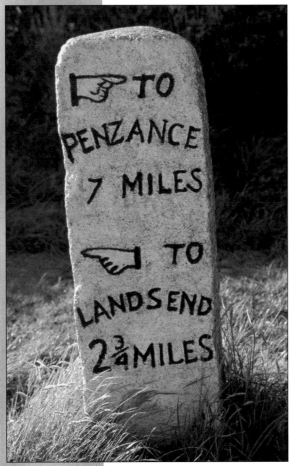

A milestone

Another convention says that the nodes to the left have lower numbers than the nodes to the right. Most projects will meet unforeseen circumstances to some degree over their duration, and it is not impossible that new significant points will have to be inserted. In order to keep to our convention we have to leave numbers free in case this happens. Traditionally, therefore, we allocate numbers to milestones in intervals of 10. Looking at our example again, the following is a more conventional list of our milestones:

- **10** Start of project
- **20** End of activity 1
- **30** Delivery of JCB
- **40** End of activity 2
- **50** End of project

Step 3 – Construct a network diagram

In this section you arrange the nodes and draw lines between them to represent the activities. The lines should be labelled indicating which activity it is and how long this is going to take (see Fig. 8.4.5). To complete your network diagram you include all the activities and nodes. Each node should appear only once (see Fig. 8.4.6).

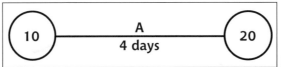

Figure 8.4.5 A PERT connection

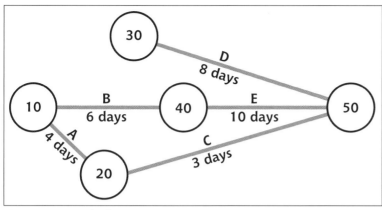

Figure 8.4.6 Multiple PERT connections

Our PERT chart is not very elegant; the way it looks now makes identifying the critical path (the next stage) a little difficult. Our milestone '30' is the delivery of the JCB, seven (7) days after the start of the project. To make things a little neater we are going to add another activity (F) which we will call 'Wait for JCB'. This will take seven (7) days. The results of this can be seen in Figure 8.4.7.

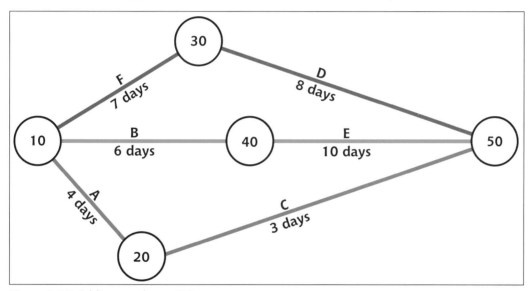

Figure 8.4.7 Adding another activity

Step 4 – Identify the critical path

The critical path is very important to a project as this identifies the series of particular tasks, connected together, which take the longest overall time and lead to the completion of the project. If any of the activities on the critical path is delayed in any way, the completion date of the project is also delayed. This is why it is called the 'critical' path. If an activity in one of the other paths is delayed, there may be a leeway which will mean that the project is not necessarily delayed. Let's look at what this means using Figure 8.4.7 as an example.

The end nodes of our project, start of project (10) and end of project (50), are shown in black. The critical path is the longest path between them, in time terms. This can often be confusing with a PERT chart as the lines are not drawn to scale (as they are in a Gantt chart), therefore what looks the longest path is not necessarily the one that takes the longest time.

In our example we have a red path (milestones 10 to 30 to 50). If we add up the times each of the activities take in this path we get: 7 days + 8 days = 15 days. If we follow the same procedure for the green and the blue path we get 6 days + 10 days = 16 days for the green path and 4 days + 3 days = 7 days for the blue path. The critical path is therefore the green path, and we cannot allow the activities in this path to slip. In the red path we have a leeway of one day before we start pushing back the completion date. Meanwhile, we can afford the activities in the blue path to slip by 9 days.

Following the project

Both the Gantt chart and the PERT chart are good diagrammatical ways of planning your project. With the PERT chart it is probably easier to identify the critical path and with the Gantt chart it is easier to see which tasks take the most time. Producing our initial plan, however, is not the last time we visit these charts. As you will see we have to review our plan regularly and adjust the chart accordingly.

ACTIVITY 1 Produce a project plan ◀

George Bailey has bought a plot of land on which he wants to build a house. The house will be two storeys high and will be built by a number of contractors. George has broken down the building of the house into the following activities and has made estimates of the time each activity will take:

Dig the foundations	2 days
Lay the foundations and let them dry	6 days
Lay the ground floor and let it dry	2 days
Build the ground floor external walls	4 days
Lay the first floor and erect ground floor ceiling	3 days
Insert the ground floor windows and doors	3 days
Build the ground floor internal walls and doors	3 days
Plaster the downstairs walls and ceilings and let them dry	4 days
Erect the stairs	1 day
Build the first floor external walls	4 days
Erect the roof joists and first floor ceiling	5 days
Build first floor internal walls and doors	3 days
Plaster first floor walls and ceilings and let them dry	4 days
Tile the roof	5 days

The foundations cannot be laid until they have been dug and no other work can take place on the house until the foundations are dry. Once the foundations are dry work can start on the external walls and on laying the ground floor. The ground floor external walls have to be complete before the doors and windows can be put in. The ground floor has to be covered before the internal walls can be erected or any plastering takes place (to protect from the weather). The stairs can only be erected once the first floor is in place. The bricklayers can

Continued on the next page

continue laying the first floor external walls as soon as the ground floor walls are complete, but the roof joists and ceiling cannot be laid until all the external walls are complete. Once again the internal walls and plastering cannot take place until the first floor is protected from the weather (i.e. the ceiling is in place) and of course the tiles cannot be laid until the roof joists are in place.

1 Draw a Gantt chart to show a plan of this project.
2 Draw a PERT chart to show a plan of this project.
3 Identify the critical path.
4 How long do you estimate the project will take, assuming there are no glitches?

Project activities
▶ Breaking them down

Whichever charting method you use you are faced with the problem of splitting the project into activities and estimating how long each activity will take. Estimating times is not as easy as it may first appear. In fact, to do so accurately takes experience. Many estimates are to some extent guesses and this can cause difficulties later on. Fundamentally, however, the shorter the task, the smaller any errors are likely to be, so it makes sense to split your project into smaller activities if you can. To show you the effect this can have let us for the moment revisit Activity 1.

ACTIVITY 2 Compare estimate with actual ◀

George has allowed a total of 8 days to build the external walls. Imagine that the bricklayers can each lay 4 bricks a minute and that there are two bricklayers. They work for 8 hours a day and have a hod-carrier to keep them supplied with bricks. The house plans show that approximately 15 000 bricks will be needed to build the house.

Using these figures, how close was George in his original estimate?

George's initial estimate was actually quite good. So far, however, we have just broken down the project into the project life cycle phases; we did this before we actually merged the design and development phases.

These estimates are not detailed enough so we need to split them down into smaller activities. These smaller activities are all going to combine to make the larger activity above in a form of hierarchy. The time the larger activity takes will then be the sum of the times of the smaller activities.

It is easiest to do this by using a diagram. There isn't one especially designed for this activity so we are going to borrow one from another area of ICT. The Structure Diagram was developed as a process specification for a modular program, but it has many properties that are useful in this area: it allows us to define hierarchical processes or activities and to define repeating groups of processes. It also allows the definition of selections of processes (IF or Case statements), but we will not need those. There is more about structure diagrams

We made an initial estimate of timings in our project proposal which we used to get the go ahead. Note, however, that these were figures almost off the top of our head, and actually bear little relationship to our final timings.

in Unit 12. A suggestion, however: when you start to draw a structure diagram, make sure you use a large piece of paper.

▶ Defining the smaller activities

We have to start somewhere so let us start with the project life cycle. We used this earlier to estimate times. Since then, we have not only changed the product life cycle phases, we have also completed two phases of it so we now only need to worry about the remaining two. These are design and development, and handover. So the rest of our project can be drawn as being split into these two phases. They are chronological, which means that we have to finish one before we start another. Using our structure diagram format this can be shown as in Figure 8.4.8.

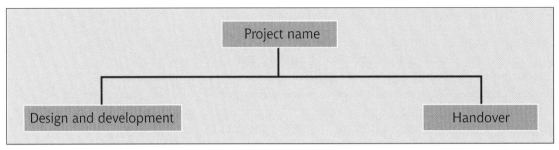

Figure 8.4.8 Defining the smaller activities

Each of these phases can then be broken down. Let us start with the design and development phase. How can we break this down? Well, we have already done this. In our definition of scope we have stated a number of objectives. We should not use subjective ones like 'The system will be easy to use', but the more practical ones like, 'The system will be capable of adding, deleting and editing up to 140 different customer records'. All of these objectives could be our next level of activities (see Fig. 8.4.9).

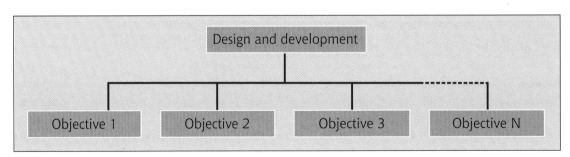

Figure 8.4.9 Objectives of each activity

This is where the structure diagram gets more complex, as you can specify whether a particular activity repeats and also specify the condition when it will stop repeating. A repeating activity is shown with an * in the top right-hand corner of the box.

What is it that we need to repeat? Our whole design and development system is built on prototyping: we design and develop a bit, get feedback, then design and develop based on the results of this feedback, and so on until our customer is satisfied. Figure 8.4.10 shows how we show this in the structure diagram.

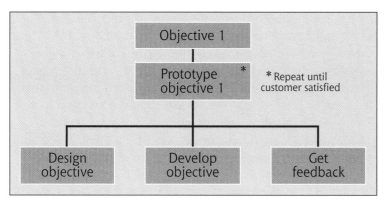

Figure 8.4.10 Repeating activity

Obviously this can be repeated for each of your objectives. Can we break it down even more? The feedback might be difficult to break down, but we can break down both the design and the development. All systems, remember, are made up of inputs, processes and outputs, so each of our objectives can be broken down in this way. We have to take account of these in both the design and the development. For the input activity, we are designing and developing how data gets into the system so we are looking at something like an input form. The process is what happens to it once it is there: how it is changed. Here we are looking at formulae or queries or other processing. Finally, we have outputs, which is how the information gets to the user. This could be output forms or reports. The next level of the structure diagram would therefore look like Figure 8.4.11.

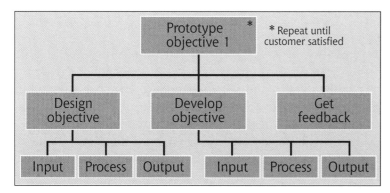

Figure 8.4.11 Inputs, processes and outputs

This pretty much completes this side of the structure diagram. It shouldn't be necessary to split down the design and development phase any further; what is more, this sort of split will work for most ICT projects. If you wanted to you could include formative testing as a separate box in your prototyping phase (e.g. design, develop, test and get feedback), but normally one would always expect this to be done as part of the development process.

Now we need to look at handover. Splitting up the handover doesn't have as many levels but does have many of the same features. It is important that your customer is involved in all of the handover activities including the design of the testing. The handover has three phases: summative testing, transition and post-project review. Summative testing is the testing you do at the end of the project.

> ### Formative testing
> Formative testing is the testing you do, almost automatically, as you develop. For example, when you put a button on a form you test it by clicking it as soon as it is created, just to make sure it does what it should. If it doesn't do what it should you correct it there and then. This is an example of formative testing and explains why it probably doesn't need its own process box.

More than anything it is a confidence-builder for your customer, since if your formative testing has been rigorous, you shouldn't have any trouble at this stage. Repeating all the tests you have already done is a little bit of a waste of time, so your summative testing should be based on your load, capacity and throughput objectives. For example, your customer may have specified a minimum number of transactions in a set time, or the fact that the system should hold at least 'x' number of records. This is also where you test out your subjective objectives, such as ease of use, by simply asking your customers what they think. These sorts of tests are always better if done in a live environment.

'... is equipped with many user-friendly features such as this dial which slows down the blade for maximum pain.'

Transition is the method you will use to hand over. We have mentioned two of these methods before: parallel running and phased handover. The boxes you put in your structure diagram depend on which of these you choose. The final box in this section is the 'end of project' review. There will be more on this later; for now, let us just say that this is where it will be decided if your project is a success or not.

Conclusion ▶ ▶ ▶

The success of all projects is to some extent measured against time, since time often equates to money. The examination board will expect you to produce a plan which breaks down your project into scheduled activities. You will be expected to assign times to these activities and the progress of your project will be measured at frequent intervals against these timings.

Your success as a project manager will be judged on the quality of the product delivered, your management of budgets and resources (human and material), and how well you stick to your timings, so it is important that your planned schedule is as accurate as possible. The less experience you have at estimating timings the more likely the timings are to go wrong. It is easier to estimate the timing of a small activity than it is a large one, so the smaller you can break down your activities the better.

The project roadmap and further planning

Introduction

As part of the specification, the examination board advises you to use project management software. This makes planning much easier since it allows you to set the hours and days that you work on the project. For example, when you estimate the time an activity will take, e.g. '4 weeks', the software will automatically take into account rest days. It allows you to link activities and set different start dates. It will make automatic adjustments to dates of activities if the completion date of a related activity is changed.

For the rest of Unit 8 we will therefore be organising our project using project management software. The application we will be using is Microsoft Project.

Creating the project roadmap

So far we have created our project proposal and have also created most of our definition of scope. The bits of the definition of scope outstanding are the initial project roadmap and assigning of resources, both of which we can do using our project management software.

▶ Setting the parameters

When you open the project management software it allows you to enter some parameters for the running of the project (see Fig. 8.5.1).

Figure 8.5.1 Entering parameters

Setting a project start date

The project start date is the first date from which all activities are scheduled. When the software is given this date it will, unless told otherwise, schedule a task starting at this date. The project, for us, started some time ago with the production of our initial concept. We still have to plan the project though, so we will need to leave a little time for that. When you set the project start date, set it for a couple of days' time to give you plenty of time to come up with a good plan.

Setting the project's general working times

The next step is to set the general working times of your project. It would be unusual if you were prepared to work 12 hours a day, 7 days a week on your project. On the other hand if you say you are going to work for 6 hours a day (which may initially seem reasonable) and in the end you only work 3, all your predicted timings are going to be out. We must also be aware that ICT is not the only subject you study, so for several hours a day you will not be available to work on your project. It may also be tempting to say that you have every single evening to work on your project, but again we have to allow you a little bit of a life outside work, just as you would have in the real world.

What would be reasonable, then? Your software will provide you with a number of templates from which to choose. Figure 8.5.2 shows the timings of the default 'standard' template. As you can see this shows general working hours of 08:00 to 12:00 and 13:00 to 17:00, Monday to Friday. This may seem a reasonable timetable if you are in a full-time job, but is a little excessive for just one of your A-level courses.

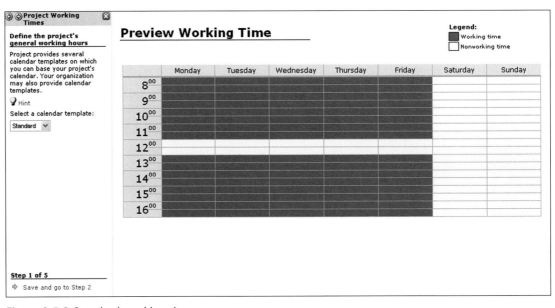

Figure 8.5.2 Standard working time

Let us look at the case of Adrian Kennett, who is undertaking the Atha's Ice Cream project. For Unit 8 ICT, Adrian receives 3 x 2-hour lessons per week: Monday 09:00 to 11:00, Tuesday 11:30 to 13:30 and Thursday 14:30 to 16:30. In addition, he has a free period on Friday morning from 09:00 to 11:00, which he is willing to dedicate to his project. He is also prepared to give an hour each evening (Monday to Friday) between 18:00 and 19:00 to the project, but this will be using his home computer and not the school network. Figure 8.5.3 shows the results of resetting the general working hours.

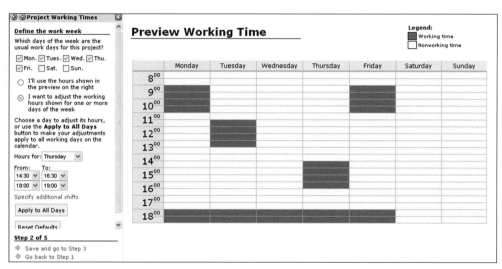

Figure 8.5.3 Customising working time

The software lets you set time off and holidays, so if your project extends over a holiday you can specify this. For instance, perhaps 13–17 February is half term and Adrian is away during that period (see Fig. 8.5.4).

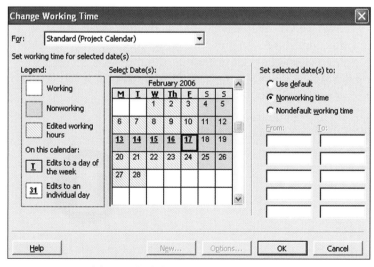

Figure 8.5.4 Building in holidays

The software will now need you to specify what constitutes a day's work, a week's work and a month's work. Our standard template saw us working 8 hours a day, 5 days a week. This gives us about 20 working days a month. In Adrian's case a day's work on his project is about 3 hours, and this only really happens 4 days a week (although he does work for an hour at home on Wednesdays).

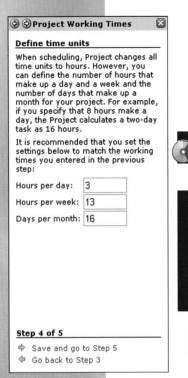

Project Working Times

Define time units

When scheduling, Project changes all time units to hours. However, you can define the number of hours that make up a day and a week and the number of days that make up a month for your project. For example, if you specify that 8 hours make a day, the Project calculates a two-day task as 16 hours.

It is recommended that you set the settings below to match the working times you entered in the previous step:

Hours per day: 3

Hours per week: 13

Days per month: 16

Step 4 of 5

➪ Save and go to Step 5

⇦ Go back to Step 3

Figure 8.5.5 Defining work periods

A day's work to Adrian, therefore, will be 3 hours on each day except Wednesday, so a week's work would be 13 hours and he will work for on average 16 days a month. The software requires you to set these times so that it can work out the timings for you (see Fig. 8.5.5).

Now when we tell the system that an activity takes a day's work it knows that we actually mean 3 hours' work. Similarly, if we say an activity takes a week's work we are scheduling 13 hours. If we allocate a month's work to a project we are actually talking about 48 hours. A demonstration of this process can be viewed from the ActiveBook.

ACTIVITY 1 Schedule your project ◀

Using your project management software set the start date and working times for your own project. Check your timetable carefully and only allocate what you are prepared to stick to. Enter any holiday times or other times when you are unable to work on the project for whatever reason.

▶ Listing the activities

Having set our time available we now have to list the activities in the project. We suggest you undertake the top-down process used for creating the structure diagram in Unit 8.4.

The two phases of the project left to plan are the design and development (prototyping) phase and the handover phase, so this is where we should start. Activities are entered in the section of the software shown in Figure 8.5.6. As you can see, we have entered our design and development and our handover phases already. That is all we have done, everything else has defaulted. The first column is obviously the activity number. This will be adjusted if we insert more activities. The information sign (see Fig. 8.5.7) heads a column where the software enters flags or indicators. This is where you will see if a task is overdue or if it is complete. We have left the duration to default, this is signified by the '?' after the 1 day. We are not too concerned about timings at the moment, so we can just leave these to default. As we have left the start date to default it has entered the project start date we set in the general working times section.

ⓘ	Task Name	Duration	Start	Finish	Predecessors	Resource Names
1	Design & Development	1 day?	Fri Jan 27, '06	Tue Jan 31, '06		
2	Handover	1 day?	Fri Jan 27, '06	Tue Jan 31, '06		

Figure 8.5.6 Entering activities

Figure 8.5.7 Information sign

The completion date is interesting. If the activity starts on 27 January and takes one day it should finish on 28 January but it actually finishes on 31 January. The software recognises that no one works on the project at the weekend. The software has also started a Gantt chart for us (see Fig. 8.5.8). We can change the patterns and colours. At the moment we will let them default but we may well change them later.

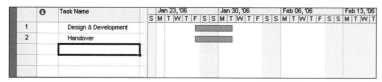

Figure 8.5.8 Gantt chart

We now have to break down the two phases into the next level in our structure chart. For the moment we will ignore the handover phase and concentrate on the design and development. As we said in Unit 8.4, at the next level we are going to put our objectives.

We only want the objectives which require us to do things. The more subjective things like 'The system should be considered easy to use by Mr Atha's sons' are something we keep in mind as we do our designs. In other words we don't need to allocate them time.

Let's remind ourselves of Adrian's objectives. The ones we are going to allocate time to are:

- The system will be able to store, delete and modify the name, price, and current number on the van of up to 30 products. (Store Data)
- The system will be able to select the price of these products by pressing a button on a touch screen. (Retrieve Price)
- The system will be able to calculate the total price of a transaction. (Total Price)
- The system will be able to cancel a transaction. (Cancel Transaction)
- The system will be able to clear totals ready for the next transaction. (New Transaction)
- The system will put out a message if a button is pressed and there is no stock of that item on the van. (Out of Stock)
- The system will be capable of inputting the amount of money tendered and calculating the change required. (Calculate Change)
- The system will keep a total of the amount of money which should be in the till (including the £10 float). (Amount Taken)
- The system will be able to list the stock on the van. (List Stock)
- The system will be able to clear the stock on the van when it is removed. (Clear Stock)

You will note that after each objective we have entered a label in brackets. This is what we are going to call our objectives so that we don't have to enter the complete objective in the application.

We are going to enter these objectives as sub-tasks which means that they need to be inserted in between our two major phases. It is quite easy to do this: you simply select the handover activity and press the 'Ins' button. A new line will be inserted automatically above, and we can type in our sub-task (see Fig. 8.5.9).

	ⓘ	Task Name	Jan 23, '06								Jan 30, '06				
			S	M	T	W	T	F	S	S	M	T	W	T	F
1		Design & Development													
2		Store Data													
3		Handover													

Figure 8.5.9 Inserting sub-tasks

Notice that at the moment the software has assigned it simply as another task. It has the same details as default. We do not want it to be this way: the new task, with others, makes up the design and development task, so we don't want it to appear to be a separate task. We organise tasks and sub-tasks using the buttons shown in Figure 8.5.10.

Figure 8.5.10 Buttons for organising tasks and sub-tasks

	❶	Task Name	Jan 23, '06							Jan 30, '06					
			S	M	T	W	T	F	S	S	M	T	W	T	F	S
1		⊟ **Design & Development**													
2		Store Data													
3		Handover													

Figure 8.5.11 Organising tasks and sub-tasks

If we were to select our task and click the right-pointing arrow then this will make this task a sub-task of the task above (see Fig. 8.5.11). Notice that the bar on the Gantt chart has changed shape. This signifies the fact that this is the major task, the one below is a sub-task, and the main task is highlighted. How this is helpful to us doesn't really become apparent until a little later. The other thing that is interesting now is that if we insert another task, the software will assume that this task is also a sub-task. If we didn't want this assumption to be made we would have to click on the left-pointing arrow in Figure 8.5.10. However, we do want our other tasks to be sub-tasks so we can simply insert them (see Fig. 8.5.11).

Note that we have let all the times default to one day. We now have 10 tasks each taking a day's work, all starting on 27 January and all finishing (taking into account Saturday and Sunday) one day later. Isn't this impossible? In theory it actually isn't: what the software is assuming is that we have an infinite number of team members, each of whom could be assigned to a different task. We will tell the system that this isn't the case later.

ACTIVITY 2 Enter tasks into your schedule ◀

Using your project management software enter as tasks the two main phases; then enter your practical objectives as sub-tasks of the design and development phase. Leave everything else to default at the moment. You can view a demonstration of Adrian doing this from the ActiveBook.

Even if we did have an infinite number of team members there are problems with running all our activities together. Certain activities are dependent on the completion of others: for instance we cannot read the price of a product (task 3 in Figure 8.5.11) until we have a method to store the price (task 2). So task 3 depends on the successful completion of task 2. We need to look at which activities are dependent upon the completion of other activities. It is probably easiest to do this in the form of a table (see Table 8.5.1).

Table 8.5.1 Task dependency

Task number	Dependent on tasks
2	
3	2
4	2, 3
5	2, 3, 4
6	2, 3, 4, 5
7	2, 3
8	2, 3, 4, 5
9	2, 3, 4, 5, 6
10	2, 3
11	2

We need to tell the software about these dependencies as it means that the overall duration of the project will be greater than currently shown. To do this we simply add the number of the task a particular task depends on in the section marked 'predecessors' (see Fig. 8.5.12). We do not have to put in the whole chain, just the final number in the chain. For instance if task 3 depends on task 2, and task 4 depends on task 3 and task 2, we need only enter task 3 as a predecessor to task 4.

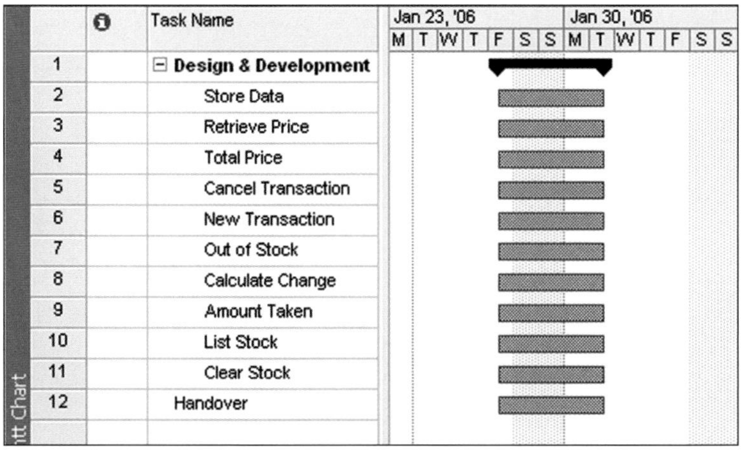

Figure 8.5.12 Indicating dependencies

One thing we haven't considered is the fact that we really cannot start the handover phase until we have completely built the system. In terms of our project, therefore, what is currently task 12 (handover) is dependent on the completion of task 1 (design and development). We will need to put 1 in the predecessors section of task 12 (see Fig. 8.5.13).

As you can see this changes the Gantt chart quite significantly (see Fig. 8.5.14). Firstly, the duration of the design and development phase has increased to 6 days (although this is probably still too short). Secondly, the links are now shown.

	ℹ	Task Name	Duration	Start	Finish	Predecessors
1		⊟ **Design & Development**	**6 days?**	**Fri Jan 27, '06**	**Tue Feb 28, '06**	
2		Store Data	1 day?	Fri Jan 27, '06	Tue Jan 31, '06	
3		Retrieve Price	1 day?	Tue Jan 31, '06	Fri Feb 03, '06	2
4		Total Price	1 day?	Mon Feb 06, '06	Thu Feb 09, '06	3
5		Cancel Transaction	1 day?	Thu Feb 09, '06	Mon Feb 20, '06	4
6		New Transaction	1 day?	Tue Feb 21, '06	Fri Feb 24, '06	5
7		Out of Stock	1 day?	Mon Feb 06, '06	Thu Feb 09, '06	3
8		Calculate Change	1 day?	Tue Feb 21, '06	Fri Feb 24, '06	5
9		Amount Taken	1 day?	Fri Feb 24, '06	Tue Feb 28, '06	6
10		List Stock	1 day?	Mon Feb 06, '06	Thu Feb 09, '06	3
11		Clear Stock	1 day?	Tue Jan 31, '06	Fri Feb 03, '06	2
12		Handover	1 day?	Wed Mar 01, '06	Mon Mar 06, '06	1

Figure 8.5.13 Indicating predecessors

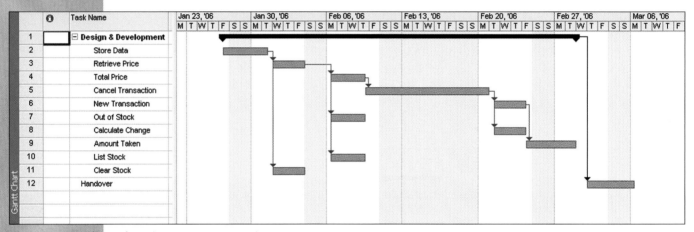

Figure 8.5.14 Effect of predecessors on Gantt chart

ACTIVITY 3 Create a dependent tasks table ◀

Create a table similar to the one above showing which of your tasks are dependent on the completion of a previous task. Update this information in your project management software.

In Unit 8.4 we suggested that each objective should be split into three phases: design objective, develop objective and feedback. We will need to put these in as sub-tasks for all our objectives. As this is the bottom of our hierarchy we will need to estimate times. In doing this it will be very useful to assume that our project is susceptible to Murphy's Laws, the most famous of which is 'Anything that can go wrong, will go wrong'. Adrian has looked at each of his sub-tasks and, somewhat optimistically, decided each will take half a day to design, half a day to build and half a day to get feedback. We will need to build some slack into the system so it may as well be here. He has decided to put in an extra sub-task for each, timed at half a day, to give him a bit of leeway. The other thing we must remember here is that we cannot develop before we finish the design, we cannot get feedback until we have developed, and there is no point in having leeway running in parallel with our tasks. We therefore have to set the predecessors accordingly (see Fig. 8.5.15). Having inserted this information not only has the duration of the project expanded but also the Gantt chart is starting to look a bit more interesting (see Fig. 8.5.16).

	❶	Task Name	Duration	Start	Finish	Predecessors
1		⊟ Design & Development	12 days	Fri Jan 27, '06	Mon Mar 27, '06	
2		⊟ Store Data	2 days	Fri Jan 27, '06	Fri Feb 03, '06	
3		Design	0.5 days	Fri Jan 27, '06	Mon Jan 30, '06	
4		Develop	0.5 days	Mon Jan 30, '06	Tue Jan 31, '06	3
5		Feedback	0.5 days	Tue Jan 31, '06	Thu Feb 02, '06	4
6		Leeway	0.5 days	Thu Feb 02, '06	Fri Feb 03, '06	5
7		⊟ Retrieve Price	2 days	Mon Feb 06, '06	Mon Feb 20, '06	2
8		Design	0.5 days	Mon Feb 06, '06	Tue Feb 07, '06	
9		Develop	0.5 days	Tue Feb 07, '06	Thu Feb 09, '06	8
10		Feedback	0.5 days	Thu Feb 09, '06	Fri Feb 10, '06	9
11		Leeway	0.5 days	Fri Feb 10, '06	Mon Feb 20, '06	10
12		⊟ Total Price	2 days	Tue Feb 21, '06	Tue Feb 28, '06	7
13		Design	0.5 days	Tue Feb 21, '06	Wed Feb 22, '06	
14		Develop	0.5 days	Thu Feb 23, '06	Fri Feb 24, '06	13
15		Feedback	0.5 days	Fri Feb 24, '06	Mon Feb 27, '06	14
16		Leeway	0.5 days	Mon Feb 27, '06	Tue Feb 28, '06	15
17		⊟ Cancel Transaction	2 days	Wed Mar 01, '06	Thu Mar 09, '06	12
18		Design	0.5 days	Wed Mar 01, '06	Thu Mar 02, '06	
19		Develop	0.5 days	Fri Mar 03, '06	Mon Mar 06, '06	18
20		Feedback	0.5 days	Mon Mar 06, '06	Tue Mar 07, '06	19
21		Leeway	0.5 days	Tue Mar 07, '06	Thu Mar 09, '06	20
22		⊟ New Transaction	2 days	Thu Mar 09, '06	Fri Mar 17, '06	17
23		Design	0.5 days	Thu Mar 09, '06	Fri Mar 10, '06	
24		Develop	0.5 days	Mon Mar 13, '06	Tue Mar 14, '06	23
25		Feedback	0.5 days	Tue Mar 14, '06	Thu Mar 16, '06	24

Figure 8.5.15 Refining predecessors

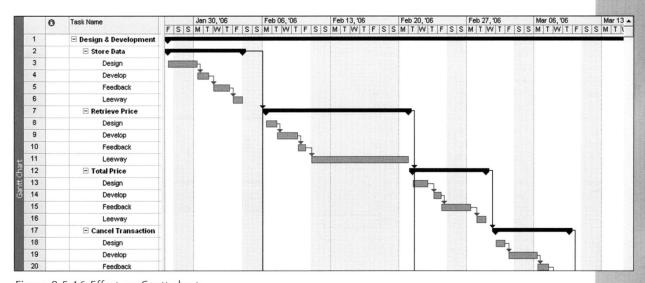

Figure 8.5.16 Effect on Gantt chart

ACTIVITY 4 Refine your project plan ◀

Insert design, development and feedback tasks into your project plan. Estimate and enter an estimated time for each phase and add a Leeway task to each. Don't forget to link them as predecessors to each other. What date is your project now due to finish?

Have we missed anything?

Before we go onto breaking down our handover, we need to ask ourselves if we have forgotten anything. If we look back at Adrian's definition of scope and look at what he has promised to deliver, he is going to have to produce a systems manual and a user guide. These will take time to write. The prototyping approach we are using allows us to develop these manuals as we go along. We could assign half a day at the end of each process but that might be a bit excessive. Writing the user guide and the systems manual could almost be a fill-in activity when we cannot move on the project for some reason. But we don't want writing the manual to stop us from starting the next phase, so let us assign documentation its own task. We simply insert it before handover. We have to click the left-pointing arrow otherwise the software thinks it is another sub-task of the previous task. We can then split this task into user guide and systems documentation. We are going to assign 3 days' work to each.

As we said earlier, this can be done in parallel with the design and development of the objectives but we will need to have something in place before we can write about it. Our suggestion is that we link both of these to the end of the first objective, that way we can write up the first objective as we are designing and developing the second one, and so on (see Fig. 8.5.17).

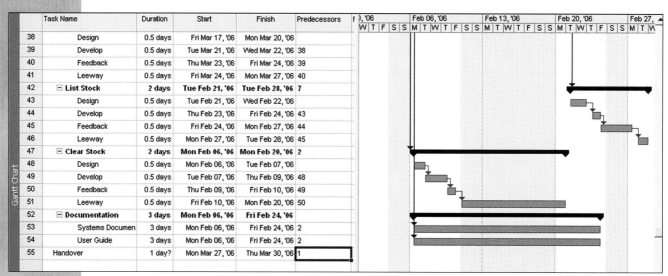

	Task Name	Duration	Start	Finish	Predecessors
38	Design	0.5 days	Fri Mar 17, '06	Mon Mar 20, '06	
39	Develop	0.5 days	Tue Mar 21, '06	Wed Mar 22, '06	38
40	Feedback	0.5 days	Thu Mar 23, '06	Fri Mar 24, '06	39
41	Leeway	0.5 days	Fri Mar 24, '06	Mon Mar 27, '06	40
42	⊟ List Stock	2 days	Tue Feb 21, '06	Tue Feb 28, '06	7
43	Design	0.5 days	Tue Feb 21, '06	Wed Feb 22, '06	
44	Develop	0.5 days	Thu Feb 23, '06	Fri Feb 24, '06	43
45	Feedback	0.5 days	Fri Feb 24, '06	Mon Feb 27, '06	44
46	Leeway	0.5 days	Mon Feb 27, '06	Tue Feb 28, '06	45
47	⊟ Clear Stock	2 days	Mon Feb 06, '06	Mon Feb 20, '06	2
48	Design	0.5 days	Mon Feb 06, '06	Tue Feb 07, '06	
49	Develop	0.5 days	Tue Feb 07, '06	Thu Feb 09, '06	48
50	Feedback	0.5 days	Thu Feb 09, '06	Fri Feb 10, '06	49
51	Leeway	0.5 days	Fri Feb 10, '06	Mon Feb 20, '06	50
52	⊟ Documentation	3 days	Mon Feb 06, '06	Fri Feb 24, '06	
53	Systems Documen	3 days	Mon Feb 06, '06	Fri Feb 24, '06	2
54	User Guide	3 days	Mon Feb 06, '06	Fri Feb 24, '06	2
55	Handover	1 day?	Mon Mar 27, '06	Thu Mar 30, '06	1

Figure 8.5.17 Building in time for documentation

Activity 5 Plan for documentation ◀

Decide on how you will plan to create any documentation and add it to your system.

Handover

The only activities we need to look at now are the handover activities. What makes a successful handover? In Unit 8.4 we suggested three phases: summative testing, transition and end-of-project review. We will leave summative testing for the moment but Adrian reckons that he needs 3 days for transition. This is what he has planned.

The vans will go out carrying the new system for 3 days. On the first day the sons will operate the system with a parent in each van in case things go wrong. Adrian himself will be at the venue on his mobile phone ready to go to either of the vans should there be a problem. The second time the vans will go out with Mr Atha who will attend to a van if there is any problem; otherwise, the sons will run the vans using the system. Adrian will be on call in case of a serious problem. On the third day the vans will go out with only the sons to man them. Adrian and Mr Atha will be on call in case of problems.

After the transition Adrian plans to hold a meeting with all the Atha family to do an end-of-project review. This should only take a couple of hours but adding the write-up, he has decided it will take a day's work.

Returning to the summative testing: in Adrian's case his transition plans involve testing in a live environment, so all he really needs in addition is a test plan that tries out all the major objectives. He feels this will take half a day to plan and half a day to run, so another day's work.

As far as dependencies go the testing has to be completed before the transition can start, and the system needs to be handed over before we can do the end-of-project review. Adrian's plan has therefore been updated as shown in Figure 8.5.18.

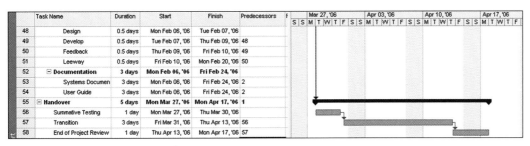

Figure 8.5.18 Building in time for testing

ACTIVITY 6 Refine your project plan further ◀

Using your project management software complete the process of breaking down the tasks of your project by analysing the handover of your project and setting up the task accordingly.

Conclusion ▶ ▶ ▶

In Unit 8.5 we have analysed our project and split it up into tasks. We still haven't completed the planning section as we still have to assign resources, but we have a plan with built-in leeway that should allow us to implement our project on time. It may seem that we are spending a lot of time on the planning and not too much on building the actual system itself. Do remember, however, that this is a project-management unit: it is the project plan and your ability to implement the plan that you will be assessed on. The actual assessment of the system will be covered in either Units 10, 11 or 12, depending on which you are using for your project.

Introduction

We are now about to enter the final phase of getting our plan together, by assigning resources to each of the activities. 'Resources' means anything you require to get the task finished. You can think of the resources as the tools for the job: and as any DIY enthusiast will tell you, a job is much easier when you have the right tools. Once you have assigned resources to your project you are ready to get started; the second half of Unit 8.6 will be an overview of what to do once the project starts.

Resources

It is all very well us saying that the right tools make the job easier; the problem with resources is that you are largely limited to what you have available. This is especially true in the environment you will be working in. Your school or college does not have a never-ending supply of hardware and software; it is possible that it may not have a piece of equipment you need for your project development. For example, Adrian's college does not have any touch-screen monitors and Mr Atha will not be buying them until he is sure that the project is going to be successful. In fact, it is more than likely that Mr Atha does not exist and this is an assignment set by the college with Adrian's teacher taking the part of Mr Atha. Whatever the reason, Adrian will not have access to a touch-screen monitor during most of his project.

'... and exactly why is this a vital resource for your spreadsheet project Hayley?'

Let us look at the sort of resources you may need and what you will be able to rely upon. We suggest that you use one of your optional units to implement your project, although you do not have to. If you take our advice you will either have a spreadsheet project, a multi-media project or a customised application project. For most spreadsheet or customised application projects, you would normally only need the software and the hardware to develop it, and a team of developers (which will usually end up being you). Unless you require specialist hardware, such as a touch-screen monitor or a bar code reader, that's pretty much it. Assuming your school or college has the right software you will be able to develop your system on its network, which will be available to you at almost any time. This makes scheduling quite straightforward, as you do not have to make adjustments

Figure 8.6.1 Availability of equipment

for the availability of resources. The multi-media project may be slightly more problematic in that you may have to schedule some tasks according to the availability of specific equipment (see Fig. 8.6.1).

As an example, one of the authors used to teach a class of multi-media students at a school in Berkshire. This school was lucky enough to have a complete recording studio with mixing equipment. As a result three separate members of the author's class wanted to create a promotional website for the bands of which they were members. They each wanted to film a recording session for their band; for obvious reasons, the studio was also in demand from other areas of the school. So the students needed to handle the logistics of booking the studio, the filming equipment, someone to do the filming, and of course, getting the rest of the band together, all at the same time. For two of the students this coming together of equipment and people could only occur once during the duration of the project: consequently, the whole project needed to be arranged around this one immovable time.

▶ Assigning resources

Human resources

A large real-life project can involve hundreds or even thousands of people, all with different skills and specialisms that the project manager can use. Unfortunately for you, your staff will be limited and you may be tempted to assume, in the sort of project you are managing, that the only human resource you have is yourself. To a large extent this is true but the picture is not absolutely clear-cut. You may also be able to call on a little help, however, like Adrian, for whom one of the school administration staff is doing some data entry. You may also have people supplying feedback, and you will also need people to help you test. You may agree with a classmate, as Adrian has done, that you will provide each other with feedback. Remember, however, that your collaborator will have his or her own project to worry about, so you will have to schedule meetings. You will also need to arrange meetings with your customer; your customer will be busy, so these will also have to be scheduled carefully.

ACTIVITY 1 List the human resources needed on your project

Make a list of the people (other than yourself) you think will make contributions to the development of your project. Describe how they will contribute and what they will be doing.

Adrian's list appears in Table 8.6.1.

Table 8.6.1 Adrian's list of people who will be contributing to his project

Resource	Contribution
Mrs Rose	Mrs Rose is the school secretary and has offered to enter data onto my system for me. She has allocated me 2 hours. She is very busy and I will have to book her time at least 2 weeks in advance.
Paul Atha Snr	Paul Atha is the owner of Atha's Ice Cream vans. He will be required to give feedback and attend the progress meetings. He will also have to be present for most of the handover sessions as he not only provides a backup in case a problem occurs, but will also have to be confident enough to accept the system at the end of the project.
Shelagh Atha	Shelagh Atha will contribute to some of the progress meetings but will mainly be involved as a backup when parallel running takes place.
Paul Atha Jr	Paul Atha Jr is an ice cream van operator and will be involved in all the live tests.
Lee Atha	As above.
Sophie Bendix	Sophie Bendix is another ICT student. She is required to provide feedback at various points in the project.

The next thing we have to do is to assign working times for our human resources if they differ from the norm. The general working hours should be set based on your availability, because this is the standard. You have to be involved with almost everything, not much progress can take place on your project if you are not there. You should only assign times for your other resources which coincide with yours. All your other resources' timings should be a sub-set of the general times.

As an example, let us look at Adrian's human resources. We will start with Mrs Rose, who only works school hours. Although she will actually be there for more time than Adrian has allocated, he will only have access to her during the times when he has a lesson, and he must bear this in mind. He has allocated an hour in the evening when Mrs Rose will not be available. Her time profile will look like Figure 8.6.2.

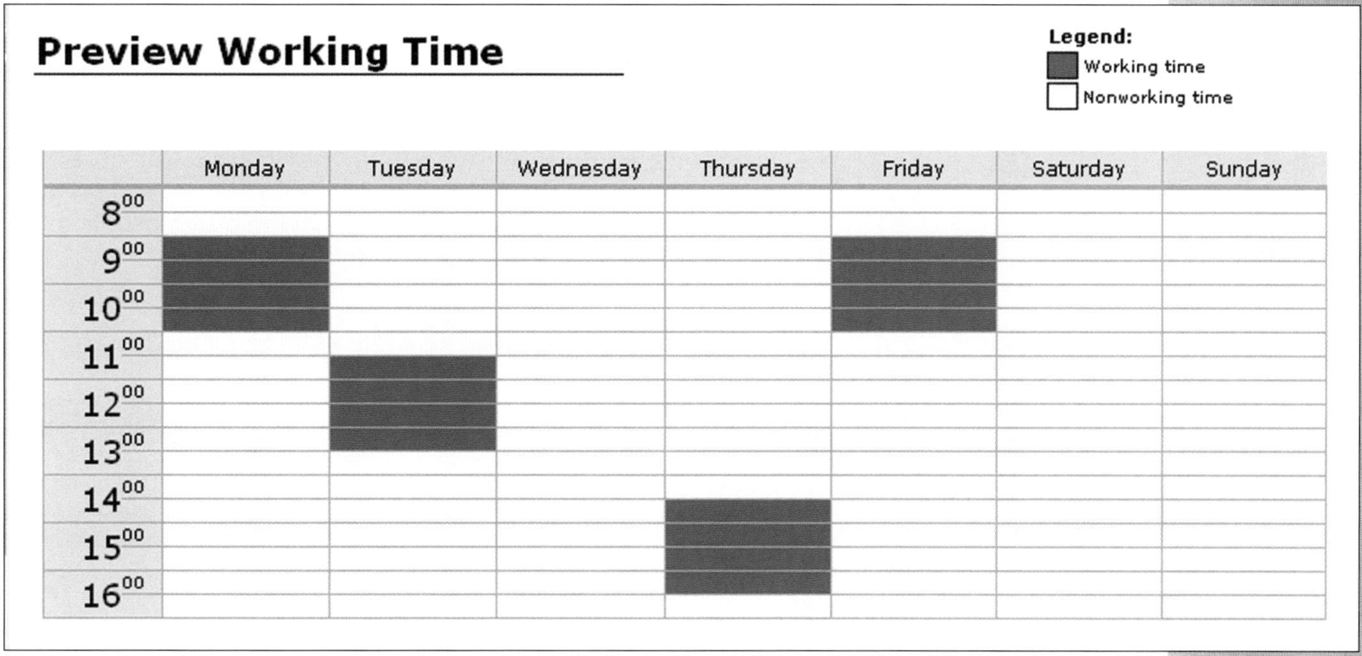

Preview Working Time

Legend:
- Working time
- Nonworking time

	Monday	Tuesday	Wednesday	Thursday	Friday	Saturday	Sunday
8^{00}							
9^{00}	working				working		
10^{00}	working				working		
11^{00}		working					
12^{00}		working					
13^{00}		working					
14^{00}				working			
15^{00}				working			
16^{00}				working			

Figure 8.6.2 Allocating time to Mrs Rose

As opposed to Mrs Rose, all the Athas, assuming they are real people, are only available after school. They may be available at weekends: but at the moment Adrian is not scheduled to work on Saturdays. As they are a family unit we can give all the Athas the same working hours (see Fig. 8.6.3).

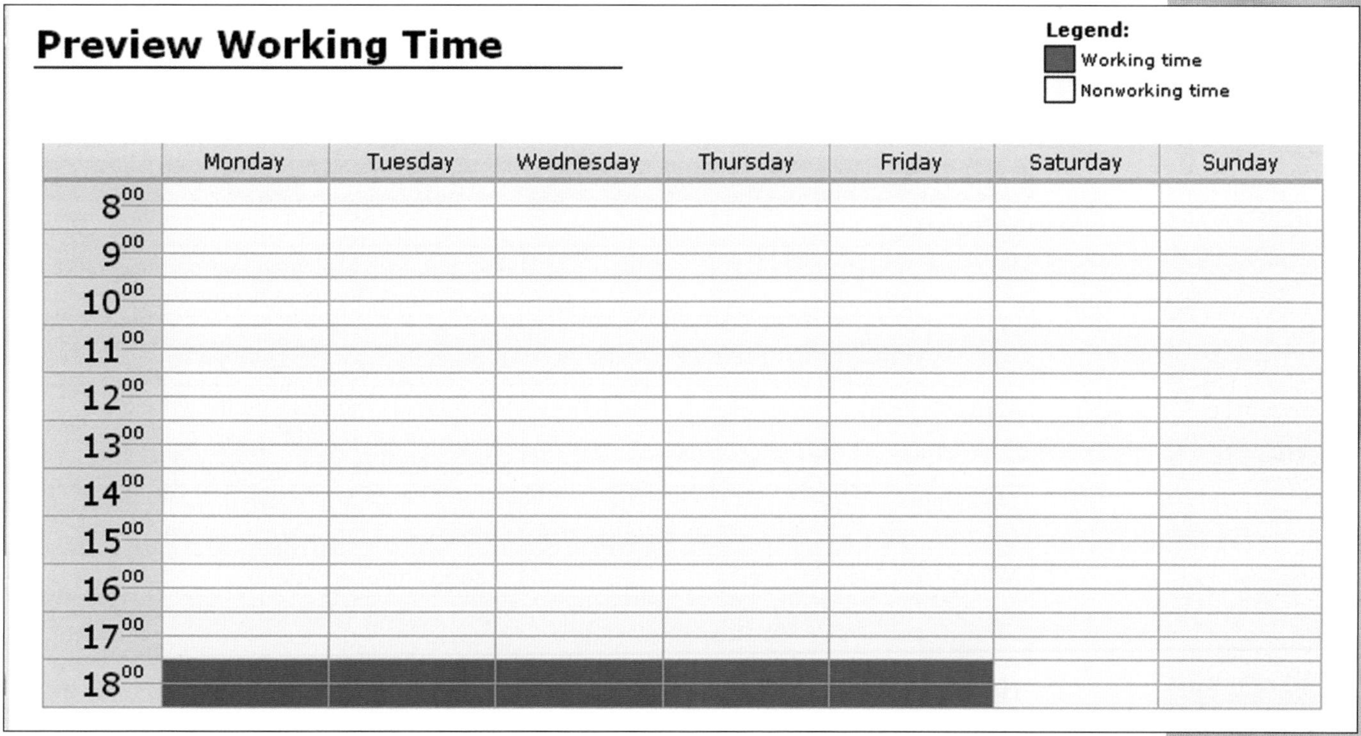

Preview Working Time

Legend:
- Working time
- Nonworking time

	Monday	Tuesday	Wednesday	Thursday	Friday	Saturday	Sunday
8^{00}							
9^{00}							
10^{00}							
11^{00}							
12^{00}							
13^{00}							
14^{00}							
15^{00}							
16^{00}							
17^{00}							
18^{00}	working	working	working	working	working		

Figure 8.6.3 Allocating time to the Athas

This leaves Sophie Bendix. We will assume that Sophie is actually a member of Adrian's class and is therefore available during class hours. If we assume that Adrian and Sophie don't necessarily see each other out of school then Sophie's times will be much the same as Mrs Rose's.

For our example Adrian has to create two extra base calendars. One for Mrs Rose and Sophie, and another for the Athas. This demonstration shows how to create a new calendar; this demonstration shows you how to assign people to it.

ACTIVITY 2 Create calendars for your human resources

Using your project management software create calendars for your human resources and assign times for them.

Other resources

When managing a project you not only have to manage the people involved, you also have to manage all the other resources. In many ways physical resources are as difficult to manage as human ones. We know humans are fallible and will fall ill, but machines are not perfect either and will crash or break down. You manage machines in a similar way to your human resources. The first thing you have to do as a project manager is to work out what physical resources you need. As we have mentioned before, for the sort of project you are doing for Unit 8, this task should not be difficult. On the whole you need software to develop your project and hardware to develop it on. Unless you need specialist hardware, that is pretty much it. As an example, let us have a look at what Adrian thinks he wants; Table 8.6.2 contains Adrian's thoughts.

Table 8.6.2 Adrian's resource list

Resource	Reason for need
Software	
Microsoft Project	Required for keeping an eye on the project and planning for what happens when
Microsoft Excel	Spreadsheet package for developing the main part of the system
Microsoft Word	Word processing software for writing the systems manual and the user guide. It will also be used to type up minutes
Adobe PDF Creator	Converts files of different types into PDF format for inclusion in the eportfolio
Macromedia Dreamweaver	Used to create eportfolio
Microsoft PowerPoint	Used to create presentations for meetings with the customer
Hardware	
Computer at school	To enable me to work on the project during school hours

Continued on the next page

Resource	Reason for need
Computer at home	To enable me to work on the project when at home
Pen drive	To backup work
Two laptops	To try out the system in a live environment
Two touch-screen monitors	To try out the system in a live environment

Adrian's situation as far as software is concerned is fairly simple. His school network contains all the software he needs, so when he is at school he can do everything he wants. Unfortunately, he doesn't have a PDF creator or Dreamweaver at home, and neither does he have Microsoft Project. However, although he needs these they are not necessarily required for all of the tasks he has listed in his project. This means he is able to work on most of the tasks either at home or at school. He can transfer data between the two systems using a pen drive. At school he has access to the network during all the time he has scheduled in. His computer at home belongs to him, so obviously he can access it at anytime. The two laptops and the touch-screen monitors are more problematic: Mr Atha has said that he wants to be sure he is going to get a working system before he is prepared to fork out the money for these pieces. Should the project go according to plan they will be ordered for arrival on 3 April.

Accepting that most of the software is linked to the machines and that he carries his pen drive with him at all times, the resources Adrian will have to schedule are as follows:

School computer
Home computer
Laptop with touch screen monitor 1
Laptop with touch screen monitor 2.

Activity 3 List the electronic resources needed on your project ◀

Undertake an exercise similar to the one Adrian has just undertaken, for your own project. Make a table of the hardware and software you will need and where it is available to you. Analyse this to identify your key resources and list them as above.

As we have said, we treat physical resources in much the same way as we do human resources. This means that they will need an availability calendar. For the home and school computers we already have a calendar, since the school computer is available during the times we defined in the 'Secretarial' calendar. The home computer is available at much the same time as the Athas, so we can use the 'Atha' calendar. The same could be true of the laptops, except that they are not available until 3 April. The way we get over this is to assign them to the 'Atha' calendar and then set their availability date to 3 April.

How to set an availability date for a resource

1 Select view/resource sheet
2 Select the resource you wish to change the availability date of
3 Click the right button and select resource information
4 In the resulting window click on the general tab
5 Select the drop down arrow in the first 'Available from' field (see Fig. 8.6.4)
6 Choose an 'Available from' date from the resulting calendar (see Fig. 8.6.5)
7 Close the resource window by clicking OK.

Look at this demonstration from the ActiveBook.

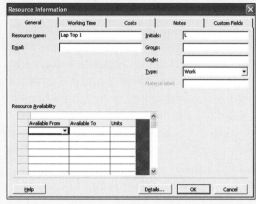

Figure 8.6.4 Selecting 'Available from' field

Figure 8.6.5 Selecting a date from the calendar

Assigning resources to tasks

Having defined our tasks and our resources we have to decide which resources we need to complete each task. Bearing in mind that you are the only real developer you are going to have to decide what proportion of your time you will assign to each task when you are doing things in parallel. In Adrian's case some of his design and development activities can be done in parallel so he could effectively have two development strands, one at school and one at home. Occasionally, he could be doing three things in parallel. This is possible, but he would have to split his time which makes things more complicated. It is probably best just to have the two strands and run them sequentially.

The way Adrian has set-up his project there are a large number of pre-requisites already. One particular strand contains the following sequential path:

Store Data
Retrieve Price
Total Price
Cancel Transaction
New Transaction
Out of Stock
Calculate Change
Amount Taken.

Each one of these has to be completed before the next one can start. They also each contain a design section, a development section, a feedback section and a leeway section. For the design and development section Adrian will need a computer to work on. His decision was that these sections would be done at school. He would use Sophie to do the feedback for most of the sections, but for the fourth and the last sections he would use Mr Atha. For the leeway sections he would need both computers and someone to give feedback. He has chosen to do this at school as well and use Sophie for all the leeway feedback. So basically all these tasks require Adrian and the school computer, while the feedback sessions and the leeway sessions require Sophie. That is, except for feedback numbers 4 and 8, when we need Mr Atha. We will need to set these on our project management software.

Assigning a resource to a number of tasks

1 Select resources
2 Click on assign people and equipment to tasks
3 Select the tasks you wish to assign resources to
4 Click on assign resources
5 In the assign resource window (see Fig. 8.6.6) choose the resource and click on assign
6 Repeat 5 until all resources are selected then click on close.

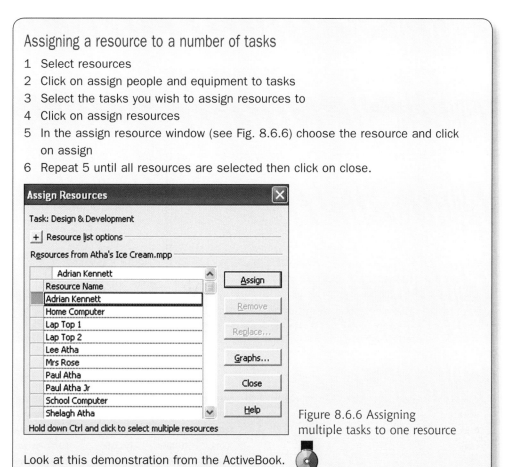

Figure 8.6.6 Assigning multiple tasks to one resource

Look at this demonstration from the ActiveBook.

This leaves Adrian with the out of stock, list stock, clear stock and documentation. As these will form the other stream he will have to assign the home computer to them. Given that Sophie isn't available for these times, Mr or Mrs Atha will have to provide the feedback. First things first, however: he will not be able to start one before he finishes another, so he will have to specify them as pre-requisites.

Finally, we have to look at the issue of the handover and for all this we need Mr Atha. For the testing we also require the two sons and Mrs Atha. We also need the new laptops. Once he has assigned these resources, Adrian's planning is complete except for one small issue, which we already know about: the laptops are not available until 3 April, so the summative testing cannot start until that date. We tell the project management software about this by setting a starting constraint, i.e. that the task cannot start until this date.

Setting a constraint

There are many different kinds of constraint, setting a particular start date is only one of them. A similar method to this can be used to set a deadline for a particular task:

1 Select view/Gantt chart
2 Select the task on which you want to set a 'start from' date and click the right button
3 Select task information
4 From the resulting window select the general tab (see Fig. 8.6.7)
5 Select the drop down arrow on the start date field and click on the required start date.

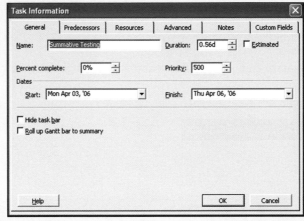

Figure 8.6.7 Setting a constraint

Look at this demonstration from the ActiveBook.

Resource levelling

	ⓘ	Resource Name	Type	Material Label	Initials	Group	Max. Units	Std. Rate	Ovt. Rate	Cost/Use	Accrue
1	◈	Adrian Kennett	Work		A		100%	£0.00/hr	£0.00/hr	£0.00	Prorat_
2		Mrs Rose	Work		M		100%	£0.00/hr	£0.00/hr	£0.00	Prorate
3		Paul Atha	Work		P		100%	£0.00/hr	£0.00/hr	£0.00	Prorate
4		Shelagh Atha	Work		S		100%	£0.00/hr	£0.00/hr	£0.00	Prorate
5		Paul Atha Jr	Work		P		100%	£0.00/hr	£0.00/hr	£0.00	Prorate
6		Lee Atha	Work		L		100%	£0.00/hr	£0.00/hr	£0.00	Prorate
7		Sophie Bendix	Work		S		100%	£0.00/hr	£0.00/hr	£0.00	Prorate
8		School Computer	Work		S		100%	£0.00/hr	£0.00/hr	£0.00	Prorate
9	◈	Home Computer	Work		H		100%	£0.00/hr	£0.00/hr	£0.00	Prorat
10		Lap Top 1	Work		L		0%	£0.00/hr	£0.00/hr	£0.00	Prorate
11		Lap Top 2	Work ▼		L		0%	£0.00/hr	£0.00/hr	£0.00	Prorate

Figure 8.6.8 Overuse of resources

Adrian still has a problem. If you look at his resource list, both he and his home computer are overused (see Fig. 8.6.8). This means that at some point he is trying to do too much. It probably means he is trying to do two things at once. Project management software provides you with a tool to overcome this. It is called **resource levelling**. The software will find out where the overuse is and put off part of the task until there is time for it to be done.

Levelling resources

1 Select view/resource sheet
2 Select tools/level resources
3 From the resulting window click on level now (see Fig. 8.6.9)
4 From the next window select entire pool and click on level now.

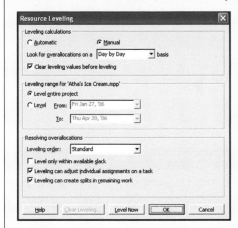

Figure 8.6.9 Levelling resources

ACTIVITY 4 Assign tasks

Use your project management software to assign resources to tasks. Sort your tasks into order and decide which activities should be linked. Set start dates for any resources which will not be available until later in the project. If you have any overstretched resources, level your project.

Baselining

Your initial project plan is more or less complete. This plan is essentially what you measure progress against so you need a copy. You can save the project as it stands now within the project management software using a process called baselining. Later on you can save other versions of the plan and at any time analyse your progress based on this baseline.

Taking a baseline save

1 Select tools/tracking/save baseline
2 In the resulting save baseline window (see Fig. 8.6.10) click on OK.

Your baseline will be saved.

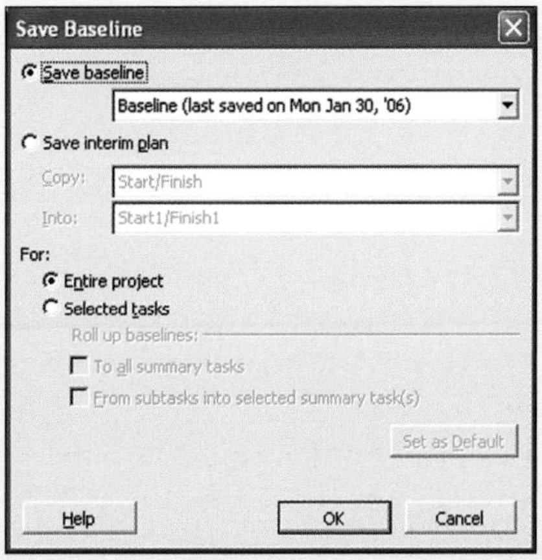

Figure 8.6.10 Taking a baseline save

We will look at the baseline and how you compare your project against it in Unit 8.7. For the moment you just need to know that you can change your plan and still know what it was like at the beginning.

ACTIVITY 5 Save a baseline ◀

Save a baseline for your project.

Conclusion ▶ ▶ ▶

We have finally set up our initial plan. It has taken a long time but we should make no apologies for that, it is a crucial process. Successful plans are always well thought out in the beginning; when plans are unsuccessfully carried out, this is very often due to something you missed early on. The next step is putting the plan into practise: actually doing what you set out to do. Right at the beginning you committed yourself to a certain amount of work and the times when you would do this work. If you want your project to be successful you have to make every effort to do what you set out to do. There will be enough things you come across as you develop the project that will be out of your control and which may make a mess of your plans. The last thing you need is to add to these unnecessarily.

8.7 The role of meetings

Introduction

At last we have come to the part where you start work on the actual development of the product itself. Having said this, the physical building of whatever it is you intend to produce is of only vague interest to us in Unit 8. For help with your actual projects you are going to need to refer to the other units in this book. In Unit 8.7 we will guide you through the process of running a project, reviewing progress and making remedial decisions based on these reviews. Remember that there are a number of stakeholders in the project, all of whom will need to be kept informed about progress. People are often awkward to deal with and you will need to demonstrate good interpersonal skills if your project is to be successful.

Although we are now at the phase where we are starting to develop our product, Unit 8 is about managing the project and, perhaps more importantly, providing evidence in your portfolio about this management process. Unit 8.7 is about how to supply that evidence (see Fig. 8.7.1).

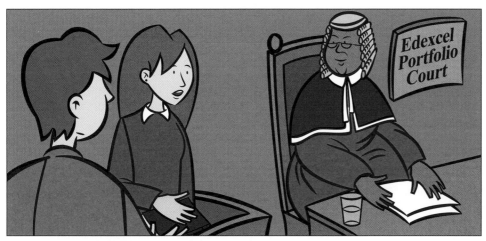

'... that the evidence I shall give will be the truth'

Running the project

▶ Storing the evidence

You may be inclined to tackle your project head-on and then worry about providing the evidence for your portfolio later. This can be a very frustrating business as you often have to provide evidence of progress. This you may have overwritten as the project developed, discarding vital pieces of evidence. It is worthwhile from the outset to start to save things. You will be tracking your progress mainly by saving versions of your plans and also the minutes of meetings. We would suggest that at this point you create a project folder to store all your work in. We would also suggest that you create a 'documents' folder to hold, amongst other things, your initial project proposal and your definition of scope. Other things you can put in this folder are your functional specification and any letters you need to send. We would suggest you use a separate folder for printouts of your project plans at different times. These need to be viewed by your assessor sequentially, so if you were to include the date in the document title that would be helpful. You will be attending and running a number of meetings which will need to be minuted. Once again your assessor will need to know the order, so it would be helpful if you put the date in the title of the document.

The initial project plan

Figure 8.7.1 Presenting the plan

Our initial project plan is important because it is against this original plan that everything else is measured. It is helpful to keep a copy of that externally to the project management software. The software that we are using allows us to convert our Gantt chart into a PDF file. This means that we can save a copy of the plan and simply link it into our eportfolio when the time comes. If we have the dates in the title we will know which plans were produced in which order.

We have to present this plan both to our customer and our senior managements (see Fig. 8.7.1). All we are looking for in this case is approval for the plan. We therefore need to minute the meeting in which this takes place.

Reviews and meetings

During the course of the project you will attend and even run a number of meetings. A little later we will look at a number of different meetings you may need to set up; for the moment we will take a short look at meetings in general and how to make them successful.

'Let's schedule a meeting about it'

Effective meetings

When used properly, meetings are an efficient and effective method of decision making. At their best the attendees of a meeting can amount to more than the sum of their parts. Unfortunately, a lot of meetings are not run properly and consequently a lot of time is wasted. Often this is caused by the chair of the meeting allowing it to go off on tangents. This can sometimes be useful, as it can occasionally lead to innovative approaches to problem solving. It is not time-efficient, however, and this slackness of agenda should only be allowed if you have time to spare. In your project you probably do not have this luxury, and neither will your customer. If your teacher is acting as your customer then he or she will be doing the same for 20 or more other students. The time he or she can spend in a meeting with you is therefore limited. It is important, therefore, that your meetings are efficient and do what they set out to do in the minimum of time.

There are a number of things you can do to make sure this happens. When setting the agenda for the meeting go into detail about what you are going to discuss. The more information the other members of the meeting have, the better prepared they will be. Be clear about exactly what is expected from the meeting. If you want feedback on something, make sure the members of the meeting are aware of this. Equally importantly, if you are not looking for feedback, make this clear. During the meeting, make sure you stick to the point and don't go off on a tangent. When decisions are made, make a note of them for the minutes later. A quick rule of thumb is that all discussions should end either in a decision or an action – something someone has to do. If the result is an action make sure you state a date and time by which this action has to be completed.

Most of your meetings will have the same people in attendance, but be aware there are different types of meeting you will have to attend and that they each will have a slightly different focus.

Project proposal meeting

The first meeting you will attend is the project proposal meeting, although you will have had some conversations with your customer beforehand. The major and overriding objective of this meeting is to get the go-ahead both from the customer and your manager (your teacher). You should come out of the meeting with a signed piece of paper confirming that you can start your project. You will also be presenting some initial design ideas, so the meeting is also your first opportunity to get some feedback on these. Minute the feedback carefully and try to adjust the next design accordingly. For your GCE qualification, the assessor needs to be able to identify where you have changed the design based on the feedback. If it may be difficult to see where you have made these changes, so highlight them in some way.

Agreement for the statement of scope and the functional specification

This is a similar meeting to the previous one; the objective is to gain your customer's agreement to what you have planned. Notice that we are suggesting combining the statement of scope from Unit 8 with the functional specification from the optional unit. This is because they cover much of the same ground; indeed, the functional specification can almost be made up from bits of the statement of scope. Once again, this is an opportunity to elicit some feedback which you should note down carefully.

Meeting to agree the initial plan

Before you attend this meeting, save a copy of your plan. Although this appears to be similar to earlier versions there is a slight difference at this stage: you are going into more detail, for example explaining to your customer what will happen, where and when. For assessment purposes, therefore, it is important to save this latest and subtly different version of the plan.

At this meeting your customer may have issues with the timings of things which involve him or her, so you may have to compromise on some of the meeting times and when the customer can be involved with testing. If these compromises endanger the deadline of your project you must use your interpersonal skills to persuade the customer to make the time available.

Figure 8.7.2 Project review meeting

Project review meeting

These meetings will occur at various stages throughout the project. They will involve, in theory, all the stakeholders in the project or at least their representatives. In practice, the ongoing project review may take place as a series of individual meetings, since it is extremely difficult to get all the stakeholders together at one time. These meetings should be timed to take place at key points in the project; for your project we would suggest at least four review points. Before each of these you should save yet more copies of your plan. If your project management software allows you to make a comparison with the baseline plan, then you should do this and take the printout along to the meeting.

Comparing the current plan against the baseline
Checking the progress of the project

The first thing you have to do when you fail to complete a task or a set of tasks on time is to adjust your plan. Depending on your project management software there are a number of ways of detecting if you have a problem. Probably the easiest way is to look at your resources sheet (see Fig. 8.7.3). Our project management software puts a little sign against the resources which are causing difficulty. As you are key to this project it is almost invariably going to be you who has the problem. You can then either adjust your plan or level it to create a new one. Your new plan now looks fine on paper, but if you compare it against the original plan it will mark certain tasks as being late (see Fig. 8.7.3).

Continued on the next page

	ⓘ	Resource Name	Type	Material Label	Initials	Group	Max. Units	Std. Rate	Ovt. Rate	Cost/Use	Accrue ▲
1	◈	Adrian Kennett	Work		A		100%	£0.00/hr	£0.00/hr	£0.00	Prorat_
2		Mrs Rose	Work		M		100%	£0.00/hr	£0.00/hr	£0.00	Prorate
3	◈	Paul Atha	Work		P		100%	£0.00/hr	£0.00/hr	£0.00	Prorat
4		Shelagh Atha	Work		S		100%	£0.00/hr	£0.00/hr	£0.00	Prorate
5		Paul Atha Jr	Work		P		100%	£0.00/hr	£0.00/hr	£0.00	Prorate
6		Lee Atha	Work		L		100%	£0.00/hr	£0.00/hr	£0.00	Prorate
7		Sophie Bendix	Work		S		100%	£0.00/hr	£0.00/hr	£0.00	Prorate
8		School Computer	Work		S		100%	£0.00/hr	£0.00/hr	£0.00	Prorate
9	◈	Home Computer	Work		H		100%	£0.00/hr	£0.00/hr	£0.00	Prorat
10		Lap Top 1	Work		L		0%	£0.00/hr	£0.00/hr	£0.00	Prorate
11		Lap Top 2	Work		L		0%	£0.00/hr	£0.00/hr	£0.00	Prorate

Figure 8.7.3 Late tasks

To check a plan against the original plan:
1 Select view/Gantt chart
2 On the viewing toolbar (see Fig. 8.7.4) select track

Figure 8.7.4 Checking a plan against the original plan

3 Click on the 'Check the progress of the project' and your overdue tasks will be marked (see Fig. 8.7.5).

	Task Name	Status Indicator	% Work Comple
1	⊟ Design & Development	⊘	2
2	⊟ Store Data	✓	10
3	Design	✓	10
4	Develop	✓	10
5	Feedback	✓	10
6	Leeway	✓	10
7	⊟ Retrieve Price	✓	10
8	Design	✓	10
9	Develop	✓	10
10	Feedback	✓	10
11	Leeway	✓	10
12	⊟ Total Price	✓	10
13	Design	✓	10
14	Develop	✓	10
15	Feedback	✓	10
16	Leeway	✓	10
17	⊟ Cancel Transaction	⊘	
18	Design	⊘	
19	Develop	⊘	
20	Feedback	⊘	

Figure 8.7.5 Overdue tasks

Item 1 – Check plan against original

At any particular point in a project all tasks will either be completed, partially completed or not started. Each one of the first two types needs to be discussed, or at least reported on (unless a task was reported complete at the previous meeting). If those tasks that should have been completed have not been, you will need to say why. Any delay will have a knock-on effect on the rest of the project and you will have to explain what these effects will be. New interim deadlines may have to be agreed and it is possible that the dates of the remaining review meetings will have to be changed.

Partially completed tasks also have to be reviewed. At any particular point, according to your plan, there is an expectation that a partially completed task will be finished to a certain percentage degree. It is possible that you haven't achieved as much as you had hoped, or that you may not have even started. If this is the case once again you will have to explain why, and try to predict the likelihood of this causing a delay. You may feel that you can make up the time, but remember you have already planned your project based on a realistic assessment of the amount of time you were prepared to work on it. If you are trying to catch up, the only way you can do so is to allocate more time to the project.

Having looked at what is complete you now need to look ahead to the tasks you have coming up. Will you be ready to start them on time? If not, why not? Do you have all the resources you need to complete the task? If not, you need to check whether you will have them by the time you are due to start it. It may sound obvious, but tasks that do not start when they are supposed to generally don't finish when they are supposed to either.

During your discussions about the tasks, especially those that don't look like they will complete on time, you will come to a point where someone has to do something to get you back on track. This is called an action and should be minuted. Actions need to be assigned to someone and a target date should be set for completing them. Someone looking at a set of minutes should also be able to identify the actions.

Item 2 – Assigning and reassigning tasks

Often the project review meeting is used to assign tasks to members of the team and to check on their progress (though this is unlikely to happen in your project as you are the team). It may be that you need to involve other people; if they are at this meeting it is a good time to agree dates and times.

▶ Prototyping feedback meeting

It is expected that during the development of your project's product you will use a prototyping approach to development. This will mean showing your product to your customer (or someone else) and getting their opinions and suggestions about it. In order that the assessors have evidence of you using this approach you should minute the entire meeting where you will be getting feedback. Often you will have an item in your project review meeting where this can occur, but on other occasions feedback will simply be the result of a fairly casual conversation and demonstration. The fact that it is casual does not mean that it is unimportant, however, so make sure you carefully note what is said on these occasions as well. The assessor will be looking for how feedback affects your plan. The minutes of such 'casual' meetings do not need to be as formal as those of the scheduled review meeting, but they still need to be included in your eportfolio.

Agendas and minutes
▶ The agenda

There are general conventions to follow when you organise a meeting. The first important point to consider is that all the participants should be able to recall what has happened in the previous meeting. But it may have taken place some time ago and they may have difficulty remembering. You should have sent out the minutes of the previous meetings to all concerned within 3 days of it finishing, so the attendees should have these to bring to the next meeting. Human nature being what it is, however, this often doesn't happen as people lose or forget their copy of the minutes. It is therefore useful to attach a copy of the previous minutes to the next meeting's agenda when you send it out. If there are unfulfilled actions on the minutes it may prick a few consciences.

Your agenda should be headed by the title of the meeting and should also list the location, date and time the meeting is to take place. Traditionally, the first item on an agenda is 'Apologies for absence'. In a formal meeting this is a list of the people who cannot attend and the reasons they gave for their non-attendance. As most of your GCE meetings will probably have only two attendees, an absence would mean the meeting not taking place, so you could probably skip this bit.

The next item on the agenda is usually 'Minutes of the previous meeting'. Initially this is to agree that the previous minutes are an accurate reflection of what took place at that meeting. But its real importance lies in the fact that it goes over the previous minutes and checks that the actions assigned there have been completed. This can act as something of a spur to team members to make sure they do what they have agreed to: they would not wish to go through the embarrassment of making their excuses at the meeting.

After these traditional items you can put any items you need to discuss on the minutes. You must invite other attendees to suggest agenda items, since they are just as much stakeholders in the project as you are; in your particular circumstances it is likely to be you who is the stakeholder and therefore you who sets the items. Commonly in the world of work, agendas have a series of one-line item titles and that is all you get. For your GCE we would suggest that you expand on this approach with a short paragraph describing exactly what you want to discuss. This will allow other attendees to prepare themselves and bring along any documents they feel might contribute to the discussion. If they are not sure exactly what you want to discuss, they cannot be fully prepared and this may lead to wasted time in the meeting.

We now come to the item 'Any other business', sometimes shortened these days to 'AOB'. You will often see this at the bottom of an agenda; it is there in case a stakeholder has something important to raise that has occurred between the distribution of the agenda and the actual meeting taking place. In practice, individuals may sometimes use this item to draw attention to their own pet issues. Items that are discussed in this way will come as a surprise to all the other attendees, leaving them somewhat unprepared for a proper considered response. It is therefore advisable to proceed with caution before taking any major decisions within the 'AOB' section of the meeting.

▶ Minutes

Sometimes the minutes of meetings in the world of work are almost a transcript of everything that is said. In your portfolio for the GCE you can keep things shorter: just note down in a document all the important points of the discussion. It should be laid out in the same order as the agenda items and should contain all the actions agreed at the meeting, who will perform them, and by what date. Other than that there aren't really any hard and fast rules for what the minutes should look like, though they should always have a title containing the location, date and time the meeting took place. Here is an example:

> **Minutes of the Atha's Ice Cream project review meeting**
> **held on**
> **Tuesday, 21 February 2006**
> **at**
> **Faraday College conference room.**

Underneath you should list the attendees and any apologies for absence, for example:

> *Attendees: Mr Paul Atha, Mrs Shelagh Atha, Adrian Kennett*
> *Apologies: none*

Finally, in the header you need to copy in those parties who are interested in the meeting but did not attend, for example:

> *c.c. Mr F Phelps*

Underneath these headings you simply write out the important points of each of the agenda items in the order they were discussed:

Look at these examples of:

- an agenda

- the corresponding minutes.

Close down and end of project review

We have discussed a number of different types of meeting which you may have to organise or attend. We have delayed talking about one of the most important, namely the end of project review. This meeting would normally be between you and your customer. In this circumstance it will need to be between yourself and your teacher, preferably with your customer attending if this isn't your teacher.

The first thing to note in the case of your GCE is that the date of the end of project is not necessarily when you have finished everything, but rather the deadline your teacher has set. If your project has overrun due to circumstances beyond your control, then as long as you have managed the project as well as could be expected, the overrun will not disqualify you from the higher grades in Unit 8.

The end of project review **must** take place, however, even if your project isn't quite finished. At this meeting you will go back over your objectives and your key success criteria and decide between you how well your project has gone. You will need to get your teacher's opinion of how well you have performed; you also need to note down your own evaluation of your performance. All this must be written in the minutes of the meeting and included in your eportfolio.

If you are undertaking a project in conjunction with another unit you will have to complete it for that unit, but as far as Unit 8 is concerned, the project is finished once you have done the end-of-project review.

Conclusion ▶ ▶ ▶

Throughout the course of the project your plan for developing it may need to be adjusted several times. There will almost inevitably be issues arising which you didn't consider when you set out your initial plan. For your eportfolio you will have to supply evidence of **managing your project**, showing how you made and altered plans to accommodate these changing circumstances. You will need to document what happened and how you changed your plans because of it. The main evidence for this will be copies of your plans at different stages during the project, and the minutes of the meetings you attended. All of these must be included in your eportfolio.

'... and finally item 1373: proposed 50% pay rise for the chairman. Any objections?'

Introduction

Hopefully, the information in Unit 8 has enabled you to run a successful project. Your eportfolio should contain the evidence that you have done so. The assessors and moderators of your work will have to delve through a large amount of information to find evidence that you have attended to certain points. This is not an easy task, and if the information is difficult to find they might miss it. It is in your interest, therefore, to structure your eportfolio in such a way as to make life easy for the assessors. Unit 8.8 will suggest a structure with this in mind.

The eportfolio

▶ ## Home page

Throughout your project you have generated a large number of documents. These include your project proposal, your definition of scope, various versions of plans, and the minutes and agendas of many meetings. The assessors will have to wade their way through these looking for evidence. They will be working from a section in the specification called the Assessment Criteria. Taking a good look at this document (it is on the <u>Edexcel</u> website) could be very illuminating for you.

The assessment criteria are split up into five strands; we suggest you structure the home page of your eportfolio to match the strands (see Fig. 8.8.1).

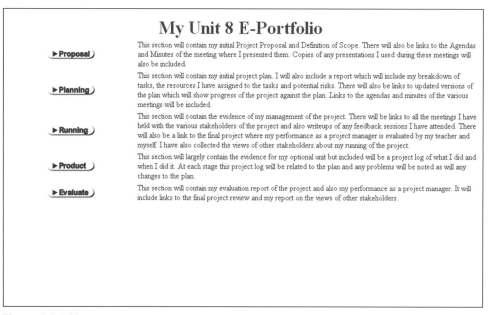

Figure 8.8.1 Home page structure

Loosely, the strands can be categorised under the following headings:
a Proposal and definition of scope
b Initial project planning
c Managing the project
d The product of the project
e Evaluation of performance.

▶ Proposal and definition of scope

As the title suggests, this section will be about the initial project proposal and, once the proposal has been agreed, the definition of scope or the boundaries of the system. The section carries a maximum mark of 6 out of 60 and is designed to assess your ability to define your project accurately.

Clearly, your project proposal document should have a link on this page and so should your definition of scope. But you should also link to the minutes and agenda of any meetings or feedback discussions and, if you did a presentation to present either of the two major documents, it would also be useful to link to an html version of this. To get the highest marks you will need to include a research document (see Fig. 8.8.2). In the research document you need to show a complete understanding of the situation itself and should include the results of any surveys you did, major points of any interview, any document analysis or a write up of your observations. It is also worthwhile seeing if there is a ready made product which will meet the objectives of your product. If there is you would probably have to justify continuing with your project on the grounds of cost or functionality.

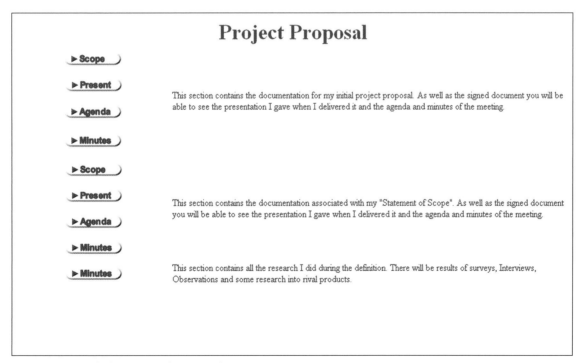

Figure 8.8.2 Including research material

▶ Initial project plan

There are 12 marks out of a total of 60 for this section. It will contain information about how you developed the initial project plan and how this changed over time. The first thing you need to show is the initial plan itself. It would help if you present a series of notes with it which describe how you developed the plan. This document would start by describing how you split your plan into logical phases, and how you decided which tasks depended on the completion of which others. For top marks you will need to identify areas of risk, in other words try to predict where your plan is likely to go wrong. Again, you will have presented your plan, so you should supply links to the agenda and the minutes of the meeting at which you presented this to your customer. Throughout the course of the project you will run at least four review meetings which may well have caused the plan to be adjusted. For each of these you will need a link to a printout of the plan, the agenda, and the minutes of the meeting (see Fig. 8.8.3).

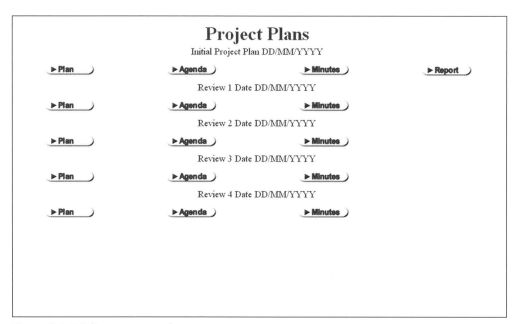

Figure 8.8.3 Adjustments to plan

▶ Managing the project

There are 20 marks out of a total of 60 for this section and it is a tricky one to provide evidence for. You are assessed on how well you ran the project. How you provide evidence for something as subjective as this may seem problematic, so here are some pointers. To begin with you will need to include links to all the agendas and the minutes of all the meetings you have run. It would also help if the links were associated with a date and time and the type of meeting you had. Even though you already have links on other pages, you should include the project proposal meeting, the definition of scope meeting and all the planning meetings. You must also include the minutes of the final project review meeting, as this will contain comments from your teacher and your customer about how well you ran the project. Including a testimonial from your classmate reviewer will also be important.

These pieces of evidence will provide the assessor with a picture of how you ran the project. As there are so many different types of evidence for this section it is impossible to suggest a definitive framework. You will need to look through the evidence you have and design your pages accordingly.

▶ The product of the project

This section carries a maximum mark of 10 out of a total of 60, and will be where you put your evidence for the optional unit you chose to do your project on. For whatever project you chose the assessment grid will be similar. You will need to provide:

a A functional specification
b Design work
c The project itself
d Testing
e Evaluation.

In these five sections, if you have done your project in one of the optional units you will have 60 marks available for either Units 10, 11 or 12. Remember of course that you also have 60 marks available for Unit 8, so how are you going to ensure you are awarded these as well? We suggest you keep a log during this process saying what you did during each session. It is very important that in your log you relate the tasks you do to the plan, and that whenever you complete a task you state whether it is on target, late, or even early. The product page would therefore look something like Figure 8.8.4.

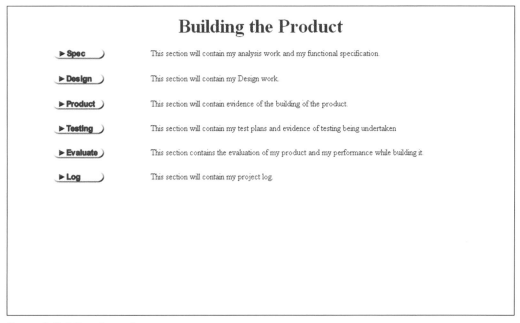

Figure 8.8.4 Keeping a log

▶ Evaluation of performance

Although you can back this section up with what your teacher says in the final review meeting and the comments of your customer, the main part of the evaluation will be your assessment of your own performance. Being self-critical is a difficult skill. When you think carefully about how the project went, however, there will always be something you think you could have done better. So be honest about this as it will not lose you marks.

Conclusion ▶ ▶ ▶

The examination board will not have seen you perform as a project manager. The only thing the assessors will have to go on in marking your work is the evidence you produce for your eportfolio. Clearly, the higher the quality of the content of your portfolio, the higher your final mark will be. Making this evidence easy to find is also essential, however. Assessors are less likely to miss bits of evidence if all aspects of your portfolio are logically ordered, linked and positioned. A well-structured portfolio is not a guarantee of a good mark, but it will help to ensure that you get the marks you deserve.

Using Multimedia
Software

Multimedia basics

Make sure you have:

- revisited the work you did on creating and storing multimedia in Unit 1.
- access to, and have used, a graphics package, sound-recording software, a digital movie camera or digital still camera with movie recording facility, and a CD burner.
- understood the essence of developing and managing a project, as explained in Unit 8.
- revisited, if you have time, the work you did in Unit 1 on design and navigation.

Multimedia is one of the most exciting and immediately obvious uses of ICT in our modern world. As text, graphics, sound, animation and video converge in the use of PCs and other devices such as hubs for education, business applications and entertainment, multimedia applications have become indispensable. In Unit 10.1 we will examine the software currently available to produce quality multimedia applications, and the major principles and techniques underlying the production of multimedia. We will then introduce the demonstration project that you will be working on throughout Unit 10 as practice for completing your own project.

You have already studied multimedia applications quite extensively throughout Unit 1 while producing your e-book on The Information Age. In Unit 10 you will be expected to apply and extend the knowledge you gained there to manage a full multimedia project, first by defining the functional specification, then by designing, developing and testing your product.

ACTIVITY 1 Define multimedia ◀

Use your favourite search engine to find definitions of 'multimedia'. Adapt your favourite two or three to come up with an original definition of multimedia.

Early applications

Figure 10.1.1 Example of character-mapped screen from Ceefax weather

Interactive multimedia is not a new idea, though the term is. Back in the early 1980s microcomputers (now called PCs) mainly output text to black-and-white monitors. The monitors were often 'character-mapped' screens, so that the only graphics available looked something like the Ceefax screen shown in Figure 10.1.1. Yet one white 'blob' making its animated way across the screen could conjure up games of tennis, football, hockey and even simulate rockets being fired at space invaders. Even without graphics, interactive text adventure games abounded where users could issue commands like 'go north', 'pick up axe' and 'throw axe at dragon'; sometimes the computer might respond irritatingly with 'axe bounces off dragon'. Even with limited resources, then, an imaginative mind, good design and careful construction could produce an interactive product that people enjoyed using.

ACTIVITY 2 Investigate some multimedia products ◀

Visit the <u>Teachers Evaluating Educational Multimedia</u> website (see Fig. 10.1.2). Look at the tours of multimedia products. Choose three products for Key Stage 3 and/or Key Stage 4, and for each of these summarise what the purpose of the product is and what the evaluation says about it.

Continued on the next page

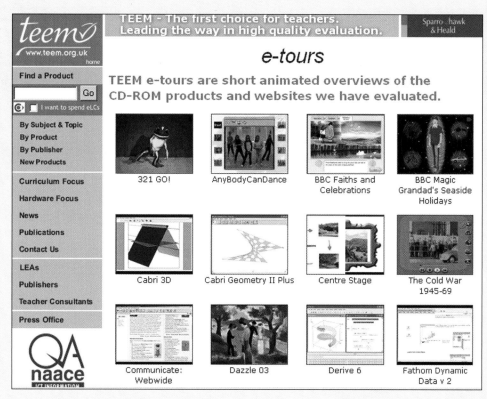

Figure 10.1.2 Teachers Evaluating Educational Multimedia website

Activity 3 Research multimedia on the internet ◀

Work in small groups to complete this activity. Choose one of the areas below to research and present to the rest of the class.

Task 1

Use the internet and other sources to research the variety of multimedia applications that are used in one of the following areas:
- education and training
- marketing, advertising and product promotion
- entertainment
- gaming
- publishing.

Create a small multimedia presentation using a web page development package (e.g. Macromedia Dreamweaver) to present your results. Each page should contain an introduction and links to relevant websites that demonstrate the various applications of multimedia.

Continued on the next page

The New York Philharmonic website

The BBC Radio website

Ben & Jerry's ice cream website

Task 2

Evaluate the multimedia applications found. Consider the purpose, audience, benefits, limitations, enhancements and alternatives for each.

Figure 10.1.3 Examples of some multimedia websites

ACTIVITY 4 Investigate multimedia and the ActiveBook

This book is published as both paper and electronic texts. Investigate the multimedia features of the ActiveBook. Comment on how they enhance the text.

Multimedia components

There is a vast array of applications that can be, and is, used to create multimedia. You do not have to use all of them in your project, but it is important to use each application you choose effectively. Creating multimedia requires the use of multiple applications, with which you will have need to some proficiency.

An important skill you will develop throughout Unit 10 is to select the correct tool for a particular job, then integrate its output with other outputs into a single coherent product. The format of the final product is also flexible. There are no absolute constraints imposed by the exam board, provided the product can be viewed in a fifth-generation browser.

An obvious application you might choose to use to develop your product would be a web development tool; presentation applications might also be used, provided they offer web output. In Unit 10 we will mainly use Macromedia Dreamweaver with Fireworks, Flash and Windows Movie Maker to explain concepts and techniques. As far as possible the unit is intended to demonstrate and build transferable skills, rather than simply show you how to use particular applications; it is therefore important that all activities are attempted using the multimedia software you have available, whatever that may be.

ACTIVITY 5 Identify the tools available for a multimedia project

Open this file, which contains Table 10.1.1. Match the software you have available with the tool you need for your multimedia project. (*Note*: You may be able to use the same software in more than one tool.)

Table 10.1.1

Basic tool	Software
Bitmap graphics editor	
Photo editor	
Vector graphics editor	
GIF animation	
Vector animation	
Sound recorder	
Sound editor	
Video editor	
Integration tool (HTML or presentation editor)	
Others	

The demonstration project

In order to develop further your skills in using multimedia, and in managing a multimedia project prior to undertaking the coursework for Unit 10, you will first build a small demonstration project using a combination of resources provided for you (that you can access from the ActiveBook) and assets you construct yourself, based on the activities in Units 10.2 and 10.3. As you work through these two sections, you should bear in mind the scenario that will be used for the demonstration project.

▶ The demonstration scenario

The local town council is keen to give local tourism a boost, but has limited funds to do this. It wants an interactive CD, called *Our Town*, to be available in local libraries, council offices and other public places, extolling the town's attractions in a way that would encourage visitors to stay longer and come back for more. The CD needs to be fun, using appropriate text, sound, photography, animation, video and colour. It should be easy to navigate, allowing the user to meander through the material, and include quizzes and puzzles. At this stage the council only wants a first draft of the product before it decides who the work will be commissioned from.

ACTIVITY 6 Set up a project folder ◀

Create a folder for the demonstration project and save all your resource files into it. Many of these are provided via the ActiveBook, and you will create others as you progress through the unit. Put the file you created in Activity 5 in the folder.

Conclusion ▶ ▶ ▶

Unit 10.1 has looked at current multimedia software and investigated the major tools, principles and techniques needed to create a multimedia product. Unit 10.2 will put these principles and techniques into practice, using the demonstration scenario to provide a focus.

In Unit 1 you covered creating graphics, screenshots and digital images, editing photographs, movies, animations and sound, and their common file formats. Unit 10.2 looks at the following fundamental principles and techniques for creating a multimedia product:

- the use of colour
- resizing, filtering and compression
- vector graphics, fonts and spacing
- stop-motion animation
- tweening
- motion tweening
- tweening using motion guides
- shape tweening
- creating and editing video clips
- creating and editing sound.

Images

▶ Colour

Colour is a fundamental building block of multimedia. Multimedia packages use a mix of a colour palette and a code number system that represents specific mixes of red, green and blue (RGB). To be consistent, you should choose a colour you want, and then note the colour's number so that you use the exact colour you want every time (of the 16 777 216 available in a 24-bit colour system).

Macromedia packages such as Dreamweaver, Flash and Fireworks automatically convert a selected colour to its RGB value in its colour palette (see Fig. 10.2.1), though RGB values can be seen if the System Color Picker option is selected from this palette. Packages like Microsoft FrontPage and Jasc Paint Shop Pro provide the hexadecimal value as well as the three separate decimal ones in the same window.

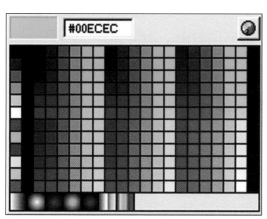

Figure 10.2.1 Flash colour palette

Figure 10.2.2 Fireworks' eyedropper tool

One means of 'copying' a colour from an existing image is to use the eyedropper tool. Many graphics packages (e.g. Fireworks, Adobe Photoshop, Paint Shop Pro) have this tool (see Fig. 10.2.2). The dropper is used to pick up the colour from an image pixel. It will usually then display the RGB pixel value in decimal or hexadecimal format and change the active colour in the palette.

Activity 1 Use the eyedropper tool ◀

1 Save this GIF file into your project folder. Then open it in your graphics package.
2 Use the dropper in your package to find the colour value of the letter 'T' in 'Our Town'.
3 Make sure you have worked out the decimal and hexadecimal values of the colour.

You can see a demonstration of this from the ActiveBook. *Note:* In Fireworks ensure you open the fill or line colour palette first.

▶ Contrast, brightness and hue

Sometimes when you have a photographic image it is either too light or dark, or perhaps not quite the right colour. For example, you might want to give a picture an old-fashioned sepia look. Making a picture lighter or darker is generally fairly straightforward, and graphics packages like Paint Shop Pro, Adobe Photoshop and Microsoft Office Picture Manager have options to change the contrast and brightness. *Tip:* If you want to brighten a dark image, increase both the brightness and contrast together.

Changing the hue lets you change one or more colours in an image. To change just one colour, use something like a hue map. If you want to shift all the colours then usually you can change the hue by shifting the colour wheel through a number of degrees. For example, if you change all the red pixels to green, then the green pixels turn to blue and the yellow pixels turn to cyan. In the next activity, you will change just one colour.

Activity 2 Change the hue ◀

1 Save this photo into your project folder as 'sax.jpg', then open it in your graphics package.
2 Using the hue map facility in your package, shift the red colour 120 degrees to green.
3 Compare your modified image with this file.

You can see a demonstration of this from the ActiveBook. *Note:* Different graphics packages have different interfaces for the same effect. In Fireworks you need to be in Bitmap Mode, then choose 'Filters', 'Adjust Color', 'Hue/Saturation'.

Finally as regards colours, it is worth being aware of web-safe colours. These are the 216 colours that are 'guaranteed' to appear the same in any web browser.

ACTIVITY 3 Use web-safe colours ◀

1 Use the internet to investigate web-safe colours (e.g. look at <u>Lynda.com</u>).
2 Use your graphics package to snap to web-safe colours (e.g. in Macromedia packages chose the 'Colour Palette' and select 'Snap to web safe colours').

Are web-safe colours as important now as they were in the past? If not, why not?

▶ Cropping, resizing, and filtering

It is not possible to cover all of the other features of graphics packages and the tools available for image manipulation. However, in the next activity, we will look at two of the more essential features together: resizing and filtering. Resizing is an important facility for ensuring that an image fits correctly into a multimedia page; the filtering facilities, if not overused, can add quite stunning effects to enhance an image.

ACTIVITY 4 Use cropping ◀

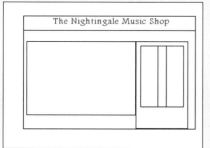
a   Mock up of a shop window

b   One possible outcome of Activity 4

Figure 10.2.3 Using advanced cropping techniques

1 Use the saved image 'sax.jpg', or save it again from this file. Open the image in your graphics package.
2 Cut out the saxophone using the magic-wand facility, or possibly using the freeform selection tool. (If you're not sure how to do this look at this demonstration from the ActiveBook.)
3 Save this image (see Fig. 10.2.3a) as 'musicshop.jpg'. Then open it in your graphics package. Paste the cropped version of the saxophone image onto it. (If the saxophone image is too large, resize it to a smaller size before pasting.)
4 Position the saxophone, repeat for a second saxophone (it might look something like Figure 10.2.3b) and then save the image as 'music_shop_with_saxes.jpg'.

> ### Aspect ratio
> The aspect ratio is the ratio between the horizontal width and vertical height of an image. By default the aspect ratio will be locked so that scaling will be applied equally to the horizontal and vertical sides of an image, thereby avoiding accidental distortion. Of course, interesting effects can be achieved by deliberately manipulating this ratio.

Activity 5 Resize and filter ◀

1 Find an image of a famous painting on the internet. In order to get a good quality image rather than a 'thumbnail', try to ensure that only the image is displayed on the screen. Save the image to your project folder.
2 Open the image in your chosen graphics package.
3 Look at the image's properties (e.g. 'Modify', 'Canvas', 'Image Size' in Fireworks; 'Image', 'Image Information' in Paint Shop Pro) and make a note of the image's dimensions (e.g. 750 × 318 pixels) and pixels per inch (e.g. 200).
4 Reduce the image size by resizing the height and width to 80% of the original (e.g. use the same menu as before in Fireworks; in Paint Shop Pro use 'Image', 'Resize'). Make sure that the aspect ratio is locked in order not to distort the image while scaling.
5 Now try adding different filter effects to it, such as 'Charcoal', 'Sepia' or 'Page Curl' in Paint Shop Pro (all available from the 'Effects' menu). Note that Fireworks' filters are available from the 'Filters' menu. Different graphics packages have different effects and it is often worth using a package simply to use one of its filter. Photoshop, for example, has a particularly extensive range of exciting filters; Flash 8 also has some interesting filter effects. Save the file, but under a new name.

▶ Compression

So far, we have been saving files without checking the compression ratio. Although compressing images is useful for reducing file sizes, it can result in lower quality. It is important, therefore, to get the right balance between small files, which can then be displayed by web browsers much more quickly than large files, and acceptable quality. Too much compression can lead to pixelated images. That is, the pixels can be seen by the viewer.

Activity 6 Compress images ◀

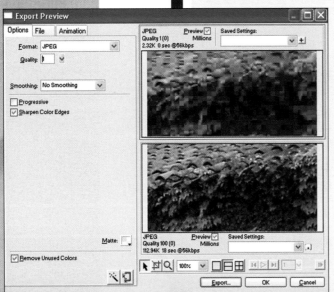

Figure 10.2.4 Compression quality

1 Open the original image you saved in the previous activity in your chosen graphics package.
2 Save or export the image under a different name, but with the highest compression factor possible. For example, in Fireworks, choose 'Export Preview', and select the doubled up view. In the bottom pane select 100% quality and in the top pane 1% quality (see Fig. 10.2.4).
3 The 1% image should appear very pixelated.
4 Compare it with the original.
5 Find the lowest compression that still gives acceptable quality for viewing on the screen (*Note*: This will often be quite low if used with a photograph, as these are often optimised for high resolution printers.)

Vector and bitmap graphics

In a **bitmap** image, also known as a **raster** image, the image is made up of individual picture elements (**pixels**) which form the individual dots that appear on the screen or other output device. Thus, the quality of a bit-mapped image is determined by the number of pixels it uses, that is, its **resolution**. Digital cameras, for example, take pictures in bitmap formats (e.g. jpg). **Vector graphic** images are made up of geometric objects, such as circles and curves, along with colour information. The mathematical formulae that draw these objects are stored in the image file itself, which means that the image can be scaled to different sizes without a reduction in quality. Vectors are therefore usually much lower in file size than bitmaps. Graphics packages such as Fireworks allow you to use vectors for text, lines and shapes alongside bitmap graphics, but it is still important to understand the difference between them, since their behaviour will be different under different conditions.

ACTIVITY 7 Compare bitmaps and vectors ◀

a   Original

b   Vector file with crisp text and line

c   Bitmap version with muddy text

Figure 10.2.5 Vector and bitmap graphics

Continued on the next page

1. Save this file to your project folder, then open it in Flash (a true vector editing package).
2. Enlarge the image to double its current size to see the effect of vector editing – to do this press 'CTRL + Y' (see Fig, 10.2.5b).
3. This is the same file saved as a bitmap. Save it to your project folder then open it using a painting application. Scale it to 200% (see Fig. 10.2.5c) and compare the two.

Activity 8 Use fonts in vector drawing

Figure 10.2.6 Composition

Create the drawing shown in Figure 10.2.6 in your vector drawing package (e.g. Flash). Note how in a vector drawing you can use shapes to line up elements as they can later be moved or deleted. The font used is Bell at different sizes and different character spacings. Fonts themselves can be used to create interesting graphic effects. Varying the character spacing means that the ascenders and descenders can be put into gaps rather than obscuring another word. The graphic balls use the gradient fill that is part of the Flash palette. Try changing the colours, the spacing, the fonts and so on to alter the composition. Note that the overall composition can be changed quite radically by quite small changes in the different elements. Compare this with what can be achieved with a conventional bitmap graphics package.

Animation

Animation refers to the ability to simulate movement by displaying a sequence of images in successive frames. In each frame the positioning of an object or objects is altered slightly, so that as each frame is looked at in turn movement seems to occur. When you look at a film in the cinema you are looking at 24 frames/second animation. To distinguish between video and animation, however, we tend to think of animation as consisting of moving physical objects (**stop motion** or **stop-frame animation**), moving clay figures (**claymation**), cartoons (**animated drawings**), **animated vector graphics** or some combination of these. Most graphics packages (including Fireworks) allow us to create and/ or edit animations, and there are free packages available (e.g. Microsoft Gif Animator). Vector animation packages are also widely available (including Macromedia Flash and its many emulators).

More about animation

There are many websites about animation:
- Wikipedia
- Museum of Unnatural Mystery
- Stop Motion Pro
- The Virtual Art Room
- The Art of Stop-Motion Animation.

Activity 9 Use stop-motion animation

By moving from one picture to the other very quickly you can simulate movement, that is, the wooden man falling over and climbing up again.

Watch this demonstration from the ActiveBook showing how to create a stop-frame animation in Fireworks. Now watch this demonstration showing how to create a stop-frame animation in Flash.

Continued on the next page

1 Save this zip file to your project folder. It contains 16 images of a wooden man (see Fig. 10.2.7) in slightly different poses. Use these 16 GIF files to create an animation using your GIF animation package.
2 Save the animation as 'woodman.gif' and compare it with the animation you can view from the ActiveBook.
3 Test that the animation runs with your browser. You can usually do this with your web browser without needing to write any html. Use the right button on your mouse and click on the GIF file in Windows Explorer. Select the 'Open With' option, and then choose your browser.

Figure 10.2.7 First scene of wooden-man animation

Activity 10 Create your own stop-motion animation

1 In a group of three or four, brainstorm ideas for an animation for *Our Town*. Here are some seed ideas: Monopoly, Lego, clay shoppers, model cars, animated brochure, zoom in from a distance ...
2 Create a project (sub) plan for assembling resources, shooting, editing and post-production.

Activity 11 Create a simple cartoon animation

1 In a group of three or four brainstorm an idea for a simple cartoon mascot for *Our Town*.
2 Sketch an initial drawing then develop it into a fully-fledged illustration for animation.
3 Insert new frames by duplicating the initial frame and making a small change.

When you have 10 frames or so, save and test your animation.

Tips

1 If you are not good at drawing base your drawing on an existing image.
2 If you are not confident, to start off with you could take either the goose image or the goose animation from the ActiveBook and refine it (see Fig. 10.2.8).
3 Try adding little dashes of colour to a monochrome mascot.

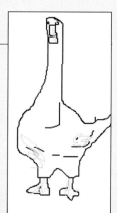 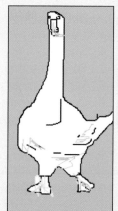

Goose image   Goose animation

Figure 10.2.8 cartoons of goose

Tips for stop-motion photography for multimedia

- Have a theme, story, twist or something to say.
- Plan carefully before you start; preferably using storyboards for key frames.
- Set your camera to a low resolution such as 640 × 480. A higher resolution is not needed, nor indeed useful, for PC multimedia projects.
- Use a tripod! It is essential that the camera does not move between shots in the same scene, or the animation will seem jerky.
- Consider making a background for your scene. It could either be one colour or a detailed scene. Either will be better than a mixed and out-of-scale moving background.
- It is possible to use supports for figures and edit them out using the art tools, but minimise their use to avoid masses of detailed editing.
- Keep it short.

ACTIVITY 12 Create a time-lapse animation

Take multiple shots of your town at different times of the day. Combine them using your animation package to represent your town.

▶ Tweening

Tweening is an animation tool that places appropriate intermediate frames between two key frames. It is a technique widely used in TV, advertising and other motion presentations. It can be used to animate a transition between one scene and another or, alternatively, to animate objects (or symbols or 'sprites', as they are commonly known) without having to tediously capture each individual frame.

ACTIVITY 13 Animate symbols in Fireworks

Look at demonstration showing how to create a transparent goose from the goose animation in Activity 12 using Fireworks. Then look at this demonstration to see how to create an animated goose walk using Fireworks.

Now look at this animation to view the finished effect (see Fig. 10.2.9).

Figure 10.2.9 Still from the goose walk animation

1   Save this file to your project folder. Then open it in Fireworks.
2   Use the export wizard to create a GIF with a transparent background (selecting blue as the matte colour, the transparent part of the image).
3   Save it as 'transparentgoose.gif'.
4   Save this file to your project folder. Then open it in Fireworks.
5   Resize the image to 400 pixels width.
6   Set the image to be copied across all frames.
7   Open the transparent goose and copy and paste it onto the restaurant.
8   Drag it to resize it to an appropriate size and move it just to the right of the door.
9   With just the goose selected, choose 'Modify', 'Animation', 'Animate Selection'.
10 Choose five frames (or more). Allow Fireworks to add frames.
11 Drag the line to follow the path.
12 Export it as an animated GIF.
13 Export it as an SWF (Flash) file.

Keyframes

Keyframes are the building blocks of animations and of tweening. In Flash, in particular, a Keyframe is in effect a control point in an animation. They are the points at which user-defined changes occur. In between Keyframes, shapes can be changed or objects moved using tweening techniques, but these are controlled by Flash itself and should not be edited by the user.

ACTIVITY 14 Use motion tweening in Flash ◀

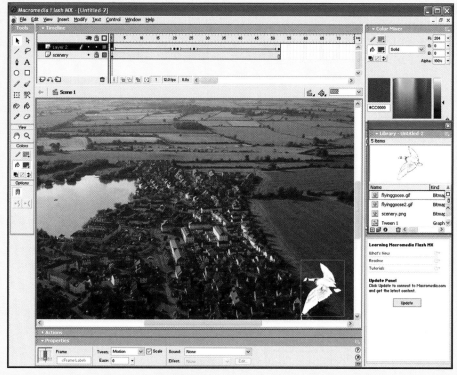

Figure 10.2.10 Flash-tweened animation

Look at this demonstration from the ActiveBook to see tweening in operation.
  Now look at the finished animation.

1 Save these images into your project folder as 'scenery.jpg' and 'flyinggoose.gif'.
2 Open a new Flash Movie sized 550 × 400 pixels.
3 Import the background photo and the flying goose image into the library. Add the background photo to the first layer, insert 50 frames and lock the layer to act as backdrop scenery.
4 Insert a new layer.
5 Add the flying goose image to the bottom right and convert it to a symbol called 'goose' (see Fig. 10.2.10).
6 Add a Keyframe at the 20th frame.
7 Highlighting the two Keyframes, select 'Insert', 'Motion', 'Tween'. This will add a path.
8 Now move the symbol to the end point at the top left.
9 Look at the intermediate frames to see how the program has tweened the motion between the two Keyframes.
10 Insert a Keyframe at frame 21.
11 Transform the symbol by flipping it horizontally.
12 Insert a Keyframe at frame 50.
13 Highlight the Keyframes at 21 and 50 and create a motion tween.
14 Move the goose near to the bottom left to make it fly to this point.
15 Test the movie.
16 Save it as goose.fla.
17 Export it as a Flash movie 'goose.swf 'and test it in your browser.
18 The goose should now be flying over and around 'Our Town'.

Layers

Layers are an essential element of virtually all vector and mixed-mode graphics packages. In Flash they are particularly important. Each new effect (Motion Tween, Shape Tween, Interaction etc.) should be created in its own layer. Each layer is stacked so that layers on top in the timeline window are shown on top in the presentation.

Locking layers

An extremely important technique in managing layers is to lock layers using the padlock tool while you are not working on them. This ensures that you only edit the layer you mean to. This is particularly important when working with background images that will otherwise be selected unintentionally virtually every time you attempt to select a higher level object.

How to stop Flash movies looping

By default Flash movies will loop. To run a movie through a single time rather than looping one of two techniques should be used:
1 For movies embedded in HTML set the 'HTML Publish' settings by unchecking the 'Loop Checkbox'.
2 For all movies, add the Actionscript action 'stop();' to a Keyframe at the very end of the movie (ideally on a separate actions layer).

ACTIVITY 15 Create more *Our Town* animations

1 In a small group brainstorm a number of tweened animations for the *Our Town* presentation.
2 Create an image-based animation.
3 Create a text-based animation.

ACTIVITY 16 Use motion guide and shape animation

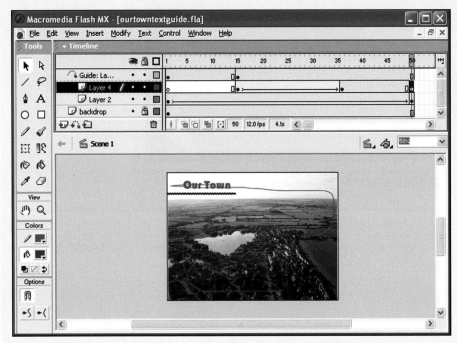

Figure 10.2.11 Flash motion tweening with guide

Look at these demonstrations from the ActiveBook of animation using the motion guide and animation using shape tweening.

Watch the finished Flash movies to see the type of effects you are going to create:

- animated text
- animated shape.

Creating the text animation

1 Create two layers as before with a 50-frame backdrop (using this image) and an animation layer.
2 Write the text 'Our Town' in the font you require onto the animation layer and convert it to a symbol.
3 Add a Keyframe at frame 50.
4 Put the frame pointer at the first Keyframe and open the Properties window.
5 Set Motion Tweening and Orient to 'Path'.

Continued on the next page

6   Close the Properties window.
7   With the animation layer highlighted select 'Insert', 'Motion Guide'.
8   Choose the pencil and draw a path.
9   Select the first Keyframe and drag the symbol until it snaps to the start of the line.
10 Select the last Keyframe and drag the symbol until it snaps to the end of the line.
11 Test it, save it and export it as a movie.

Creating the shape animation

1   Now add a new layer for shape animation.
2   Insert a Keyframe at the end.
3   Highlight the Keyframe at the start.
4   Draw a short line.
5   Select 'Properties' and choose 'Shape Animation'.
6   Highlight the final frame and extend the line to the intended final length.

ACTIVITY 17 Use other animation techiniques ◀

Open at this spreadsheet from the ActiveBook. It uses VBA to move a button shape around the Excel Window and play a couple of sound files when the button hits the edges.

> **Security settings**
>
> Your computer's security settings may prevent you from using this spreadsheet. To adjust these see the help section, or you may need help from a network administrator.

Video

Video can play an important part in a multimedia production. Usually for this type of production it is better to restrict the output to a few segments of carefully edited and focused video, rather than a single long piece. This has two major implications. First, it is possible – and perhaps even preferable – to create all the video using a digital still camera with movie facility. It is also important that you know exactly what you are trying to shoot before you shoot it. If you are lucky you will then capture a short segment that is exactly what you want in video and audio terms. More likely though, you will still have to edit the video. Therefore, it is usually preferable to record audio separately, as well as in the video. This gives maximum flexibility when you are editing.

ACTIVITY 18 Create a short video clip using Windows Movie Maker ◀

From the ActiveBook you will be able to access a video about a cycling club which needs some editing. Save this video to your project folder so that you can edit it. The plan is to overlay a title on a section, capture Derek's segment between 'it's a very active club' and 'good cycling on road and off road', and then fade out. Compare the original clip in the saved file with the finished video here.

Continued on the next page

Flash video

The method we recommend for integrating video into your presentations is to splice your videos in your normal manner, but then to add the video to your Flash movie where titles, animation, credits and audio – even user interaction – can all be integrated in a controlled and synchronised manner on a frame-by-frame or tweened basis. The final output will also be a Flash movie, so there will be no issue over whether your computer has the right CODEC (compression and decompression algorithms) for viewing the output.

Figure 10.2.12 Video editing with Windows *Movie Maker*

1 Open your movie editing package and import the original clip from the resources.
2 Drag the movie onto the timeline (switch to Timeline View if you are in Storyboard View).
3 Play until just before Derek says 'It's a very active club' (i.e. just before 2.6 seconds).
4 Select 'Clip', 'Split'.
5 Move along until after he says 'active club' (just before 11 seconds) and split again.
6 Right click on the audio for the first segment and mute it.
7 Add a title sequence of your choice over the top of the first segment. (*Note*: This step is actually better achieved in Flash if you have access to it – see the margin.)
8 Delete the third segment.
9 Drag the Fade Out To Black effect onto the end segment.
10 Test it.
11 Save it as a movie file, as video for broadband (512 kbps), i.e. at 320 x 240 pixels.
12 It is now a more focused product with a total file size of less than 20% of the original.

Activity 19 Edit and test more videos

1 Save the three video clips here to your project folder. In a group of between three and six, view the videos showing:
 • a duckpond
 • someone talking about a local bookshop
 • someone talking about public transport.
2 Decide how they might be used in the final production of *Our Town* and how they might be improved by editing, adding audio, titles etc. The idea is to make them more focused and to make them consistent with each other.
3 Each person should choose one video and edit it to the group's specification.
4 Another person should test and evaluate the video.

ACTIVITY 20 Create further video sequences ◀

Decide on short video sequences that would further enhance the product. Shoot and edit them.

Sound

There was a brief introduction to sound and sound formats in Unit 1. For Unit 10, however, we need to go much further. For example, we need to know how to link sound with images or movie clips. Movie clips created with a digital camera or digital camcorder usually have audio included, but how do you associate sound with an image? In the following activity, we use Windows Movie Maker, although similar techniques can be used with Flash and other packages.

ACTIVITY 21 Link sound and image ◀

1 Save the files as:
 • 'music_shop_with_saxes.jpg'
 • 'softly.wav'
2 Open Windows Movie Maker and start a new project (menu option 'File', 'New Project'. Use the menu option 'File', 'Import into Collections' and import the saved files (see Fig. 10.2.13a).

a Movie Maker collection

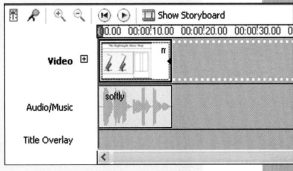

b Movie Maker timeline

Figure 10.2.13 Movie Maker imported files

3 Drag each clip onto the timeline at the bottom of the window (see Fig. 10.2.13b).
4 Make sure that each clip is the same length in the timeline and starts at the same place, as shown in Figure 10.2.13b, otherwise they will not be synchronised (e.g. the picture disappears before the sound finishes).
5 Use the menu option 'File', 'Save Movie File' to save the combined image and sound in WMV format as 'music_shop_with_sound'.
6 Movie Maker should now run this in Windows Media Explorer as a test, but it is worth testing it from Windows Explorer itself by double clicking on the file. Compare your file with this file you can open from the ActiveBook.

Using existing sounds as in Activity 21 is fine, but what if you want to use your own sounds? Fortunately, the Windows operating system has its own built-in Sound Recorder that can make WAV files. For MIDI files, specialist software such as Band-In-A-Box is needed. To keep things simple, the next activity looks at creating your own WAV files.

Activity 22 Create WAV files

1 Ensure that the microphone is set on. (This assumes that you have a multimedia computer with appropriate soundcard.) For this, you need to open the Volume Control. To do this click on the 'Start' button, then 'All Programs', 'Accessories', 'Entertainment', 'Volume Control'. From the 'Options' menu select 'Properties' then 'Recording' (see Fig. 10.2.14). Check that the microphone is on. Also check that the volume is high enough.

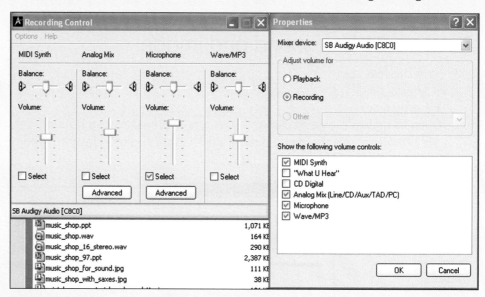

Figure 10.2.14 Recording properties

2 Now connect a microphone to the microphone socket on your soundcard (usually a specified jack input at the back of your computer). *Note*: it is possible that your computer already has a microphone attached (e.g. most modern laptops have built-in microphones).
3 Open the Sound Recorder software, available from the same 'Accessories', 'Entertainment' list as the 'Volume Control'.

Figure 10.2.15 Sound recorder

4 Click on the red record button (see Fig. 10.2.15) and start speaking into the microphone (e.g. 'This is a nice looking music shop. I wonder how much the saxophones cost?'). The displayed green wave line should fluctuate with your voice. Stop the recording when you have finished and save the recording as a WAV file.

Continued on the next page

5   Test that the WAV file has been saved properly by double clicking on the file name in Windows Explorer. It should play back in Windows Media Player (or another associated media player).

6   As an additional exercise you change the quality of the recording in your sound recorder software. Do this by selecting 'File', 'Properties', then clicking the 'Convert Now' button (see Fig. 10.2.16). From the Sound Selection list displayed (see Fig. 10.2.17) select a high-quality option, for example 16 bit rather than 8, and then record at this setting.

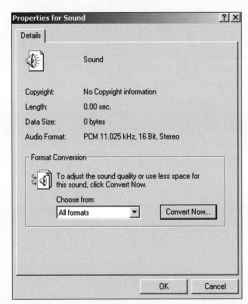

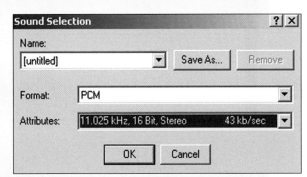

Figure 10.2.16 Properties for Sound window   Figure 10.2.17 Sound Selection window

7   Compare the different qualities when played back in Windows Media Player. Note the different file sizes. For example, compare the following files:
    • 16 bit WAV file
    • 8 bit WAV file
    • MIDI file

by saving them and comparing their sizes (in Media Player, go for 'File', 'Save Media As'). The 16 bit WAV file uses more bytes than the 8 bit WAV file. The MIDI file only uses only 2 kbytes – a much smaller file. MIDI files, however, do not include actual sounds, but information on how to make these sounds.

There is a good chance we will want to edit a sound file once it has been saved; for example, cutting out pauses or coughs at the beginning of the recording. Although this can be achieved using the sound recorder, more specialist software is often better, particularly if it displays the sound in waveform (e.g. Audacity and GoldWave). Also, such software often provides many more audio effects. In Activity 23, it is important that you use such a program.

Sound compression

In their purest form, audio files can be extremely large, and therefore very slow for downloading and streaming. Just as compression techniques have been developed for images (e.g. JPG files), so compression techniques have been developed for audio. File size is reduced without losing too much in the way of quality. A number of different formats exist, such as MP3, WMA and RA (real audio). Each has its own set of *compressor-de*compressor (CODEC) algorithms for compressing and then decompressing the audio.

ACTIVITY 23 Edit sound

1 Save this file to your project folder and name it 'musicshop.wav'. Then open it in a suitable audio software package and display its waveform (see Fig.10.2.18).

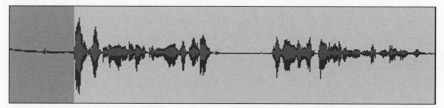

Figure 10.2.18 Waveform

2 Use your package's editing tools to select the opening part of the file where there is no sound (the dark grey area in Figure 10.2.18).
3 Use the appropriate menu option (e.g. 'Edit', 'Cut') to remove this area.
4 Play back the sound to check that it is correct and then save it under a new name.
5 As additional activities, try the package's reverse effect and fade-in effect, if these are available. (*Note:* you will normally need to select the area of the waveform that you want to apply the effect to.)

Music editing

Music in multimedia presentations will vary enormously. It is possible to use music created by others in MP3, midi or other forms – with permission. If you are at all musical you could record your music onto a minidisk, a tape player, a hard disk mixer or even straight onto your computer. Many schools and colleges have a range of music hardware and software, including keyboards and other instruments and sequencers (see Fig. 10.2.19), which will help in music production. Try to make use of this to enrich your final production. Even if you are not musical you could create a simple sound effect, but if you are you could create a score.

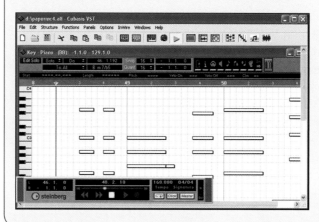

Figure 10.2.19 Editing midi and audio using the Cubasis sequencer

Activity 24 Brainstorm sounds ◀

1 In a group of three or four create a mind map of where sounds might enhance the presentation (e.g. the introduction) and where they are absolutely required (e.g. with a 'talking heads' video).
2 Ensure you consider the following in your deliberations:

score	theme music
interviews	voiceover
commentary	pre-recorded music
sound effects	video.

Activity 25 Choose sounds for your *Our Town* presentation ◀

In a small group:
1 Save this zip file to your project folder. Extract the audio files it contains and examine them.
2 Decide which sounds are appropriate to your presentation 'as is', and which need to be edited to fit.
3 Edit and integrate the sounds as necessary.

Activity 26 Create sounds for your *Our Town* presentation ◀

In a small group:
1 Decide what sounds you still need to create.
2 Create, edit and integrate these sounds as necessary.

Conclusion ▶ ▶ ▶

In Unit 10.2 we have explored a number of the principles and techniques behind multimedia production. Inevitably this is just skimming the surface of what can be achieved by a skilful producer. There are so many separate skills to learn that it can appear daunting, but it should also be fun. This is a creative and interesting area that you can throw yourself into. The real skill is, as usual, in the concept and the design. Unit 10.3 looks briefly at how all of these separate techniques and principles can be put together to make a unified presentation.

10.3 Multimedia integration and production

Authoring tools

We recommend that an authoring tool based around web page development is used to provide the framework for the production, and that individual elements are integrated within Flash wherever sensible, to provide the close control and synchronization that this tool allows.

In Unit 10.3 we consider how the various elements of the multimedia production (the colour, text, images, animations, sound and video) can be integrated to create a finished multimedia product, and how interactive elements can be used to add extra interest to the production by examining in turn:

- integrating sound
- integrating video
- masking elements
- overlaying animation and video
- integrating animation
- interactive controls
- interactivity
- creating buttons in Dreamweaver
- creating navigation buttons in Flash
- creating a self-running presentation in Flash and Dreamweaver.

Integrating sound, video and animation with text and images

Figure 10.3.1 Adding sound

In general the optimal place to integrate sound is directly into your Flash presentation (see Fig. 10.3.1). This is normally a three-step process. Firstly, import the sounds you want into the library. Secondly, create Keyframes on a layer you create for sounds. Finally, with the Keyframe selected, add the sound using the Sound drop down. To include background music and narration simply use two layers.

ACTIVITY 1 Synchronise sounds ◀

1 Watch this demonstration from the ActiveBook showing how to add sound.
2 Save this file to your project folder. Then create a backdrop similar to that in Figure 10.3.1 and add background music to it (e.g. this piano music).
3 Save the Flash file and publish.

Adding video occurs via almost exactly the same process as for sounds. Import the video to the library; add it to the scene in its own layer; if necessary expand the timeline on the other layers to match the video. Of course, it is possible to do a great deal more than this with video. Using different layers you can synchronise an animation with your video. In Figure 10.3.2 we have used the simpler technique of masking part of the video.

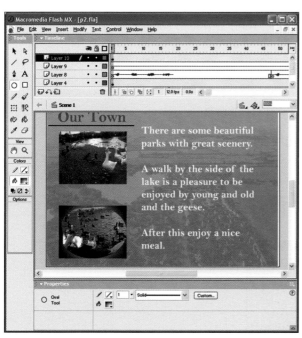

Figure 10.3.2 Adding video

ACTIVITY 2 Add and mask video ◀

1 Watch this demonstration from the ActiveBook that shows how to add and mask a video.
2 Save this file to your project folder. Then open it in Flash and apply a filter to it to reduce the contrast, as in Figure 10.3.2.
3 Add text and images as appropriate in separate layers.

Continued on the next page

Synchronising sounds

'Event Sync' simply causes a sound event to be played until complete from the Keyframe. 'Start' is the same, but prevents sound repeating over the top of itself (in a movie loop). Either of these should be used routinely. 'Stop' stops the specified sound at the Keyframe. 'Stream' synchronises with the timeline very precisely. It should only be used when synchronising sound, for example, to the moving lips of a cartoon character.

Flash-embedded video

It is useful to embed your videos in Flash when deploying in mixed environments, as Flash-enabled websites will be able to view your creation more simply than if you use a mix of AVI, WMV and MOV formats.

4 Save these files into your project folder as:
   - 'duckpond.avi'
   - 'duck.wav'
   - 'piano.wav'

5 Import the files into the library and add each one to a new layer in the scene.
6 Draw a solid rectangle over the video.
7 Draw a solid oval in the same style over the rectangle to expose the mask.
8 Test, save the Flash file and publish.

Activity 3 Combine animation and video ◀

1 Save this file to your project folder and name it 'publictransport.avi'.
2 In a small group, design a short movie combining the video with an overlaid animation, adding background music and a voiceover.
3 Save it as 'p.6' and publish the SWF with an HTML file.

Normally GIF animations would be added to web pages as normal GIF images. It is also possible to add them to a Flash presentation if needed (e.g. if importing as separate frames there would be some technical issues). The optimal method is to add the animation to the library; then add it to the scene and convert it to a movie clip symbol. It can then be treated as any other symbol. This same method can also be applied to Flash animations (SWF files) and video clips.

Activity 4 Add an animation ◀

1 Create the text and background as shown in Figure 10.3.3.
2 Save this file into your project folder as 'goosewalking.gif' and import it into the library.
3 Place and position it on the scene. Convert it to a movie clip symbol.
4 Test, save the Flash file and publish.

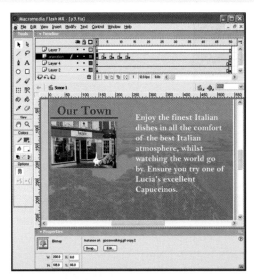

Figure 10.3.3 Adding GIF animation

Publishing files

Publishing a Flash movie creates an SWF movie file and the HTML necessary to run it. If you are running the whole presentation as linked Flash files then this is all that is required. If you are using the Flash movie as one element in a larger HTML presentation (e.g. a Dreamweaver web page) then you can copy the code required to embed and play the movie by the method you require from the published HTML file. The only caveat is to ensure that the settings are correct for the output you require using the Publish Settings dialogue (see Fig. 10.3.4). Publish Settings determines how the Flash will be played in an HTML page. The settings determine, for example, the size of the output, the quality of the output (how much compression Flash will apply), and crucially whether the movie should loop or play only once.

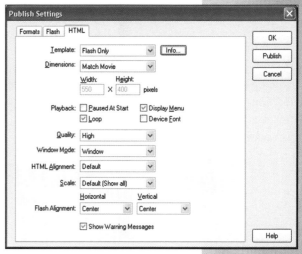

Figure 10.3.4 Publish settings

Interactivity

ACTIVITY 5 Add interactivity to your presentation

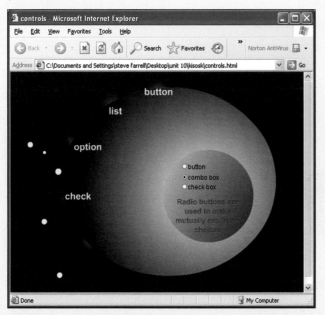

Figure 10.3.5 Examples of controls for interaction

Open this web page (see Fig. 10.3.5) in the ActiveBook to view what each control is in a short multimedia presentation.

Embed and standards

Virtually all multimedia clips can be linked to a web page using standard HTML link <a> tags or embedded in a web page using the <embed> tag. Embed is not, however, a standard HTML tag and thus cannot be guaranteed to be future-proof. There is not a cross-browser standard that works reliably; therefore we recommend it as the best solution for the moment. Review these websites to see how it works:

- W3C Website
- Netscape
- World-Voices
- Idocs.

ACTIVITY 6 Identify the elements – interactivity quiz ◀

Open this interactivity web page from the ActiveBook and try the quiz. Remember to look at the source code for each page. Much of it was automatically generated in Dreamweaver.

ACTIVITY 7 Create a quiz ◀

In a small group brainstorm quizzes that would be useful in the *Our Town* presentation. Choose the best one and create it using Dreamweaver or Flash.

ACTIVITY 8 Discover more elements ◀

Open this interactivity web page from the ActiveBook and look at the additional interactive methods. Remember to look at the source code for the additional interactive methods page.

ACTIVITY 9 Identify control types ◀

Figure 10.3.6 *Our Town* introduction menu

1 Look at the *Our Town* demonstration website (see Fig. 10.3.6). The opening page has all the controls necessary to navigate to each page created as part of the site template in Dreamweaver.

2 Identify the same eight menu items on the Flash presentation, shown in Figure 10.3.6. Note how almost any element of a presentation can be turned into a navigation element.

Compare the navigation elements of this presentation with the controls presentation. The navigation 'buttons' can be in any form that you are capable of drawing.

ACTIVITY 10 Create a button to navigate a website in Flash

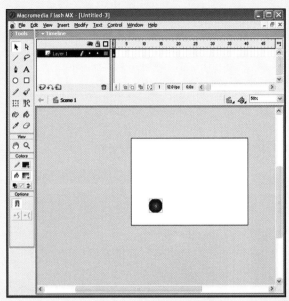

1 Draw any image (or text) and convert it to a symbol of type button

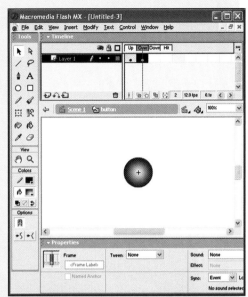

2 Edit. Insert Keyframe for rollover state. Change the image in some way.

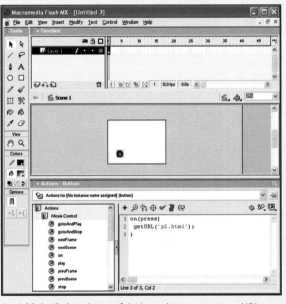

3 Add the little snippet of Actionscript to get a new URL when the button is pressed.

Figure 10.3.7 Create a button to navigate to a new web page

1 Watch the demonstration from the ActiveBook showing how to create a button.

2 Create a button to navigate to a page in a website (see Fig. 10.3.7, steps 1 and 2).

3 Add the following code snippet to the button (see Fig. 10.3.7, step 3):

```
on (press){
   getURL('pagename.html');
}
```

4 Save, publish and test.

ACTIVITY 11 Create interactive text in Flash ◀

1 Watch the demonstration from the ActiveBook showing how to create interactive text
2 Create a button to navigate to a page in a website.
3 Save, publish and test.

Note: Activities 10 and 11 together give you almost limitless possibilities for creating navigation in your multimedia presentations.

ACTIVITY 12 Auto-run kiosk presentation ◀

p1.html

p2.html

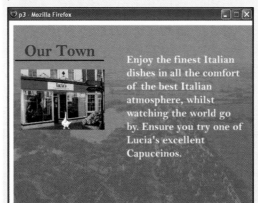
p3.html

p4.html

p5.html

Figure 10.3.8 Kiosk auto-running website presentation

Continued on the next page

1 View this kiosk website (see Fig. 10.3.8) from the ActiveBook to see how it runs round a set of slides in sequence and then starts again. Look at the source code of the index page to see how it is created (it can be adapted for all such presentations).
2 Watch this demonstration from the ActiveBook to see how the automatic change of page is achieved using the same simple scripting on a Keyframe (getURL("p2.html")) as you previously added to a button event.
3 Save this zip file and extract the kiosk website and the Flash file for page 5. Open 'p5.fla' in Flash and make the last keyframe jump to 'p6.html'. Save the file and export the SWF and the HTML file into the kiosk folder. Open the 'p6.fla' you created in Activity 3 and make the last keyframe jump to 'p1.html', then save the SWF and the HTML pages to the folder.

Conclusion ▶ ▶ ▶

In Unit 10.3 you have seen how to integrate all the different elements of a multimedia production and add navigation components to create a coherent and navigable multimedia presentation. The last vital ingredient to add is imagination. To help feed this, watch adverts, introductions to TV programmes and films, short animations, product presentations and training presentations. Note down your favourite effects and how you think they have been achieved.

In Unit 10.4, we will look at the main stages involved in creating a professional multimedia product. These include:

- the functional specification
- the design
- prototyping, construction and testing
- documentation and distribution issues
- burning the CD.

Remember that our scenario is the *Our Town* CD project outlined in Unit 10.1.

Functional specification

A functional specification is always needed at the beginning of a software project. So what is it? It must describe what our finished multimedia product should do. We might think that the scenario set out in Unit 10.1 is an example of this. However if it is, then it is a poor one, though as an initial introductory overview it is not a bad start. To appreciate how limited it is as a specification do Activity 1 before proceeding any further. In practice, on large-scale projects functional specifications can run into hundreds of pages.

Activity 1 Develop a functional specification ◀

1 After re-reading the scenario, write a list of some of the additional detail we need from the local council before we can start constructing the multimedia CD. If we created the CD without any more feedback from the council what mistakes and false assumptions might we make?
2 If you have not listed at least 10 items, re-read the scenario and try again.

Here are just some of the questions we should be asking ourselves:

- Are we clear on who the target audience is? We know that visiting tourists are a large part of the audience, but is anyone else?
- What hardware will the interactive CD run on? Does it need to run on Apple and Linux operating systems as well as PCs?
- What input devices can be used? Touch screens or just keyboard and mouse?
- What drivers are available?
- How fast should the multimedia product work?
- What software can we use to create the product in? Is Microsoft PowerPoint acceptable, does the council want it in HTML or another format?
- What version numbers of these applications can we use?
- Will we be restricted to certain file formats?

- What are the main features of the town they want us to cover?
- Where do we get the material from?
- Are there any copyright issues?
- Are there particular council logos or colours that must be used?

The functional specification should answer these questions and contain screenshots and diagrams to clarify things further. It is important to keep in constant contact with the client; this means that as the project develops, so the functional specification grows. The more specific the criteria are the better your functional specification will be. For example:

- 'The presentation must be viewable at resolutions of 800×600 and 1024×768' is much better than 'The presentation must be viewable at different resolutions'.
- 'A large text version (body text>14 point) must be provided' is better than 'Accessibility must be taken into account'.

The more specific the criteria the more straight forward it will be for the developer and the client to judge and agree whether it has been a successful project.

We will assume that after further discussions with the council, the following points are added to the functional specification:

- As this is only a demonstration version, some, but not all, of the material will be provided by the council in appropriate file formats (e.g. DOC, JPG, GIF, MOV, AVI, WAV, MIDI).
- The navigation structure is to be determined by the council.
- Quizzes and puzzles are to be left to the imagination of the designer.
- The main colour scheme is to be provided by the council.
- Accessibility issues must be taken into account.
- There will be eight feature pages, covering accommodation, eating out, leisure, local scenery, local services, puzzles and quizzes, shopping and transport.
- At this stage, only one page is required for each feature.

ACTIVITY 2 Write the functional specification ◄

Given the previous questions and information, write a functional specification for the *Our Town* project, specifying more clearly and in more detail what it is that the council want and who it is for. You can use bullet points, but make sure that you have a separate heading for each topic, e.g. target audience, hardware requirements.

Note: you may not have all the detail for all these points (e.g. hardware) but it will clarify what information you still need to obtain.

Design

In Unit 1, we looked at how we could use storyboards and navigation design structures to create an e-book. We can use these same techniques with this project. We need to get the structure and navigation of our pages worked out from the outset, otherwise we will not produce a professional-looking CD that is properly integrated and works smoothly.

ACTIVITY 3 Create a navigation structure ◀

1 Create a navigation structure using appropriate software.

The council want the following pages on the CD:
- an opening Welcome page that displays the town logo and mascot ...
- ... this page should link to the main menu page
- the main menu page should be linked to the eight feature pages, in a 'complex navigation structure with added sequential links'.

With the exception of the opening page, therefore, each page is linked to every other page, and there is also a sequential link that links the eight feature pages in alphabetical order.

2 Make sure that each page is labelled in the diagram.

3 Print out the diagram and check that all the links shown should work in theory. *Note:* The diagram will be part of your design documentation.

▶ Consistency, layout and graphical design

Since we need to ensure that there is consistency in the layout and look of our pages, the next step is to design a template for a typical page. The template should only include features that need to appear on every page (though some multimedia authoring packages allow individual template features to be turned off for specific pages).

ACTIVITY 4 Design your page layout ◀

1 Using appropriate software (e.g. Word or a graphical design package), design and print out a typical page layout that would help a developer to create a template for the *Our Town* pages. The page should include written details on:
- the position and size of any logo, page title, navigation buttons (menu system), other possible controls, content etc.
- font sizes, style and colour for any text
- any background colours
- any borders.

Thought should be given to:
- where the viewer will first focus on the page
- the use of web-safe colours
- accessibility issues
- usability issues.

Note: This material will be part of your design documentation.

2 As an additional exercise, use the internet to investigate accessibility issues (e.g. Web Content Accessibility Guidelines) and usability (e.g. Usability News) *Note:* This material will be part of your design documentation.

> **Usability and accessibility**
>
> **Usability** is about how easily and intuitively people can use a website. A website is considered to be **accessible** if it can be used as effectively by people with disabilities as those without.

Prototyping, construction and testing

For the construction of the product we will use evolutionary prototyping; that is, the product is gradually developed and tested as we go along. This type of prototype is a model that helps us and the client envisage what the final product might look like. You must test *and log* each development stage thoroughly. and encourage client feedback to demonstrate the use of prototyping.

Therefore, before we start any construction, it is essential that we have worked out in some detail what it is we are going to test. For example:

- Navigation buttons: do they take us to the correct pages?
- Links: do they all work?
- Colour scheme: does it meet the council's requirements?
- Multimedia objects (e.g. movie clips, animation, photos): do they work as expected?
- Quizzes: do they give the right answers?
- Layout: is there consistency?
- Usability: do users find the product easy to use and is there any built-in help?

A common method for logging the results of these tests is to create **test data tables**. These should be set up as early as possible and not be left until after the project is completed. They should be used as the project develops. The next activity looks at setting up a test data table.

ACTIVITY 5 Produce test data tables ◀

1 Produce initial test tables for each of the areas previously identified that need testing. Each table should look something like Figure 10.4.1.

Date:

Tester name:

Test description:

Test no.	Test data	Expected results	Observed results	Comments
1				
2				

Figure 10.4.1 Typical test data table

A 'Test description' might be 'Outcome of pressing navigation buttons'. For test number 1, 'Test data' might be 'click on transport button', while 'Expected results' would be 'user taken to transport page'.

2 Make sure the 'Test data' and 'Expected results' columns are completed.
3 Print out the tables.

As tests are carried out on the completed parts of the project, the 'Observed results' column is filled in. It is good practice for someone other than the developer to undertake the tests. For example, for the current project it would be useful if someone else could undertake some of the tests on usability.

Now we have the test tables set up, we can start constructing the product.

ACTIVITY 6 Gather additional material

1 Save the zipped folder here to your project folder. It conatins back-up files for existing materials already provided for you to build the *Our Town* product. In this activity you will create the additional materials required.

Table 10.4.1 Material needed for Our Town product

Page title	Existing material	Material still required
Welcome		GIF or Flash animation for the town mascot (a teddy bear)
Accommodation		Information about bed and breakfasts or hotels
Eating out		Information about cafes, inns and restaurants
Leisure	Cycling club video clip Swimming baths picture	Information about arts and crafts activities, cinema, the football club and theatre
Local scenery	Canal photo Ducks pond videoclip Ducks in the park picture Ducks quacking sound clip Local scenery picture	
Local services		Information about the library, tourist information office and town hall
Puzzles and quizzes	Quiz	More puzzles and quizzes
Shopping	Italian delicatessen picture Local bookshop video Music shop (created by you in Activity 21, Unit 10.2)	
Transport	Bus picture Public transport clip Ted's Bike Hire	Car hire Taxis Trains

2 Table 10.4.1 lists the pages, existing assets (with one exception available from the zipped file) and details of materials still required. Complete this document and expand it to form the basis of your project plan in your design documentation.
3 Now create the components you need to complete the project.

Now that we have clarified the design and collected enough multimedia material we can start on the first prototype.

ACTIVITY 7 Construct the first prototype

Although in this activity Macromedia Dreamweaver is the application referred to when creating the prototype, you may use the multimedia authoring package of your choice. Save and extract this zip file from the ActiveBook. It contains the beginnings of a solution to this activity.

1 Create the template that will be used as the basis for all the pages. An example is given in Figure 10.4.2, but yours can be different (and, hopefully, better). *Note*: the council have specified four colours in RGB format: a red of RGB(204, 0, 0), a grey of RGB(153,153,153), a background grey of RGB(192,192,192) and pure white: RGB(255,255,255).

Which of these is not a web-safe colour?

Figure 10.4.2 Template page

2 From this template create the eight features pages, plus main menu and opening page. You may wish to leave out the multimedia components until all pages have been set up.
3 Make sure that all the navigation buttons etc. are in place.
4 Add the multimedia components.
5 Save the logo from the ActiveBook as 'ourtownlogo.gif' and add it to the opening page. The council has not provided any text for each page. Use your imagination and supply your own. Apart from the logo, the council prefers the Arial font.
6 Test that the prototype works and update your test log. If you can, ask someone else to undertake the testing and provide feedback for any evaluation.

Once the product is finished, we need to burn the product onto a CD, but first we must:
- complete our documentation
- decide what files we need on the CD to ensure that it runs properly.

Documentation for the CD

This should include:
- A printable (PDF format) *Getting started with... : User Guide*, with clear instructions on how to use the product, preferably with screenshots.
- A printable (PDF format) *Technical Guide* that enables an administrator to troubleshoot or add additional features where possible. The guide should include:
  - diagrams of the navigation structure
  - details of the fonts, colours and layouts used
  - lists of all the multimedia objects used and any hyperlink paths to the linked files.

A *Readme* (.txt) file written in unformatted text (e.g. Windows Notepad) that would assist an administrator if the product was not working properly.

Distributing the product

Just because the product works on *your* computer it does not mean it will necessarily work on other computers. Have all your potential users got the right software to view the product? Will the CD autoplay? If the files are downloaded off the CD onto a hard disk, will all the files be in the right folders? Most multimedia presentation packages provide a 'Pack and Go' facility to cover some of these issues. This facility adds all supporting files and, often, a viewer for users without the application software.

▶ File association

Most of the multimedia objects should display and work fine, but remember that Windows uses **file association** to link filename extensions e.g. JPG, WAV, MOV to their associated application and **object linking and embedding (OLE)** to launch these associated applications. If the filename extension is not supported by OLE, then the object will not run. So make sure you have tested all the multimedia components in the authoring package thoroughly.

Burn the CD

Now you can burn the CD, with any appropriate 'Pack and Go' files, plus the documentation.

Final testing

As a final test, run the CD on a computer that does not have the authoring package. Try it with your monitor at different resolutions. Also, if possible, run it under a different operating system, such as an earlier version of Windows, and try it on a slow machine. In other words, undertake a proper **systems test** so that you know the product's limitations. Log the results.

Evaluation

Consider how well your final product fulfils its purpose; how suitable it is for its audience, what benefits it has, what limitations it still has; what one enhancement would improve it most and what alternative methods you might have used. Consider the same headings for your own performance and really try to focus on what will help you make a better product the next time.

Tackling the Unit 10 assessment

Having finished the trial assessment you will now be in a position to attempt the actual coursework. Clearly you will use many of the same techniques and tools, but the multimedia will all be sourced and/or created by you. Make sure that your eportfolio for this unit contains all the requirements set out in the Unit 10 specification's Assessment Evidence.

Conclusion ▶ ▶ ▶

- Ensure that your functional specification is clear and detailed before launching into any real development. Use screenshots for the functional spec. If you write in the present tense, then some of this writing can be used in other documentation (e.g. the user guide and technical guide).
- Spending time getting your core design right by planning it is not wasted time. It saves time in the long-run. Make sure you keep the different versions of your design as you update it and give each a different version number. Keep all your design documentation together.

- Prototyping is a very useful method for getting feedback from the client *and users*. Keep all your prototypes as proof that you have taken this approach, and make sure you log the feedback. A good way of getting feedback, which will also help with your evaluation, is to get a friend to test your prototype and make notes.
- Make sure you have drawn up test data tables early on. Test *everything* – even the user guide.
- Future proof your solution as much as possible. For example, can additional pages be added easily to the product, and would your technical documentation help a developer to achieve this?
- Finally, read the specification very carefully to ensure you meet all the requirements for the mark bands you are targeting.

Using Spreadsheet Software

Software

11.1 Introduction

The unit specifications

In Unit 3, you learnt the basics of using a spreadsheet. In Unit 11 you will learn how to create technically complex spreadsheets.

Although the rest of this unit refers to Microsoft Excel, there is no reason why the activities cannot be undertaken using another spreadsheet package. Most have similar functions and similar layouts. The main differences are likely to be in the steps required to produce charts. However, it should still be possible to create the same results, following relevant instructions in the package's user manual.

Covering the unit specifications

Here is a true story. Every month a company imported data from a text file into a spreadsheet. Statistics, tables and charts were automatically produced from the figures and were inserted into reports for senior management. One day an IT professional was asked to enhance the system. He noted that summary information on the worksheets stated that 65 536 rows of data had been imported. He thought this was a bit of a coincidence, as the spreadsheet had exactly 65 536 rows. On investigation, he discovered that the text file actually contained 80 000 rows of data. Nearly 15 000 rows had been lost by the import process and nobody had noticed. Decisions had been based on this false spreadsheet analysis for the previous five years.

Although this particular kind of error is fairly rare, it can be disastrous. In addition, there are many other kinds of errors which users can fail to spot. A common one is when new data is added at the top of a block of data and the SUM function does not automatically update. How can we ensure that this kind of error is not built into any solution we create?

The answer is to make sure that we take each stage of the development process equally seriously. Errors can be introduced, unintentionally, at every one of the development stages: functional specification, design, construction, testing and even documentation. It may seem odd that errors can occur at the testing stage itself, but having remedied an error after running a test, it is possible that the remedy itself creates further errors elsewhere. In any case, leaving *all* the testing to the test stage of development is a mistake. Errors that have arisen in the functional specification stage are much more costly to remove if they are not detected until later stages.

Ensure that you read all the following sections in this unit:
- 11.2 Functional specification
- 11.3 Design and prototyping
- 11.4 Construction and advanced techniques
- 11.5 Testing and documentation.

It may be tempting to go straight to Unit 11.4, but don't!

The final section, 11.6, provides useful advice on tackling the unit assessment.

Finally, to make the activities in Unit 11 realistic, we use the following scenario throughout. It is important that you read this scenario carefully.

The scenario

Tina has just been appointed Head of the Project Division of an international energy company. She is now responsible for five worldwide project teams that are investigating new sources of energy that can be utilised by the company. As well as long-term projects, each project team can run up to six smaller projects lasting up to a year. Tina wants to track the progress of these smaller projects in a more automated and systematic way. She knows that each team submits proposals for these projects in December, and provides estimates of monthly costs over the coming year. The teams also make a very rough end-of-year estimate of how much energy they think the project would generate. Tina is looking at ways of collecting all this initial data into a master spreadsheet, and then gathering further information, month by month, to measure each project's success. She is also hoping to use this information for additional statistical analysis: for example, to see whether renewable energy projects are more productive than non-renewable energy projects, and to see which teams are the most successful. Finally, her senior manager wishes to know how much income these projects are likely to generate if they were adopted on a permanent basis. She intends to use some 'what-if' analysis here.

Other scenarios

The previous scenario will enable us to cover much ground, but it is not possible to cover everything in one example. Although other uses of spreadsheets (e.g. forecasting) have already been covered in Unit 3, it is worth looking at a few additional examples, although do not worry too much about the techniques used; much will be covered in the rest of Unit 11:

- statistical examples
- break-even example (this also refers to cost–benefit analysis)
- simulation example.

Conclusion

We now have an idea of what the rest of Unit 11 will be covering and why we need to cover these areas. In addition, a scenario has been set out that provides a typical example of the kind of task that spreadsheets are used to tackle in industry. This scenario can be used to help to lay the foundations for undertaking the Unit Assessment.

Although functional specification, design and prototyping are dealt with separately in Units 11.2 and 11.3, they should be seen as interrelated. The **functional specification**, setting out what the client wants, may change after the client has seen the first **prototype** (that is, a model) of the solution. This in turn will mean the **design** needs updating. The result will be a much better solution for the client. It is important that, as updates occur, we not only make new versions of these documents and models, but we also archive the old ones as well, in case we need to go back to them. (This is also crucial for the assessment for this unit – see Unit 11.5.)

Functional specification

A functional specification is always needed at the beginning of a software project. Sometimes it may be referred to as a **requirements specification** or even just a **spec**. Which name is used is not that important; more important is an understanding of why we need one and whether we have one that is detailed enough.

So what is it? A functional specification should describe what our spreadsheet solution is supposed to do. We might think therefore that the scenario set out in Unit 11.1 is an example of such a specification. If so, then it is a poor one; though as an initial introductory overview it is not a bad start. To appreciate how limited it is as a specification, you should undertake Activity 1 before proceeding any further. In practice, on large-scale projects, functional specifications can run into hundreds of pages.

Activity 1 Write a functional specification

1 Re-read the scenario set out in Unit 11.1.
2 Write a list of some of the additional details we need to get from Tina before we can start constructing a spreadsheet solution. To help you, imagine building a solution with the limited knowledge we have, then handing it to Tina. What might Tina say we have left out, or misunderstood, or just got plain wrong?
3 If you have not listed at least 10 items, re-read the scenario.

Pivot tables

A pivot table provides a means of viewing data in a summarised way. More information on pivot tables is given in Unit 11.4.

The questions we would want to put to Tina could include the following:
- How many charts does she want, what type and what should the layout be?
- Are pivot tables required?
- Are any other reporting facilities required (e.g. a scenario manager)?
- Is each team to have its own workbook?
- Can the teams use a common spreadsheet template to store their data?
- Do the teams have access to a common shared drive or will the workbooks be emailed?

- How will the data be input by the teams?
- Does Tina want the teams to give a breakdown of the monthly costs (e.g. buildings, consumables, expenses, wages) rather than provide totals only?
- Will the teams' workbooks be storing financial data in a local currency (e.g. Japanese yen, Chinese renminbi or US dollars) or a common currency?
- If the financial data is in a local currency, does it need to be converted to a common currency (e.g. sterling)?
- What unit of measure will be used for the generated energy values? A common unit of measure? And who will write the formula to do this?
- Is any security (e.g. passwords) required?
- Which version of Excel will the spreadsheet be running on, and on which operating system?

Some of these questions may seem to have obvious answers, but we could easily be wrong in our assumptions. It is just possible, for example, that one team can only submit its data in delimited text file format and not via a workbook.

However, let us assume that after further discussions with Tina and users of the new system, we are able to write a fairly comprehensive version (1.0) of our specification. For the sake of brevity, we will only list a few of the highlights.

> ## Highlights from functional specification version 1.0

Introductory overview

Consists more or less of what is written in the scenario.

Outputs

'What-if' calculations

- By assigning an EU (energy unit) different monetary values, potential loss-making, revenue-generating and break-even projects can be identified.

Pivot tables

- Users can view totals and subtotals by pivoting the following variables: team name, project name, project type, actual values and estimates (see Fig. 11.2.1).

Charts

- Line chart of monthly actuals against estimates by team and by type (see Fig. 11.2.2).
- Column chart of surplus revenue by team and by type.

> ### Clients and users – drawing up a specification
>
> Tina is our main contact for drawing up the specification, but we must remember that the users of the proposed system include many people other than Tina: the project team members who will be inputting data, and Tina's assistants, who may actually end up running and administering the new system. It is important, if possible, that we get some early involvement from them. We could leave this to the design stage, but potential users may spot problems in the specification that Tina would miss.

Annual Actual EUs Generated - 2006

Team	Project Type HY	NR	RE	Grand Total
Team A	829,015	971,117	875,704	**2,675,836**
Team B	790,831	911,746	910,552	**2,613,129**
Team C	1,108,684	961,620	766,020	**2,836,324**
Team D	1,074,407	1,065,298	811,364	**2,951,069**
Team E	984,771	709,703	655,139	**2,349,613**
Grand Total	**4,787,708**	**4,619,484**	**4,018,779**	**13,425,971**

HY= Hybrid
NR = Non-Renewable
RE= Renewable

Figure 11.2.1 Example of required pivot table

Continued on the next page

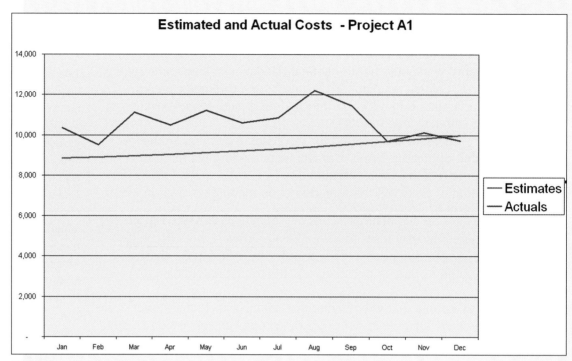

Figure 11.2.2 Example of required chart

Archiving

- All the previous year's workbooks must be archived.

Inputs and structure

Project team estimates

- One standard workbook, based on a common template, exists for each project team.
- This workbook consists of a summary sheet, showing the estimated monthly total costs for each project (in local currency), the annual total of these costs (in local currency) and an estimated total of the annual energy generated.
- The energy figure is expressed in a common energy unit measure (an EU) e.g. 1 500 000 EU.
- Converting energy sources to EUs is undertaken by the project teams prior to data entry, so this is *not* a requirement for the assignment.
- Data is entered directly into the worksheet cells (see Fig. 11.2.3).

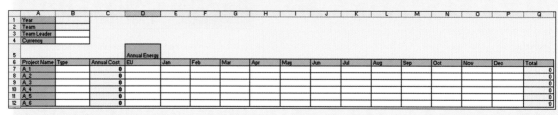

Figure 11.2.3 Project teams' estimate workbook

Continued on the next page

Project team progress

- One standard workbook, based on a common template, exists for each project team.
- This workbook contains a worksheet for each month, displaying the breakdown of actual costs by buildings, consumables (e.g. stationery), environment, equipment, expenses, rates (local taxes), wages, and actual EU output for each project.
- This workbook contains a summary sheet, showing the actual monthly total costs for each project, the annual total of these costs and the monthly and annual totals of energy generated.
- Data is entered directly into the worksheet cells (see Fig. 11.2.4).
- The summary sheet automatically sums the monthly values (see Fig. 11.2.5).

	A	B	C	D	E	F	G	H	I
1	Month	January							
2									
3	**Costs**								
4	Project Name	Buildings	Consumables	Environment	Equipment	Expenses	Rates	Wages	Total
5	A_1								0
6	A_2								0
7	A_3								0
8	A_4								0
9	A_5								0
10	A_6								0
11									
12									
13									
14	**Energy**								
15	Project Name	EU							
16	A_1								
17	A_2								
18	A_3								
19	A_4								
20	A_5								
21	A_6								
22									
23									

Instructions \ **Jan** / Feb / Mar / Apr / May / Jun / Jul / Aug / Sep / Oct / Nov / Dec / Summary /

Figure 11.2.4 Monthly sheet from the project teams' progress workbook

	A	B	C	D	E	F	G	H	I	J	K	L	M	N	O	P
1	Year	2006														
2	Team	A														
3	Team Leader	Janet Long														
4	Currency	Euro														
5			Monthly Costs													
6	Project Name	Annual Cost	Jan	Feb	Mar	Apr	May	Jun	Jul	Aug	Sep	Oct	Nov	Dec	Total	
7	A_1	0													0	
8	A_2	0													0	
9	A_3	0													0	
10	A_4	0													0	
11	A_5	0													0	
12	A_6	0													0	
13																
14																
15																
16			Monthly Energy													
17	Project Name	EU	Jan	Feb	Mar	Apr	May	Jun	Jul	Aug	Sep	Oct	Nov	Dec	Total	
18	A_1	0													0	
19	A_2	0													0	
20	A_3	0													0	
21	A_4	0													0	
22	A_5	0													0	
23	A_6	0													0	
24																

Jan / Feb / Mar / Apr / May / Jun / Jul / Aug / Sep / Oct / Nov / Dec \ **Summary** /

Figure 11.2.5 Summary sheet from the project teams' progress workbook

Continued on the next page

The workbooks also need to store the project type (e.g. renewable energy), the team leader name and the project team name.

Master workbook

- Stores raw summary sheet data from the project team's workbooks.
- Converts local currencies to common currency.
- Provides analysis, summaries, pivot tables, charts and 'what-if' analysis.

Storage

- The five estimate workbooks (one for each project team) and five progress workbooks are stored on a shared drive. The administrator of the new system puts them there. Appropriate members of each project team have access to this drive.
- The master workbook accesses these workbooks, but is not on a shared drive.

Security

- All workbook cells are locked, except where data is to be input.
- The master workbook is passworded.

Business rules

- The summary sheet on the master displays all the financial values in a common currency. The user is able to change the common currency.
- Values having zero decimal places are acceptable;
- Projects that are over their estimated total cost are flagged red, those under their estimate are flagged yellow and the rest are white.
- The percentages that determine what is an overestimate or an underestimate can be varied by the user.
- Project codes include the team name.

User interface

- Instructions are provided in each workbook on how to input the data and output data (if appropriate), and how to navigate the workbooks.
- Drop-down list boxes are used extensively to provide ease of data entry and data validation.

Notice that, after the 'Introductory overview', we started with 'Outputs'. This is because the whole purpose of the exercise is to get what Tina wants *out* of the system. We should be clear on what this is; using screenshots at this stage is very helpful. Once we know what we are trying to get out of the system we can start thinking about the inputs needed to get these results. Again, screenshots are very useful here.

ACTIVITY 2 Create workbook structure ◄

A functional specification is much clearer if it contains screenshots of what the user requires. Figures 11.2.3, 11.2.4 and 11.2.5 provide an idea of what Tina would like the project teams' estimate and progress workbooks to look like. (To some extent, this also gives us some idea of the diagrams we might use for the design of the solution.)

1 Create the two workbooks as shown in these figures. The estimate workbook has two worksheets, called 'Summary' and 'Instructions'. The margin box explains how you can do this efficiently.

2 Save the workbooks as 'estimate_template.xls' and 'progress_template.xls'.
   - In both workbooks, the white cells imply that users can enter data; other colours imply that the cells are locked.
   - In the 'estimate_template.xls' workbook, the zeroes in the 'Total' column suggest a SUM function formula is used; the zeroes in the 'Annual Cost' column are a copy of the 'Total' column, purely for ease of reading.

3 Produce a screenshot of each, ready for placing into a functional specification.

Compare the layout and structure of your workbooks with these sample workbooks:
   - the estimate workbook
   - the progress workbook.

Activity 2 should not be too time-consuming, particularly as neither workbook contains numeric data at this stage. But how do we generate data like that shown in Figures 11.2.1 and 11.2.2? In Figure 11.2.1, we need to enter at least 15 realistic looking numeric values and for the chart we need 12. Later on, when we design and prototype, we are going to need to generate even more values. Fortunately Excel has a very useful random function which is excellent for creating this 'dummy' data. We will use this function in Activity 3 and throughout much of the prototyping and design stage. As long as the figures are fairly realistic (and we can check this with Tina), we can also use these values as part of our testing process (see Unit 11.5).

ACTIVITY 3 Create representative data ◄

In this Activity we create the data and screenshot for Figure 11.2.1 – the 'Required pivot table'. (This is not an actual pivot table, only a mock up of one. A full explanation is given in Unit 11.4.)

1 Create a new workbook.

2 Enter all the text and colour as in Figure 11.2.1, but no numeric values.

3 In cell C6, where the first numeric value is required, type in the following formula:

   =INT(RAND()*600000) + 600000

Continued on the next page

Creating similar worksheets

Creating 12 monthly worksheets can be time-consuming if created individually. Try one of the these methods:

Method 1   In the progress workbook construct the January worksheet first; then use 'Edit', 'Move or Copy Sheet...' to copy this 11 times (you must check the 'Create a copy' box). Then rename the sheets and any appropriate cell labels.

Method 2   Create the 12 sheets, using 'Insert', 'Worksheet' from the menu. Select all 12 worksheets by holding down the shift key and clicking on the first worksheet name tab (e.g. 'Jan') and last worksheet name tab. (If you're not sure about how to do this watch this demonstration.) Any text entered in the first worksheet will now appear in all the others. That is, you have selected multiple worksheets. When you have completed the entries, click on any other worksheet to deselect this multiple selection.

 Screenshots

If you're not sure how to take and save a screenshot, watch this demonstration from the ActiveBook.

This uses the random function, RAND(), to generate the random value. Initially, it generates a random fractional value between 0 and 1 (e.g. 0.025 467 8). We then multiply this by 600 000 to get a random value between 0 and 600 000. We use the INT() function to convert it to a whole integer number (e.g. 121 055 instead of, say, 121 055.738 2). We add 600 000 because Tina thinks all projects should create at least 600 000 EUs.

4 Copy this formula across to the other two columns to the right, and down four rows. The values should vary.

5 Use the SUM function to get the grand totals for each row and column, e.g. =SUM(C6:E6).

Note: Every time you undertake a calculation, the random figures change. To stop this, highlight the range of values, use 'Edit', 'Copy' from the menu, then 'Edit', 'Paste Special', 'Values'. This overwrites the formulae.

6 Save the workbook.

7 Take the screenshot and paste into an appropriate application.

 Compare your prototype 'simulated' pivot table with this simulation.

Documentation

The reason for writing the functional specification in the present tense is so that it can be easily adapted for the design, technical and user guide documentation. So, instead of writing 'this workbook will contain a summary sheet' we write 'this workbook contains a summary sheet'.

Version numbers

Also, note that we have called the specification 'version 1.0'. As we make changes to the specification, we must save a different version to disk and archive the old one. A small change might make it version 1.1, but a significant change would make it 2.0.

Conclusion

Unit 11.2 has concentrated on showing how important it is to get the functional specification clearly stated right from the start. Failure to do so can lead to errors that can be very costly to remove later on. Unit 11.2 has also provided information on what should be included in such a specification and shown how spreadsheets themselves can be used to provide some of this material.

Design and prototyping

When it comes to design, there are many different methodologies. One of the most useful, and the one we will use, is a form of prototyping called **evolutionary delivery**.

Prototyping involves developing a **model** of how the final product will look to the user and how the user will navigate it. It involves getting feedback from the user/client and covers much of the area of **human–computer interaction**. A typical prototype would display the buttons to be used, any input forms to be used, typical input data, output data, onscreen help, required charts and worksheets. This should give the client an idea of how the finished product will look. Hardly any spreadsheet functions or formulae are required as, in theory at least, prototypes are only models and should eventually be thrown away. On the other hand, **evolutionary delivery**, although similar to prototyping, *will* include the functions or formulae. It is not a throwaway model but a gradual development of the solution. The client will get a chance to provide feedback, and the developer can move towards completing the job. We will use both methods.

Design

We have already created two workbooks from Activity 2 in Unit 11.2. Assuming that Tina is happy with the look of these, we now need to develop the functional specification into a more detailed design document on which we can build our evolutionary delivery. Tina has provided a lot of additional information, but there are still a number of design issues, including the following:

- What naming conventions do we use for the folder names and workbook names?
- Where do we store team name, team leader name and project type? In every workbook?
- Will each workbook open to an instructions worksheet?
- How many sheets will the master workbook have?
- What data type should the data be?
- What data validation do we need for data entry?
- How do we stop or remove the duplication of data?
- Will we need named ranges?
- How will the password be determined?
- What labels, headings and styles will we use on the worksheets, charts and pivot tables?
- How do we future-proof the solution? For example, will our solution work in two years' time? Will archiving previous year's workbooks cause all the external links to fail?

In the following sections we will look at the design issues relating to inputs, outputs, structure and processing.

Inputs and structure

Our functional specification has given us a good idea of what data is to be input and how it is to be input. It also covers where data is to be stored. However, from a design point of view we must ensure that this storage is logical, consistent and robust. Looking at just one of these issues, having a consistent naming convention for folders, workbooks and worksheets, it can all seem a bit over the top at this stage. Does it really matter? Surely we can change the names later? So, try Activity 1.

ACTIVITY 1 Name the parts ◀

Tina wants our solution up and running from next year. (*Note*: For the purpose of the examples below, we assume that 'this year' is 2007.)

1 Write down the names you want to call the project team estimates workbooks.
2 Write down the names you want to call the project team progress workbooks.
3 Write down the names of worksheets to be used.
4 Write down the names of the folders for each.

The two major considerations when naming objects are:
- Do we have a consistent style? (For example, everything in lower case, underscore symbol for all spaces)
- Is the name future proofed?

If you have chosen names like 'team_a_project_estimates_2007.xls' problems could occur next year when everything needs to be renamed to 2008. All the external links to filenames that appear in the master workbook would need to be updated accordingly. This could be a very costly process, and prone to error, so thinking this through early on is very important.

In addition, formulae could start to look a bit long with such lengthy names. Therefore, a name like 'a_est.xls' might be better. As long as we archive last year's versions to a different folder, we can use the same name every year.

For the purposes of our current project we will use the names 'a_est.xls', 'b_est.xls' etc. for the five estimate workbooks to be stored in a folder called 'team_est' (see Fig. 11.3.1). There will only be two worksheets in each, called 'Instructions' and 'Summary'. For the five progress workbooks we will use 'a_pro.xls', 'b_pro.xls' etc to be stored in a folder called 'team_pro' (see Fig. 11.3.2). The worksheets in these workbooks will be called 'Instructions', 'Jan', 'Feb' etc. and 'Summary'. That is, 14 worksheets in all.

ACTIVITY 2 Create the project teams' workbooks ◀

Create all ten workbooks (five estimate and five progress ones) and the two folders, as just described, using the templates from Activity 2 in Unit 11.2. The margin box explains how you can do this efficiently.

Naming conventions for files

Spaces in file names can cause a headache for Visual Basic for Applications programmers, so it is better either to use the underscore for spaces or use no spaces at all with a capital letter at the start of each new word e.g. TeamAEstimate.xls, TeamCProgress.xls. It does not matter which method we use as long as we are consistent throughout.

Creating multiple workbooks

Method 1 Use 'Edit', 'Copy' (or 'Ctrl + C') at the Windows Explorer level to copy the template and then use 'Edit', 'Paste' ('Ctrl + V') to create each workbook. Rename each copy (e.g. from 'Copy of estimate_template. xls' to 'a_est.xls').

Method 2 Open up 'estimate_template.xls', then use the menu option 'File', 'Save As...' to keep saving the workbook with different names. Be sure to save each copy in the right folder.

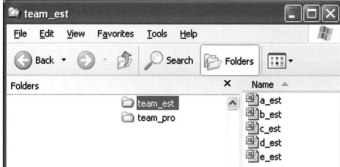
Figure 11.3.1 The estimate workbooks in their folder

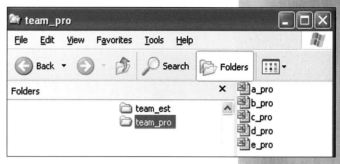
Figure 11.3.2 The progress workbooks in their folder

Reducing data input error

'Garbage in, garbage out'. It is at the design stage that we can reduce much of the possible input error. Incorrect output can arise from errors such as the accidental duplication of data entries, mistyping of data entries and entries of the wrong data type (e.g. text data that should have been numeric). Errors can also occur because of incorrect processing (e.g. the wrong formulae are used), but it is important to recognise that a lot can go wrong even at the input stage.

▶ Duplication

It is important that data is only input once. If the same data is entered twice or more there is a good chance that mismatches will occur. For example, assume the team leader for project team D is called Amy Cheung, and we enter her name in the estimate workbook. If we also enter her name in the progress workbook we might accidentally type Amy Chueng. The names are different and this will cause problems when we analyse data by team leader name. To avoid this problem we enter the team leader name only once. In our present project, we will put the name into the estimate workbook. If the name needs to be displayed elsewhere (e.g. the master workbook) we will use a formula to link the cell to the estimate workbook cell.

Other values that need entering only once include: year, team name and local currency.

ACTIVITY 3 Avoid duplicates ◀

In this activity you will add the year, team name and local currency to the estimate workbooks.

1 Use the layout of year, team, team leader and local currency as in the Project teams' estimate workbook in Unit 11.2, and shown in Figure 11.3.3.

2 Add the values in Table 11.3.1 to each of the estimate workbooks' summary worksheets:

Figure 11.3.3 Layout for the estimate workbooks

Continued on the next page

Table 11.3.1 Duplicated data in the estimate workbooks

	a_est.xls	b_est.xls	c_est.xls	d_est.xls	e_est.xls
Year	2007	2007	2007	2007	2007
Team	A	B	C	D	E
Team Leader	Janet Long	Bob Jones	Tim Smith	Amy Cheung	Charlie Wood
Currency	EUR	EUR	EUR	USD	REN

▶ Incorrect input values

Imagine a spreadsheet solution that requires users to enter the name of a country. What are the chances that a user might mistype the name (e.g. 'Agrentina' instead of 'Argentina') or misspell the word (e.g. 'Argentinia') or accidentally add an extra space at the end of the word (e.g. 'Argentina ')? All these kinds of errors will make our analysis and results inaccurate. The hardest one to spot is where an additional space has been added at the end of a word. This means that the totals of values for 'Argentina' will not include values for 'Argentina '.

This is where drop-down list boxes can be very useful. Try Activity 4.

ACTIVITY 4 Use lists ◀

1 Given the functional specification, identify where drop-down list boxes would reduce error in the project teams' workbooks.
2 Write down the list of values each of these drop-down list boxes should display.

At the design stage, we should have identified all the drop-down boxes needed, plus the list of values to be displayed in these boxes. In the Unit 11.4 we will set these up.

▶ Data validation and data types

We have already covered Excel's data validation feature in Unit 3 and we will use this in the Unit 11.4 when we construct the solution. At the design stage, however, we should identify the data validation we want.

ACTIVITY 5 Consider data validation ◀

When users enter costs and energy unit values, what kind of validation can we undertake?

Outputs

The functional specification has provided us with a lot of detail, but we still need more at the design stage. This is where prototyping is very useful. We can mock up charts, pivot tables etc. and discuss them with Tina and her team until we have identified exactly what is required. We need to consider:

- the precise analysis Tina requires
- the data source needed to achieve this
- how these results should be laid out, including headings, other labels, fonts and colour schemes.

We will assume that all Tina wants at this stage are:
- colour coding for budget performance (see functional specification)
- the pivot table as in Figure 11.2.1
- a similar pivot table for teams and budget performance (whether actual spending is over, under or on target)
- a chart for each team as in Figure 11.2.2
- the ability to change the value of an EU in the 'what-if' analysis so that actual project cost can be compared with possible revenue generated
- the ability to view the break-even points in this analysis (that is when the total costs equals the total projected revenue)
- all the above financial values to be displayed in a common currency and this common currency to be changeable
- separate sheets for charts, 'what-if' analysis and colour coding; while both pivot tables to be on one sheet.

Tina is not interested, at this stage, in the predicted totals of energy units created by each project.

We now have some good design ideas for data output and we have also created the workbooks for data input. We must now think about the design of the intermediate stages and the processes needed to achieve these outputs.

Structure of the master workbook

- How many worksheets do we need?
- What names are the worksheets to be given?
- How is data imported?
- What data is to be stored on each worksheet and do we need any additional columns for intermediate calculations?
- Should any named ranges be used?
- Which cells and/or worksheets are to be protected?
- How do we archive the master workbook?

▶ Importing data

Developers familiar with Excel's programming language, Visual Basic for Applications, might consider an import solution that involves automatically opening each project teams' workbooks, copying the data and then pasting it into the master workbook. As we are not using a VBA solution, we will use Excel's facility to link cells in one workbook to cells in another workbook.

ACTIVITY 6 Use master worksheets ◀

Given the information you have so far, complete the worksheet details given in Table 11.3.2. Add more rows as necessary.

Table 11.3.2 Additional worksheet details

Worksheet name	Data to be stored/displayed	Comments, objects, named ranges	Security
Instructions	How to use the master workbook	Text box(es) containing instructions. Navigation buttons to take you to each worksheet would be useful.	Worksheet protected

 There are many possible working solutions to Activity 6, but this is the file we will use in Unit 11.4.

▶ Archiving the master workbook

The ability to link workbooks is an excellent feature of Excel, except that problems can arise when the workbooks from which the data is coming are moved or deleted. This is not an uncommon problem. Tina wants the master workbook archived each year in the following way: renamed to 'master_yyyy.xls', where 'yyyy' represents the year (e.g. 'master_2007.xls'), and stored in a new folder with the project teams' estimates and progress workbooks. This action would cause the links to fail. One solution would be to copy the data, then use the 'Paste Special...' option from the 'Edit' menu and paste only the 'Values' back. We will investigate this further in Unit 11.4.

Processing

Although we are using a prototyping method, we should still have some idea, at the design stage, of how we are going to tackle the processes. For example:

- What formulae will we need for converting the currency?
- How will imported data get colour coded?
- Are there any additional processes for reducing error?

Some detail should be written at the design stage, providing descriptions (e.g. steps in each process, formulae and functions to be used) and diagrams (e.g. flow charts), where appropriate.

For the sake of brevity, the actual processes will be looked at in the Unit 11.4, but it will be assumed that some design has already been provided.

Conclusion ▶ ▶ ▶

While Unit 11.2 laid out the client/user requirements, Unit 11.3 has looked at the design side of development. That is, how we are going to achieve these requirements. As with the functional specification, it is important to get this specified clearly and in some detail before rushing into the construction of the solution. However, by using a prototyping method, we can start to develop part of the solution early on and gain a much more interactive relationship with the client/user. This should mean that we are much more likely to get the final product right.

Construction and advanced techniques

In Unit 11.4 we complete the project set out in Unit 11.1. Not all the advanced Excel techniques that you might find useful when tackling your assignment can be covered by this one project, so there is a further section to cover some of these additional techniques.

Constructing the workbooks

Armed with our functional specification, design, and prototypes, we are in a good position to complete the project as requested. Even better, not all the prototypes are throwaway models. The projects teams' workbooks we have created can be used as part of our solution. We will start with these and gradually work through until the master workbook produces all the required outputs.

▶ Drop-down list boxes

In Activity 4 in Unit 11.3 you were asked to identify where drop-down list boxes would reduce error in the project teams' workbooks. You should at least have identified currency, energy type and team leader. Also, that these only need to be in the estimates workbooks. Year and team name, displayed as locked cells on the summary sheet in the estimate workbooks, could also be included for use by the administrator. However, for the sake of brevity, in Activity 1 we will only add lists for currency, energy type and team leader.

Named ranges

The ability to give a single cell or a block of cells its own unique name is a very useful feature of spreadsheets. For example, it is easier to remember 'CurrencyList' than B2:B6, and we can select the name from the 'Go To...' dialogue box (Function key F5). We can also use named ranges in formulae. For example, '=Price*Quantity' means more than '=D92*AA46'. Finally, it is also clearer when setting up lists. To name a range of cells (you can also see a demonstration of this process):

1 Click on the Name box at the left end of the formula bar (see Figure 11.4.1).
2 Type the name for the cells
3 Press 'Enter' (this is important, otherwise the name is not stored).

	A	B	C
	TeamLeader	**Currency**	**EnergyType**
2	Amy Cheung	EUR	HY
3	Bob Jones	GBP	NR
4	Janet Long	JPY	RE
5	Tim Smith	REN	
6	Charlie Wood	USD	

CurrencyList ▾   *fx* EUR

Name box

Figure 11.4.1 Example of a named range

Continued on the next page

If a mistake is made, use the menu option 'Insert', 'Name', 'Define...' to get the 'Define Name' dialogue box (see Fig. 11.4.2). Select the named range then, either edit it, or delete it, and start again.

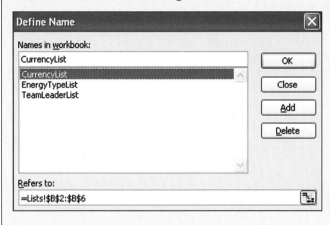

Define Name

Names in workbook:

CurrencyList

CurrencyList	OK
EnergyTypeList	Close
TeamLeaderList	Add
	Delete

Refers to:

=Lists!$B$2:$B$6

Figure 11.4.2 Use the 'Define Name' dialogue box if you make a mistake

ACTIVITY 1 Use drop-down list boxes ◀

Note: Before we start this activity, it should be clear that it would have been better to have added these lists in our original estimates template before generating the five team workbooks. This would have cut down the work. This is a good example of rushing ahead a bit too fast before completing the design. Remember this when you undertake your assignment. However, sometimes we have to learn from our mistakes.

1 Open the workbook, 'a_est.xls', that you created in Activity 2, Unit 11.3.
2 Insert a new worksheet and name it 'Lists'.
3 Add the lists shown in Figure 11.4.3 starting at cell A1:

a_est

	A	B	C
1	**TeamLeader**	**Currency**	**EnergyType**
2	Amy Cheung	EUR	HY
3	Bob Jones	GBP	NR
4	Janet Long	JPY	RE
5	Tim Smith	REN	
6	Charlie Wood	USD	
7			

Instructions / Summary \ Lists /

Figure 11.4.3 Text for the drop-down lists

4 Select cells A2:A6 and name the range of cells 'TeamLeaderList'. (See the margin box if you are not sure how to do this.)
5 Select cells B2:B6 and name the range of cells 'CurrencyList'.
6 Select cells C2:C4 and name the range of cells 'EnergyTypeList'
7 Open the Summary sheet and place the cell pointer on cell B3, where the team leader's name is to go.
8 Use the data validation option 'Data', 'Validation...' to enter the team leader list. Under 'Allow' select 'List', then in 'Source', type in the text '=TeamLeaderList' (see Fig. 11.4.4).

Continued on the next page

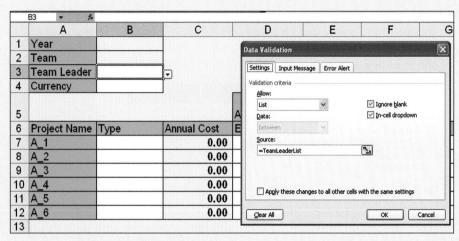

Figure 11.4.4 Adding a drop-down list

9 Check that you get the desired drop-down list box in cell B3 (see Fig. 11.4.5).

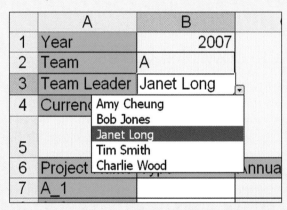

Figure 11.4.5 The drop-down list of team leaders

10 Repeat this for the other two lists and the other four workbooks.

Look at this example of the completed lists.

▶ Master workbook worksheets

How many worksheets do we need in the master workbook? As stated in Unit 11.3, there are a number of possible answers. For our present purposes, we will assume that Figure 11.4.6 meets our requirements.

Figure 11.4.6 Master worksheet names

For easier viewing, Tina decides she would like the following data in separate sheets:
- the raw data for actual energy units produced per month (sheet 'RawEU')
- the raw data for actual and estimated costs per month (sheet 'RawCosts')
- the actual and estimated costs per month, after conversion into a common currency, with colour coding of budget performance (sheet 'ConvertedCosts')

- pivot tables (sheet 'PivotTables')
- budget performance charts (sheet 'ChartBudget' as first example)

In addition, for processing purposes, we will create the following worksheets:
- 'CurrencyTable' to store currency conversion rates for the common currency
- 'ProjectLookupTable' to store a lookup table for project fields
- 'Settings' to store any additional settings for the administrator, e.g. percentages for colour coding.

ACTIVITY 2 Use master worksheets ◀

Create the initial version of the master workbook, making sure that it has all the worksheets shown in Figure 11.4.6. Compare your workbook with this file.

▶ Linking external data

The raw data in the master workbook will come straight from the project teams' workbooks as externally linked data. For example, the first entry in the master workbook 'RawCosts' worksheet will be something like '=[a_pro. xls]Summary'!H7'. However, there are a lot of cells to fill in. There are 30 projects with 12 months worth of cost values in both the estimates and progress workbooks, plus the actual energy values: a total of 1080 cells. We therefore want to copy formulae down and across as much as possible.

In addition, it is a good idea to test our formulae as we go along, rather than leave all the testing until the end. The more errors we remove now, the better in the long run. Without values in the project teams' workbooks this would be a bit difficult to undertake, but in Activity 3 of Unit 11.2 we learnt how to create 'dummy data' very quickly.

In the next Activity we will link the workbooks' data, but only after you have created **dummy data** in each workbook.

ACTIVITY 3 Link external data ◀

1 Make sure that each of your project teams' workbooks has monthly values displayed. For the progress monthly worksheets for each individual cost (e.g. buildings) per month use something like:
    =INT(RAND()*6000)+2000

As we saw in Unit 11.2, we can speed up this process by selecting multiple worksheets for the months 'Jan' to 'Dec', and then following these steps. Enter the formula as shown in Fig. 11.4.7, step 1. Copy the formula across and then copy it down (Fig. 11.4.7, step 2). Remember, the figures change each time we do a calculation, and so we need to keep the cells selected and then copy them using 'Edit', 'Copy' from the menu. Finally, use 'Edit', 'Paste Special...' and select 'Value' (see Fig. 11.4.7, step 3). As a result the cells now contain values, not the formula. This process should be repeated for each of the following areas, enabling worksheets to be populated in seconds. You can view a demonstration of this from the ActiveBook.

Continued on the next page

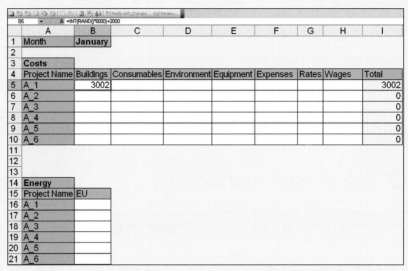

1 Enter formula for one cell

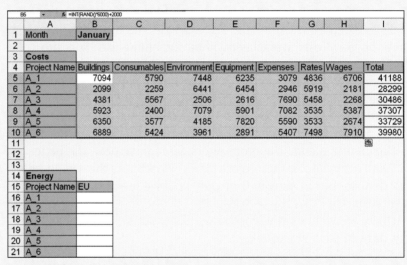

2 Copy the formula across and down

3 Use 'Paste Special...' to copy the values

Figure 11.4.7 Creating data to populate a spreadsheet

For monthly energy units, use something like:

$$=INT(RAND()*50000)+50000$$

For the estimates summary sheets for each monthly costs use:

$$=INT(RAND()*40000)+2000$$

and for the estimated EU quantity use:

$$=INT(RAND()*600000)+600000$$

Look at examples of these formulae in these workbooks:

- estimates workbook
- progress workbook.

Continued on the next page

2 Make sure that the layout for the 'RawEU' and 'RawCosts' worksheets in the master are as in Figures 11.4.8 and 11.4.9. You may wish to use, or at least look at, this workbook.

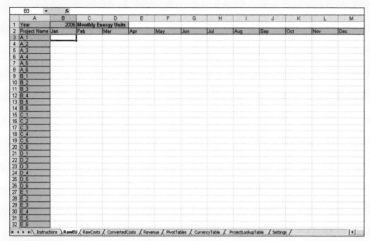

Figure 11.4.8 Check your layout for the worksheet 'RawEU' matches this

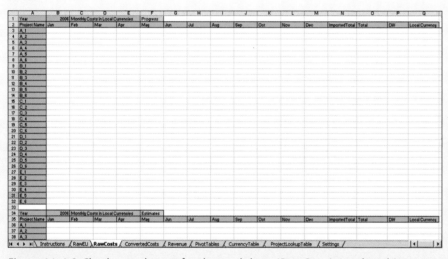

Figure 11.4.9 Check your layout for the worksheet 'RawCosts' matches this

Note that extra columns are in the RawCosts workbook for double checking and displaying the local currency. Make sure that there are rows for all the actual (progress) costs for each project and estimated costs.

3 Make sure that all the workbooks are in the correct sub folders (that is, 'team_est' and 'team_pro').

4 We will now link our first piece of data. Make sure that both the master and first progress workbook 'a_pro.xls' are open. Place the cursor in cell B3 in the 'RawCosts' sheets and either type the formula as in Figure 11.4.10 or type the equals sign then click on the appropriate cell on the Summary sheet of 'a_pro.xls'. Press 'Enter'. The formula ' =[a_pro.xls]Summary!$C$7' is inserted. Don't worry that the value inserted is different to the one in Figure 11.4.10, this is just due to the randomly generated figures.

Continued on the next page

This is a start, but we need to remove the fixed referencing (the $ signs) if we want to copy the formula across and down and pick up other appropriate values.

B3	▼	*fx* =[a_pro.xls]Summary!$C$7	
	A	B	C
1	Year	2006	Monthly Costs
2	Project Name	Jan	Feb	Mä
3	A_1	38166	
4	A_2		
5	A_3		

Figure 11.4.10 Link progress data

5 Remove the $ signs from the formula, then copy down *only* for team A projects. Copy across to December (see Fig. 11.4.11).

B3	▼	*fx* =[a_pro.xls]Summary!C7											
	A	B	C	D	E	F	G	H	I	J	K	L	M
1	Year	2006	Monthly Costs in Local Currencies			Progress							
2	Project Name	Jan	Feb	Mar	Apr	May	Jun	Jul	Aug	Sep	Oct	Nov	Dec	
3	A_1	38166	33964	31131	32853	36936	32621	40119	35714	30351	28252	30893	35083
4	A_2	40349	33470	34627	34868	39064	36151	33307	28345	40602	32803	33672	25153
5	A_3	37483	38378	30129	38011	39122	36352	37701	39533	40403	28925	36697	31257
6	A_4	38041	38004	39101	31863	27991	34064	32108	34148	40069	31833	41415	36784
7	A_5	38487	32751	37951	36564	34988	35019	43558	35956	36998	33283	34874	34355
8	A_6	33231	33342	32836	29730	36267	38944	37908	37308	34287	38874	39490	36460
9	B_1	0	0	0	0	0	0	0	0	0	0	0	0
10	B_2												

Figure 11.4.11 Data linked into the master worksheet from team A progress sheet

6 Place the cursor in cell B9 and repeat the steps from 4 above, but for 'b_pro.xls'.

7 Repeat for each team, opening the appropriate workbook.

8 Repeat for the estimated values further down the 'RawCosts' worksheet, using the estimate workbooks.

9 Repeat for the 'RawEU' worksheet, taking data from the progress workbooks.

10 For the local currency column in 'RawCosts', we can use fixed cell referencing by linking the currency name in the estimate workbook. For project A_1, the formula will look like:

=[a_est.xls]Summary!$B$4

This can then be copied down for the other five team A projects without any need to remove the $ signs. For team B projects the first formula is:

=[b_est.xls]Summary!$B$4

and so on.

Figure 11.4.12 Update links option

As long as all the teams' workbooks (the **source** files) stay in the same place on the disk drive, the master workbook (the **destination** file) will update without problems. So, as the teams enter their monthly data, the master can be updated. The option to update the master with the latest figures in the source workbooks occurs every time we open the master (see Fig. 11.4.12).

▶ Editing links

What happens if the source files are moved? The answer is, the links are broken. If you have chosen 'Update' when opening the master workbook, then Excel opens up the Open dialogue box and asks you to find each of the missing files. If you cancel, then '#REF' appears in every cell. The alternative is to choose 'Don't Update' when opening the master. We then use the 'Edit' menu to select 'Links...' and change the source files accordingly (see Fig. 11.4.13).

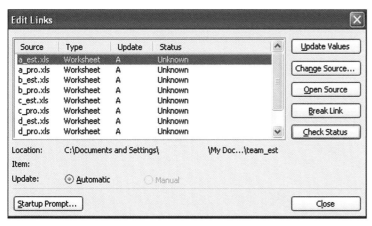

Figure 11.4.13 Edit links dialogue box

▶ Double checking

The column headed 'Diff' (see Fig. 11.4.9) is only there to double check that the imported totals are the same as summing the monthly imported values. This process is not strictly necessary, but does operate as a double check if one of the source workbooks gets modified incorrectly. The 'Total' column simply uses '=SUM(B3:M3)' in the first row, then copies this down. The 'Diff' column simply displays the difference between the two totals: '=N3−O3'.

When you undertake your assignment, it might be worth thinking of your own double-checking routines.

▶ Data validation

Some data validation has been undertaken already, with drop-down list boxes, but we could include data validation for the inputting of numeric and financial data. Again, it would have been quicker if this had been set up in our original templates, but better late than never.

Activity 4 Use more data validation ◀

Tina has decided that all energy values and costs must be whole numbers equal to or greater than zero.

Open each of the source workbooks and add appropriate data validation to the input data cells. You can view a demonstration of this process from the ActiveBook.

▶ Currency conversion

For the process of converting the values imported from their local currencies to a common, base, currency, we will use a formula in the 'ConvertedCosts' worksheet to internally link to the data in 'RawCosts' and then multiply it by the appropriate exchange rate, using the VLOOKUP function. We will set up a currency table in the worksheet 'CurrencyTable' and give it the named range 'tbl_currency'. (It is a standard naming convention to use 'tbl' rather than 'table'.) We will also use a named range for the local currency column in the 'ConvertedCosts' worksheet so that the formula will be easier to understand. That is:

> =RawCosts!B3*VLOOKUP(local_currency,tbl_currency,2, FALSE)

rather than:

> =RawCosts!B3*VLOOKUP(N3,C3:D8,2, FALSE)

 Note: Use a copy of this version of the master workbook for some of the following activities; save it as 'master_with_raw_data.xls'. To avoid problems with broken links, so that you can concentrate on the following exercises, the raw data is *not linked* to external data.

ACTIVITY 5 Use VLOOKUP ◀

1 Using the file 'master_with_raw_data.xls', enter the data in Table 11.4.1 on the worksheet 'CurrencyTable' and name it 'tbl_currency'.

Currency	Sterling
EUR	0.67583
GBP	1.00000
JPY	0.00479
REN	0.07153
USD	0.57800

Table 11.4.1 Currency conversions based on sterling

2 The 'ConvertedCosts' worksheet required is more or less a copy of the 'RawCosts' worksheet, so delete the existing blank 'ConvertedCosts' worksheet, make a copy of the 'RawCosts worksheets ('Edit', 'Move or Copy Sheet...' – make sure you copy rather than move!) and rename it as 'ConvertedCosts'.

3 Add columns at the end for 'Budget' and 'Type' (columns R and S).

4 Delete the 'ImportedTotal' and 'Diff' columns

5 Select all the names in the local currency column (e.g. row 3 to 65) and name the range 'local_currency'.

6 In cell B3 (Project A_1, Jan) type:

> =RawCosts!B3*VLOOKUP(local_currency,tbl_currency,2,FALSE)

7 Copy this across to December then copy it down to the last project (row 32). Values in GBP will stay the same, but those in other currencies will change.

You can view a demonstration of this from the ActiveBook.

8 Repeat for the Estimates values by placing the cursor in cell B36 and entering the same formula with B36 instead of B3. Copy this across to December then copy it down to the last project (row 65).

9 Use the SUM function in the 'Totals' column.

Continued on the next page

10 Now we *must* test that it works fine with other currencies. So change the values in the currency table to those in Table 11.4.2.

11 Check that the values in 'ConvertedCosts' worksheet have changed.

Currency	US dollars
EUR	1.169256
GBP	1.730103
JPY	0.008287
REN	0.123754
USD	1.000000

Table 11.4.2 Currency conversions based on US dollars

VLOOKUP

VLOOKUP is an excellent function for extracting a value from a table e.g. a tax table, mileage claim table. The VLOOKUP function consists of the following four parts:

- the value to be looked up
- where the table with the values is
- which column contains the answer to be brought back
- whether an exact match is needed for the looked-up value or whether a boundary limit will do.

These parts are called parameters and are contained within the brackets of the function, each separated by a comma. In Activity 5 the parameters we used were local_currency, tbl_currency, 2, and FALSE. This means that the function went to the table called 'tbl_currency', it looked vertically down the first column of the table for the value, 'local_currency' (in our first row this was 'GBP'). When found, it went to the second column ('2') and extracted the value there (in this case, 1.000 00). We wanted an exact match with GBP, not the nearest value, so we used the word FALSE.

If our table had been laid out differently, so that lookup values went across, rather than down, then we would have used HLOOKUP, for a horizontal lookup. As our currency names went down the first column in the table, 'tbl_currency', we used VLOOKUP.

If we were looking for numeric values, rather than text values, then we might use TRUE instead of FALSE, if exact matches were not required. The values, however, would need to be in order. For example, a table for mileage claims might look like Table 11.4.3. Anybody claiming for 99 miles would be paid 46p a mile, even though 99 is not in the first

Table 11.4.3 Mileage costs

Distance	1	100	500	2000
Cost per mile	0.46	0.44	0.42	0.40

row. Anyone claiming for 501 miles would be paid 42p. The distances are in ascending order (otherwise we would get incorrect results). We would use HLOOKUP here.

Colour-coding budget performance

After doing these activities, the 'ConvertedCosts' worksheet should look like Figure 11.4.14.

	A	B	C	D	E	F	G	H	I	J	K	L	M	N	O	P	Q
1	Year	2006	Monthly Costs in Local Currencies			Progress		2006						ImportedTotal	Local Currency	Budget	Type
2	Project Name	Jan	Feb	Mar	Apr	May	Jun	Jul	Aug	Sep	Oct	Nov	Dec				
3	A_1	17,913	16,471	19,240	18,142	19,408	18,343	18,756	21,130	19,817	16,765	17,524	16,806	220,315	GBP		
4	A_2	19,770	15,246	14,886	13,981	14,166	17,055	15,619	15,516	14,059	17,815	15,567	20,043	193,723	GBP		
5	A_3	15,784	16,753	18,441	17,566	17,721	14,261	16,522	14,471	13,756	17,369	17,545	13,888	194,076	GBP		
6	A_4	15,569	17,631	15,225	16,609	15,566	15,754	14,856	16,315	16,720	15,462	18,287	14,972	192,967	GBP		
7	A_5	16,185	13,827	16,704	17,211	17,699	19,429	15,144	17,195	18,533	18,616	14,680	16,706	201,929	GBP		
8	A_6	12,893	11,364	11,631	11,687	11,329	13,103	11,717	11,867	11,157	11,622	10,457	10,362	139,188	EUR		
9	B_1	13,745	12,430	12,260	12,745	13,106	10,246	10,633	12,848	12,139	11,793	13,218	13,048	148,211	EUR		
10	B_2	11,439	10,864	11,088	11,075	11,068	11,171	11,759	10,008	12,543	10,774	12,511	9,839	134,138	EUR		

Figure 11.4.14 'ConvertedCosts' worksheet

We now want to process this data with colour coding. In the budget column we want to display whether the actual costs are over or under budget, and colour code accordingly. However, we want the user to set what percentage determines whether a project is over or under. The first task then is to set up these variables on the 'Settings' worksheet.

ACTIVITY 6 Use colour coding

1 Open the 'Settings' worksheet.
2 Type the data in Figure 11.4.15 onto the sheet:

Colour code	Progress/estimate costs
Yellow	90%
Red	110%
White	in between

Figure 11.4.15 Colour settings

We have only put 90% and 110% in for test purposes and these can be changed at any time. They are not locked cells.
3 Select the cell with 90% in it and name it 'under_budget'.
4 Select the cell with 110% in it and name it 'over_budget'
5 Open the 'ConvertedCosts' worksheet and place the cursor just below the 'Budget' heading (cell P3 in Figure 11.4.14)
6 Type in the following formula:
   =IF(N3/N36>=over_budget,"Over",IF(N3/N36<=under_budget, "Under",""))

Note 1: If the 'Totals' column in your version of the workbook is not column N, then change the formula accordingly.
Note 2: The formula being used calculates 'actual costs/estimated costs' (e.g. N3/N36) and then compares this with what the user sets as over or under budget. So if actual costs/estimated costs gives 0.91, but the user sets underestimate to be 0.90 (that is, 90% on the 'Settings' sheet), then the cell is left blank. If actual costs/estimated costs gives 1.11 and the user sets overestimate as 1.10 (that is, 110% on the 'Settings' sheet), then the cell displays 'Over'.

Continued on the next page

7 Drag the formula down to the last project (row 32). Cells should contain either 'Over', 'Under' or nothing

View a demonstration of setting the formula from the ActiveBook.

8 We can now colour code the cells using the conditional formatting techniques we learnt in Unit 3. (That is, using the menu option 'Format', 'Conditional Formatting...' – see Figure 11.4.16. You can also see a demonstration from the ActiveBook.)

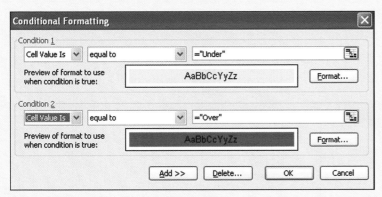

Figure 11.4.16 Colour coding cells using conditional formatting

9 Test that this works fine by changing the values on the 'Settings' sheet.

▶ A brief note on testing

So far we have been carrying out quite a few tests as we progress. Although testing will be looked at in more depth in the Unit 11.5, it is important that an ongoing log is kept of all the testing that we undertake. This should include not only what it is we are testing, but also the data we have used in these tests (e.g. 90% and 110% in the example above) and whether our test was successful or not.

▶ Pivot tables

In Unit 11.2, we saw that Tina wanted pivot tables available in the master workbook. As a reminder, here is the figure from Unit 11.2 again (see Fig. 11.4.17).

Pivot tables allow us to get different views of our data very quickly. In the proposed pivot table, although we have 30 projects, we can view totals by project type and by team in a neat tabular form. We can see which teams are the costliest overall, but we can also see which teams are the costliest for a particular type of project. We could even set up a pivot table to see which team is most often over budget (see Fig. 11.4.18).

Annual Actual EUs Generated - 2006

Team	Project Type HY	NR	RE	Grand Total
Team A	829,015	971,117	875,704	**2,675,836**
Team B	790,831	911,746	910,552	**2,613,129**
Team C	1,108,684	961,620	766,020	**2,836,324**
Team D	1,074,407	1,065,298	811,364	**2,951,069**
Team E	984,771	709,703	655,139	**2,349,613**
Grand Total	**4,787,708**	**4,619,484**	**4,018,779**	**13,425,971**

HY= Hybrid
NR = Non-Renewable
RE= Renewable

Figure 11.4.17 Pivot table design

Project Spending	Budget ▼			
Team ▼	Over	Under	OK	Grand Total
Team A	2	1	3	6
Team B	4	1	1	6
Team C	4		2	6
Team D	3		3	6
Team E	6			6
Grand Total	19	2	9	30

Figure 11.4.18 Pivot table showing how often each team has gone over budget

	C	D	E	F	G
1	Currency	Team	Budget	Estimated Costs	Progress Costs
2	GBP	Team A	Over	111,923	127,342
3	GBP	Team A	Over	40,606	111,972
4	GBP	Team A		116,165	112,176
5	GBP	Team A		104,766	111,535
6	GBP	Team A	Over	50,001	116,715
7	EUR	Team A		74,894	80,451
8	EUR	Team B	Under	98,642	85,666
9	EUR	Team B	Over	34,770	77,532
10	EUR	Team B		86,023	82,521
11	EUR	Team B	Over	24,699	75,576
12	EUR	Team B	Over	10,556	78,228
13	EUR	Team B	Over	35,433	78,887
14	EUR	Team C	Over	70,593	87,576
15	EUR	Team C	Over	37,039	79,121
16	EUR	Team C		73,692	74,683
17	EUR	Team C	Over	31,577	79,480
18	EUR	Team C		83,100	76,113
19	EUR	Team C	Over	6,036	78,810
20	USD	Team D		72,785	72,922
21	USD	Team D	Over	37,560	67,798
22	USD	Team D	Over	7,900	68,309
23	USD	Team D	Over	4,188	66,224
24	USD	Team D		64,129	68,852
25	USD	Team D		69,153	67,841
26	REN	Team E	Over	5,858	9,302
27	REN	Team E	Over	7,156	8,573
28	REN	Team E	Over	1,413	8,288
29	REN	Team E	Over	5,035	8,263
30	REN	Team E	Over	490	8,060
31	REN	Team E	Over	5,435	8,513

Figure 11.4.19 Pivot table data

Creating a pivot table, using Excel's pivot table wizard, is quite easy, *as long as the data is laid out correctly*. That is, data should look like records in a database table, with appropriate field headings. For our analysis this means we need a worksheet with the data as in Figure 11.4.19.

We could use the 'ConvertedCosts' worksheet and add a few more columns for 'Type' and 'Team' etc., but this could get confusing for the user who only wants converted costs on that sheet. It is much better to have it on our PivotTable worksheet, so that we, and the user, can see what is happening. It will also make it easier to add other pivot tables in the future.

There are a number of ways we can get this data into the worksheet. 'Project Name', 'Currency', 'Budget', 'Estimated Costs' and 'Progress Costs' can all come from linked cells in the 'ConvertedCosts' sheet (e.g. '=ConvertedCosts!A3 in cell A2'). 'Type' and 'Team', however, will have to come from the estimates workbooks. We could use some clever coding for the team name by picking up the first letter in the 'ProjectName' cell and adding the word 'Team' in front of it. For example,

   ="Team " & LEFT(A2,1)

While this works, it is a good example of how trying to be clever can weaken the integrity of the data. What happens if the team names change in the estimates workbooks? We have already discussed this type of problem in the section on duplication, in Unit 11.3.

In the next activity we will create one of the required pivot tables.

ACTIVITY 7 Create a pivot table

1 Using your 'master_with raw data.xls' file, set up the 'PivotTable' worksheet so that it looks like Figure 11.4.19.

You can view a demonstration of the following process from the ActiveBook.

2 Name the block of data, including headings 'tbl_pivot_data'
3 Select 'Data', 'Pivot Table...' from the menu.
4 Leave the option as 'Microsoft Office Excel list or database' and click on 'Next' (see Fig. 11.4.20).

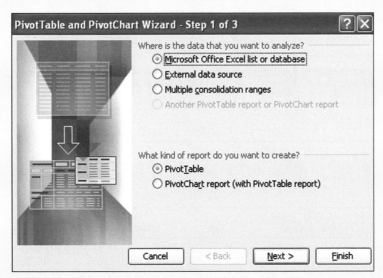

Figure 11.4.20 Pivot wizard step 1

5 Type in the name of the data range and click on 'Next' (see Fig. 11.4.21).

Figure 11.4.21 Pivot wizard step 2

6 Type in where you want the table to go (e.g. cell $I$13), but click 'Layout', *not* 'Next' or 'Finish' (see Fig. 11.4.22).

Figure 11.4.22 Pivot wizard step 3

Continued on the next page

7 In the Layout window (see Fig. 11.4.23), drag the 'Team' button on the right to the ROW area. Drag the 'Type' button to the COLUMN area. Drag the 'Progress Costs' button to the DATA area. Then click 'OK'. Then click 'Finish' on the Step 3 dialogue box (see Fig. 11.4.22).

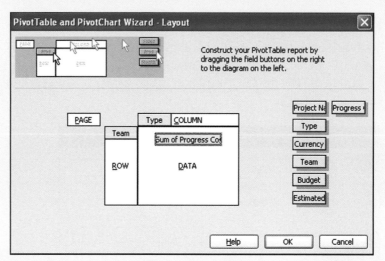

Figure 11.4.23 Pivot wizard step 4

8 We should get something like Figure 11.4.24.

Sum of Progress Costs	Type			
Team	HY	NR	RE	Grand Total
Team A	191985.803	112176	356029	660190.803
Team B	236983.844	163198.077	78227.9983	478409.92
Team C	234403.526		241380.794	475784.32
Team D	140719.88	134532.968	136692.954	411945.802
Team E	8059.85734	25063.3252	17874.4886	50997.6712
Grand Total	812152.911	434970.37	830205.235	2077328.52

Figure 11.4.24 The resulting pivot table

9 We will now tidy up the numeric values to zero decimal places. We could have achieved this at step 4 above by double clicking on the 'Sum of Progress Costs' button, bringing up the Field Settings dialogue box (see Fig. 11.4.25) and making changes then. However, we can still bring up the Field Settings dialogue box by highlighting all the numeric values in the pivot table, using the right mouse button to display the drop-down menu and then selecting 'Field Settings'.

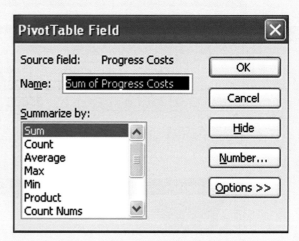

Figure 11.4.25 Pivot table field settings

10 Select the 'Number...' option and change the format to 'Number, zero decimal places'.

Pivot tables have an enormous number of features, and it is impossible to cover them all in this Unit. However, it is useful to know how to actually pivot the data, and to do this we need to use the 'PAGE' area shown in Figure 11.4.23.

You can try these additional pivot table exercises.

ACTIVITY 8 Pivot the table

1 Use the wizard again, but this time place the data below the previous pivot table and on the Layout window drag the 'Budget' button onto the PAGE area. Fill in the other areas as before.

2 This time we can view the data as before but by budget as well. So change the budget drop-down box to 'Over' (see Fig. 11.4.26).

Budget	Over			
Sum of Progress Costs	Type			
Team	HY	NR	RE	Grand Total
Team A			356029	356029
Team B	154463	77532	78228	310223
Team C	158290		166698	324988
Team D	67798	134533		202331
Team E	8060	25063	17874	50998
Grand Total	388611	237128	618829	1244568

Figure 11.4.26 Pivot table showing over budget projects by team

3 Now let's pivot the data. On the pivot table itself, on the worksheet, drag the 'Budget' button down to the team area on the pivot table and let go. You immediately get a more complex layout. Fine, but we want it clearer. Drag the 'Team' button up to where the 'Budget' button had been (see Fig. 11.4.27).

Team	(All)			
Sum of Progress Costs	Type			
Budget	HY	NR	RE	Grand Total
	423542	112176	211376	747094
Over	388611	237128	618829	1244568
Under		85666		85666
Grand Total	812153	434970	830205	2077329

Figure 11.4.27 Pivot table Teams

4 Use the drop-down list boxes for 'Type', 'Team' and 'Budget' to restrict the view of what is displayed.

▶ What-ifs

Tina wants to undertake some 'what-if' analysis to assess the financial implications of the projects.

ACTIVITY 9 Use 'What-if' analysis ◀

In this activity we will use the Goal Seeking facility in Excel to work out what price we should charge for each energy unit (EU) in order to balance revenue with costs exactly; that is, no surplus. This is the break-even point.

1 Open the 'Revenue' worksheet and use internal links to get the data looking as in Figure 11.4.28. The EUs come from the 'RawEU' sheet and are the annual totals for each project. You may need to sum these values in the 'RawEU' sheet before linking them to the 'Revenue' sheet. Use a cell to store the 'Price per EU'.

- Use the headings: 'Project Name', 'EUs', 'Actual Costs', 'Projected Revenue' and 'Surplus'.
- 'Actual Costs' are the progress costs (e.g. '=ConvertedCosts!O3').
- 'Projected Revenue' will be the value in the 'EU' column multiplied by the eu_price (see step 3).
- 'Surplus' is simply 'Projected Revenue' minus 'Actual Costs' (e.g. '=D2-C2').
- Use the SUM function for the totals.

	D2	▼	ƒx =B2*eu_price					
	A	B	C	D	E	F	G	H	I
1	Project Name	EUs	Actual Costs	Projected Revenue	Surplus		Price per EU		
2	A_1	671,309.00	127,342	134,261.80	6,919.80		0.20		
3	A_2	699,011.00	111,972	139,802.20	27,830.20				
4	A_3	836,630.00	112,176	167,326.00	55,150.00				
5	A_4	762,429.00	111,535	152,485.80	40,950.80				
6	A_5	656,472.00	116,715	131,294.40	14,579.40				
7	A_6	721,193.00	80,451	144,238.60	63,787.80				
8	B_1	751,636.00	85,666	150,327.20	64,661.02				
9	B_2	603,194.00	77,532	120,638.80	43,106.91				
10	B_3	847,507.00	82,521	169,501.40	86,980.53				
11	B_4	597,352.00	75,576	119,470.40	43,894.36				
12	B_5	918,290.00	78,228	183,658.00	105,430.00				
13	B_6	731,622.00	78,887	146,324.40	67,437.47				
14	C_1	853,840.00	87,576	170,768.00	83,191.92				
15	C_2	654,453.00	79,121	130,890.60	51,769.15				
16	C_3	713,384.00	74,683	142,676.80	67,993.53				
17	C_4	833,334.00	79,480	166,666.80	87,186.49				
18	C_5	713,794.00	76,113	142,758.80	66,645.47				
19	C_6	720,059.00	78,810	144,011.80	65,201.91				
20	D_1	708,708.00	72,922	141,741.60	68,819.39				
21	D_2	783,988.00	67,798	156,797.60	88,999.93				
22	D_3	727,911.00	68,309	145,582.20	77,273.58				
23	D_4	739,637.00	66,224	147,927.40	81,703.05				
24	D_5	633,371.00	68,852	126,674.20	57,822.26				
25	D_6	744,531.00	67,841	148,906.20	81,065.18				
26	E_1	641,695.00	9,302	128,339.00	119,037.24				
27	E_2	851,016.00	8,573	170,203.20	161,630.47				
28	E_3	705,715.00	8,288	141,143.00	132,855.18				
29	E_4	525,977.00	8,263	105,195.40	96,932.90				
30	E_5	919,664.00	8,060	183,932.80	175,872.94				
31	E_6	657,311.00	8,513	131,462.20	122,949.20				
32									
33	Totals	21,925,033	2,077,329	4,385,007	2,307,678				
34									
35									
36									

Figure 11.4.28 Data for What-if analysis

2 Name the cell that contains the total surplus, 'surplus'.
3 Name the cell that contains the price per eu, 'eu_price'.
4 Make sure the 'Projected Revenue' column stores the 'EU' column multiplied by the 'eu_price' (e.g. 'B2*eu_price').
5 Type a value into the 'Price per eu' cell (e.g. 0.20) and check that a realistic total appears for the surplus. (Carry out a few more test and log them.)
6 Use the menu option 'Tools', 'Goal Seek...' and complete the dialogue box as in Figure 11.4.29. This process is shown in the demonstration you can view from the ActiveBook.

    We want Excel to change the 'eu_price' until the 'surplus' cell (the 'Set cell:') ends up as zero.

Continued on the next page

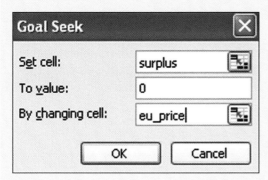

Figure 11.4.29 Goal seeking dialogue box

7 On clicking 'OK', you will be given the option to save the calculation or leave the worksheet as it was. Choose to accept the changes.

In this example, the value returned to the 'eu_price' was 0.09.

As well as using goal seeking, Tina can simply change the 'eu_price' to what she thinks is acceptable and see whether the surplus is within acceptable limits. Excel also has a more sophisticated facility, Solver, which allows for the changing of more than one variable. In our example we only have one variable, price, but in your own assignment you might have more, so Solver is worth investigating further.

▶ Charts

Unit 3 has already covered much on charting and Tina's requirements are fairly limited here (see the functional specifications). However, to make sure that you are familiar with all the chart objects and their properties, try Activity 10.

ACTIVITY 10 Use chart objects and properties ◀

1 Open this workbook from the ActiveBook.
2 Open the 'ChartBudget' sheet.
3 Double-click on as many items (objects) on the chart as you can and make a note of the name of the dialogue box that appears. You should find at least six. Each of these allows you to change the properties of the object you clicked on. But what if the objects are too small? This is where the chart toolbar comes in very handy.
4 If the chart toolbar is not already visible (see Fig. 11.4.30) use the menu option 'View', 'Toolbars', 'Chart'.

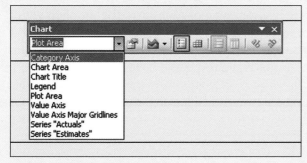

Figure 11.4.30 Chart toolbar

Select each of the objects in the drop-down list.

Continued on the next page

5 Now try the 'Data Table' button on the chart toolbar to get a data table at the bottom of the chart.

6 Finally, note that you can change the type of chart by simply selecting the chart type button on the chart toolbar. (Use 'Edit', 'Undo' if you want to get back to the original chart!)

You can view a demonstration of this from the ActiveBook.

It is also worth noting that when we created the pivot table we also had the option to store this as a chart (a pivot table report).

ACTIVITY 11 Create a pivot chart

1 Open the 'PivotTable' sheet.

2 Select one of the pivot tables (ensure that you have highlighted all the pivot table cells).

3 Click on the mouse's right button and, from the drop-down menu select 'Pivot Chart'.

4 A pivot chart is automatically created, based on this table. If you change any of the data displayed (e.g. view only team A), this is what will appear on the worksheet. The chart and table are linked, as any chart is, to data.

▶ Security and passwords

There are different levels of protection for Excel workbooks. Protecting worksheets is covered in Unit 3. It is worth adding, however, that colour coding is quite important here. It is usually assumed that cells that have colour set to 'No fill' (i.e. basically white) are there for data entry. That is, the cells are unlocked. *Tip*: it is usually quicker to lock all the cells in a worksheet and then unlock the ones for data entry as there are fewer of them. Pressing 'Ctrl + A' is a quick way to select the whole sheet. If this only selects a block of data on the sheet, then repeat a second time. Protecting the whole workbook, via the menu option 'Tools', 'Protection', 'Protect Workbook...', stops actions like the deletion of worksheets. Finally, it is possible to protect the workbook at the 'Save As' level so that it cannot be opened without the correct password. This option is available by selecting from the option 'Tools', 'General Options' in the 'Save As...' dialogue box. We can even encrypt our workbook at this level.

If protection is to avoid accidental damage then a password at the worksheet, workbook and 'Save As' level is probably not necessary. The problem with passwords is that sometimes people forget them or the person who knows the password leaves the organisation. This is not uncommon. If passwords are to be used, it is always better to ensure that two people have the password and that it is stored somewhere safe.

For now, assume that Tina only wants cell locking, except for data entry cells.

▶ The user interface

We have a more or less complete solution, but is it easy to use? For example:
- Does Tina know how to use the goal seeking facility?

- Does Tina know that the 'Revenue' worksheet has been set up for the what-if analysis she wants?
- Is it easy to get from one worksheet to another?
- Are the colours and fonts easy on the eye?
- Can an administrator add new features readily?

Good user guides and technical documentation are helpful in this regard, but the workbook should be as self-explanatory as possible. **Accessibility** is also becoming very important in software application development. For example, can the visually impaired use our workbook without difficulty? You could investigate accessibility issues further on the internet. For our current project we cannot cover all the issues in human–computer interaction (HCI), but we can at least undertake one or two activities that will move us in the right direction.

ACTIVITY 12 Create the user interface 1 ◀

In this activity, you will provide clear instructions to the user on Goal Seeking.

1. Open the 'Revenue' sheet in the master workbook.
2. 'Copy' and 'Paste' a screenshot of the Goal Seek dialogue box onto the worksheet (see Fig. 11.4.29).
3. Insert a text box onto the workbook using the Drawing Toolbar ('View', 'Toolbars', 'Drawing').
4. Write instructions in the text box, explaining to the user how to use Goal Seek on the 'Price per EU' to obtain a break-even value (that is, a total surplus of zero). Give the text box a background colour that is easy on the eye. The <u>Lighthouse International</u> website provides some useful guidance on this.
5. Position the objects (text box and picture), and use arrow objects from the drawing toolbar, to ensure that the instructions are clear.
6. Test the clarity by getting someone (e.g. a fellow student or family member) to follow your instructions. Don't forget to put this test in your test log.

A similar approach could be taken for the 'Settings' sheet, explaining how the different values affect the 'ConvertedCosts' sheet.

We could also add a worksheet of project details (like the 'ProjectLookupTable' worksheet in this workbook). We would need to clear this with Tina, but users might find this useful to get important background data.

Finally, we need to tidy up the 'Instructions' sheet.

ACTIVITY 13 Create the user interface 2 ◀

1. Open the 'Instructions' sheet in the master workbook.
2. Insert a text box onto the workbook and list all the worksheets in the workbook and what they are for. (Any hidden sheets can be referred to in the technical documentation.)

Continued on the next page

3 If you know how to use Excel's macro recorder, provide navigation buttons on the Instructions sheet to take users to the appropriate sheets. That is:
- turn on the recorder ('Tools', 'Menu', 'Record New Macro...')
- provide a meaningful name for the macro (e.g. 'GoToConvertedCosts')
- click on cell A1 in the 'ConvertedCosts' worksheet
- stop the recorder
- return to the 'Instructions' sheet
- add a button from the 'Forms' toolbar ('View', 'Toolbars', Forms)
- when the 'Assign Macro' dialogue box pops up, double-click on the 'GoToConvertedCosts' macro
- provide the button with suitable text
- continue for every worksheet
- provide 'ReturnToInstructions' buttons on each worksheet.

You can see a demonstration of this from the ActiveBook.

4 Insert text, or text boxes, at the top of the 'Instructions' sheet, displaying:
- the name of the system (e.g. Team Project Analysis)
- which version number it is (e.g. v1.0)
- when it was constructed.

5 As always, test the text box instructions and navigation buttons and log all this in the test log.

Additional advanced techniques

We have used a number of Excel's advanced features. However, it is likely that when you begin the assignment for Unit 11 you will need some additional features. To cater for this, additional workbooks with instructions can be opened from the ActiveBook. These workbooks cover:

- Excel's Database functions (e.g. DSUM). Useful for analysing tables of data

- referencing cells to find the position of a value, or the value of a position (e.g. MATCH, INDIRECT)

- increasing a chart's data series automatically

- creating a floating bridge graph.

Conclusion

Constructing the solution to the scenario has meant learning about Named Ranges, Dropdown Boxes, LookUp tables, Pivot Tables, Linking Data and much more. Unit 11.4 has provided many practical activities to help the reader learn these spreadsheet techniques. However, as it is not possible in one scenario to cover all the important spreadsheet features, other advanced techniques have been covered in a number of additional spreadsheet examples that you can access from the ActiveBook. Together, the material in Unit 11.4 should give the reader enough knowledge and understanding to tackle the Unit Assignment.

Testing and documentation

Spreadsheets can manipulate data to produce complex results quickly. However, the results produced are not guaranteed to be correct. Formulae may be wrong, logic may be incorrect, data at the boundaries may be left out. To ensure that our solution is working correctly we need to undertake thorough testing, including checking the following:

- linking of data – have we linked the correct cells?
- the formula for converting local currencies to a common currency – is it correct?
- budget performance status messages (i.e. over, under and blank) – are they the correct messages?
- colour coding of budget performance
- values in the pivot tables
- chart values – is the series data correct?

We also need to test what happens when a user inputs invalid values, e.g. text instead of numbers or negative numeric values. Much of this was covered in Unit 11.4 in the section on data validation, but we must not be complacent. What we need is a test plan and test tables (also known as test data tables).

Test plan and test tables

Test plans set out how we are going to carry out our testing. For example, we can test our developing workbooks as we go along (that is, **incremental testing**) and we can test the whole system when we have finished (that is, **system testing**). We should also list all areas we are going to test. This needs to be detailed. Just stating 'User interface' tells us little. 'Testing the navigation buttons' is a bit more specific.

The test tables then provide the detail of how we expected our tests to fare and what actually happened. Hopefully, you have been logging your incremental testing results as you have gone along. However, it may well be that your test tables are not properly laid out. So, try Activity 1.

Activity 1 Use test table ◀

On the 'Settings' worksheet of the master workbook users can enter percentages to represent over and under budget. Do our two cells only accept valid values? The test table (see Fig. 11.5.1) sets out the tests we need to undertake to check that the cells are set up correctly. The table is incomplete.

Continued on the next page

Date:_____

Tester name:_____

Test description: Data validation – over budget and under budget values on the 'Settings' worksheet

Test No.	Type	Test data	Expected results	Observed results	Comments
1	Valid	12%			
2	Valid	120%			
3	Valid	1			
4	Valid	120			
5	Valid	11.9732%			
6	Valid – boundary	0%			
7	Valid – boundary	-1%			
8	Invalid	bob			
9	Invalid				
10	Invalid				

Figure 11.5.1 Test table

1 Open a copy of Figure 11.5.1 from the ActiveBook. Complete the grey cells in the 'Test data' and 'Expected results' columns.
2 Carry out the tests on your copy of the master workbook and complete the 'Observed results' column. Add any useful comments (e.g. possible remedy) to the 'Comments' column.

An example of a ready to use test table and further information on testing spreadsheets can be found on the ActiveBook CD-ROM.

Documentation

So far we have created the following documentation: a functional specification and a design and test plan, with test tables. A user guide and technical documentation are still required. Is it time now to start writing them?

▶ User guide and technical documentation

As stated in Unit 11.2, we should not see the development of our solution as having entirely separate stages. In a prototyping and evolutionary delivery model, all stages are interactive. We should be developing our user guide and technical documentation as we progress. As we refine our understanding of what Tina and her team want – through constant prototyping and feedback

– our functional specification and designs are updated. Our evolutionary model then faces additional modification and testing, and we update our test logs, user guide and technical documentation. When the first version of the solution is complete, we can go through our draft user guide and make it more professional, accurate and user-friendly. However, we do not have to start from scratch. We should already have much of the text and screenshots.

When the documentation is complete, we still need to test it just like everything else. It should be included in our test plan. A good test here would be to get someone else to work through the guide and give feedback.

Finally, the main difference between the two documents is that the user guide should explain to the user how to *use* the system. (Additional advice on user guides is available from the ActiveBook.) The technical documentation is more concerned with how an administrator *maintains* the system. In our present project it would include:

Figure 11.5.2 User and technical guides are essential to help the client make the most of your solution

- a list of all the workbook names, folder names and named ranges
- how the various workbooks relate to each other
- how to re-set links
- how to add additional charts and sheets
- protection, passwords and other security issues
- troubleshooting (at minimum, who to contact)
- test plan and test log if the client requests them.

Conclusion

Although testing is often seen as a stage that occurs at the end of building a spreadsheet solution, it is important to recognise that thinking about testing and setting out test plans are activities that should be started early in the development process. So, ensure that you have read the additional material on testing that you can view from the ActiveBook.

Documentation is not something that should be considered as an optional extra. It is an essential part of providing a solution to a problem and is nearly always specified as a requirement by the client. Users will want some guidance on how to use your product (the user guide) and administrators will want a technical guide that sets out how to maintain the product (e.g. insert new features, modify settings) and troubleshoot any problems. A good user guide and technical guide are invaluable.

Most of what you need when tackling the assignment has already been addressed in Unit 11 and in Unit 3 (and evaluation was covered in Units 1, 2 and 8). However, it is still useful to have a quick recap.

- Ensure that your functional specification is clear and detailed before launching into any real development. Use screenshots for the functional spec and write in the present tense. Then some of this can be used in the other documentation.
- Spending time getting the design right is not wasted time. It saves time in the long run. Make sure you keep the different versions of your design as you update it and give each a different version number.
- Look for quick ways of generating dummy data and multiple worksheets and workbooks. We created five workbooks for the estimates data. Should we have used one Excel .xlt template rather than copy an .xls file?
- Prototyping is a very useful method for getting feedback from the client *and users*. Keep all your prototypes as proof that you have taken this approach, and make sure you log the feedback. Also, distinguish between the throwaway prototypes and the *evolutionary delivery* ones.
- Make sure you have drawn up a test plan early on and keep a detailed test log with test tables. Test *everything* – even the user guide.
- Future-proof your solution as much as possible. One obvious weakness in our solution to Tina's request is what happens if Tina decides on seven projects per team instead of six? If Tina changes her mind right at the end this would involve a lot of additional work, so raise future-proofing issues with the client early on.

Conclusion ▶ ▶ ▶

If you have undertaken all the activities in Unit 11, then you should be able to tackle the Unit Assessment. However, 'practice makes perfect' is very applicable to IT (although it still needs to be based on some sound ideas), so the more practice you get at trying out some of the ideas and techniques set out in Unit 11 the better. A good approach, then, is to set yourself a very small spreadsheet problem, with minimum complexity at this stage (e.g. a spreadsheet solution to handle a mileage claim) and see if you can solve it using the stages specified in this Unit: functional specification, design, prototyping, construction, testing and documentation. After this, you may have a better feel for tackling the real assessment.

Unit 12

Customising Applications

The unit specifications

> **Event-driven programming language**
>
> Specific features of a program written in an event-driven programming language (e.g. importing data, creating a chart) are activated by an event (e.g. a mouse click or key press). Usually these events are initiated by the user.

This unit covers the design, development and testing of a custom solution to a problem requiring the use of either database or spreadsheet software, with added functionality provided by an event-driven programming language, such as Visual Basic for Applications (VBA). As Unit 3 (The Knowledge Worker) and Unit 7 (Using Database Software) have already provided a good introduction to spreadsheet and database software, this unit devotes much of the time to developing the event-driven programming skills required to build such a custom solution.

Good programmers of languages like VBA are aware that developing a successful solution to a problem requires many stages, plus clear answers to a number of crucial questions:

1 Do I really understand what the client/customer wants?
2 Does the client fully understand what he/she wants?
3 How can I be sure that my design will meet these client requirements?
4 When the solution is up and running will a user, or another programmer, be able to make useful modifications to my program?

The first two questions cover what is called **user requirements**, the third question would cover **design methodology and testing**, while the last question is concerned with **program maintenance**. All the various stages involved in successfully solving a problem from beginning to end are sometimes referred to, collectively, as the **software life cycle**.

Covering the unit specifications

Given the unit specification, it is tempting to cover all the material relevant to this unit in the order given above. Issues such as user requirements and design would be looked at first before any coding (e.g. VBA coding) was introduced. Then we would look at testing, maintenance and so on. Although this is the correct way to tackle a real problem, this is not very helpful for the newcomer to programming, as it can all seem very abstract and incomprehensible. Generally, it helps to have a bit of a feel for programming first.

Therefore, the approach taken in this unit is to start with a fairly typical spreadsheet problem, which we can solve with a relatively small amount of Excel VBA code, and build much of our understanding around this. The problem we will use is set out in the scenario below.

In Unit 12.2, we will generate some potentially useful VBA code for solving this problem, using the built-in **macro recorder** in Excel. Important concepts such as **top–down design** and **modular programming** will also be introduced in a practical way. In Unit 12.3 the essential structures and skills that are required in programming will be investigated. Unit 12.4 introduces the more professional approach to programming, where we work through all the software life cycle stages in the correct order. It also shows us how useful **prototyping** can be. Unit 12.5 covers more of the advanced programming code and techniques. The emphasis is on automated database solutions, though spreadsheets are not ignored. The final section, Unit 12.6, provides assistance on tackling the assessed coursework assignment.

The problem

The problem given in the following scenario is not an uncommon one for spreadsheet users. It involves daily repetition, and can easily result in mistakes when undertaken manually. It is crying out for an automated solution. This scenario is often referred to in Unit 12, so it is important that you read it carefully.

The scenario

Tom works in the finance team of a large retail store. Each day his colleague, Ali, sends him a spreadsheet providing all the previous day's sales figures for the store, department by department (e.g. clothes, food, gardening). Although not every section provides their daily figures, most do. One of Tom's daily tasks is to produce a column chart from these figures for his boss, Sheila, who then puts them in a report. There is a standard layout for the chart, covering font, background colour, scale etc., and this must be adhered to. Tom is fed up with going through more or less the same keystrokes each day to create the chart and thinks there must be a way of automating the process.

Tom reckons that he ought to be able to create the chart once, in one main spreadsheet, and then simply copy and paste the daily data from Ali's spreadsheet into this. Then, hey presto, at the press of a button a new chart is automatically created and the new version saved to disk, with a file name containing yesterday's date, ready to be sent to Sheila.

Conclusion ▶ ▶ ▶

We now have an idea of what the rest of the unit will be covering and why they are covered in the particular order that they are. In addition, a scenario has been set out that provides a typical example of the kind of task that VBA solutions are used for. This scenario can, therefore, be used to help to lay the foundations for undertaking the Unit Assessment.

In Unit 12.2, we will use the Macro Recorder in Microsoft Excel to generate some potentially useful code for solving the problem set out in the scenario. Once the code has been generated, concepts, such as **classes**, **objects**, **methods**, **properties**, **collections** and **events**, can be explained in a more meaningful way.

Activity 1 Create a chart using the Macro Recorder

Before turning the Macro Recorder on, we need to set up a spreadsheet with the kind of data that Tom might be expecting from his colleague, Ali. So, let us assume that Ali has sent Tom the spreadsheet data in Figure 12.2.1.

	A	B	C
1	Sales at:	10/11/2005	
2			
3		**Department**	**Value(£)**
4		Carpet	2,500
5		Children's Clothing	3,000
6		Electrical	4,000
7		Food	9,250
8		Furniture	3,000
9		Gardening	1,700
10		Hardware	1,400
11		Lighting	975
12		Men's Clothing	900
13		Women's Clothing	3,500
14			

Figure 12.2.1 Daily sales figures

You can see a demonstration of the following steps from the ActiveBook.

1   Enter this data into a workbook and save the file to disk as 'daily_sales.xls'. We can use the Macro Recorder to get an idea of the sort of VBA code we might need when we eventually develop an automated solution to Tom's problem. However, at this stage, we will only use the recorder to create a simple column chart.

2   Turn on the recorder ('Tools', 'Macro', 'Record New Macro...') and make sure that the drop-down box labelled 'Store macro in:' is displaying the option 'This Workbook'. Do *not* click the 'OK' button at this stage. We need to change the macro name.

Continued on the next page

One way of telling a poor programmer from a good one is to look at the macro names that the programmer has used throughout the VBA code. If the code is littered with names like Macro1, Macro2 etc., then the programming is usually poor. Using meaningful names early on is crucial for later **debugging and maintenance**.

3 Type 'CreateColumnChart' into the 'Macro name:' text box (see Fig. 12.2.2). Click on the 'OK' button.

4 Now that the recording has started, go through the following steps to create the chart:

   i Highlight all the data, including the labels (see Fig. 12.2.3).

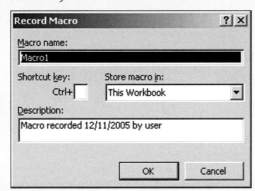

Figure 12.2.2 Naming a new macro

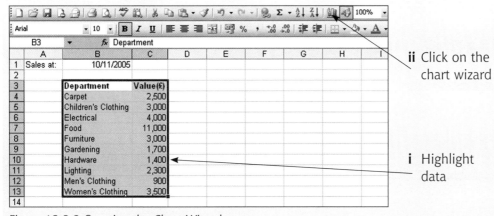

ii Click on the chart wizard

i Highlight data

Figure 12.2.3 Opening the Chart Wizard

Naming conventions

Since we are trying to record the keystrokes to create a column chart, it would make more sense to call the macro 'create column chart' rather than Macro1. Macros, however, do not like spaces in their names, so we could call the macro 'createcolumnchart'. As this is quite hard to read a number of different naming conventions have arisen. One convention is to keep the name in all lower case letters and use the underscore for spaces; that is, 'create_column_chart'. Programmers who are used to working in a Unix environment tend to prefer this method as Unix is case sensitive. The main alternative is to use a capital letter for the start of each new word, but not use any spaces; that is, 'CreateColumnChart'. Either method is acceptable as long as we are consistent.

ii Click on the 'Chart Wizard' button.

iii In Chart Wizard Step 1 (see Fig. 12.2.4) select the 'Column' chart and first sub-type, then click the 'Next' button. In Chart Wizard Step 2 (see Fig. 12.2.5) simply click the 'Next' button.

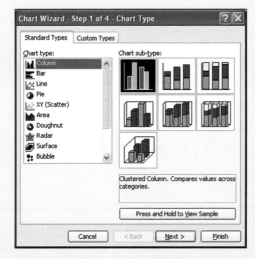

Figure 12.2.4 Chart Wizard Step 1

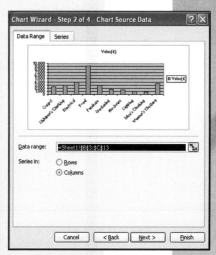

Figure 12.2.5 Chart Wizard Step 2

Continued on the next page

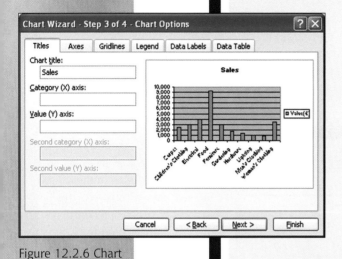

Figure 12.2.6 Chart Wizard Step 3

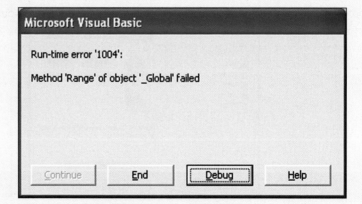

Figure 12.2.7 Chart Wizard Step 4

iv For Chart Wizard Step 3 (see Fig. 12.2.6) change the 'Chart title' to 'Sales', then click the 'Next' button.

v For Chart Wizard Step 4 (see Fig. 12.2.7) select the 'As new sheet:' option, but leave the name as 'Chart1'. (We need this for a later activity.)

Finally, click the 'Finish' button.

vi The column chart should appear as in Figure 12.2.8.

vii Turn the Macro Recorder off (either by clicking on the 'Stop Recording' button or using the menu option 'Tools', 'Macro', 'Stop Recording').

5 Return to the worksheet and test that the macro has been successfully recorded. That is, use the 'Tools', 'Macro','Macros...' menu option, select 'CreateColumnChart' from the list and click the 'Run' button. If clicking on the 'Run' button creates another column chart, 'Chart2', then the macro has been created successfully.

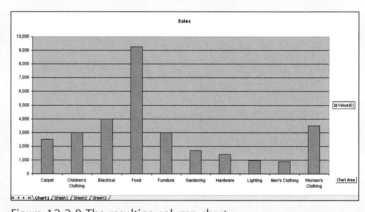

Figure 12.2.8 The resulting column chart

Error messages

If on the other hand we get something like the dialogue box in Figure 12.2.9, then a mistake has been made.

Figure 12.2.9 Error message dialogue box

Continued on the next page

For example, we may have tried to run the macro from the chart window rather than the worksheet window, or retyped 'Chart1' into the text box in the Chart Wizard final step (see step 4v).

We should get used to this run-time error message box as it is likely to appear quite often when we try to run incorrect code. By the end Unit 12.2, we should have a better idea of how to remedy this sort of problem.

6 Finally, we will look at the code in what is called the **Visual Basic Editor**. One of the options available via the Macro dialogue box (generated by 'Tools', 'Macro', 'Macros...') is the 'Edit' button. Using this is the simplest way of getting to see the macro's code (see Fig. 12.2.10).

```
daily_sales.xls - Module1 (Code)
(General)                                    CreateColumnChart

Sub CreateColumnChart()
' CreateColumnChart Macro
' Macro recorded 02/03/2006 by user


    Range("B3:C13").Select
    ActiveWindow.Zoom = 150
    Columns("B:B").ColumnWidth = 15.43
    Charts.Add
    ActiveChart.ChartType = xlColumnClustered
    ActiveChart.SetSourceData Source:=Sheets("Sheet1").Range("B3:C13"), PlotBy _
        :=xlColumns
    ActiveChart.Location Where:=xlLocationAsNewSheet
    With ActiveChart
        .HasTitle = True
        .ChartTitle.Characters.Text = "Sales"
        .Axes(xlCategory, xlPrimary).HasTitle = False
        .Axes(xlValue, xlPrimary).HasTitle = False
    End With
End Sub
```

Figure 12.2.10 Macro code

The text shown in the Visual Basic Editor is our VBA code. It can look pretty daunting, particularly with all those dots between the words. What does it all mean? To make sense of the code fully, we need to understand terms like **objects**, **methods**, **properties**, **collections** and **events** – look at the panel about these.

Classes, Objects, Methods, Properties, Collections and Events

Object-orientated programming has been around for some time and the term can sound very mystifying. In fact, the purpose behind it is to make programming easier.

Forget about Excel for a minute and think about a game like draughts or even chess. Imagine that we would like to write a computer program to play one of these games, where we pit the wits of the computer against the user. Wouldn't it be nice if someone had already written a draughts or chess programming language where most of the work had already been done for us? For example, a language that allows us to state very easily the things that we want at the start of this game of draughts or chess; that is, a board, pieces, players and a rule book. The language would be even better if it made it easy for us to state what we wanted these things to do; for example, in the case of a piece, move or take another piece. Finally, the ability to describe these things would also be great; for example, give the players a name and give the pieces a colour.

In our imaginary language, we would be able to write things like:

Players(1).Name = "bob's computer"
Players(2).Name = "Sheila"
Pieces("Black_King").Move (4,5)

Continued on the next page

The first two lines would let the program know what the players' names were. The third would move the black king to position (4, 5) on the board.

We still need to write the rest of the program, but it is so much easier if we already have these features available. In fact, in an object-orientated language, the 'things' referred to above, such as board or player, are called **objects**. An activity associated with an object, like 'move' or 'take', is called a **method** and a characteristic of an object, like a name or colour, is referred to as a **property**. In a way, we can think of objects as a bit like nouns, methods as a bit like verbs and properties as a bit like adjectives.

Technically, we should use **class** when referring to a *type* of thing and only use object when we refer to an *instance* of it. For example, 'Players' is a class in this example but 'Players(2)', which refers specifically to 'Sheila', is an object/instance of that class.

So what is a **collection**? In this case we are referring to all the similar objects we have created in our program. In our game of draughts we have a collection of two players and a collection of 24 pieces.

Finally, **events**. When the program is written, what activity gets our program running? Does the user click a button, press a key or use a joystick? All these are possible events to get the program started.

ACTIVITY 2 Name the parts ◀

After reading the panel above, a line of code like 'Charts.Add' (see Fig.12.2.10) should make a lot more sense.

1 Is the term 'Charts' a class, object, method, property or event?
2 Is 'Add' a class, object, method, property or event?

'Charts' in VBA is a class and 'Add' is one of its methods. The full stop between the words 'Charts.Add' is used to show that this method belongs to this object or class. (In object-orientated language the term **encapsulate** is often used here.) So what does the line of code do? It creates a new chart for our workbook.

However, at this stage, we have not said what type of chart we want; that is, the chart's properties. The line that reads 'ActiveChart.ChartType = xlColumnClustered' begins setting a number of these properties:
- 'ActiveChart' is the object
- 'ChartType' is one of the chart's properties
- 'xlColumnClustered' is the value of that property.

The lines that follow set other properties like the range of worksheet cells to be included in the chart, the title of the chart and whether the chart is to be located on the data worksheet or have its own sheet (that is, 'ActiveChart.Location Where:=xlLocationAsNewSheet'). To make Excel VBA easier to read, many property values are provided in text form rather than as numbers. So, the location property could have been set as 'ActiveChart.Location Where:=1'.

A value '2' would have left the chart displayed on the worksheet. If we can use 'xlLocationAsNewSheet' or xlLocationAsObject' instead, it is so much easier to work out what is going on. Excel refers to these text values as **constants**.

ACTIVITY 3 Modify the code ◀

Just to check that we have understood all this, we will change one of the properties of the chart and see its effect. You can also see a demonstration of this from the ActiveBook.

1 Edit the line:

```
.ChartTitle.Characters.Text = "Sales"
```

to:

```
.ChartTitle.Characters.Text = "Daily Sales by Department"
```

2 When you have completed this, return to the worksheet. It is important you do this before running the code, otherwise VBA brings up an error message as it tries to run the code in the VB Editor and cannot find the chart sheet there. You can return to the worksheet a number of ways. One method is to select the menu option 'File', 'Close and Return to Microsoft Excel', another is to use the shortcut key 'Alt + Q'.

3 Now, when the macro is re-run, a second chart is created, this time with the title 'Daily Sales by Department'. It is worth noting that the macro has not changed the title for chart 1.

4 If this has all worked correctly, make sure that this new version of the code is saved, via the menu option 'File', 'Save'.

Before moving onto Unit 12.3, where the more formal structures and skills of programming can be dealt with, and where we can add a bit more depth to our scenario solution, we can still pick up a few more useful concepts from these activities. These are: **Literals**, **Subroutines**, **Comments** and **Events**.

Literals

When writing programs, we should try to avoid typing in the **literal** value of something. We look at alternatives to this in Unit 12.3. In Activity 3, when we changed the property from 'Sales' to 'Daily Sales by Department', we changed it from one literal value to another. Similarly, the cell range 'B3:C13' is a literal value.

Subroutines and parameters

In Figure 12.2.10 the name of our macro, 'CreateColumnChart', appears in the following line of code: 'Sub CreateColumnChart ()'. There is also an 'End Sub' at the bottom of the subroutine. The reason for this is that in the various Basic programming languages the term **subroutine** is used when grouping a set of instructions together, rather than the term **macro**. In fact, the term 'macro' itself has more than one meaning in computing. Additionally, some languages use other words. The programming language Pascal prefers the term 'procedure', while C prefers the term 'function'. However, keeping things simple, we can roughly say that a subroutine or procedure, even our macro, groups a set of instructions together. The more precise and specific the set of instructions, the easier it is to check for errors in a program, or trap for user errors (this is covered in Unit 12.3) and even reuse code.

In our subroutine, we have grouped a set of instructions together to create a column chart from a range of cells. Why the brackets '( )' though? At the moment these are empty, but we could put what are called **parameters** into them. This is covered in Unit 12.3, but spreadsheet users should not find the concept too difficult. For example, Excel uses the function Today(), with nothing in the brackets, whereas the Sum() function must have values in the brackets. In other words, the Sum function takes parameter values.

Comments

Just below 'Sub CreateColumnChart ()' there are a few lines that start with apostrophes (the ' character) and are coloured green. These are **comment** lines and are there to provide essential information to programmers when they need to improve programs, add new features, remove bugs or simply remind themselves how they wrote the code in the first place. The comments in our subroutine are far too limited but at least we have the date when the subroutine was written. In Unit 12.4 we explore how using good commenting can enhance the future use of a program dramatically; in many of the activities that follow, the comments are left out simply to reduce typing errors.

Object Browser and other useful help facilities

So far, our macro recording exercise has only created a small amount of VBA code: a few objects, a few methods and a few properties. Just what is available to us in VBA? How many objects (or, more correctly, classes) are there?

ACTIVITY 4 Use the Object Browser ◀

Excel provides a very useful tool to find out just what objects are available and what methods, properties and events can be associated with them. This tool is the **Object Browser**. In this activity we will use the browser to see how many methods and properties are associated with the class Charts. You can also see a demonstration of this from the ActiveBook.

1 Open the workbook 'daily_sales.xls'. Launch the VB Editor from the worksheet, either by using the shortcut key 'Alt + F11' or using the menu

Continued on the next page

option 'Tools', 'Macro', 'Visual Basic Editor'. You should get a screen looking something like Figure 12.2.11.

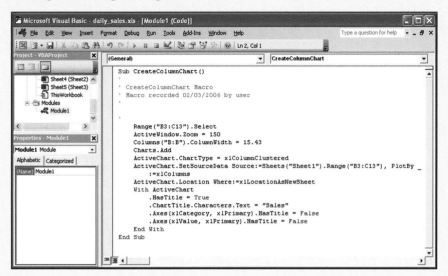

Figure 12.2.11 Visual Basic Editor

Whether your screen looks exactly like this depends on what state it was left in last time. Often the Editor displays three windows: Project Explorer, the Properties Window and Code Window, but any of these could be closed. For the Object Browser, it does not matter. We select this from the VB Editor menu.

2 Use the shortcut key 'F2' or the menu option 'View', 'Object Browser' and you should get a screen similar to Figure 12.2.12.

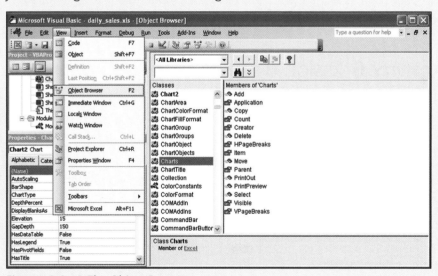

Figure 12.2.12 The Object Browser

3 Select the word 'Charts' (not 'Chart') from the 'Classes' list and look at the list alongside it. We can see that seven methods, including 'Add' and 'Select', are given a green icon; the eight properties, including 'Count' and 'Visible', are given the property icon – a hand holding a piece of paper.

4 Not only can we see all the methods and properties for a class this way, but Excel also has a built-in context-sensitive help system – if you hit the

Continued on the next page

'F1' key when a word is highlighted, Excel can generally pull up some help on that word. So, with 'Charts' selected, hit the 'F1' key. You should get a window of help information explaining the Charts collection.

We have not covered events yet, but we can use the Object Browser to show us what events can be associated with objects.

ACTIVITY 5 Find object events

Use the Object Browser to look up the object called 'Chart' (not 'Charts').

1 List the events you can find.
2 What symbol is associated with events?

In the case of the object 'Chart', one of the events is 'Activate'. (The symbol to identify an event is the lightening symbol.) This means that we could associate a subroutine with this particular event. In other words, we could display a pop-up message every time the user activated the chart. Altogether, you should have found at least 10 events including 'MouseDown', 'MouseUp' and 'Resize'. For the moment, however, we will only use one event with our existing subroutine; clicking a button to run the code.

One of the simplest and most useful events for running and testing code during program development is that of clicking a button to run the code. With the existing subroutine, 'CreateColumnChart', this means putting a button on the worksheet, with a helpful text label that states something like 'Click here to create a new chart'. On clicking the button, a new chart is automatically created.

ACTIVITY 6 Assign a button to the subroutine

The simplest button to use is the one supplied with the Forms toolbar.

1 To obtain this button, use the menu option 'View', 'Toolbars', 'Forms'. Do not use the Control Toolbox toolbar. Although this provides a button it is far too complicated to use at this stage.

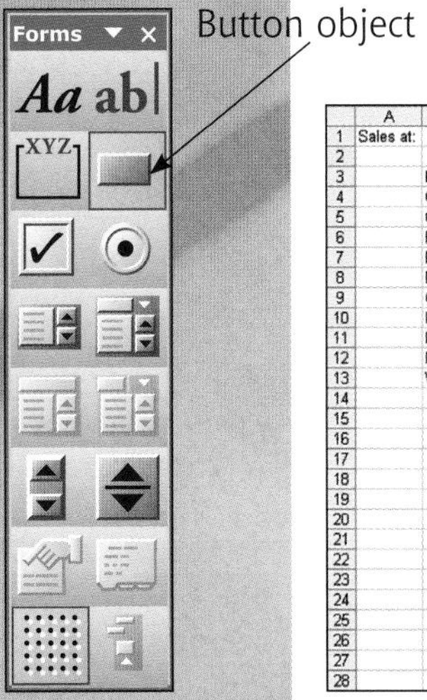

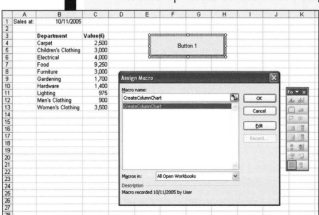

Button object

Figure 12.2.13
Forms toolbar

Figure 12.2.14 Assign macro

2 When the Forms toolbar appears (see Fig. 12.2.13), click on the button image in the toolbar once; let go of the mouse button; move the mouse to where you want the button to appear; then use your mouse to click and drag over a rectangular area for the button size.

3 On releasing the mouse you should get the dialogue box shown in Figure 12.2.14.

4 Make sure that you select the subroutine, 'CreateColumnChart', before clicking the 'OK' button.

Continued on the next page

5   Change the text in the button object (by clicking on the button object, see Fig. 12.2.15) to 'Click here to create a new chart'. You can view a demonstration of this from the ActiveBook.

6   Click on the button and a new chart should be created automatically. In fact, every time you click a new chart appears, labelled 'Chart2', 'Chart3' etc. If you need to change the text on the button, click on the button object with the right button on your mouse. This brings up a menu with an 'Edit Text' option.

Figure 12.2.15
Button object

Conclusion ▶ ▶ ▶

The Excel macro recorder has been used in Unit 12.2 to generate a small amount of VBA code to enable us to get a better idea of what constitutes an object-orientated programming language. The concepts are not that difficult and once we know what is meant by an object, a method, a property and even an event, it becomes much easier to program in other applications that use VBA. So, while in Excel we may want objects like workbooks, worksheets and ranges, in a database package like Access we might want a database, recordset, form or textbox. In addition, a few program design features have been covered to ensure that any code we write is readable, easily maintainable and professional: that is using subroutines and comments, and avoiding literals. However, we have not yet covered enough to tackle the original scenario in a professional manner. Unit 12.3 will help us to do this.

Program structures and skills

In Unit 12.3, we undertake practical activities to cover a number of essential concepts and issues. These include:
- programming structures
- logical and relational operators
- subroutine calls
- variables and constants
- data types and data structures
- parameters
- global variables versus parameter passing
- validation
- error trapping.

Where appropriate, the activities will refer to the scenario in Unit 12.1.

Programming structures

Like other programming languages, VBA uses the three main **constructs** (that is, **con**trol **struct**ures): **sequence**, **selection** and **iteration**. There is a fourth construct, **transfer**, but as we shall see it is discouraged, though it is extremely useful in error trapping.

▶ Sequence

When executing a subroutine, VBA starts at the first statement and works its way through, executing one statement after another, that is, in sequence. Therefore, when we run the subroutine we created in Unit 12.2 ('CreateColumnChart'), the statement 'Range("B3:C13").Select' is executed first, the statement 'Charts.Add' is executed next and so on.

The exceptions are where we *call* another subroutine within our subroutine or we use the transfer statement, 'GOTO'. These are discussed further in the sections on subroutine calls and error trapping, but it is worth noting that even when a subroutine goes off to run another subroutine it still returns to where it left off.

▶ Selection

To understand selection, we will use the scenario set out in Unit 12.1. We will not use the macro recorder this time, but type the code manually.

ACTIVITY 1 Understand selection ◀

Let us assume that before Tom pastes in the new set of daily figures into his master workbook, 'daily_sales.xls', he wants to be able to press a button that deletes all the old charts left over from the previous day's figures.

1 Open your copy of 'daily_sales.xls', created in Unit 12.2, and ensure that there are at least four charts created. If there are not, click on the button to create a few more.

2 View the subroutine 'CreateColumnChart'. This can be achieved either by using the menu option 'Tools', 'Macro', 'Macros…', then selecting 'CreateColumnChart' in the Macro dialogue box, then clicking the 'Edit' button or by using the VBE shortcut key 'Alt + F11'. In this latter case, you may need to use the 'View' menu option to select the 'Project Explorer' and then click on 'Module1' in the Modules folder, itself in 'VBAProject(daily_sales.xls)'.

3 Just below the 'End Sub' of subroutine, 'CreateColumnChart', type the following:

```
Sub DeleteAllCharts
  ActiveWorkbook.Charts.Delete
End Sub
```

Notice that when you press the enter key, after typing 'Sub DeleteAllCharts', the VB Editor puts the brackets in for you and the statement 'End Sub'. In addition, when you hit the full stop after typing 'ActiveWorkbook', a drop-down box appears supplying all the methods, properties and events for that object – very useful indeed. Just hit the 'Tab' key when you have selected 'Charts' from the drop-down list.

4 Go back to the worksheet and assign a Forms toolbar button to this new subroutine, 'DeleteAllCharts' (see Activity 6, Unit 12.2 for how to do this). Give the button a text label like 'Delete all charts'. This process is shown in the demonstration you can view from the ActiveBook.

5 Test the button and see if all the charts are deleted. (Initially, Excel will display a dialogue box to check that you want to delete all the charts.) If the code does not work and you get the error message box, similar to the one mentioned in the Unit 12.2, click on the 'End' button in the error message and check your code again. That is, **debug** the program. Are the brackets there? It should read:

```
Sub DeleteAllCharts()
  ActiveWorkbook.Charts.Delete
End Sub
```

If absolutely nothing happens, this is probably because you did not assign the button to the 'DeleteAllCharts' subroutine, so create another button and try again.

6 When all the charts are deleted, click on the button again. The code should now fall over (that is, crash)! So, click on the 'End' button in the error message to stop the code running. Why do you think the subroutine fell over?

Continued on the next page

7 We need to modify this routine in order to avoid trying to delete charts when there are no charts to be deleted (which is why it falls over). For this, we need a conditional statement. So, modify the code to read:

```
Sub DeleteAllCharts()
If Charts.Count > 0 Then
   ActiveWorkbook.Charts.Delete
Else
   MsgBox "There are no charts to delete"
End If
End Sub
```

8 Test the delete button again and check to see that it displays the message 'There are no charts to delete'. if the workbook has no charts. Create a few more charts with the other button, and check that the delete button still works correctly. This process is shown in the demonstration you can view from the ActiveBook.

One of the many lessons we should have learnt from Activity 1 is just how important testing is. If we had only tested the button when our workbook contained charts, we might have thought that it worked fine. Testing for all possible situations is an essential part of testing.

Relational operators

Another useful insight that we can gain from Activity 1 is that when we set up a conditional statement we generally use what is called a **relational operator**. Examples of relational operators are the equals sign (=), greater than sign (>), less than sign (<) or even a combination like greater than or equals (>=). So, in Activity 1, the statement 'Charts.Count > 0' used the greater than symbol. This statement, sometimes called a **conditional statement**, is tested for **true** or **false**. If true, then one statement of code will be executed; if false, the other statement(s) will be.

As for selection, VBA has provided the programmer with an **If-Then-Else-End If** selection construct. This is not dissimilar to the **IF** function that is used in Excel workbooks. The first line of this code carries out a test. That is, if you count all the charts in the workbook is the result greater than zero? ('Charts.Count' provides a useful **method** for the charts **collection** in the workbook.) If the test is true (there is at least one chart) then the statement 'ActiveWorkbook.Charts.Delete' is executed. If the statement is false then the **Else** part of the selection structure is executed – in this case, displaying a message. Finally, the whole of the selection construct is rounded off with an **End If**, so that VBA knows what statements go with this selection construct. The general layout for this structure is therefore:

If test is true **Then**
    execute the following statements
Else
    execute these statements instead
End If
    now get on with the rest of the program

You can have as many statements as you like and the test can contain more than one condition; for example,

```
Charts.Count > 0 AND Charts(1).ChartTitle.Characters.Text = "Sales"
```

This would stop any charts getting deleted if the first chart did not have 'Sales' as the title. As well as the **logical operator**, **AND**, VBA also provides **OR** and **NOT**.

Activity 2 Use logical and relational operators ◀

In this activity, both a logical operator, NOT, and a relational operator, >, are used.

Write a second version of the 'DeleteAllCharts' subroutine, called 'DeleteAll ChartsMethod2', but use the NOT operator to test for there not being more than zero charts. Here is the bulk of the code. Complete the missing bits.

```
Sub DeleteAllChartsMethod2()

    If NOT (Charts.Count > 0) Then
        _____
        Else
        _____
        End If
    End Sub
```

You can compare your code with this workbook.

> ### Security settings
>
> Your computer's security settings may prevent you opening this and other Excel speadsheets and Microsoft Access databases. For further information on changing these settings see the Help Section. You may need help from a network administrator.

If our code should ever require a lot of tests before a statement or set of statements is executed, the VBA reserved words **Select Case-Case-Case Else-End Select** might be better. Activity 3 provides an example and an exercise.

Activity 3 Select Case ◀

1 Open up this workbook.
2 Run the subroutine and look at the code.
3 Undertake the exercise described in the worksheet text box.

The code in Activity 3 could have been achieved using four separate IF statements, but the Select Case is more efficient. Once the correct result has been found, for example, the text is horizontal, no more testing is undertaken, but with four IF statements each would be tested even if the correct answer was found in the first IF statement.

> ### Module sheets and scope
>
> Activities 1 and 3 refer to the module sheet, Module1. So what is a module sheet? It is probably best to think of it simply as a sheet of paper on which we can write our VBA code in subroutines. We can have many module sheets and these are created by using the VB Editor menu option 'Insert', 'Module'. We can even rename the module through the Properties Window in the VB Editor. The main reason for having more than one module sheet is to keep our work organised better. For example, we might have all our mathematical subroutines on one module sheet and all our graphical subroutines on another. Although these subroutines would not be on the same module sheet they can still use each other (that is, **call** each other). The **scope** of a subroutine allows it to be available to all the other subroutines in any modules in the workbook. However, module sheets should not be confused with **modular** programming, which is touched upon in Unit 12.4. Finally, be aware that code can also be associated with objects on worksheets and database forms. This will be covered in Unit 12.5.

▶ Iteration

Iteration refers to repetition, and VBA provides a number of options. For a fixed number of repetitions use the **For-To-Next** keywords. If a conditional statement is required as well (e.g. repeat until the active cell is blank) then a number of options are possible; for example, **While-Wend** or **Do-While-Loop** or **Do-Loop-While** or **Do-Until-Loop** or **Do-Loop-Until**.

Activities 4 and 5 provide a couple of examples that will give us some useful code when we eventually tackle the main scenario.

ACTIVITY 4 Use fixed repetition, For-To-Next ◀

In this activity, the subroutine, 'InsertAToZ' inserts all the letters of the alphabet in the first 26 rows of column A using the **For-To-Next** repetition structure. The code contains no comments, simply to reduce typing error. Normally, comments should be included. Also, we will create a new module for the first time.

1 Open a new workbook.

2 Open the VB Editor and make sure that the workbook name is selected in the Project Explorer. (We do not want the module inserted into the wrong workbook!) Use the menu option 'Insert', 'Module'. This will create a new sheet.

3 Type in the following code:

```
Sub InsertAToZ()
    Dim intLoop As Integer

    Range("A1").Select

    For intLoop = 1 To 26
        ActiveCell.Value = Chr(intLoop + 64)
        ActiveCell.Offset(1, 0).Select
    Next intLoop
End Sub
```

4 Add a button on the worksheet, save the workbook and test the code.

5 Note how the code is indented. All the lines between 'Sub' and 'End Sub' have used the tab key to move the text right. All the text between 'For' and 'Next' has been tabbed again. This indented layout is much easier to read and debug. You should always use indentation in all your programming.

6 In case you are wondering about the second line that starts 'Dim intLoop...', this is dealt with later in this section under 'Variables'.

Naming conventions again

Just as we have seen that there are naming conventions for subroutines, so there are naming conventions for constants and variables. Generally, three-letter prefixes are put in front of the variable or constant name to give us an idea of its **data type**. This is very useful when we want to update or debug an existing program. Here is a list of typical prefixes:

bln for Boolean	lng for long
cur for currency	obj for object
dat for date	sng for single
dbl for double	str for string
int for integer	var for variant

So a variable to store someone's surname might be called 'strSurname', while a variable to store their birthday might be 'datBirthday'.

Data type basics

Before you go further, make sure you know about:

- data types

If not, refer back to the work you did in Unit 2.

In Activity 4, a section of code is repeated exactly 26 times. First time round the loop, the statement 'ActiveCell.Value = Chr(intLoop + 64)' puts ASCII value 65 (which is character 'A') into cell A1. This is because 'intLoop' stores the value 1 first time round the loop. Add 64 to it and you get 65. The next statement, 'ActiveCell.Offset(1, 0).Select' moves the cursor down one row, but stays in the same column. Second time round the loop, the statement 'ActiveCell.Value = Chr(intLoop + 64)' puts ASCII value 66 (which is character 'B') into cell A1. This is because 'intLoop' now stores the value 2. The next statement, 'ActiveCell.Offset(1, 0).Select' moves the cursor down one row, but stays in the same column. This continues until the section of code has been executed 26 times.

More useful is the ability to include a condition with the repetition. An example is given in Activity 5.

Arithmetic operators and a warning

Anyone familiar with Excel spreadsheets should already know that formulae can use the **arithmetic operators**: that is, +, - , / , * (multiply), ^ (the power of) and brackets ( ). In addition, a spreadsheet user should know that there is an order in which these operators are executed. Brackets are first, followed by ^, then / or *, then + or - . Thus, on a worksheet, '= 2 + 3 * 4' should give the result 14, whereas '= (2 + 3)*4' returns the result 20. VBA also uses these operators in the same way, but it does have an additional division symbol, \, for integer division. This means that while we would expect 6/4 to return 1.5, 6\4 would only return the whole part of the number, that is, 1 (see data types later in Unit 12.3 for more detail). So when you use the division sign in a formula, make sure you use the right one!

ACTIVITY 5 Use conditional repetition, Do-While-Loop

In this activity, the subroutine, 'FindFirstBlankCell', moves the cursor down a block of data in a column until it reaches a blank cell. That is, the cursor moves down a cell if it is not blank. This is a very useful piece of code and we could use it later in our solution to the scenario. It could be used to find out the boundaries of the block of data that Tom pastes into his main workbook.

1 Use the workbook created in Activity 4 and make sure that the letters A to Z are in the first 26 rows of column A.

2 Open the VB Editor and open Module1 in that workbook.

3 Type in the following code below the first subroutine:

```
Sub FindFirstBlankCell ()

    Range("A1").Select

    Do While Activecell.Value <> ""
      Activecell.Offset(1,0).Select
    Loop

  End Sub
```

4 Add a button on the worksheet, save the workbook and test the code.

5 When you have tested that it works, run it again after you have:

i removed a few of the last letters

ii removed a middle letter.

Did the cursor stop where you expected?

 In Activity 5 the **Do-Loop** provides the repetition, whereas the **While** does the testing. The test in this case is that the value in the cell that the cursor is on, 'Activecell.Value', is not blank. The 'not' is represented by the greater than and less than symbols, <>, and 'blank' is represented by two double quotes with nothing between them, "". As the test is undertaken first, this is a **pre-conditional loop**. Look at this example of a **post-conditional loop**.

Subroutine calls

Before looking at the importance of variables and constants to programming it is worth noting that subroutines are able to have subroutines inside them. In fact, this is how we run a number of subroutines together; we simply wrap another subroutine around the lot of them and associate a button with this routine.

For example, our solution to Tom's problem might start to look like this:

```
Sub CreateDailyChart()
    DeleteChartsAndDataFromMainWorkbook
    ImportNewData
    CreateNewChart
    SaveNewChartToDisk
End Sub
```

Each of the statements in the main subroutine, 'CreateDailyChart', is a subroutine itself with a 'Sub...End Sub' further down the Module Sheet. As 'CreateDailyChart' is run, each subroutine is executed in sequence. That is, each is **called** by the main subroutine, 'CreateDailyChart'. We will undertake an activity that uses the ability of one subroutine to **call** another later on in Unit 12.3.

Variables, constants and Option Explicit

▶ Variables

In Activities 3 and 4 the word 'Dim' appeared in statements like 'Dim intResult As Integer'. Dim does not mean stupid, but is a short name for dimension. We are instructing the computer to put aside some memory (that is, **dimension** a piece of memory) to store a value. In this case, the value it will store will be a whole number, that is, an integer. However, we do not know what that number is yet. Since the number can vary, we use the term **variable**. We use the word **integer** to tell the computer what its **data type** is. As for the 'intResult' part of the statement, this is the word we give the piece of memory store. When we want the computer to put a number into it, or overwrite an existing number in it, or tell us what the number is, we simply refer to this name. We could have called it 'Rhubarb', but we should really choose a name that reminds us what the store is for and what its data type is; thus the 'int' part of the name.

At the beginning of a subroutine it is important to state what variables we are going to use. To use the jargon, we should **declare** all our variables. This not only shows that we have thought about what our routine needs to do, but it also reduces potential error, particularly if we put the term 'Option Explicit' at the top of our code. This forces all variables to be declared and stops the programmer accidentally mistyping them as he/she goes along. Try Activity 6 to test this.

ACTIVITY 6 Use Option Explicit and declaring variables ◀

You can also see a demonstration of this activity from the ActiveBook.

1   Open up the workbook containing the 'InsertAToZ' subroutine that you created in Activity 4.
2   View the routine in the VB Editor.

Continued on the next page

3. Create an error by changing the word 'intLoop' in 'ActiveCell.Value = Chr(intLoop + 64)' to 'inLoop'.

4. Run the subroutine from the worksheet.

5. You should get lots of @ symbols.
   Excel has assumed that 'inLoop' is a quite different variable from 'intLoop'. This means you can make up variable names on the fly. Very dangerous indeed!

6. Go back to the code and type 'Option Explicit' at the very top, then run the code from the worksheet.

7. You should get the error message 'Compile Error: Variable not defined', and the variable, 'inLoop', should be highlighted.

8. Click on 'OK' in the error message box.

9. Stop the subroutine still running by using the menu option 'Run', 'Reset'.

10. Change 'inLoop' to 'intLoop' and run again. Save the workbook.

Note: From now on, in all future activities, it will be assumed that you are saving your work as you go along! You will not be reminded anymore.

Option Explicit is very important, so set the VB Editor to do this automatically in the future. Use the menu option 'Tools', 'Option', select the 'Editor' tab, then check the 'Require Variable Declaration' box.

Once a variable is declared, then it can be **assigned** a value. This could be a literal value, for example 'intMyAge = 92' or a value referenced somewhere else. Thus, in Activity 3, intResult was assigned the value of the active cell's orientation. That is, 'intResult = ActiveCell.Orientation'. This process is shown in the demonstration you can view from the ActiveBook.

▶ Constants

Constants are used where we want to retain a fixed value throughout a program, or we want to be able to change a value throughout a program quickly, or we want the code to be more readable and avoid literals. Constants normally appear at the top of programs above the first subroutine.

Here are some examples of where we might use constants. Supposing our program accessed a lot of worksheets and we always wanted the cursor to start in cell A1. Rather than write 'Range("A1").Select' throughout the program, we could write 'Const strStartCell = "A1"' and then write 'Range(strStartCell).Select'. Not only is this easier to understand, but if for some reason we decide the cursor should start at cell A2 (especially if the first row is always full of headings) then we only need to change the constant once and the change will ripple through the program. Otherwise we would have to search for appropriate "A1" references and change them to "A2".

ACTIVITY 7 Use constants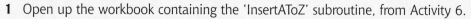

1 Open up the workbook containing the 'InsertAToZ' subroutine, from Activity 6.

2 View the routine in the VB Editor.

3 Just above the subroutine, but below 'Option Explicit', type:

```
Const A As Integer = 1
Const Z As Integer = 26
```

4 Now edit the subroutine to contain the line:

```
For intLoop = A To Z
```

Instead of:

```
For intLoop = 1 To 26
```

5 Run the routine from the worksheet button.

The code should work as before, but the code is probably a bit easier to understand, and we can get an idea of what the loop is doing. If you are having problems, compare your code with this workbook.

Local/global variables and scope

Constants can be declared and assigned a value at the top of the module sheet. Can we do the same with variables? The answer is yes, but there are repercussions. If a variable is declared with a 'Dim' statement above and outside the subroutines, then it can be used by all the subroutines in that module. So each subroutine can potentially change the value.

What we are referring to here is the **scope** of variables; sometimes we want a variable to be available to a number of routines in the module. Even better, we may want the variable to be available to subroutines in other modules, that is, make it **global**. We have only used one module so far, 'Module1', but we can create more if we want. To make a variable available to all the modules in our program we would use the word 'Public'. For example, 'Public intResult As Integer'.

A **local** variable is one that is declared within the subroutine itself, as we have done in Activities 4 and 5. This means that no other subroutine can access it, and it also means that another subroutine could use the same variable name without a problem. Activity 8 gives us a practical example of this.

ACTIVITY 8 Use global and local variables ◄

1 Open up this workbook.

2 Run the subroutine, then look at the code. The variable 'strUserName' has been given the scope Public (though Dim would have been just as good as we only have one module). Now we will try running the code with a local variable instead.

3 Inside the subroutine, 'GetUserName', just below 'Sub GetUserName()', type:

```
Dim strUserName As String
```

4 Now run the code again from the worksheet button.

What has happened and why?

The word 'User' should appear in cell B1, but cell B2 should remain as before. This is because the subroutine 'GetUserName' is storing the user name, typed into the input box, in a *local* variable. However, we are asking the computer to display the value stored in the *global* variable, a quite separate piece of computer memory. As no value has been assigned yet to the global variable, it displays nothing in the cell. The lesson is, always use local variables when no other subroutines need access to the values; otherwise use global ones (though below you will learn that **parameter passing** with local variables can be safer – but much harder to understand).

One very important reason for declaring the right data type is that we can then use VBA's built-in **functions**. For example, in Activity 4 we were able to use Excel VBA's function Chr() to convert a whole number into an ASCII value; for example 65 to the letter A. The statement that we used, 'Chr(intLoop + 64)', would fail if we had declared intLoop as, say, data type String. Activity 9 provides another example of this.

ACTIVITY 9 Use data types ◀

One of the tasks we need to undertake, in order to meet Tom's user requirements is to save a new version of the workbook to disk, with a file name containing yesterday's date. In the following activity, if we use the right data types, then we can use built-in Excel VBA functions **Now()** and **Format()**.

1 Create a new workbook, insert a new VBA module, then type in the following code:

```
Sub AddYesterdaysDateToFilename()
    Dim strFilename As String
    Dim strFileExtension As String
    Dim datYesterday As Date
    Dim strYesterday As String

    strFilename = "daily_sales"
    strFileExtension = ".xls"
    datYesterday = Now() - 1
    strYesterday = Format(datYesterday, "yy_mm_dd")
    MsgBox strFilename & "_" & strYesterday & strFileExtension
End Sub
```

2 As no reference is made to any worksheets, we can run this subroutine from inside the VB Editor. So, place the cursor somewhere inside the subroutine and use the menu option 'Run', 'Run Sub' or use function key F5 or even the run button (▶).

3 A message box should appear stating something like 'daily_sales_05_11_ 26.xls' where the first two digits represent the current year, the second two the current month and the last two yesterday's date.

4 Assuming you have successfully achieved this, change the data type of 'datYesterday' to Integer and run the subroutine again. It should fall over: wrong data type!

If you are having problems, compare your code with this workbook.

So far, our constants and variables have only been storing one value. However, there are occasions when we want to store a lot of values of the same data type in memory, and then do a quick sort or search on them. While it is possible to undertake sorting and searching data via a worksheet, doing all the processing in memory is so much faster. This is where the data structure called an array comes in handy. Activity 10 gives a small example of how an array works. There are also additional notes on arrays, on the worksheet provided.

ACTIVITY 10 Use an array

1 Open this workbook.
2 Run the subroutine and look at the code.
3 Undertake the exercise described in the worksheet text box.

Parameters

Parameters usually go between brackets. As stated in Unit 12.2, spreadsheet users should be used to parameters because they often put values between the brackets of functions. For example, the IF function uses three parameters in the brackets: one for the test, one for true and one for false; for example '= IF(age > 20, "old", "young"'. We can use a simple example to show how to use parameters with subroutines. In Activity 4 we saw that you could move the cursor down one row with the statement 'ActiveCell.Offset(1, 0).Select'. For clarity, and error testing, this statement should really be in its own subroutine, called, say, 'DownCell'. Thus:

```
Sub DownCell()
    ActiveCell.Offset(1, 0).Select
End Sub
```

This is fine, but what if we want to move down, say, 10 cells. A number of solutions are possible. For example, one solution might be to change the statement to 'ActiveCell.Offset(10, 0).Select'. However, we cannot later re-use this code if we want to go down five cells. Another possibility is to use the FOR...TO...NEXT repetition structure and call the subroutine this way. However, a neater solution is to use parameter passing. That is, we pass the values 10, or 5, as a parameter to the calling subroutine, by writing 'DownCell(10)' or 'DownCell(5)'. Activity 11 provides the code to test this out.

ACTIVITY 11 Use parameters and parameter passing

1 Create a new workbook, insert a new VBA module, then type in the following code:

```
Sub MoveCursor()
    DownCell (10)
End Sub
```

Continued on the next page

```
Sub DownCell(intNumberOfTimes As Integer)
    ActiveCell.Offset(intNumberOfTimes, 0).Select
End Sub
```

2 Run the subroutine, 'MoveCursor', from the worksheet.

3 The cursor should move down 10 rows from wherever it was.

What row would the cursor need to be in to make the code crash? (See the section on error trapping.)

If you are having problems, compare your code with this workbook.

Global variables versus parameter passing

Activity 12 compares using parameter passing with using global variables. This is a complex subject, but worth looking at.

ACTIVITY 12 Compare global variables with parameter passing

1 Open up this workbook.

2 Run the subroutine and look at the code.

There is no exercise with this Activity, but the code is worth investigating.

Validation

When users input data it is important to check that it is of the correct data type before proceeding with the rest of the program, otherwise the program might crash. For example, you ask the user for their age and, instead of writing in a number, they write in text, e.g. 'nineteen'. A good tip, therefore, is to ensure that you always read user input as a string. If it needs to be of another data type, test that it is valid first; then convert it to its appropriate data type if it is OK, else display an error message. Additionally, we can also test for acceptable values at the same time. A negative value for someone's age is clearly not valid so we can reject it. Activity 13 gives an example of this.

ACTIVITY 13 Use validation

In this activity the subroutine should reject any non-numeric values.

1 Create a new workbook, insert a new VBA module, then type in the following code:
```
Const strAgeCell As String = "A2"
Sub GetAge()
```

Continued on the next page

```
        Dim strAge As String

        strAge = InputBox("Type in your age.")
        If IsNumeric(strAge) Then
            Range(strAgeCell).Value = Val(strAge)
        Else
            MsgBox "Digits only please."
        End If
    End Sub
```

2 Run the code from the worksheet. It should accept a numeric value, but not a text value, and copy it to cell A2.

Add code to reject negative values.

What happens if you hit the 'Cancel' key on the input box? This workbook, which you can view from the ActiveBook, demonstrates a solution to the problem that can occur here.

Excel provides much data validation of cells values on a worksheet via the menu option 'Data', 'Validation...'. This includes data type validation, text length, numbers within specified ranges and so on. All this can be achieved via VBA as well.

ACTIVITY **14** Use text length validation ◀

1 As an exercise, use the VBA function Len() and see if you can write a program to accept or reject whether a National Insurance Number is valid in terms of length (that is, it must be nine characters long).

2 Improve this program to only accept two letters, followed by six digits, followed by one letter. VBA functions like LEFT() or MID() will be useful here.

Error trapping

One of the reasons for keeping subroutines small is so that we can identify the cause of an error if they fall over. We then add our own user-friendly error-trapping messages and possible remedies. If a subroutine is very large, it is often difficult to identify the cause of the error. It could be one of many things. As an example, refer back to Activity 11 where you were asked 'What row would the cursor need to be in to make the code crash?'. The answer is any row from 65 527 onwards, as moving the cursor down 10 cells would cause the program to try and go to a row that does not exist. So, even a simple routine like this can go wrong. Activity 15 provides some error-trapping code to handle this.

ACTIVITY 15 Use error trapping ◀

1. Open the workbook created in Activity 11 and place the cursor on row 65527.
2. Run the macro from the menu option 'Tools', 'Macro', 'Macros...'.
3. The VBA run-time error message should appear.
4. Click on the 'End' button.
5. Now, change the code to read:

```
Sub MoveCursor()
    DownCell (10)
End Sub


Sub DownCell(intNumberOfTimes As Integer)
    On Error GoTo ErrorHandler
    ActiveCell.Offset(intNumberOfTimes, 0).Select
    Exit Sub

ErrorHandler:
    MsgBox "The cursor cannot go beyond row 65536."
    End
End Sub
```

6. Test this code thoroughly and check that it error traps when the cursor is on row 65527.

 If you are having problems, compare your code with this workbook.

This is one of the few times when the VBA GOTO word is considered professionally acceptable, as was mentioned earlier in Unit 12.3. In this case, if there is no error, the cursor is moved and 'Exit Sub' neatly ends the subroutine successfully. In the event of an error, code execution jumps to the line starting 'ErrorHandler:' This is known as a **label** and it always ends with a colon. The label does not have to be called 'ErrorHandler', but 'ErrorHandler' or 'ErrHandler' are the words most commonly used. In other words, the line to move the cursor is skipped and code execution only starts from the label. This puts a message on the screen (our own) and then ends the program with 'End'; that is, no other subroutines are run. The more error trapping we do the better our code.

In Unit 12.4 we start to look at a more professional approach to programming.

Conclusion ▶ ▶ ▶

Although VBA is an event-driven object-orientated programming language, it still retains, quite rightly, the main features of standard programming languages: that is, the ability to handle statements in sequence, selectively and iteratively (with repetition). Arithmetic, logical and relational operators are also provided. One major difference (and potential danger) is that variables do not need to be declared at the beginning of a routine. However, it is always good practice to do so and Option Explicit should, therefore, appear at the top of every module.

Specify, design, test and document

Units 12.2 and 12.3 have concentrated on VBA code, in order to give newcomers to programming a flavour of what it is all about. We now need to return to a discussion of all the stages in the software life cycle: the specification, design, implementation, testing and documentation. Any professional programmer should have a good understanding of what these stages entail and why they are so crucial – only poor programmers try to skip them.

Functional specification

A functional specification is always needed at the beginning of a programming project. Sometimes it may be referred to as a **requirements specification**, or even just a **spec**. Which name is used is not important; more important is an understanding of why we need a spec and whether we have one that is detailed enough.

So what is it? A functional specification should describe what the program is supposed to do. We could say, for example, that the scenario is one. However, if it is, then it is a very poor one. To appreciate this, start with Activity 1.

ACTIVITY 1 Create a functional specification ◀

1 Re-read the scenario.
2 Now imagine that you are a programmer about to code in VBA. Write down a list of all the information you still need to get from Tom, who is both client and user, before you can be absolutely certain that Tom will be happy with your program. This should be a detailed list.
3 If you have not listed at least 10 items re-read the scenario.

Before looking at some of the extra information you should have listed in Activity 1, it is worth bearing in mind some of the research that has been undertaken on this subject. According to Steve McConnell in his book *Code Complete* (2nd edition, Microsoft Press, 2006), errors in requirements detected during the coding stage are 10 times more expensive than if they had been detected at the requirements stage itself. In other words, if Tom has not spelt out exactly what he wants, he will probably fail to get what he wants and also create inconsistent requirements.

Referring back to Activity 1, some of the questions we still need to ask Tom are:

1 Which version of Excel will the program be running in?
2 Which operation system is being used?
3 Does Tom want to automate the copy and paste routine?

4 Does Tom want separate buttons for clearing old data, importing new data, creating charts and saving the new version to disk?

5 Will these buttons be on the data worksheet or should they be on a separate worksheet?

6 What size should the buttons be?

7 Should the buttons be coloured?

8 What are the standards referred to (scale size, fonts required etc.)?

9 Should these standards be picked up by the VBA program from user input?

10 Should the saved versions be stored in a separate folder from the current one?

11 Should saved versions only contain the data and charts, and no module sheets?

12 Is any security required (e.g. passwords)?

For large projects there will also be requirements for acceptable speeds of processing, disk space, simultaneous access by a number of users, and so on.

It is therefore useful to have examples of required outputs (e.g. reports, charts) and inputs (e.g. forms to be filled in, workbooks to be imported) in this specification. Screenshots can be very helpful here, as well as tables setting out any required standards.

Activity 2 Complete a functional specification ◀

1 Assume that you have spoken to Tom in some detail. Write a detailed functional specification for the scenario. Refer to the questions listed after Activity 1 and make your own judgement as to what the answers are.

2 Use screenshots to give some indication as to what the worksheet(s) should look like.

3 Use a table to list the properties required for the chart objects (e.g. colour of bar, scale of axes).

4 Complete the specification in a professional manner using a word-processing package.

5 Compare your specification with other people in your class. Who has the most professional-looking specifications?

Design

When we have the detailed functional specification we still do not start coding until we have worked out the design. Some programming students still insist on producing their design plans *after* coding. This is bad practice: after all, we would not expect a house to be built without some design plans first.

There are many different design methodologies using such techniques as **top–down design**, **flow charts**, **system charts**, **state transition diagrams**, **prototyping**, **Structured Systems Analysis and Design Methodology (SSADM)**, **data-flow diagrams** and, in the case of database solutions, **entity** and **relationship diagrams**. We can only cover a few of these, so we will concentrate on the more practical ones.

▶ Prototyping and evolutionary delivery

One useful device is the prototype. Prototyping involves developing a **model** of how the final product will look to the user and how the user will navigate it. It involves getting feedback from the user/client and covers much of the area of **human–computer interaction**. A typical prototype would display the buttons to be used, any input forms, input data, output data, onscreen help, required charts and worksheets. This should give the client an idea of how the finished product will look. Hardly any code is required as, in theory, prototypes are only models and should be thrown away. On the other hand, **evolutionary delivery**, although similar to prototyping, *will* include code. In other words, it is not a throwaway model but a gradual development of the solution. The client should get a chance to see and make comments, as with a prototype. Where possible, we will use this method.

▶ Top–down design and modular programming

At some stage we will need to work out what subroutines our programming solution is going to need. We do not need to worry too much at this stage about *how* they are going to work, only *what* they should do and how they relate to each other (e.g. the order in which they are to be executed). A useful device is the structure chart. Figure 12.4.1 shows an initial structure chart that could be used for our scenario. It is based on the assumption that Tom wants the data imported automatically, that he wants the chart standards to be picked up from a worksheet, and that he wants the whole lot executed at the press of one button.

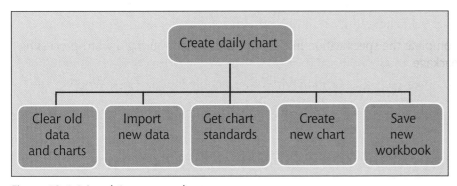

Figure 12.4.1 Level 1 structure chart

Activity 3 Create a structure chart diagram ◀

Figure 12.4.1 displays the main subroutines we want for the solution.

1 Try to produce a lower level of boxes (nodes) for each box at level 1. That is, add level 2. For example, the 'Save New Workbook' box could have the following boxes connected to it from below:
   - Create filename with yesterday's date
   - Locate workbook folder
   - Save workbook

   This is only a start, as you might want to include a routine to copy only the data sheet and chart to the new workbook, and not the standards-setting sheet and VBA module sheet behind.

2 Compare your diagram with other people in your class. As there are many solutions to this exercise it is unlikely that any two will look the same.

Design diagrams

This section looks at structure chart diagrams, but there are many other types of diagrams that can be used in the design process. For example, in the case of a database solution, we would need to produce an entity relationship diagram. (For further information on this, refer to Unit 7.3.) Flow charts are not considered to be as useful these days as they were once, though some designers still use them to identify sequence, selection and repetition within a routine.

Because we start at level 1 and then work out what we want at level 2, then level 3 and so on, this approach is often called **top–down design**. In addition, when creating a structure chart, as in Activity 3, we are involved in **modular programming**. We have broken the whole problem down into small parts (modules) in order to work on a solution to each. Each separate solution, however, will have to fit into the overall solution and not cause any conflict. That is, we must have an **integrated** solution, which neatly brings us to the **skeleton program**, **integrated development** and **integrated testing**.

Skeleton program, integrated development and integrated testing

Skeleton program

Once we know what modules we need we can start laying down a skeleton outline of the solution in VBA. This contains subroutine headings and endings, with no code in between, but much comment, setting out what we need to do. At the top of the program there should be comments stating any assumptions we need to make about the program, who wrote it, when it was written and what version number it is. We can even associate a button with this code, ready to test our program as it develops. Activity 4 provides an introduction to this approach.

Activity 4 Produce a skeleton program ◀

In this activity we will use the diagram in Figure 12.4.1 to set up the outline code for our VBA solution. For the sake of simplicity, we will assume that Tom is happy with our assumptions; that is it all happens at the press of *one button only*.

1 Create a new workbook, insert a new VBA module, then type in the following code:

Continued on the next page

```
Option Explicit

'Create Daily Chart Program
'Author: Joe Bloggs
'Date: 15/11/2005
'Version: 1.0
'Program to create a chart from imported data
'
'Public variables to store the chart standards
'Public variables and constants to store folder names, workbook names

Sub CreateDailyChart()
    'clear old data and charts
    ClearOldDataAndCharts
    'import new data
    ImportNewData
    'get chart standards
    'create new chart
    'save new workbook
End Sub

Sub ClearOldDataAndCharts()

End Sub

Sub ImportNewData()

End Sub
```

2 Assign a button to the subroutine 'CreateDailyChart' and test it. Nothing should happen as the code only contains comments.

3 Only two level 1 subroutines have been set up: 'ClearOldDataAndCharts' and 'ImportNewData'. No code is in them yet. Complete the other subroutines.

4 Which two subroutines will refer to the chart standards variables and constants?

If you are having problems, look at this workbook.

Note: In Activity 4 that we have set up comments to remind us to store any public variables or constants we may need. In a real situation, these should be identified and set up before any code is implemented. In other words, do we need arrays, and what size and data type? What will the names of the chart standards' constants be and what will their type be? If we do not identify these early, then errors will occur later.

Test plan

Testing is a science in itself, so this is only a brief overview. It is advisable, therefore, to read this document before proceeding. Testing is also covered in Units 7.2 and 7.4.

All large programs are likely to have some errors in them. If the program is designed properly the number of errors will be reduced substantially. However, testing provides the means of removing errors we might have missed. Some clients rightly insist on seeing a **test plan** before making the final payment for a program: they want to know that you have systematically searched for, and removed, errors. A test plan written early would set out what is to be tested. For example:

1 security (e.g. is the password working?)
2 navigation of the system (e.g. do the buttons work?)
3 the graphical user interface (e.g. are forms given clear headings and is there any help?)
4 completeness with respect to user requirements (e.g. has anything been left out?)
5 adhering to business rules and functions
6 speed of processing
7 data validation
8 mathematical manipulation and accuracy
9 mandatory fields (e.g. are required database fields set properly?)
10 multi-user access
11 stress testing
12 documentation (e.g. is the user guide correct?).

The test plan would also include **test data tables**. These list the data values to be used to check whether something works correctly, what result is expected from the test and then, after testing, what result was obtained. Comments would follow each. Do not write the test plan *after* a project is completed. A professional programmer can *always* make these programs fall over. In Activity 5 we will create a test data table for data validation.

ACTIVITY 5 Create a test data table ◀

Assume an input box asks the user for their age. Age is of the type integer. If the user is 18 or over the message 'You can vote' appears, otherwise the message 'You cannot vote' appears.

1 Create the test data table shown in Table 12.4.1.
2 Add extra rows and provide some additional test data and expected results.

Table 12.4.1 Data validation test for age input box

Test data	Expected result	Actual result	Comment
twelve	reject	Wrong data type	

 An example with additional rows is given in this document.

Integrated development and integrated testing

We should, therefore, draw up test data tables for each of the subroutines in our program, then test that each works correctly (this is known as **unit testing**). But will all the subroutines work together? Fortunately, our skeleton program approach allows us to check this as we go along via **integrated testing**. We develop a subroutine (e.g. 'ClearOldDataAndCharts') and click the 'Forms' button to check that it works. If it does, we develop the next subroutine (e.g. 'ImportNewData') and click the 'Forms' button to check that the two work together. We progress like this, developing and testing each subroutine until the program is complete. This can seem a bit slow to the novice programmer, but in the long run it pays off, more than compensating for time spent debugging programs.

Documenting

Finally, a few bullet points on documentation:
- Make sure that your code is readable by:
  - using clear names for subroutines, variables and constants
  - sticking to the naming conventions
  - indenting code with the tab key (see Activity 4, Unit 12.3)
  - using lots of comments.
- Produce a test plan, with test data tables, at the design stage. You can always add further tests as the project is developed.
- Where possible provide a built-in help facility for the user or administrator of your program. This can simply be a series of text boxes on a worksheet or database form.
- Provide a user guide with plenty of screenshots on how to use and navigate the program. (For further guidance, see this document.)
- Provide a technical guide so that the program can be updated (maintained) easily. For example, include:
  - any named ranges you have used (for spreadsheet solutions)
  - relationship diagrams (for databases)
  - the code and where it is (e.g. module, form and worksheet names)
  - who to contact in the event of a problem.

Additional material is available from the ActiveBook in this document.

Conclusion ▶ ▶ ▶

Unit 12.4 has shown how important it is to get the functional specification clearly stated right from the start. Failure to do so can lead to errors that can be very costly to remove later on. As with the functional specification, it is also important to get the design specified clearly and in some detail before rushing into the construction of the solution. However, by using an evolutionary development (prototyping) approach, combined with integrated testing, we can start to develop part of the solution early on and gain a much more interactive relationship with the client/user. This should mean that we are much more likely to get the final product right.

The main purpose of Unit 12.5 is to provide those pieces of code that may be essential for an assignment, but are not easy to work out or find. Running the macro recorder is a good way of finding some complex code for spreadsheet solutions (e.g. clearing data off a worksheet), but it is not available in Microsoft Access. However, remember that Access and Excel also have the VB Editor, with its Object Browser and Help facilities providing good examples of very useful code. Neither should the internet be ignored. However, some code is just hard to come by.

Spreadsheet solutions

▶ Naming a block of cells

The ability to give a block of data a named range crops up quite a bit with spreadsheet solutions, particularly where we are never certain how much data we are going to get. The beginnings of a solution are given in this workbook.

▶ Using the Control Toolbox buttons

Many programmers prefer to run code via the Control Toolbox objects (e.g. buttons, drop down lists, shapes) than the Forms button. Not only are there more objects available, but the properties and events are numerous. To see how a control toolbox button works, open this file. This workbook has onscreen explanation in a text box. There is also a demonstration that you can view from the ActiveBook.

▶ Data duplication

This workbook demonstrates one method of testing for duplicate data.

▶ Opening all the workbooks in a folder

The need to automatically open workbooks, process them and then close them is common to a lot of VBA solutions. Code is provided in this workbook. It is worth noting that this code can also be used from within a Microsoft Access module as long as it also references the Excel VBA library and provides the correct Excel objects in the code. An example of this is given later.

ACTIVITY 1 Develop a solution ◀

With the 'opening workbooks' code now supplied, it should be possible to provide a good solution to Tom's request.
1. Re-read your functional specification for this scenario (Activity 2, Unit 12.4).
2. Produce a prototype, design diagrams, list of variables required etc.
3. Produce the skeleton program with initial comments.
4. Start a test plan.
5. Use evolutionary delivery and integrated testing to provide a solution in VBA.
6. Produce documentation.

Database solutions

The examples in this section have been produced in Microsoft Access 2003 (version 11). However, earlier versions from 97 onwards should work fine in most cases.

▶ Module sheets

Access uses module sheets in the same way as Excel. They are just coding sheets.

▶ Option Explicit

'Option Compare Database' appears at the top of each module sheet. It is used for string data comparison. However, as explained earlier, make sure that Option Explicit is on the next line.

▶ Objects and events

Just as we saw that Excel had objects such as workbooks, worksheets, charts, ranges and controls, so Access has tables (called recordsets), queries, forms and controls, such as labels, textboxes and buttons. Methods, Properties and events can be associated with these.

Activity 2 provides a small example of where these might be used within a larger database solution.

ACTIVITY 2 Use form objects ◀

Save and open this database file.
1. Read the explanation and look at all the code.
2. The database contains an additional module called mBackup. Create a new form with a command button to run the backup subroutine in this module.

Note: This may only work in Access 2003, but at least you should get the get the error handler message in other versions.

Save and open this database file, which is an additional example of a form control with VBA.

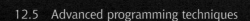

The next activity assumes that workbooks data has already been imported into the 'tbl_data_imported' table referred to in Activity 2. You do not need to import this data. This time, however, we want to:
- find the number of records in the table
- check for duplicates.

Activity 3 Read a Recordset ◀

Save and open this database file.
1. Read the information textbox and look at all the code for the three command buttons.
2. Put a textbox on the settings form to display the Imported Data Table record count. Modify the code for the first command button so that it displays the result in this text box, rather than a message box.

Finally, we look at how Access and Excel VBA can communicate with each other (or any other VBA application such as Word, PowerPoint and Outlook).

Activity 4 Link Access and Excel VBA ◀

Save and open this database file.
1. Read the information text box and look at all the code for the command button and 'mGetWorkbookName' module.
2. Modify the code to display the first worksheet name in each workbook.

Note: It is possible in this activity to leave a copy of Excel in memory every time the code fails. It is worth using the task manager to remove any additional instances of Excel.

Linking applications together can be very productive. However, care must be taken to ensure that the correct libraries are referenced and that error trapping is included.

Conclusion

It is important to study Unit 12.5 along with the examples on the CD. Some useful code has been provided here that you may find helpful when tackling the assessment. If you understand the code, it is much easier to adapt it accordingly.

For the Unit 12 Assessment you are required to submit a working solution to a problem requiring the use of either database or spreadsheet software, with added functionality provided by an event-driven programming language. The evidence must be in an **eportfolio**.

Your eportfolio should include:

1 a functional specification
2 an initial design
3 a fully working custom solution
4 technical documentation
5 evidence of formative and summative testing
6 an evaluation.

Units 12.1 to 12.5 have covered points 1 to 5, and evaluation has already been covered in Units 1, 2 and 8. The scenario specified in Unit 12.1 has been used extensively throughout this unit, so that to some degree you should already have a good example of portfolio material. The purpose of Unit 12.6 is to re-emphasise some of these points and provide a few additional tips.

> ### Assessment basics
> Make sure you know how to:
> - create an eportfolio (see earlier units)
> - undertake an evaluation of your work (see earlier units).

Choosing a project

The scenario we have used can appear very simple. Tom wants to copy some data onto a worksheet and then create a chart, all at the press of a button. However, once a functional specification is drafted, the task can become quite complicated; for example, the importing data routine. *Tip*: Write a draft functional spec first to get an idea of the complexity of the required solution. Do not start by dabbling with code.

Possible projects, based on the kind used in industry and commerce, could be:

- A program that checks to see that the temperature readings of a company's buildings are within a range specified by health and safety. Assume the readings are already in a text file. This is a good project for a spreadsheet.
- A program that reads in the daily logs files from a website and counts page impressions, different IP addresses etc. This is a good project for a database.
- A program that pulls data from a set of workbooks provided by an international company's sales reps, into separate worksheets within a master workbook. It then converts the sales figures into a common currency (e.g. sterling, euro or dollar) and also provides a summary sheet.

Assessment evidence

Read the assessment evidence criteria for this unit as laid out in the Edexcel specification. This might seem obvious, but a number of students ignore this to their cost. *Make sure you are not one of them.* The rest of Unit 12.6 looks at some of the things you might easily miss.

▶ Documentation

This is often a last-minute consideration for poor programmers. *Tip:* If you write the functional specification in the present tense rather than the future, much of this can be re-used in user guides, technical documentation and testing. For example, 'The user will be able to click on a button to...' should read 'When the user clicks on the button...'. Many professional software houses use this technique.

▶ Form design

Think carefully about the user interface. Can the user input values easily (e.g. via a database form or dedicated worksheet) and is the output clear (as well as meeting the user requirements)? *Tip:* A good way to find out is to test it on someone.

▶ Prototyping

The specification for the design states 'plus evidence of your use of prototyping to improve and refine the design'. So, if you do not provide a prototype you could have some problems!

Finally, remember to stick to the order of development laid out in Unit 12.4.

Conclusion ▶ ▶ ▶

Unit 12 has provided a basis for tackling the assessment. A complete VBA solution has not been provided in order to remove the temptation to copy and paste. However, with a good understanding of event-driven object-orientated programming techniques, plus the professional approach to program design, you should be well equipped to undertake the work.

Index

1NF *see* first normal form
2NF *see* second normal form
3NF *see* third normal form
2012 Olympic Games 129–30
abnormal data 112
accessibility 236, 279
action queries 79–83
activities
    project breakdown 163–6
    project management software 170–7
    project roadmapping 158–62
    small activities definition 164–6
actual input 114
advanced techniques 260–80, 320–2
agendas 191, 194–5
aggregate calculations 106
aggregation (total) functions 77, 78
aliases 18, 75
analysis of users' requirements 17
AND 72, 301
animated vector graphics 214
animation 214–19, 226–8
'Any other business' (AOB) 195
'Apologies for absence' 195
applications
    customising 285–324
    databases 2–14
    multimedia software 204–8
archiving 84–5, 248, 258
arithmetic operators 303
aspect ratio 211
assignment
    resources 184–5
    tasks 194
ATM *see* automated teller machines
atomic data 37
attributes 27–36
audio *see* sound
authoring tools 226
auto-generated primary keys 9
auto-run presentations 232–3
automated teller machines (ATM) 4
automatic testing 115–17
AutoNumbers 53

backing up 19, 86
banking databases 4
bar codes 3
baseline 187–8, 192–3
basic form 108
basic joins 74
basic queries 66–8
BCNF *see* Boyce–Codd normal form
benefits 153–4
bitmap graphics 213–14
black-box testing 112
Boolean data 43–4
bottom-up modelling 18, 27
bottom-up testing 112
bound controls 93
boundary data/testing 112, 113

Boyce–Codd normal form (BCNF) 38
brightness 210
budgets 134
Buncefield Oil depot 23
burning CDs 241
business rules 250
buttons
    Control Toolbox 320
    subroutines 296–7

calculated controls 98
calculated fields 75–6, 98–100
calculations (aggregate) 106
calendars 180–2, 183–4
calls 301, 304–5
cardinality of relationships 29–31
cartoons 214, 215
cascaded deletes 63–4
cascaded updates 63–4
CASE *see* computer-aided software
    engineering
cells, naming blocks 320
characters 43–4
Chart Wizard 289–91
charts
    functional specifications 247–8
    Macro Recorder 288–92
    spreadsheets construction 277–8
Chen, Peter 27
class 292
claymation 214
clearing systems 4
clients 134, 139, 247
close down meetings 196
Codd, Dr 5–6
codes 19
collection 292
colour
    coding on spreadsheets 270–1
    customising forms 91
    images 209–11
    schemes 209
combining actions 84–7
Combo Box Wizard 92
combo boxes 92–3, 109–10
Command Button Wizard 93–4
comments 62, 294
commercial database applications 3–4
completion dates 156
components, multimedia 206–7
composite primary keys 5, 8, 53
compression 212, 223
computer-aided software engineering
    (CASE) 36
concept phase of project life cycle 148
conditional formatting 95–6
conditional repetition 304
conditional statements 300
conformance to requirements 153
consistency 236
constants 303, 305, 306–7

constraints
    definition of scope 155
    projects 134
    setting 186
construction
    multimedia software 237–40
    spreadsheets software 260–80
contrast 210
control
    sources 98
    test plans 114
Control Toolbox buttons 320
copying colour 210
costs of projects 145
critical paths 161–2
cropping 211
crossing lines 33
currency conversion 268
customers 134, 139, 247
customised working time 169
customising applications 285–324
    advanced programming techniques 320–2
    design 314–19
    documentation 319, 324
    eportfolio 323
    event-driven programming 286, 288–97
    functional specifications 313–14
    program structures and skills 298–312
    testing 316–19
customising forms 89–94

data
    atomic 37
    capture 22
    conversion 19, 23
    database functional specifications 22
    dictionaries 18, 27, 47
    duplication 38, 255–6, 320
    importing 19, 257
    input error reduction 255–6
    input testing 112–14
    integrity 38–41
    linking external data 263–6
    modelling 17–18, 27–48
    names 43
    redundant 38
    specifications 42–8
    types 43–4, 53–4
    validation 44, 45–7, 54–61, 256, 267
    verification 44–5
database management systems (DBMS) 5
databases
    applications 2–14
    commercial 3–4
    data modelling 27–48
    development lifecycle 15–20
    functional specifications 20–6
    key terms 5
    menus 107–11
    personal records 2–3
    querying 11, 66–87

Acknowledgements

We are most grateful to the following companies for permission to reproduce their website material:

BBC Ceefax
BBC Radio
Ben&Jerry'sTM
www.firstdirect.com
iTunesTM
New York Philharmonic
www.teem.org.uk
Wikipedia

We are grateful to the following for permission to reproduce copyright photographs:

Alamy: pg1 © STOCK IMAGE/PIXLAND / royalty-free; pg3 (t) © Motoring Picture Library; pg15 © Swerve; pg24 © Kader Meguedad; pg131 © LightworksMedia; pg192 BrandX / royalty-free.
Bubbles: pg2 (Clarissa Leahy).
Corbis: pg23 © HANDOUT/epa; pg129 © Stephen Hird/Reuters; pg130 © Kim Sayer; pg160 © Adam Woolfit.
Education Photos (www.educationphotos.co.uk): pg179 © Linda Westmore.
Getty Images: pg190 © Jasper James.
Purestock RF: pg283.

Every effort has been made to trace the copyright holders and we apologise in advance for any unintentional omissions. We would be pleased to insert the appropriate acknowledgement in any subsequent edition of this publication.

IMPORTANT: READ CAREFULLY
WARNING: BY OPENING THE PACKAGE YOU AGREE TO BE BOUND BY THE TERMS OF THE LICENCE AGREEMENT BELOW.

This is a legally binding agreement between You (the user or purchaser) and Edexcel Limited. By retaining this licence, any software media or accompanying written materials or carrying out any of the permitted activities You agree to be bound by the terms of the licence agreement below. If You do not agree to these terms then promptly return the entire publication (this licence and all software, written materials, packaging and any other components received with it) with Your sales receipt to Your supplier for a full refund.

SINGLE USER LICENCE AGREEMENT

YOU ARE PERMITTED TO:	YOU MAY NOT:
• Use (load into temporary memory or permanent storage) a single copy of the software on only one computer at a time. If this computer is linked to a network then the software may only be installed in a manner such that it is not accessible to other machines on the network. • Make one copy of the software solely for backup purposes or copy it to a single hard disk, provided you keep the original solely for back up purposes. • Transfer the software from one computer to another provided that you only use it on one computer at a time.	• Rent, lease or sell the software or any part of the publication. • Copy any part of the documentation, except where specifically indicated otherwise. • Make copies of the software, other than for backup purposes. • Reverse engineer, decompile or disassemble the software or create a derivative product from the contents of the databases or any software contained in them. • Use the software on more than one computer at a time. • Install the software on any networked computer in a way that could allow access to it from more than one machine on the network. • Include any material or software from the disk(s) in any other product or software materials. • Use the software in any way not specified above without the prior written consent of Edexcel Limited.

ONE COPY ONLY

This licence is for a single user copy of the software.

EDEXCEL LIMITED RESERVES THE RIGHT TO TERMINATE THIS LICENCE BY WRITTEN NOTICE AND TO TAKE ACTION TO RECOVER ANY DAMAGES SUFFERED BY EDEXCEL LIMITED IF YOU BREACH ANY PROVISION OF THIS AGREEMENT.

Edexcel Limited owns the software. You only own the disk on which the software is supplied.

LIMITED WARRANTY

Edexcel Limited warrants that the disk(s) or CD-ROM(s) on which the software is supplied are free from defects in materials and workmanship under normal use for ninety (90) days from the date You receive them. This warranty is limited to You and is not transferable. Edexcel Limited does not warrant that the functions of the software meet Your requirements or that the media is compatible with any computer system on which it is used or that the operation of the software will be unlimited or error free.

You assume responsibility for selecting the software to achieve Your intended results and for the installation of, the use of and the results obtained from the software. The entire liability of Edexcel Limited and your only remedy shall be replacement free of charge of the components that do not meet this warranty. This limited warranty is void if any damage has resulted from accident, abuse, misapplication, service or modification by someone other than Edexcel Limited. In no event shall Edexcel Limited be liable for any loss or damage whatsoever arising out of installation of the software, even if advised of the possibility of such damages. Edexcel Limited will not be liable for any loss or damage of any nature suffered by any party as a result of reliance upon or reproduction of or any errors in the content of the publication.

Edexcel Limited does not limit its liability for death or personal injury caused by its negligence.

Pearson Education and Edexcel accept no responsibility for the content on any Website to which a hypertext link from this CD-ROM exists or for any use of personal data by the third party operating such a Website. The links are provided 'as is' with no warranty, express or implied, for the information provided within them.

This licence agreement shall be governed by and interpreted and construed in accordance with English law.

Installation instructions

Insert the Interactive Students' CD-ROM into your CD-ROM drive.

If Autorun is enabled on your computer, then the program will start after a few seconds.

Otherwise, go to your file management tools, double click on the CD drive and then double click on Launcher.